Atypical and Flexible Working

Employment Law Handbook

August 2014

IDS

Atypical and Flexible Working

Employment Law Handbook

Incomes Data Services
Finsbury Tower, 103-105 Bunhill Row, London EC1Y 8LZ
Tel: 0845 077 2911 Fax: 0845 310 5517
Email: ids.sales.support@thomsonreuters.com
Website: www.incomesdata.co.uk

ISBN 978 0 414 03346 7

IDS Employment Law Handbook, 'Atypical and Flexible Working', is published by Thomson Reuters (Professional) UK Limited trading as Incomes Data Services Limited (Registered in England & Wales, Company No. 16790446). Registered Office: Aldgate House, 33 Aldgate High Street, London EC3N 1DL.

The information contained in this journal in not intended to be a substitute for specific legal advice and readers should obtain advice from a qualified adviser in relation to individual transactions or matters.

No natural forests were destroyed to make this product: only farmed timber was used and re-planted.

A CIP catalogue record for this book is available from the British Library.

Typeset by DC Graphic Design Ltd, Swanley Village, Kent BR8 7PA
Printed by St Austell Printing Co Ltd, St Austell Business Park, Cornwall, PL25 4FD

Contents

Abbreviations

Courts

ECJ	European Court of Justice
ECHR	European Court of Human Rights
PC	Privy Council
SC	Supreme Court
HL	House of Lords
CA	Court of Appeal
Ct Sess	Court of Session
NICA	Northern Ireland Court of Appeal
QBD	Queen's Bench Division
Div Ct	(Queen's Bench) Divisional Court
KBD	King's Bench Division
ChD	Chancery Division
NIRC	National Industrial Relations Court
EAT	Employment Appeal Tribunal
ET	Employment Tribunal

Case references

AC	Law Reports, Appeal Cases
All ER	All England Law Reports
Ch	Law Reports, Chancery Division
CMLR	Common Market Law Reports
COET	Employment Tribunal folio number
EAT	Employment Appeal Tribunal unreported case number
ECR	European Case Reports
ET	Employment Tribunal unreported case number
EWCA	Court of Appeal unreported case number
ICR	Industrial Cases Reports
IRLR	Industrial Relations Law Reports
ITR	Industrial Tribunal Reports
KB	Law Reports, King's Bench Division
QB	Law Reports, Queen's Bench Division
SCOET	Scottish Employment Tribunal folio number
SLT	Scots Law Times
TLR	Times Law Reports
UKSC	Supreme Court unreported case number
WLR	Weekly Law Reports

Legislation

DDA	Disability Discrimination Act 1995
EA	Employment Act 2002
EqA	Equality Act 2010
EqA 2006	Equality Act 2006
EqPA	Equal Pay Act 1970
ERA	Employment Rights Act 1996
ERRA	Enterprise and Regulatory Reform Act 2013
ETA	Employment Tribunals Act 1996
PIDA	Public Interest Disclosure Act 1998
RRA	Race Relations Act 1976
SDA	Sex Discrimination Act 1975
TULR(C)A	Trade Union and Labour Relations (Consolidation) Act 1992

Introduction

Traditionally, employment protection legislation has been geared towards individuals with stable, regular full-time jobs working for a single employer under an open-ended contract of employment. However, working patterns and norms have changed and continue to do so. The last few decades have seen an increase in the number of individuals whose working arrangements are 'atypical', in that they fall outside the traditional model, and new types of working arrangement are constantly emerging. An individual worker may fall into none, one, or more of the various categories of atypical work at any one time, and may move between them at various points over the course of his or her working life.

The figures are instructive. Seasonally adjusted statistics based on the Labour Force Survey for January to March 2014 suggest that out of a workforce of around 30 million, there were over 8 million part-time workers, 4.5 million self-employed workers, and just over 1 million workers with more than one job. 6.4 per cent of employees were in temporary work, of whom over a third stated that the reason for this was that they could not find a permanent job. Furthermore, the Office for National Statistics estimates that in January to February 2014 there were around 1.4 million people working on contracts, such as 'zero-hours' contracts, that did not guarantee a minimum number of hours.

There are many reasons for such trends, an analysis of which falls outside the scope of this Handbook. However, the need for flexible working patterns in general is driven both by the needs of individual workers and by the economic and market pressures on employers. Contributing factors include an increase in female workers with family responsibilities, leading to more requests to work part time or in job-sharing arrangements; greater longevity, meaning that more workers need to care for elderly relatives; technological developments, which have opened up more opportunities for some people to work from home; and a rise in the cost to the individual of higher education, which has resulted in a larger number of students becoming available for temporary, part-time work. Increasing financial pressures on employers have encouraged the use of fixed-term or zero-hours contracts and agency, casual and seasonal work, which allow employers to meet fluctuating demands and respond to financial exigencies.

Given this diversity in working arrangements, the term 'atypical' is perhaps so broad as to be essentially meaningless. Some 'atypical' working patterns may nevertheless be stable, regular, and well-remunerated; while others may provide workers with little or no job security, a lack of control over the work they are given, and low pay. Indeed, the term 'atypical' is a misnomer in many industries and workplaces, where more workers are likely to work according to non-traditional patterns than otherwise.

One thing that is certain is that non-standard working patterns are here to stay, particularly now that the right to request flexible working has been extended to all employees. While one method of 'alternative' working discussed in this Handbook – the apprenticeship – has a long history and is governed to some extent by the common law, in most areas the law has developed fairly recently, driven to a large extent by the European Union's identification of the need to improve conditions for workers who previously fell outside the scope of employment protection legislation. Thus, much of the domestic legislation discussed in this Handbook implements European Directives: the Part-time Workers (Prevention of Less Favourable Treatment) Regulations 2000 SI 2000/1551 implement the EU Part-time Work Directive (No.97/81); the Fixed-term Employees (Prevention of Less Favourable Treatment) Regulations 2002 SI 2002/2034 implement the EU Framework Directive on fixed-term work (No.99/70); and the Agency Workers Regulations 2010 SI 2010/93 implement the EU Temporary Agency Workers Directive (No.2008/104). The domestic legislation allowing employees to request flexible working is an exception in that it does not directly implement a requirement of EU law.

Scope of the Handbook

This Handbook sets out the law governing a number of different 'atypical' working patterns: in particular, agency work, fixed-term work, part-time work, zero-hours contracts and other forms of ad hoc working arrangements. It also explains the right to request flexible working, and highlights the considerations applicable to three specific types of 'atypical' worker: apprentices, employee shareholders and posted workers.

Inevitably, some 'atypical' working patterns fall outside the scope of this Handbook. For example, it does not deal specifically with shift working or night working, or the issues involved in working from home, or on secondment. The rationale for not dealing with such patterns of work is that they are usually contractual arrangements, and are not generally covered by any specific employment protection legislation. Reference should therefore be made to IDS Employment Law Handbook, 'Contracts of Employment' (2009), for questions of contractual interpretation and enforcement. Where employment protections do exist, these are covered in other IDS Employment Law Handbooks. For example, protections for night workers are explained in IDS Employment Law Handbook, 'Working Time' (2013), Chapter 5, 'Night work'.

Scheme of the Handbook

The scheme of the Handbook is as follows:

- Chapter 1 examines the law relevant to agency workers, and in particular the regulatory framework surrounding their supply and employment and their rights under the Agency Workers Regulations 2010 SI 2010/93

- Chapter 2 considers the rights of fixed-term employees under the Fixed-term Employees (Prevention of Less Favourable Treatment) Regulations 2002 SI 2002/2034

- Chapter 3 addresses the rights of part-time workers, particularly under the Part-time Workers (Prevention of Less Favourable Treatment) Regulations 2000 SI 2000/1551

- Chapter 4 explains the statutory right to request flexible working under the Flexible Working Regulations 2014 SI 2014/1398, and the extent to which employees whose requests are refused may be able to claim discrimination

- Chapter 5 deals with other types of 'atypical' working arrangements, such as zero-hours contracts, casual and seasonal work, annualised hours contracts, and on-call or 'supply' contracts

- Chapter 6 examines the law governing apprenticeships, including the different contractual arrangements that may apply and the statutory rights and protections available to apprentices

- Chapter 7 explains the recently introduced employee shareholder status, and considers the legal issues surrounding the employment of employee shareholders, and finally,

- Chapter 8 looks at the law governing posted workers and sets out the rights and protections afforded by the EU Posted Workers Directive (No.96/71) to those who fall within its scope.

The law is stated as at 1 August 2014.

> **This publication aims to provide accurate, authoritative information and comment on the subjects it covers. It is offered to subscribers on the understanding that the publisher is not in business as a lawyer or consultant.**

1 Agency workers

Regulatory framework

Rights under the Agency Workers Regulations

Other statutory employment rights

Employment status

Vicarious liability

Over the past few decades, temporary employment has increasingly been used by **1.1** employers in all sectors of the UK economy to fill diverse roles, from manual labour to highly specialist work. In a typical agency arrangement a worker 'signs up' with a temporary work agency, which in turn supplies the worker to work for one of its clients as need arises. The majority of organisations that use temporary staff do so to enhance the flexibility of their workforce: temporary agency employment can provide a cost-effective way of responding to peaks and troughs in demand.

For workers, signing up with a temporary work agency (or 'employment business') can obviate the need to search for work personally. However, agency workers are potentially in a vulnerable position. The supply of work is unlikely to be guaranteed; individual assignments may vary dramatically in length; and the worker may feel insecure as to the extent of his or her rights, particularly with regard to the end-user to which he or she is assigned.

To deal with these uncertainties, and with the increasing prevalence of the **1.2** temporary agency work model, the legislature has sought both to regulate the recruitment and supply industry and to bolster the protection afforded to individual agency workers. In this chapter, we explain the regulatory framework surrounding employment businesses and recruitment agencies, before turning to consider the protection offered to temporary agency workers by the Agency Workers Regulations 2010 SI 2010/93, which implement the EU Temporary Agency Workers Directive (No.2008/104). We then set out the other statutory employment rights that may be available to agency workers and look at the employment status of such workers (which will determine what, if any, additional rights they can rely on). Finally, we discuss the extent to which an end-user may be vicariously liable for the actions of an agency worker.

Regulatory framework   1.3

The employment agency industry is regulated by the Employment Agencies Act 1973, as amended ('the 1973 Act'), and the Conduct of Employment Agencies and Employment Business Regulations 2003 SI 2003/3319 ('the 2003

1

Regulations'). This legal regulatory framework is distinct from the Agency Workers Regulations 2010 SI 2010/93, which provide certain rights and protections to workers hired out by temporary work agencies (see 'Rights under the Agency Workers Regulations' below). Unlike the 2010 Regulations, which are concerned solely with temporary agency assignments, the 1973 Act and 2003 Regulations apply to the recruitment and work agency industry as a whole. The terminology adopted in the regulatory legislation is different from that used in the 2010 Regulations, which can be confusing. The terminology used in the regulatory legislation is explained under 'Who does the legislation cover?' below, while that used in the 2010 Regulations is discussed under 'Rights under the Agency Workers Regulations – who is covered by the AWR?' below.

Note that the Government is consulting with a view to replacing the current regulatory framework – see 'Proposals for regulatory reform' below.

1.4 Who does the legislation cover?

The 1973 Act and 2003 Regulations have a wide ambit, regulating both the business of recruiting work-seekers to permanent or temporary employment, and the business of supplying work-seekers to cover temporary agency work assignments. The legislation therefore covers two distinct types of activity: that carried out by employment agencies, and that carried out by employment businesses. These terms can give rise to confusion given that many service-users tend to use the generic term 'employment agencies' to refer to both types of labour-supply firm, and workers who provide services for employment businesses are universally described as 'agency workers'. However, 'employment agency' and 'employment business' are distinct legal entities as defined in the 1973 Act – see below.

1.5 **Work-seekers and work-finding services.** The legislation uses the term 'work-seeker' to describe a person (whether an individual or a company) to whom an agency or employment business provides work-finding services (or holds itself out as being capable of providing such services) – Reg 2. The fact that a work-seeker may be a company is confirmed by Reg 32, which makes the necessary modifications to the Regulations where the work-seeker is a company and the worker is the person supplied by the work-seeker to carry out the job. Companies can, however, choose to opt out of the 2003 Regulations – see 'Opt-out for personal service companies' below.

'Work-finding services' means services (which might involve simply the provision of information) provided either

- by an employment agency to the work-seeker for the purpose of finding or seeking employment for him or her

- by an employment business to an employee of the employment business for the purpose of finding or seeking to find a hirer for the employee to work for

- by an employment business to a work-seeker for the purpose of finding or seeking to find a hirer, with a view to the work-seeker becoming employed by the employment business and acting for and under the control of the hirer – Reg 2.

Definition of employment agency. The term 'employment agency' is defined **1.6** in the 1973 Act as the business of 'providing services (whether by the provision of information or otherwise) for the purpose of finding persons employment with employers or of supplying employers with persons for employment by them' – S.13(2). In other words, they are recruitment agencies whose business it is to introduce work-seekers to a potential employer with a view to the work-seeker becoming employed by that employer (or 'end-user') on either a temporary or a permanent basis. The end-user is typically the agency's client, but in some cases the client may be the work-seeker. The work-seeker will enter into direct contractual relations with the end-user following his or her successful introduction by the agency. Following this, the agency's own relationship with the worker comes to an end. The client (end-user) will pay wages directly to the work-seeker as agencies are, in general, forbidden to pay or administer payment of remuneration – Reg 8(1) 2003 Regulations. (Exceptions to this rule are set out in Reg 8(2).)

Note that the use of the word 'persons' in S.13(2) makes it clear that employment agency activity includes the supply of companies as well as workers. Thus the Act covers, for example, the employment of a contractor who works through an intermediary personal service company. However, such contractors may opt out of the 2003 Regulations – see 'Opt-out for personal service companies' below.

In practical terms, an employment agency, as defined, will cover a wide range **1.7** of organisations, extending from the familiar recruitment agency, through a range of specialist agencies (such as entertainment and model agents), to the executive selection functions of management consultants and executive search consultants.

Definition of employment business. The term 'employment business' is **1.8** defined as the business of 'supplying persons in the employment of the person carrying on the business, to act for, and under the control of, other persons in any capacity' – S.13(3). This covers businesses that directly engage work-seekers, either under a 'professional engagement' or on a self-employed basis under a contract for services – S.13(1)(a). The business then supplies the services of the work-seeker to an end-user for particular jobs or periods of time, during which the worker is under the end-user's day-to-day supervision or control. However, the relationship of the employment business with the worker is maintained. The usual arrangement is that the end-user pays the employment business, which will then subtract its fee and pay the worker's wages. In general, the worker has a contract with the employment business but not with the organisation for which he or she actually carries out the work, although in rare circumstances an employment relationship between the worker and end-user may arise (see 'Employment status' below).

Notably, the definition of employment business in S.13(3) covers the supply of persons to work 'under the control of' others. It does not, therefore, extend to subcontractors undertaking specific tasks using their own staff who act and remain under their control. In practice, this means that where a subcontractor provides labour for a project being carried out by the main contractor, and the subcontractor remains effectively in day-to-day control of the workers, an employment business will not arise. However, in circumstances where the subcontractor forfeits control to the main contractor, the subcontractor may be seen as an employment business. A subcontractor may retain control if, for example, it has discretion over how many workers are needed for the job and when a worker should stop working.

1.9 The primary context in which employment businesses supply labour is where workers are hired out on a temporary basis, frequently called 'temping'. Such arrangements have traditionally been associated with the supply of secretarial and other office staff, but have now extended into many other areas, including professional, IT and industrial occupations.

1.10 **Dual capacity.** Some organisations act in a dual capacity, both as employment agencies and as employment businesses. There is nothing unlawful about this since a single organisation may be looking for both permanent and temporary staff for the same client simultaneously, or may seek a temporary placement for a work-seeker until permanent employment can be found. The capacity in which the firm operates in any particular case will be determined by the nature of the placement it is purporting to make with the end-user.

Regulation 14(1) of the 2003 Regulations requires the written agreement between an employment business and a work-seeker to specify whether it is operating as an agency or as an employment business in relation to that work-seeker. Furthermore, Reg 9 stipulates that an agency or employment business may not hold itself out to a work-seeker as operating on one basis while at the same time advising the end-user that it is operating on another.

1.11 **'Hirer'.** Regulation 2 of the 2003 Regulations uses the term 'hirer' to describe the client or person to whom the services of either an agency or a business are supplied. The hirer is also commonly referred to as the 'end-user', particularly in case law dealing with the employment status of temporary agency workers (see 'Employment status' below).

1.12 **Exclusions.** Section 13(7) of the 1973 Act sets out a number of businesses, agencies and services to which the Act does not apply. These include:

4

- businesses certified to find employment for ex-armed forces personnel and ex-prisoners
- childminding agencies
- services connected with the letting of vehicles, plant and equipment
- local authorities
- various police services
- members' services provided by trade unions and employers' organisations
- services provided by university appointments boards, or by certain other educational institutions.

Opt-out for personal service companies. Some self-employed contractors and **1.13** other professional workers choose to work through a 'personal service' limited company for tax reasons or to improve their chances of receiving work. Generally, the worker will be the sole director and shareholder, and will personally deliver the services supplied by the company, either directly or through an agency.

As discussed under 'Work-seekers and work-finding services' above, the definition of work-seeker under the 2003 Regulations encompasses not only individual workers but also companies. Thus, temporary workers who supply services through a personal service company are covered. However, they may choose to opt out of the Regulations in respect of their work with a particular hirer. In order to opt out, before an employment business or agency introduces or supplies the company to a hirer:

- the company and the person to be supplied to carry out the work must agree to opt out, and give notice of that agreement to the employment business or agency, and
- the employment business or agency must inform the hirer of this agreement to opt out – Reg 32(9).

However, opt-out is not allowed if the assignment would involve the worker **1.14** supplied by the company working with or attending a vulnerable person – Reg 32(12).

At any time the individual worker may give notice to the employment business or agency to withdraw the agreement to opt out, although if he or she has already started carrying out the work, the notice will not take effect until he or she stops working in that position for that hirer – Reg 32(10) and (11).

Neither an agency nor an employment business may make the provision of work-finding services to a company conditional on it, and the worker supplied to carry out the work, opting out of the Regulations – Reg 32(13).

1.15 Agreeing terms

Before providing any services to a work-seeker, an employment business or agency must agree the terms that are to apply between itself and the work-seeker – Regs 14 (in respect of employment businesses) and 16 (in respect of employment agencies).

1.16 Employment businesses. The form and content of the agreement between an employment business and a work-seeker are dictated by Regs 14 and 15. These state that the employment business must set out the agreed terms in writing in a single document (so far as possible), and copies of this document (or documents) must be given to the work-seeker before the employment business provides him or her with its services – Reg 14(2). However, this requirement does not apply if the employment business chooses to employ the temporary work-seeker under a contract of employment. In that case, the provision of a written statement of particulars pursuant to Part 1 of the Employment Rights Act 1996 suffices – Reg 14(3). (For details of written particulars, see IDS Employment Law Handbook, 'Contracts of Employment' (2009), Chapter 3, 'Written particulars'.) Once terms have been agreed and recorded, the employment business is not entitled to vary them without the work-seeker's agreement – Reg 14(4). Nor is it entitled to make the continued provision of its services conditional on the work-seeker agreeing to such a variation – Reg 14(6).

The agreed terms must include the following:

- a statement that the employment business will operate as an employment business in relation to the work-seeker – Reg 14(1)(a)

- the type of work the employment business will seek for the work-seeker – Reg 14(1)(b)

- whether the work-seeker will be employed by the employment business under a contract of service or apprenticeship, or a contract for services – Reg 15(a)

- an undertaking that the work-seeker will be paid for work done irrespective of whether or not he or she is paid by the end-user – Reg 15(b)

- the length of notice of termination that must be given by either side to end particular assignments with end-users – Reg 15(c)

- the rate (or expected rate) of remuneration and the intervals at which it will be paid – Reg 15(d) and (e), and

- holiday entitlement – Reg 15(f).

1.17 Employment agencies. Before providing services to a work-seeker for which it is permitted to charge a fee under Reg 26(1) (see 'Fees and charges' below), an employment agency must agree terms with the work-seeker – Reg 16. These terms must include:

- details of the work-finding services the agency will provide – Reg 16(1)(a)

- details of the agency's authority to act on the work-seeker's behalf, if applicable – Reg 16(1)(b)

- a statement as to whether the agency is authorised to receive money on behalf of the work-seeker – Reg 16(1)(c)

- details of any fee which may be payable by the work-seeker to the agency for work-finding services – Reg 16(1)(d)

- a statement of any notice required on either side to terminate the contract between work-seeker and agency – Reg 16(1)(e) and (f).

If the work-finding services involve including information about the work-**1.18** seeker in a publication within the meaning of Reg 26(5) (see 'Fees and charges' below), the agreement must also include a number of additional terms, set out in Reg 16(2). These include:

- that the agency will not charge a fee until the period during which the work-seeker may withdraw or cancel has elapsed – Reg 16(2)(a)

- that the work-seeker has the right, without detriment or penalty, to cancel or withdraw from the contract with immediate effect during such period – Reg 16(2)(b)

- that the agency will not include information about the work-seeker in a publication until a specified time has elapsed – Reg 16(2)(c)

- in relation to a contract with a work-seeker seeking employment in the performing arts, the agency will give him or her a copy of information published about the work-seeker, and inform him or her of the right to object to it within a particular period – Reg 16(2)(d) and (e)

- that the work-seeker is entitled to receive a full refund of the fees paid if the publication is not produced and made available to potential hirers within 60 days from the date on which payment is made by the work-seeker – Reg 16(2)(g).

If the employment agency is not permitted to charge a fee for the work-finding services it is providing, it does not need to agree terms.

Terms between employment business and hirer. An employment business **1.19** must agree terms with the hirer before providing its services – Reg 17. The employment business must record the agreed terms in writing and send a copy to the hirer as soon as reasonably practicable (unless the hirer already has a copy) – Reg 17(2). The terms must include:

- a statement that the employment business is acting in the capacity of an employment business in relation to the hirer – Reg 17(1)(a)

- details of fees payable by the hirer – Reg 17(1)(b), and

- details of the procedure to be followed if a work-seeker introduced or supplied to the hirer proves to be unsatisfactory – Reg 17(1)(c).

Most agreements between an employment business and a hirer will contain a clause requiring the hirer to alert the business if it has any grounds for dissatisfaction with a temporary worker and, as explained under 'Employment checks' below, an employment business has ongoing obligations to ensure the suitability of the workers it introduces or supplies to hirers.

1.20 If the employment business and the hirer agree to any variation in terms, the employment business must give the hirer written details of the variation as soon as reasonably practicable, stating the date on or after which it is agreed the varied terms will take effect – Reg 17(3).

Note that there is no corresponding provision in respect of terms agreed between employment *agencies* and hirers. This is left as a commercial matter for negotiation between the parties.

1.21 **Restrictions/detrimental action**
Employment agencies and businesses are prevented from including restrictive covenants in their contractual terms that would or might have the effect of inhibiting job mobility by preventing an end-user taking a temporary worker into permanent employment. In particular, Reg 6(1) of the 2003 Regulations prevents agencies/businesses from subjecting (or threatening to subject) a work-seeker to a detriment – whether by including a restrictive term in the work-seeker's contract or in any other way – on the ground that the work-seeker has:

- terminated or given notice to terminate any contract between him or her and the agency/business – Reg 6(1)(a)(i), or

- in the case of an employment business, taken up employment (or proposes to do so) for another person such as the hirer directly or through a competing employment business – Reg 6(1)(a)(ii).

Nor may the agency/business require the work-seeker to notify it or any connected person of the identity of any future employer – Reg 6(1)(b).

1.22 Although 'detriment' is not specifically defined for these purposes, it may be presumed to have a wide compass, as is the case in other employment law contexts such as discrimination. However, Reg 6(2) does make it clear that a 'detriment' will *not* include any of the following:

- the loss of any benefits that would have been payable to the work-seeker under the contract if he or she had not terminated it – Reg 6(2)(a)

- recovery by the agency/business of any losses flowing from a work-seeker's failure to carry out work he or she had agreed to perform – Reg 6(2)(b)

- a requirement in the terms agreed with the agency/business that the work-seeker give reasonable notice before terminating the contract – Reg 6(2)(c).

Regulation 6 does *not* apply where the work-seeker is or will be employed by an employment business under a contract of employment or apprenticeship – Reg 6(3). In these circumstances, the employment business would be entitled, in its capacity as an employer, to impose certain restrictions in the employee's contract of employment that would otherwise be prohibited by Reg 6. For a discussion of the law governing the use of restrictive covenants in employment contracts, see IDS Employment Law Handbook, 'Contracts of Employment' (2009), Chapter 5, 'Employee competition and confidentiality'.

Withholding pay. An employment business may not withhold (or threaten to withhold) pay due to a work-seeker on any of the following grounds: **1.23**

- that the hirer has not paid the employment business in respect of any services supplied to the hirer by the business – Reg 12(a)

- that the work-seeker cannot produce documentary evidence (such as a timesheet), authenticated by the hirer, that he or she has worked during a particular period of time. However, the employment business may satisfy itself by other means that the work-seeker worked for the period in question – Reg 12(b)

- that the work-seeker has not worked during a period other than that to which the payment relates – Reg 12(c)

- any matter within the control of the employment business (such as payroll maladministration) – Reg 12(d).

Reg 12(b) implies that if no timesheet can be produced (e.g. where the hirer is dissatisfied with the work and refuses to sign it) the employment business cannot withhold pay, but may presumably delay payment while it establishes by other means (such as contacting the hirer directly) whether or not the hours claimed were worked.

Fees and charges
1.24

Except in very specific circumstances (see 'Circumstances in respect of which fees may be charged to work-seekers' below), employment agencies are prohibited by S.6(1)(a) of the 1973 Act from charging, or receiving (directly or indirectly) a fee from, a work-seeker for providing work-finding services. Similarly, employment businesses are prohibited from charging, or receiving (directly or indirectly) a fee from, a work-seeker for placing him or her in a job, or for seeking a hirer, with a view to the work-seeker becoming employed by the employment business and acting for and under the control of the hirer – S.6(1)(b) and (c).

9

It is not unlawful to charge for ancillary services such as CV writing, training or equipment hire. However, to prevent agencies or employment businesses from insisting that work-seekers purchase such services before providing them with any work, Reg 5(1) of the 2003 Regulations makes it unlawful for an agency or employment business to make the provision of work-finding services conditional on the work-seeker using ancillary services, or hiring or purchasing goods, whether provided by the agency or the employment business or by any person with whom the agency or employment business is connected. In addition, work-seekers in the entertainment and modelling industries have a 30-day 'cooling off' period during which particular charges – such as charges for photographic services or audio recordings – may not be made and the work-seeker may cancel any contract for such services – Reg 5(3).

1.25 **Circumstances in respect of which fees may be charged to work-seekers.** There are three circumstances listed in Reg 26 where the restrictions on employment agencies charging fees to work-seekers contained in S.6(1)(a) of the 1973 Act do not apply: where the worker is seeking work in the entertainment industry; where the fee relates to a publication containing information about employers; and where the work-seeker is a company (and the work is not in the entertainment industry).

1.26 *Occupations in the entertainment industry.* Agencies (but not employment businesses) are entitled to charge fees to work-seekers for finding or seeking to find them employment in any of the occupations listed in Schedule 3 to the 2003 Regulations – Reg 26(1). The list in Schedule 3 covers performers such as actors and musicians, certain other workers in the arts and entertainment industry, models and professional sports persons. But even in these cases, with some very limited exceptions (in Reg 26(5) and (6)), fees cannot be levied up front but may only be taken out of the work-seeker's earnings once work has been found – Reg 26(2). Furthermore, the agency cannot charge fees to both the work-seeker and the hirer – Reg 26(3).

Employment agencies may charge upfront fees for including the details of workers covered by Schedule 3 – other than fashion and photographic models – in defined publications for work-seeking purposes – Reg 26(5)–(5C). However, a cooling-off period (of either seven or 30 days depending on the type of work involved) applies during which the employment agency cannot impose publishing fees and the agency worker may cancel or withdraw his or her agreement (and, in the case of those to whom a seven-day cooling off period applies, the agency must not publish the information). Workers seeking employment as an actor, background artist, dancer, extra, musician, singer or other performer (who enjoy a 30-day cooling off period) may also object to the proposed information within seven days of receiving a copy. If no published information is ultimately provided to hirers within 60 days of a fee being paid, work-seekers have the right to a refund of their fee – Reg 26(5)(d)–(g).

Publications containing information about employers. Agencies (but not **1.27** employment businesses) are entitled to charge fees to work-seekers in respect of the purchase of, or subscription for, a publication containing information about employers provided that this is the only work-finding service the agency (or any person connected with it) provides to the work-seeker and the work-seeker has been shown a copy of the publication in advance – Reg 26(6).

Work-seeker is a company. Agencies (but not employment businesses) are **1.28** entitled to charge fees to work-seekers for finding or seeking to find them employment where the work-seeker is a company and the occupation in question is *not* one of those listed in Schedule 3 to the 2003 Regulations – Reg 26(7). As mentioned above, the list in Schedule 3 covers performers such as actors and musicians, certain other workers in the arts and entertainment industry, models and professional sports persons.

Transfer fees. Once an employment business has engaged a work-seeker and **1.29** introduced him or her to a hirer, the employment business will clearly wish to protect its business interests in the event that the hirer decides to take on the work-seeker permanently, or the work-seeker's connection with the employment business is severed in some other way. For this reason, employment businesses typically charge hirers a transfer fee in respect of work-seekers they have introduced where the hirer:

- wishes to employ the worker directly (known in the industry as a 'temp-to-perm' transfer)

- seeks to re-engage the same worker through a different employment business (a 'temp-to-temp' transfer), or

- introduces the worker to a third party – often within the same group of companies – which then employs the worker directly (a 'temp-to-third-party' transfer).

Such fees are, however, restricted by the 2003 Regulations. Reg 10(4) provides **1.30** that an employment business cannot enforce any term of a contract (such as a transfer fee provision) between an employment business and a hirer which is contingent on a work-seeker:

- taking up employment with the hirer

- taking up employment with another person to whom the hirer has introduced him or her, or

- working for the hirer through another employment business

where the hirer takes on the work-seeker within eight weeks starting on the day after the end of an assignment, or within 14 weeks starting on the day the assignment started (whichever is the later) – Reg 10(5).

11

1.31 In other words, if an assignment lasted ten weeks and came to an end at the end of week ten, the hirer could re-engage the work-seeker at the beginning of week 19 without being subject to a fee. However, an employment business could charge a transfer fee where the hirer re-engaged the work-seeker two weeks after the end of an assignment. Determining the day on which the assignment started can be problematic where the work-seeker undertook a number of assignments, on and off, for the same hirer. However, so long as 42 days have passed during which the work-seeker did not work for the hirer under supply from the employment business, no account is taken of any supply that occurred prior to that period – Reg 10(6).

A further restriction is that the contract must offer the end-user the option of extending the original hire period for a set period (as specified in the contract) on no less favourable terms (e.g. at no higher rate) than before – Reg 10(1). In the absence of such a provision, the employment business cannot charge a transfer fee. An end-user who chooses the extended hire period will, at the end of the extended period, be able to employ the worker directly without having to wait a further eight weeks and without paying a fee. Such a fee is, however, chargeable if the end-user takes a worker into its direct employment during the specified extended hire period. The Regulations do not prescribe a maximum or minimum length for the extended hire period, or limit the amount of any transfer fee: these are left to be agreed between the end-user and the employment business before the assignment and will ultimately be guided by market forces.

Temp-to-temp fees are subject to the same restrictions as temp-to-perm fees. Temp-to-third-party fees, on the other hand, are subject to the timescale restrictions, but without the accompanying need to offer the extended-hire period.

1.32 Employment checks

The 2003 Regulations contain a raft of provisions setting out the requirements that need to be satisfied by employment agencies and businesses before and after a work-seeker is introduced or supplied to an end-user.

1.33 **Pre-engagement vetting.** One fundamental requirement is that employment agencies and businesses must take certain steps to satisfy themselves of the work-seeker's suitability for the position which the end-user is seeking to fill – Reg 18. Thus, before introducing a work-seeker to a hirer, an agency or employment business must obtain the following information from the hirer:

- the identity of the hirer and, if applicable, the nature of the hirer's business

- the date on which the hirer wants a work-seeker to start work and the duration, or likely duration, of the work

- the position which the hirer seeks to fill, including the type of work the work-seeker would be required to do, the location at which and the hours during which he or she would be required to work, and any risks to health and safety known to the hirer and what steps the hirer has taken to prevent or control such risks

- the experience, training, qualifications and any authorisation that the hirer considers are necessary, or which are required by law or by any professional body, for the work-seeker to carry out the work

- any expenses payable by or to the work-seeker (such as expenses incurred in attending interviews or payments to the Disclosure and Barring Service)

- (in the case of an employment agency only) (a) the minimum rate of pay and any other benefits offered by the hirer and the intervals at which the work-seeker would be paid; and (b) where applicable, the length of notice that a work-seeker would be required to give and entitled to receive, to end the employment with the hirer.

Furthermore, an employment business is prohibited from introducing or **1.34** supplying a work-seeker to a hirer unless it has obtained confirmation of the following:

- the work-seeker's identity – Reg 19(1)(a), and

- that the work-seeker has the experience, training, qualifications and any authorisation which the hirer considers are necessary, or which are required by law or by any professional body, to work in the position which the hirer seeks to fill – Reg 19(1)(b).

During initial registration, the employment business should therefore request sight of a passport, identity card, birth certificate or driving licence, and any evidence of training received, qualifications and authorisations such as certificates and registrations with professional bodies.

Similar provisions apply to employment agencies, although only where the **1.35** agency is seeking to introduce or supply a work-seeker to a hirer with a view to the work-seeker taking up a position which involves working with, caring for or attending a vulnerable person. In such circumstances, the agency must first obtain confirmation of the identity of the work-seeker, and that the work-seeker has the experience, training, qualifications and any authorisation which the hirer considers are necessary, or which are required by law or by any professional body, to work in the position which the hirer seeks to fill – Reg 19(2)(a) and (b).

Finally, neither an agency nor an employment business may introduce or supply a work-seeker to a hirer unless it has obtained confirmation that the work-seeker is willing to work in the position which the hirer seeks to fill – Reg 19(3).

Requirements imposed by law or professional bodies. As indicated above, **1.36** one of the pre-employment vetting checks involves the employment business

13

or, where relevant, employment agency, confirming that the work-seeker has the necessary experience, training, qualifications and authorisations. To this end, Reg 20(1)(a) provides that neither an agency nor an employment business may introduce or supply a work-seeker to a hirer unless the agency or business has taken all reasonably practicable steps to ensure that the work-seeker and hirer are each aware of any requirements imposed on them by law or any professional body to enable the work-seeker to carry out the work in question – Reg 20(1)(a). This means that the agency/business must be aware of any requirement in relation to particular types of work or job descriptions.

Regulation 20(1)(b) augments this requirement by placing an obligation on the employment agency or business, before introducing or supplying a work-seeker, to make all reasonably practicable enquiries to ensure that it would not be detrimental to the interests of either the work-seeker or the hirer for the placement to go ahead. It is obvious that this covers any health and safety concern, but the obligation may go wider: it may include, for example, any reasonable suspicion that the end-user company is in severe financial difficulties or is engaged in immoral or illegal practices. The obligation is without prejudice to any of the agency or business's duties under health and safety at work legislation.

1.37 *Professional qualifications or authorisation.* Regulation 22(4) provides that where the work-seeker is required by law, or any professional body, to have any qualifications or authorisation to work in a position for which the work-seeker is to be supplied or introduced to a hirer, an employment business may not introduce or supply the work-seeker to the hirer unless, in addition to the requirements in Regs 18–21, the following requirements are satisfied:

- the employment business has obtained copies of any relevant qualifications or authorisation of the work-seeker, and offered to provide copies of these documents to the hirer – Reg 22(5)(a), and

- taken all other reasonably practicable steps to confirm that the work-seeker is suitable for the position concerned – Reg 22(5)(b).

Where the employment business has taken all reasonably practicable steps to comply with the above requirements but has been unable to do so fully, it may instead comply with those requirements to the extent that it is able to do so. It must then inform the hirer that it has taken all reasonably practicable steps to comply fully but has been unable to do so, and give details of the steps that it has taken – Reg 22(6).

1.38 **Vulnerable persons.** Special precautions have to be taken where a work-seeker will be filling a position involving working with, caring for or attending vulnerable persons. A 'vulnerable person' is any person who by reason of age, infirmity, illness, disability or any other circumstance is in need of care or attention, and includes any person under the age of 18 – Reg 2. In such cases,

Reg 22 provides that before introducing or supplying the work-seeker, the employment agency or business must – in addition to the obligations imposed by Regs 18–21 – ensure that it has:

- obtained copies of any relevant qualifications or authorisations of the work-seeker and has offered to provide copies of those documents to the hirer – Reg 22(2)(a)

- obtained two references from persons who are not relatives of the work-seeker and have agreed that such references may be disclosed to the hirer, and has offered to provide copies of those references to the hirer ('relatives' having the same meaning as in S.63 of the Family Law Act 1996 – Reg 22(7)) – Reg 22(2)(b)

- taken all other reasonably practicable steps to confirm that the work-seeker is suitable for the position concerned – Reg 22(2)(c).

1.39 If the agency or business has not been able to comply fully with the first two requirements above, despite having taken all reasonably practicable steps to do so, it may instead comply to the extent that it is able to do so, and inform the hirer that it has taken all reasonably practicable steps to comply fully but has been unable to do so, and of the steps that it has taken – Reg 22(3).

1.40 **Post-engagement vetting.** Where an employment business receives or obtains information giving it reasonable grounds to believe that a work-seeker it has placed is unsuitable for the position, it must inform the hirer of that information and end the supply of the work-seeker 'without delay' – Reg 20(2). 'Without delay' in this context is defined in Reg 20(7) as 'the same day, or where that is not reasonably practicable, on the next business day'. So, for example, if a temporary teacher is supplied to a school and during the course of that supply the employment business receives information about that teacher, through a reference or other reliable report, showing that he or she is not suitable to work with children, the employment business must tell the hirer and remove the teacher from the assignment without delay.

If information is received which indicates that a work-seeker *may* be unsuitable but which does not, at that stage, give the employment business reasonable grounds for believing that he or she is unsuitable, the employment business must, without delay, inform the hirer of the information and commence further reasonably practicable enquiries as to the work-seeker's suitability, keeping the hirer informed of the progress of those enquiries – Reg 20(3). If, as a result of the enquiries, the original indication that the work-seeker may be unsuitable becomes a reasonable belief that he or she is in fact unsuitable, the employment business must inform the hirer and terminate the assignment without delay – Reg 20(4).

1.41 So far as employment agencies are concerned, where the agency receives information indicating that the worker may be unsuitable for the position, it is responsible for informing the hirer without delay. However, this obligation only applies for up to three months from the date at which the agency introduced the work-seeker to the hirer – Reg 20(5) and (6). The date of introduction presumably equates with the date on which the work-seeker starts work with the hirer.

It should be noted that the Regulations do not define 'unsuitable' for the purposes of these provisions. It seems reasonable, however, to presume that a work-seeker's suitability will be judged in light of the information that the agency or employment business is required to obtain before introducing or supplying the worker to the hirer.

1.42 **Sharing information**

Regulation 21 places a number of obligations on agencies and employment businesses to provide certain information to the hirer and work-seeker.

At the time when an agency or employment business *proposes* a particular work-seeker to a hirer, it must give the *hirer* all the information it, the agency or business, has been provided with under Reg 19 (i.e. the work-seeker's identity and details of his or her necessary experience, training, qualifications and authorisation) – Reg 21(1)(a)(i) (see 'Employment checks – pre-engagement vetting' above). In the case of an employment business, this information must include whether the work-seeker will be supplied under a contract of service (i.e. as a worker or employee) or contract of apprenticeship, or a contract for services (i.e. on a self-employed basis) – Reg 21(1)(a)(ii).

1.43 At the time the agency or employment business *offers* a work-seeker a position with a hirer, it must give the *work-seeker* all the information it, the agency or business, has been provided with under Reg 18 (see 'Employment checks – pre-engagement vetting' above) – Reg 21(1)(b)(i). In the case of an employment business that has not agreed a rate of remuneration in accordance with Reg 15(d)(i), it must also inform the work-seeker of the rate of remuneration it will pay him or her – Reg 21(1)(b)(ii).

The information may be provided to the hirer or work-seeker orally or in writing. However, where it is not given in writing (on paper or electronically) at the time the work-seeker is proposed to a hirer or offered a position with the hirer, the agency or employment business must confirm the information in paper form or by electronic means as soon as possible, and in any event no later than the end of the third business day following the day on which the information was given to the work-seeker or hirer orally – Reg 21(2).

1.44 If the work-seeker is being introduced or supplied to work in the same position with a hirer as he or she has worked within the previous five business days, and the relevant information has not changed (except for the date on which work is to start under Reg 18(b)), these information-sharing requirements will not apply, unless the work-seeker or hirer requests otherwise – Reg 21(3).

If an employment business intends to introduce or supply a work-seeker to a hirer for an assignment lasting five consecutive business days or less:

- the requirement in Reg 21(1)(a)(i) may be satisfied by the employment business giving the hirer the name of the work-seeker to be supplied and written confirmation by the employment business that it has complied with Reg 19 – Reg 21(4)(a), and

- where the employment business has previously provided the work-seeker with the information required under Reg 18 and that information remains unchanged, the requirement in Reg 21(1)(b) will be satisfied by the employment business providing him or her (on paper or electronically), the identity of the hirer and, if applicable, the nature of the hirer's business (under Reg 18(a)), and the date on which the hirer wants the work-seeker to start work and the duration, or likely duration, of the work (under Reg 18(b)) – Reg 21(4)(b).

However, where – after it has started – such an assignment is extended beyond **1.45** five business days, the information referred to in Reg 21(1) that has not already been provided must be provided in paper form or by electronic means by the end of the eighth business day of the assignment, or by the end of the assignment if sooner – Reg 21(5).

Confidentiality   1.46
Subject to the obligation in Reg 20 to give a hirer any information that indicates that a work-seeker is, or may be, unsuitable for the job, an agency or employment business must not disclose any information relating to a work-seeker without his or her prior consent, except:

- for the purpose of providing him or her with work-finding services

- for the purposes of any legal proceedings (including arbitration), or

- to any professional body of which the work-seeker is a member – Reg 28(1).

In particular, and without prejudice to the generality of that provision, an employment agency must not disclose information relating to a work-seeker to any current employer of that work-seeker without the work-seeker's prior consent – Reg 28(2). Such consent will not be valid if it has been withdrawn before any such disclosure has been made. Furthermore, an employment agency cannot make the provision of any services to that work-seeker conditional upon consent to disclosure being given (or not withdrawn).

17

1.47 **Restriction on providing work-seekers in industrial disputes**

Employment businesses are prohibited from introducing or supplying work-seekers to hirers to cover duties that would have been performed by workers who are on strike or taking part in other official industrial action (sometimes known as 'scab' labour) – Reg 7(1)(a). Nor may they introduce or supply a worker to do the work of another worker assigned to carry out the work of the person participating in official industrial action – Reg 7(1)(b). However, the employment business has a defence if it does not know, and has no reasonable grounds for knowing, that the first worker is taking part in such action.

These restrictions on providing labour do not apply if the strike or other industrial action in question is *unofficial* for the purposes of S.237 of the Trade Union and Labour Relations (Consolidation) Act 1992 – Reg 7(2) (see IDS Employment Law Handbook, 'Industrial Action' (2010), Chapter 8, 'Industrial action dismissals', under 'Dismissal during unofficial action – unofficial action'.

1.48 **Record-keeping**

In addition to client accounts (which fall outside the ambit of this Handbook), employment agencies and businesses are required to keep records to demonstrate their compliance with the 1973 Act and 2003 Regulations – Reg 29(1). In relation to every application the agency or employment business receives from a work-seeker, it must – unless it takes no action in respect of that application – keep the following particulars:

- the date the application was received

- the work-seeker's name, address and, if under 22, date of birth

- any terms which apply or will apply between the agency or employment business and the work-seeker, and any document recording any variation to them

- details of the work-seeker's training, experience, qualifications, and any authorisation to undertake particular work (and copies of any related documentary evidence obtained by the agency or employment business)

- details of any requirements specified by the work-seeker in relation to taking up employment

- names of hirers to whom the work-seeker is introduced or supplied

- details of any resulting engagement and the date from which it takes effect

- a copy of any contract between the work-seeker and any hirer entered into by the agency on the work-seeker's behalf

- the date on which the application was withdrawn or contract terminated (where applicable)

- in the case of an agency that is permitted to charge fees to work-seekers (see 'Fees and charges' above), dates of requests by the agency for fees from the work-seeker and of receipt of such fees with copies of statements or invoices, numbers and amounts; or, as appropriate, statements of dates and amounts of sums deducted from money received by the agency on the work-seeker's behalf in accordance with Reg 25, to the extent that these are not required to be comprised in records maintained in respect of a client account in accordance with para 12 of Schedule 2 to the 2003 Regulations

- details of enquiries made under Regs 19, 20 and 22 about the work-seeker and the position concerned, with copies of all relevant documents and the dates they were received or sent – Reg 29(1)(a) and (3); Sch 4.

In relation to every application the agency or employment business receives **1.49** from a hirer, it must – unless it takes no action in respect of that application – keep the following particulars:

- the date the application was received

- the hirer's name and address, and location of employment if different

- details of the position(s) the hirer seeks to fill

- the duration or likely duration of the work

- the experience, training, ability, qualifications, and authorisation required by the hirer, by law, or by any professional body; and any other conditions attaching to the position(s) the hirer seeks to fill

- the terms offered in respect of the position(s) the hirer seeks to fill

- a copy of the terms between the agency or employment business and the hirer, and any document recording any variation to them

- the names of work-seekers introduced or supplied

- details of enquiries under Regs 18 and 20 about the hirer and the position the hirer seeks to fill, with copies of all relevant documents and dates of their receipt

- details of each resulting engagement and the date from which it takes effect

- dates of requests by the agency or employment business for fees or other payment from the hirer and of receipt of such fees or other payments, and copies of statements or invoices – Reg 29(1)(b) and (3); Sch 5.

Similarly, specified particulars must be kept relating to the employment agency's **1.50** or business's dealings with other agencies and employment businesses – Reg 29(1)(c). These are listed in Schedule 6 to the 1973 Act.

The records must be kept for at least one year from the date of their creation, and those that relate to applications from work-seekers and hirers must be kept for at least one year from the date on which the agency or business ceases to provide its services to the work-seeker or hirer in question – Reg 29(2). They may be kept in electronic form, provided that the information can be reproduced legibly; and they may be kept either at the agency or employment business's premises, or elsewhere (provided certain accessibility requirements are complied with) – Regs 29(4) and (5).

1.51 Penalties for breach

If an employment agency or employment business fails to comply with any of its obligations under the 1973 Act or the 2003 Regulations, it can be sued for damages in the civil courts by anyone who suffers loss or injury as a result of the breach, including death or personal injury – Reg 30(1).

Furthermore, if an employment agency or business (or any other person) contravenes or fails to comply with the 2003 Regulations, it is guilty of a criminal offence and liable on conviction to a fine – S.5(2) 1973 Act. In addition, an attempt to charge fees or any other breach of S.6 of the 1973 Act will be an offence, liable on conviction to a fine – S.6(2) (see 'Fees and charges' above).

1.52 An employment tribunal may prohibit an 'unsuitable' person (whether an individual, company, or partnership) from carrying on or being concerned with carrying on an agency or employment business, or can impose conditions on the manner in which it does so, for up to ten years – S.3A 1973 Act. A person may be 'unsuitable' for misconduct or any other sufficient reason. Each person who was carrying on, or concerned with the carrying on of, the agency or business at the relevant time is deemed to have been responsible for what happened unless he or she can show that it happened 'without his connivance or consent and was not attributable to any neglect on his part' – S.3A(7).

1.53 Contractual terms. Contract terms that do not comply with the 2003 Regulations are unenforceable – Reg 31. Where a contractual term is prohibited or made unenforceable by the Regulations, the contract will continue to bind the parties if it is capable of continuing in existence without that term – Reg 31(1). If a hirer pays any transfer fees under a contractual term that is unenforceable by virtue of Reg 10, the hirer is entitled to recover that money – Reg 31(2) (see 'Fees and charges – transfer fees' above).

1.54 Proposals for regulatory reform

The Government considers that the current rules contained in the 1973 Act and 2003 Regulations are outdated, complicated and unduly burdensome for businesses. As a result, it issued a consultation on 17 January 2013 proposing to replace the current legislation with a simpler regulatory framework. The Government's aim is to reduce the burden on businesses while continuing to protect people who are looking for work, particularly those most at risk of exploitation.

The Government's response to the consultation, 'Reforming the regulatory framework for the recruitment sector', was published on 12 July 2013 and makes it clear that the Government intends to proceed with its proposal to replace the current legislation. Once draft legislation has been prepared, it will carry out another, shorter consultation before the new provisions come into effect.

According to the response, the new regulatory framework will: **1.55**

- ensure that employment businesses do not withhold payment from temporary workers (for example, where the employment business has not been paid by the hirer)

- continue to restrict employment agencies and employment businesses from charging fees to work-seekers (but retain current exemptions in the entertainment and modelling sector)

- clarify who is responsible for paying temporary workers where multiple businesses work together to supply a temporary worker to a hirer

- prevent employment businesses and employment agencies from penalising a temporary worker for terminating or giving notice to terminate a contract

- prevent employment businesses from enforcing unreasonable terms on a hirer when a temporary worker takes up permanent employment with that hirer

- ensure that employment agencies and employment businesses keep sufficient records to demonstrate that they have complied with the regulations governing the recruitment sector, and

- clarify that online 'job boards' are not 'employment agencies' and thus do not fall within the regulatory framework.

The Government also intends to enable individuals who are limited company contractors to opt out of the Regulations and to engage with employment businesses and employment agencies in a business-to-business relationship.

Further changes are intended for the enforcement strategy in the recruitment **1.56** sector, with the Government stating that it will focus on the most vulnerable workers by moving resources from the Employment Agency Standards Inspectorate to the National Minimum Wage (NMW) team at Her Majesty's Revenue and Customs (HMRC). The NMW team will investigate complaints of non-payment of the NMW to temporary workers. Enforcement will be carried out under NMW legislation and will be subject to HMRC sanctions. A small team will remain in the Department for Business, Innovation and Skills to enforce other aspects of the regulatory framework, including non-payment of workers earning above the NMW. Individuals will be able to enforce their rights informally and through the courts.

1.57 Rights under the Agency Workers Regulations

The Agency Workers Regulations 2010 SI 2010/93 (AWR) came into force on 1 October 2011 and implement the EU Temporary Agency Workers Directive (No.2008/104) ('the Directive'). They seek to protect temporary agency workers in three respects:

- hirers must ensure that agency workers enjoy no less favourable treatment than a comparable employee or worker in relation to access to collective facilities and amenities – Reg 12 (see 'Collective facilities and amenities' below)

- hirers must inform agency workers of any relevant vacancies during an assignment so that they may be given the same opportunity as a comparable worker to find permanent employment with the hirer – Reg 13 (see 'Information on vacancies' below)

- temporary work agencies and hirers must ensure that an agency worker who has completed a 12-week qualifying period receives the same basic working and employment conditions as he or she would be entitled to for doing the same job had he or she been recruited directly by the hirer at the time the qualifying period commenced – Reg 5(1)(a) and (b) (see 'Equal treatment: the basic principle' below).

The AWR do not affect the employment status of temporary agency workers or their entitlement to other employment rights, such as the right to claim unfair dismissal. For a discussion of these matters, see 'Other statutory employment rights' and 'Employment status' below.

1.58 The Department for Business, Innovation and Skills (BIS) published guidance to the AWR on 6 May 2011 (URN 11/949) ('the BIS Guidance'). As this Guidance is non-statutory, it has no legal force, but is helpful in obtaining a clearer view of what the AWR are intended to achieve.

Note that in the summer of 2013 the Government carried out a review of the impact of the AWR, with a view to reducing the administrative burden on agencies and hirers. According to BIS, the review's findings are currently being analysed and advice will be sent to Ministers in due course.

1.59 Who is covered by the AWR?

The AWR seek to protect 'agency workers' in their relationship with 'temporary work agencies' and 'hirers'. These terms, and the definitions that apply to them, are similar but not identical to those used in the regulatory legislation – the Employment Agencies Act 1973 ('the 1973 Act') and the Conduct of Employment Agencies and Employment Business Regulations 2003 SI 2003/3319 ('the 2003 Regulations') – examined under 'Regulatory framework' above. However, employment agencies whose function is to recruit workers for permanent roles are not covered by the AWR.

Hirer. The hirer is the end-user of an agency worker's services. For the purposes **1.60** of the AWR, a hirer is 'a person engaged in economic activity, public or private, whether or not operating for profit, to whom individuals are supplied, to work temporarily for and under the supervision and direction of that person' – Reg 2. Given that the hirer must be engaged in economic activity and must supervise and direct the work of the agency worker, those who engage agency workers in a private capacity – for example, as domestic cleaners – are unlikely to be considered 'hirers' and will therefore fall outside the scope of the AWR.

The Department of Education's non-statutory advice on the application of the AWR to supply teachers, 'Agency Workers Regulations 2010: supply teachers' (March 2014), gives specific guidance as to who is considered to be the hirer of agency supply teachers in various types of school. It advises that in foundation schools, voluntary aided schools and foundation special schools, the hirer is the school's governing body, as this is the legal entity to whom the worker is supplied and who is responsible for the supervision and direction of that worker. In community schools, voluntary controlled schools, community special schools and maintained nursery schools, the hirer is either the local authority or the school's governing body, depending on to whom the worker is supplied and who supervises and directs his or her work. In academies, including free schools, and independent schools, the hirer is the proprietor of the school.

Temporary work agency. The definition of temporary work agency (TWA) is **1.61** similar to that of 'employment business' under the 1973 Act and the 2003 Regulations. Reg 4(1) AWR defines a TWA as a person engaged in the economic activity of either:

- supplying individuals to work temporarily for and under the supervision and direction of hirers – Reg 4(1)(a), or

- paying for, or receiving or forwarding payment for, the services of individuals who are supplied to work temporarily for and under the supervision and direction of hirers – Reg 4(1)(b).

An agency may be a TWA even if it is not operating for profit, so long as its activity can be described as 'economic'. It is irrelevant whether it is operating in the public or private sphere or whether or not it is carrying on its activity in conjunction with others – Reg 4(1). If, however, the organisation supplies individuals to work temporarily for and under the supervision and direction of hirers, but this is incidental to its main economic activity, then it will not fall within the scope of the AWR. For example, the BIS Guidance suggests that where an individual is working in organisation A, but is on secondment to organisation B, who pays the individual until his or her return to organisation

A at the end of the secondment, organisation A will not be acting as a TWA as its main activity is not the supply of workers (see page 12).

1.62 While the first limb of Reg 4(1) would clearly cover a typical 'high street' agency, the second part ensures that the definition also encompasses a situation where the TWA acts as an intermediary in the labour supply chain. An intermediary could, for example, be a master vendor or management company. The Guidance points out that a hirer may appoint 'one agency (the master vendor) to manage its recruitment process, using other recruitment agencies as necessary ("second tier" suppliers)'; or it may appoint 'a management company (neutral vendor) which normally does not supply any workers directly but manages the overall recruitment process and supplies temporary agency workers through others' (see page 6). Alternatively, an individual may supply his or her services to a hirer indirectly via an umbrella company, by which the individual is employed. The umbrella company, in such a case, would be an intermediary caught by Reg 4(1)(b).

However, a person is not a TWA if it is engaged in the economic activity of paying for, or receiving or forwarding payments for, the services of individuals *regardless of whether the individuals are supplied to work for hirers* – Reg 4(2).

1.63 **Agency worker.** For the purposes of the AWR, an 'agency worker' is an individual who:

- is supplied by a TWA to work temporarily for and under the supervision and direction of a hirer – Reg 3(1)(a)

- has a contract with the TWA that is a contract of employment or any other contract with the TWA to perform work and services personally – Reg 3(1)(b), and

- is not in business on his or her own account, i.e. neither the TWA nor the hirer can have the status of a client or customer of a profession or business undertaking carried on by the individual – Reg 3(2).

This definition reflects the classic tripartite nature of the relationship between the temporary worker, the employment business and the hirer. The agency worker may either be employed by or have a contract for services with the TWA to perform work or services for the hirer: both are covered by this definition.

1.64 However, the Regulations can also encompass more complex set-ups that operate in the recruitment industry, notably where intermediaries are involved at some stage in the supply of the agency worker. As indicated under 'Temporary work agency' above, the definition of TWA is broad enough to include intermediaries. The definition of 'agency worker' is equally capacious, providing that an individual will be treated as having been supplied by a TWA to 'work temporarily for and under the supervision and direction of a hirer' (see Reg 3(1)(a)) if:

- the TWA initiates or is involved as an intermediary in the making of the arrangements that lead to the individual being supplied to work temporarily for and under the supervision and direction of the hirer – Reg 3(3)(a), and

- the individual is supplied by an intermediary, or one of a number of intermediaries, to work temporarily for and under the supervision and direction of the hirer – Reg 3(3)(b).

An individual who is treated as having been supplied by a TWA by virtue of these provisions is treated as having a contract with the TWA for the purposes of Reg 3(1)(b) – Reg 3(4).

Regulation 3(5) clarifies that an individual is not prevented from being an **1.65** agency worker simply because one of the following circumstances applies:

- the TWA supplies the individual through one or more intermediaries

- one or more intermediaries supply that individual

- the individual is supplied pursuant to any contract or other arrangement between the TWA, one or more intermediaries and the hirer

- the TWA pays for the services of the individual through one or more intermediaries, or

- the individual is employed by, or otherwise has a contract with, one or more intermediaries.

Self-employed. The definition of 'agency worker' under the AWR clearly **1.66** excludes those who are genuinely self-employed. As indicated above, a worker will not be an agency worker if he or she is in business on his or her own account – that is, where the TWA or the hirer has the status of a client or customer of a profession or business undertaking carried on by the individual – Reg 3(2).

According to the BIS Guidance, the following individual would fall outside the scope of the AWR, on the basis that his working arrangement lacks personal service and mutuality of obligation:

- an individual has set up his own limited company through which he provides IT services. He has a contract with a TWA and is supplied to work on a specific project with an anticipated duration of 12 months. He has no fixed working pattern and can determine how and when he performs the services; he can also send a substitute to perform the services at any time. Payment is made as stages of the project are delivered. However, he is subject to the hirer's reasonable and lawful instructions (see page 12).

Under supervision and direction of the hirer. But even if an individual is not **1.67** self-employed, he or she would fall outside the scope of the AWR if he or she does not work 'under the supervision and direction of the hirer' as required by

Reg 3(1). The BIS Guidance provides the following examples of working arrangements which *would* fall within the scope of the AWR:

- a company has a staff canteen managed by an in-house catering manager. One of the company's catering staff is absent and is replaced by a worker supplied by a TWA. During her assignment the worker is supervised and directed by the hirer's catering manager

- a number of factory workers are sent by a TWA to work on a hirer's production line. Because there are lots of workers on the line provided by the same TWA, the TWA sends a manager who works on-site to deal with issues such as sickness absence or any other problems that may occur in relation to the agency workers. However, each worker still does his or her job under the supervision and direction of the hirer (see page 12).

1.68 However, the Guidance suggests that the AWR would *not* cover managed service contracts under which a company provides a specific service to the hirer such as catering or cleaning, but the worker is under the direction of the contractor and not the hirer (see page 5). For example:

- an organisation contracts out the management of its canteen. The contractor manages the entire operation of the canteen and is responsible for the direction and control of its own catering staff. Although they are working on the customer's premises, the contractor's workers are not agency workers because they are not subject to the direction and control of the customer (see page 12).

1.69 *Contract with the TWA.* Equally, where the worker does not have a contract with the TWA, this will put him or her outside the scope of the AWR. Thus temporary workers who are recruited through in-house temporary staffing banks, where the hirer employs the temporary workers directly to use within the business where needed, are excluded.

1.70 *Temporary workers only.* Finally, the AWR apply only in respect of workers supplied to cover *temporary* assignments for a hirer – Reg 3(1). The EAT explored the meaning of the word 'temporary' in Moran and ors v Ideal Cleaning Services Ltd and anor 2014 IRLR 172, EAT, in which M and his colleagues were placed, from the start of their employment with ICS Ltd, with a single identified hirer, CA Ltd (or predecessor companies), which had a long-standing contract with ICS Ltd for the provision of cleaning services. None of the employees ever worked for another client, and M's written statement of terms and conditions specified CA Ltd's plant in Derby as his place of work. The employees brought a claim under the AWR but the employment tribunal and the EAT concluded that they did not qualify for protection under those Regulations. They were not agency workers, as their working arrangement with CA Ltd could not be said to be temporary. In the EAT's view, 'temporary' did not equate with 'short term', as in an employment context, a temporary contract could be for a fixed duration of many months or even years. In such a case it could properly be regarded as temporary because it was not permanent, but it could not be said to be short term. However, in this case the employment tribunal had found that the arrangement under which the employees worked was indefinite in duration: it was not temporary because it was permanent, not because it was long in duration.

The employees also argued that, regardless of what conclusion was reached on the meaning of 'temporary', the tribunal was obliged to hold that they were covered by the AWR in order to give effect to the purpose of the Directive, on which the AWR are based. The Directive was aimed at ensuring equal treatment between agency workers and those who worked alongside them. The employees argued that this purpose would be defeated if all protection was lost simply because the agency workers were assigned to an end-user on an open-ended basis. However, the EAT rejected this argument. The Directive specifically applies to 'temporary agency workers', and to adopt the interpretation put forward by the employees would run counter to the underlying purpose of the Directive. The original proposed Directive covered agency workers who were simply posted to a user undertaking. However, an amendment was introduced specifying that the Directive should apply to 'temporary' agency workers and including within the definition of that term a requirement that the worker be 'assigned temporarily in a user undertaking' (Article 3(1)). The requirement for an assignment to be temporary was therefore inserted deliberately and could not be ignored.

It is therefore important to distinguish between an assignment that is merely **1.71** long term and an assignment that is actually permanent. There are many agency workers who have been assigned to the same end-user for several years, but there is no reason to doubt that they are covered by the AWR. Usually, there is a fixed period for their assignment, which has been renewed on regular occasions. That is very different from the situation in the Moran case, where the employees were specifically recruited to work for one particular client on an open-ended basis.

A more difficult case might be where the agency worker is on an open-ended assignment with a particular client where there is nothing to indicate how long the assignment is likely to last. On a strict reading of Moran and ors v Ideal Cleaning Services Ltd and anor (above), it could be argued that because there is no limit on the duration of the assignment it cannot be said to be temporary, and therefore falls outside the scope of the AWR. In such a case, however, the overall context of the assignment would need to be considered. Arguably, there is a distinction between the position of an agency worker who happens – for the time being – to be working on an assignment with no fixed end-date and that of an employee who, like the employees in the Moran case, has been recruited specifically to work on the premises of a particular client. To hold that the agency workers in either situation are not covered by the AWR would surely be contrary to the underlying purpose of the Directive.

1.72 Access to collective facilities and amenities

Before the AWR came into force, employers would sometimes deliberately withhold access to collective facilities and amenities from agency workers in order to avoid any implication that they might be employees and accordingly have wider employment rights, including the right not to be unfairly dismissed. This is no longer possible under the AWR (and, in any event, agency workers are less likely now to be considered employees by implication – see 'Employment status' below). From 'day one' of an assignment, an agency worker has the right to be treated no less favourably than a comparable worker in relation to the collective facilities and amenities provided by the hirer, unless less favourable treatment is justified on objective grounds – Reg 12(1).

1.73 Collective facilities and amenities. The right under Reg 12 is limited to the provision of *collective* facilities and amenities. 'Collective' may mean that they are provided to the workers as a whole, or it may mean that they are provided to particular groups of workers, though there would presumably be a point at which a service would cease to be truly 'collective'. For example, it could be argued that a counselling service is not collective if it is only made available to those who are referred to it by an occupational health service.

The AWR specify that 'collective facilities and amenities' include, in particular, canteen or other similar facilities, childcare facilities and transport services – Reg 12(3). The BIS Guidance suggests that 'transport services' would include the provision of local pick-up and drop-off points and transport between sites, although it would not include company car allowances or season ticket loans, for example, as these are benefits as opposed to facilities and amenities (see page 15). And childcare facilities might include a crèche or breastfeeding facilities. The Guidance also gives additional examples of services that would fall within the definition of collective facilities and amenities, such as the provision of car parking, toilet or shower facilities, a prayer room, or a waiting room. Usually the facilities will be on-site, but if a facility such as a canteen is at another site or shared with another company, then, according to the Guidance, this could also amount to a collective facility (see page 16).

1.74 It is important to bear in mind that the right does not apply to all benefits. For example, company car allowances, season ticket loans and other benefits in kind given to directly employed staff would not fall within the scope of Reg 12. Therefore careful consideration needs to be given to company benefits to determine what is covered. For example, while the provision of access to a gym would probably constitute a collective facility, subsidised gym membership would not. (Note, however, that certain limited benefits, such as luncheon vouchers, that fall outside the scope of Reg 12 may be caught by Reg 5 – the right to equal treatment in respect of pay and working time – which is applicable after a 12-week qualifying period – see 'Equal treatment: the basic principle' below.)

Provided 'by the hirer'. Regulation 12(1) applies to collective facilities and **1.75** amenities provided 'by the hirer'. Thus, as the BIS Guidance suggests, agency workers would not be entitled to the benefit of off-site facilities and amenities that are not provided by the hirer, such as 'subsidised access to an off-site gym as part of a benefit package to reward long-term service or loyalty' (see page 16). However, this leaves open the question of whether Reg 12(1) covers on-site facilities or amenities, such as a canteen or vending machines, that are provided not by the hirer itself, but by a third party under contract. Strictly speaking, such facilities or amenities are not provided 'by the hirer', and so would not seem to come within the scope of the right. However, it is likely that a court would read Reg 12(1) purposively. If a hirer chooses to 'provide' a canteen by engaging a contractor to run it on its behalf, it is none the less providing that facility to its workers.

This interpretation is supported by the wording of the Directive, Article 6 of which requires that temporary agency workers be given access to the amenities or collective facilities *in the user undertaking* under the same conditions as workers employed directly by the undertaking. There is thus no requirement under EU law that such amenities or facilities be provided directly by the hirer.

Training. There is some uncertainty over whether the right to access collective **1.76** facilities and amenities would cover access to training. The Directive requires Member States to take suitable measures to promote dialogue between social partners in order to improve temporary agency workers' access to training (Article 6(5)). However, the UK Government resisted taking a regulatory approach to implementing this requirement and did not include training in the particularisation of collective facilities and amenities at Reg 12(3). Nevertheless, this list is not exclusive, so it would be open to an agency worker to argue that Reg 12 encompasses a right to collective training provision.

Comparable worker. Regulation 12 gives agency workers the right to be **1.77** treated *no less favourably than a comparable worker* in relation to collective facilities and amenities. A comparable worker must be an employee of the hirer (unless there is no comparable employee, in which case the comparator may be a worker) who is employed by and working under the direction of the hirer, doing the same or broadly similar work to the agency worker (having regard, where relevant, to whether they have similar skills and qualifications) at the time the breach is alleged to take place – Reg 12(4). If there is no comparable worker at the same establishment, then the agency worker may compare him or herself with a comparable worker working at a different establishment. If there is no comparable worker at the same or at a different establishment, then the right is effectively redundant, as there is no provision for comparison with a hypothetical comparator.

Clearly, given that the right is a right to be treated no less favourably than a comparable worker, an agency worker has no right to be treated *more* favourably. Thus, even if most of the permanent employees working for the hirer are entitled to use a company gym, for example, but the comparable worker is not, then neither will the agency worker be entitled to use the gym. Furthermore, if entitlement to collective facilities is subject to qualifying conditions, these will apply equally to agency workers. For instance, if there is a waiting list for a particular benefit, the agency worker would not automatically be entitled to the benefit, but would have to join the list, even if this means that he or she is unable to enjoy the benefit before his or her assignment comes to an end.

1.78 **Objective justification.** It remains open to a hirer to treat an agency worker less favourably than a comparable worker in respect of collective facilities and amenities, where it can demonstrate objective grounds for doing so – Reg 12(2). The BIS Guidance suggests that the hirer should ask itself the following question: 'Is there a good reason for treating the agency worker less favourably?' Cost may be one factor to take into account in this respect, but the Guidance cautions against relying on this factor alone to justify differential treatment. Practical and organisational considerations may also play a part (see page 16). That said, the Guidance suggests that the hirer should consider whether it is possible or feasible to offer agency workers certain access rights on a pro rata basis as an alternative to excluding them altogether.

Assistance in understanding what amounts to objective grounds for less favourable treatment may be drawn from similar provisions in the Fixed-term Employees (Prevention of Less Favourable Treatment) Regulations 2002 SI 2002/2034, which are discussed in Chapter 2, 'Fixed-term employees', under 'Equal treatment'.

1.79 **Liability.** Liability for any breach of Reg 12 lies with the hirer, not the TWA – Reg 14(6).

1.80 **Information on vacancies**
In addition to the right to access the hirer's collective facilities and amenities (see 'Collective facilities and amenities' above), an agency worker has the right from 'day one' of an assignment to be informed by the hirer of any relevant vacant posts with the hirer, in order to give that worker the same opportunity as a comparable worker to find permanent employment with the hirer – Reg 13(1).

The hirer need not personally inform the agency worker of any vacancies but can instead make 'a general announcement in a suitable place in the hirer's establishment' – Reg 13(4). For example, the hirer could post the information on a notice board or on the intranet. However, as the BIS Guidance points out, the agency worker should know where and how to access the information (see page 17).

Right to apply? On a strict reading, Reg 13 only confers a right to be informed **1.81** of vacancies, not a right to actually apply for them. However, a policy of preventing an agency worker from applying for relevant vacancies would defeat the express purpose of the provision, which is to give agency workers the same opportunity as comparable workers to find permanent employment with the hirer. While Reg 13 might seem somewhat clumsily worded if this is its intended effect, it reflects the wording of the Directive, which requires agency workers to 'be informed of any vacant posts in the user undertaking to give them the same opportunity as other workers in that undertaking to find permanent employment' (Article 6(1)).

The BIS Guidance stresses that Reg 13 'does not constrain hirers' freedom regarding… how they treat applications' (see page 17). This appears to suggest that even though agency workers must be given information about vacancies in order to be able to apply for permanent positions, their applications need not necessarily be treated in the same way as those made by comparable workers. For example, a hirer may wish to prioritise internal applications and only consider those made by agency workers at a later stage, along with other external applications. We would argue, however, that although this approach would seem technically to comply with the wording of Reg 13, it does not achieve the objective of giving agency workers the same opportunity as other workers to *find* permanent employment (i.e. to enter it, as opposed to simply apply for it).

The Guidance also states that the right in Reg 13 will not apply in the context **1.82** of a genuine 'headcount freeze', where the business is restructured or posts are ring-fenced for redeployment by existing internal staff in order to avoid a redundancy situation (see page 17). Furthermore, employers would be free to continue to require certain qualifications or levels of experience – e.g. time in service with the organisation – that agency workers are unlikely or less likely to have.

Comparable worker. A 'comparable worker' for these purposes is an individual **1.83** who is:

- working for and under the supervision and direction of the hirer

- working at or based at the same establishment as the agency worker, and

- engaged in the same or broadly similar work having regard, where relevant, to whether he or she has a similar level of qualification and skills – Reg 13(2)(a) and (b).

The comparator must be an employee of the hirer unless there is no employee satisfying these requirements, in which case the comparator may be a worker who does satisfy them – Reg 13(2)(c). However, the comparator may not be a predecessor, and, by contrast with the right to access collective facilities and amenities under Reg 12, the agency worker is not entitled to compare him or herself with a worker at a different establishment – Reg 13(3). The BIS Guidance suggests that practical difficulties could arise if 'comparable workers' included those working for the hirer at a 'geographically remote' establishment (see page 17). If there is no comparable worker, then the right is effectively redundant.

1.84 **No objective justification.** Unlike the right to collective facilities and amenities, Reg 13 does not allow for less favourable treatment of the agency worker on objective grounds.

1.85 **Liability.** Liability for any breach of Reg 13 lies with the hirer, not the TWA – Reg 14(6).

1.86 ## Equal treatment: the basic principle

The core right bestowed by the AWR is the right to equal treatment in respect of 'basic working and employment conditions'. Regs 5(1) and 7 provide that an agency worker who has completed a 12-week qualifying period must receive the same basic working and employment conditions as he or she would be entitled to for doing the same job had he or she been recruited directly by the hirer at the time the qualifying period commenced. 'Basic working and employment conditions' are restricted to terms and conditions relating to pay, working time and annual leave – Reg 6(1) (see 'Equal treatment: pay' and 'Equal treatment: working time and annual leave' below).

The right to 'equal treatment' only extends to the terms and conditions that would have been 'ordinarily included' in the agency worker's contract had he or she been recruited directly by the hirer to do the same job – Reg 5(2). This covers the terms and conditions ordinarily applicable to workers, or, if the worker would have been recruited as an employee had he or she been directly employed, the terms and conditions ordinarily included in the hirer's employment contracts – in other words, as the BIS Guidance explains, the terms and conditions that are normally set out in standard contracts, a pay scale or structure, a relevant collective agreement, or the company handbook (see page 25). By contrast, individually negotiated contract terms or one-off discretionary payments would not be caught by the 'equal treatment' rule in Reg 5. Thus large employers with defined pay structures are more likely to be caught by the AWR than small employers that directly negotiate individual terms and conditions with the workforce.

1.87 **Enhancements.** When determining the basic working and employment conditions to which an agency worker is entitled, the relevant terms and conditions are those that applied at the start of the qualifying period – Reg 5(1)(b). However, Reg 5(2) goes on to provide that any variations made to those terms *after* that point must not be disregarded. So, once the agency worker qualifies for equal treatment, he or she must be given any subsequent enhancements to terms and conditions, such as service-related increases in annual leave or incremental pay increases. This means that the obligation not to treat agency workers less favourably is ongoing.

Derogations. The Directive allows Member States to derogate from the right **1.88** to equal treatment in two respects. First, they can derogate from the right to equal treatment in terms of pay where the agency worker is employed on a permanent contract of employment that provides for pay between assignments (the so-called 'Swedish derogation') – see 'Equal treatment: pay – the Swedish derogation' below. Secondly, they can derogate in collective or workforce agreements between workers and employer's representatives. Only the first of these derogations is reflected in the AWR.

Liability. Liability for breach of Reg 5 falls on either the hirer or the TWA, to **1.89** the extent that each is responsible – Reg 14 (see 'Liability' below).

Equal treatment: the qualifying period   1.90

Although the Directive itself puts no restrictions on the right to equal treatment, Article 5(4) allows Member States to derogate from the general principle, including by the imposition of a qualifying period. The UK Government took advantage of this provision and, accordingly, whereas the rights to access collective facilities and amenities and to be informed of vacancies are so-called 'day one' rights, applicable from the start of an agency worker's assignment, entitlement to equality in respect of basic working and employment conditions under Reg 5 is only available where the agency worker has worked in the same role with the same hirer for 12 continuous calendar weeks during one or more assignments – Reg 7(1) and (2).

In practical terms, the existence of a qualifying period is significant given that the majority of agency workers are recruited only for short periods. As a result, the right to equal treatment in respect of basic working and employment conditions will simply not apply to many workers. However, Reg 7(1) and (2) will cease to have effect if an agency worker is engaged on repeated short-term assignments in violation of the anti-avoidance provision in Reg 9 – see 'Anti-avoidance provision' below.

Calendar weeks. A week will count as a calendar week if the worker works for **1.91** any part of it – Reg 7(4). Thus, an agency worker who works two days a week will qualify for equal treatment after the same amount of time as a worker who works five days a week.

According to the BIS Guidance, a calendar week begins on the day the worker starts the role with the hirer (see pages 18–19). So, if the agency worker begins work on a Tuesday, the calendar week runs until the following Monday.

1.92 **The same role.** The agency worker must work *in the same role* for the hirer for the duration of the qualifying period to become entitled to equal treatment. An agency worker works 'in the same role' unless:

- he or she has started a new role with the same hirer, whether supplied by the same or a different TWA

- the whole or the main part of the work and duties of the new role are substantively different from those of the previous role, and

- the TWA has informed the agency worker in writing of the type of work he or she will be required to do in the new role – Reg 7(3).

This wording suggests that unless there are genuine and real differences to job requirements, a change in work or duties will not amount to a new role for the purposes of the Regulations. The BIS Guidance stresses that it is not enough, for example, that a line manager has changed but not the job requirements, or that the agency worker has transferred between similar administrative functions, has moved within a single relatively small business unit or has been put on a different pay rate (see page 24). None of these things by themselves would be sufficient to show that the agency worker had ceased to work in the same role for the purpose of the qualifying period.

1.93 In the event of a dispute, the guidance suggests that a combination of factors is likely to be taken into account by an employment tribunal when establishing whether or not the work or duties are substantively different. Thus a tribunal might consider the following:

- a change in skills and competencies

- a change in pay rate

- a change of location or cost centre

- a change of line manager

- different working hours

- whether the role requires extra training and/or a specific qualification that was not needed before

- different equipment.

Thus, as the Guidance points out, simply moving an agency worker from a production line to packing the products for distribution within a warehouse would not be moving him or her into a substantively different role, as the packing role requires little training and uses most of the same skills as the production line role. The agency worker would therefore qualify for equal treatment after 12 weeks. By contrast, a move to an administrative role would be likely to be considered substantively different, triggering the start of a new qualifying period (see page 24).

Even where an agency worker has genuinely been assigned to a new role, the start of another qualifying period will only be triggered if the TWA has informed the agency worker of the type of work that he or she will be required to do in the new role. The TWA will obtain this information from the hirer in accordance with the process set out in Reg 18 of the Conduct of Employment Agencies and Employment Business Regulations 2003 SI 2003/3319 – see the section 'Regulatory framework', under 'Employment checks – pre-engagement vetting' above. The TWA should record details about the new role and notify the agency worker in writing that his or her role has substantively changed and that the qualifying period will start again.

The same hirer. Under Reg 7(2), an agency worker must work in the same role **1.94** *for the same hirer* for the duration of the qualifying period to become entitled to the right to equal treatment. In the majority of cases, it will be relatively straightforward to ascertain whether the agency worker is placed with the same hirer or not. Where a hirer is a new legal entity, it will be a new hirer. So, if an agency worker is moved around between companies within a larger group, the qualifying period will start running again each time (although a hirer that moves an agency worker back and forth across a group of companies via holding companies or subsidiaries so as to deliberately deprive him or her of a right to equal treatment is likely to fall foul of the anti-avoidance provisions – see 'Anti-avoidance provisions' below).

Conversely, where a hirer has multiple sites and the agency worker is moved around to carry out the same role, he or she will still be performing 'the same role for the same hirer' pursuant to Reg 7(2). Three examples from the BIS Guidance:

- an agency worker acting as a supply teacher for a local authority will continue to work for the same hirer while undertaking assignments at different schools within the local authority

- an agency worker working for a hospital will continue to work for the same hirer if moved to another hospital within the same NHS Trust

- an agency worker supplied to a government department to work as a PA will continue to work for the same hirer when moved to a different department to work in the same capacity (see page 23).

Involvement of multiple agencies. As we have seen above, the emphasis in **1.95** Reg 7(2) is squarely on what type of work the agency worker performs and for whom – there is no requirement for the same TWA to be involved for the duration of the qualifying period (and beyond). Accordingly, the agency worker can accumulate 12 weeks in the same job where multiple agencies have supplied him or her to perform that role with the same hirer. The BIS Guidance gives the example of an agency worker who works for a hirer for six weeks with one agency. After a three-week break, another agency places him in the same job

35

with the same hirer for a further eight weeks. Thus, after six weeks on the second assignment, he becomes entitled to equal treatment (see page 20). (The short break between assignments is disregarded for the purpose of computing the 12-week qualifying period – see 'Breaks in assignments' below.)

Conversely, an agency worker who has 'signed on' with multiple TWAs and is placed with *different* hirers on different days of the week will have several qualifying periods running at the same time. For example, a worker drives an HGV lorry for hirer A on Mondays and Tuesdays, for hirer B on Wednesdays and Thursdays, and for hirer C on Fridays. A separate qualifying period will run in respect of each individual hirer.

1.96 Given the widespread practice of individuals 'temping' for more than one TWA at any one time, it is incumbent on TWAs to ask agency workers for their up-to-date work history. If a TWA fails to conduct the necessary checks, and the worker is not accorded equal treatment as a result, the TWA will be liable for this failure and may be required to pay compensation to the worker – see 'Enforcement' below.

1.97 **Breaks in assignments.** The Regulations only confer entitlement on an agency worker after 12 'continuous' weeks in the same role with the same hirer. However, given the irregularity of many agency workers' work patterns, some breaks during or between assignments will not trigger a new qualifying period provided the break is for one of a series of specified reasons. A specified reason may either pause or keep the clock ticking for the purposes of the qualifying period.

1.98 *Breaks during which continuity is paused.* Any weeks accrued in respect of the qualifying period before the agency worker takes a break – either between or during assignments – for a specified reason are carried forward and treated as continuous with any weeks worked by the agency worker after he or she returns to work in the same job with the same hirer – Reg 7(5). This provision applies where the break is:

- for any reason and lasts no longer than six calendar weeks – Reg 7(8)(a)

- wholly due to sickness or injury and lasts no longer than 28 calendar weeks – Reg 7(8)(b) and (9). The worker must provide such written medical evidence as may reasonably be required if asked to do so by the TWA. This reason does *not* apply if the break is related to pregnancy, childbirth or maternity, and is during a 'protected period' (see below)

- related to pregnancy, childbirth or maternity and is during a 'protected period' – Reg 7(8)(c). (The 'protected period' begins at the start of the pregnancy and ends at the end of the 26 weeks beginning with childbirth or, if earlier, when the agency worker returns to work – Reg 7(10).

'Childbirth' means the birth of a living child, or a stillbirth after 24 weeks of pregnancy – Reg 7(11))

- wholly for the purpose of taking any statutory or contractual time off or leave (e.g. family leave or annual leave), or a combination of different types of time off or leave – Reg 7(8)(d)

- wholly due to the fact that the worker has been called up for jury service and lasts no longer than 28 calendar weeks – Reg 7(8)(e)

- wholly due to a temporary cessation in the hirer's requirements for any worker to be present at the establishment and work in a particular role, for a predetermined period of time according to the established custom and practices of the hirer – Reg 7(8)(f). (This would cover, for example, supply teachers during school holidays or factory workers during seasonal shutdowns)

- wholly due to industrial action at the hirer's establishment – Reg 7(8)(g), or

- wholly due to more than one of the reasons listed above other than Reg 7(8)(a) – Reg 7(8)(h).

1.99 Where, for example, an agency worker has to take two weeks off work sick after working for four weeks on an assignment, he or she will only need to work a further eight weeks on his or her return to complete the qualifying period. Alternatively, where an agency supply teacher is six weeks into a qualifying period when the school closes for the summer holidays, the qualifying period would pause at the end of the summer term and, assuming the agency worker returns to the same job with the same hirer, start again at the beginning of the autumn term. After six weeks' work in the autumn term, the worker will have completed the qualifying period for the right to equal treatment (see the Department of Education's non-statutory advice on the application of the AWR to supply teachers, 'Agency Workers Regulations 2010: supply teachers' (March 2014)).

Apart from the first of the above reasons for pausing continuity, the different types of absence can run consecutively – Reg 7(8)(h). Thus, an agency worker who is called up on jury service for five weeks and then takes two weeks off due to sickness will not be subject to a new qualifying period if he or she returns to the same role. The BIS Guidance suggests that where an agency worker has a five-week break between assignments and is then absent for two weeks due to sickness, the sickness absence will pause the clock, 'which then resumes ticking when the worker returns to the same role. In these circumstances, the break is longer than six weeks but continuity is not broken as the clock pauses after five weeks.' However, there is a difficulty with this example. Reg 7(8)(h) provides that where an agency worker's absence is wholly due to two or more of the reasons listed in Reg 8 *other than* the reason in Reg 7(8)(a) (i.e. a break that is for any reason and of not more than six calendar weeks), the reasons can effectively be run together to pause continuity. Yet the example given in the guidance appears to link a break that is for any reason under Reg 7(8)(a) with a break that is for sickness under Reg 7(8)(b), which is not permitted by Reg 7(8)(h). In our view the seven-week break would in fact break continuity, such that the agency worker would be subject to a new qualifying period upon his or her return to work.

1.100 *Breaks during which the clock keeps ticking.* There are certain family-related absences during which the agency worker will be deemed to be working and will continue to accrue time towards the qualifying period, even though he or she is unable to work. This exception applies where the agency worker has started working on an assignment but is unable to continue for a reason related to pregnancy, childbirth or maternity during the 'protected period', or because he or she takes a period of statutory or contractual maternity, adoption or paternity leave. In these circumstances, the agency worker is deemed to keep working in that role with the hirer for the original intended duration, or likely duration, of the assignment (whichever is the longer) – Reg 7(6). The clock will even keep ticking if a pregnant agency worker has actually been assigned to a different role for health and safety reasons under S.68A of the Employment Rights Act 1996 – Reg 7(7).

These provisions are more easily explained by way of a practical example. If a woman goes on maternity leave five weeks into an assignment and the assignment was meant to last for ten weeks, Reg 7(6) will keep the clock ticking for another five weeks. This is because that provision provides that the agency worker shall be deemed to be working in that role with the hirer for the original intended duration or likely duration of the assignment, whichever is the longer. If, following maternity leave, the worker is supplied to undertake the same role with the same hirer, the intermittent break (i.e. the break between the end of her previous ten-week assignment and her return from maternity leave) will be disregarded under Reg 7(5) (see 'Breaks during which continuity is paused' above) and after two weeks on the second assignment she will be entitled to the right to equal treatment.

1.101 **Anti-avoidance provision.** A system that requires workers to work for a particular qualifying period before accruing rights is clearly potentially open to abuse by unscrupulous TWAs or hirers who may deliberately prevent workers from completing the period in order to deprive them of those rights. To prevent such abuse, Reg 9 provides that an agency worker will be treated as having satisfied the 12-week qualifying period if he or she is prevented from doing so because the assignment or assignments is or are structured in a particular way, and the most likely explanation for the structure is that the hirer, the TWA or the hirer and other hirers connected with it intended to prevent the agency worker from being entitled to the right to equal treatment in Reg 5 – Reg 9(1) and (4).

A structure of assignments will be caught by this provision where the worker has:

- completed two or more assignments with a particular hirer

- completed at least one assignment with the hirer and one or more earlier assignments with connected hirers, or

- worked in more than two roles during an assignment, and on at least two occasions has worked in a role that was not the 'same role' as the previous role (i.e. was substantively different from the previous role – see 'The same role' above) – Reg 9(3).

Hirers are 'connected' if one hirer (directly or indirectly) has control of the other hirer or a third person (directly or indirectly) has control of both hirers – Reg 9(6).

In other words, it will be open to an employment tribunal to find that a hirer **1.102** and/or an agency had malign motives for moving the worker to a different job or otherwise breaking the 12-week period where one of the circumstances listed in Reg 9(3) applies and the mostly likely explanation is that the hirer(s) or agency intended to deprive the worker of his or her rights. The worker will then be entitled to equal treatment as of the date he or she would have become so entitled, had it not been for the avoidance.

The difficulty for the agency worker will be providing sufficient evidence to show that the most likely explanation for the hirer's or the agency's actions was an intention to deprive him or her of the right to equal treatment. The tribunal will take into account various factors in determining the reason behind a structure of assignments. In particular, it will need to consider the length and number of assignments; the number of times the agency worker has worked in the same and different roles with a particular hirer (or connected hirers); and the period of any break between assignments. For example, several 11-week assignments broken by periods of more than six weeks with a hirer or rotations between several 'substantively different' jobs with the same hirer would be likely to point towards an intention to avoid the effect of the Regulations.

Where a tribunal finds that Reg 9(4) applies, it can make an additional award of up to £5,000 on top of any compensation payable in respect of the breach of the equal treatment rule – Reg 18(14) (see 'Time limits and remedies' below).

Equal treatment: pay
1.103

As mentioned under 'Equal treatment: the basic principle' above, the principle of equal treatment covers basic terms and conditions, including pay. In other words, temporary work agencies and hirers must ensure that an agency worker who has completed a 12-week qualifying period receives the same pay as he or

39

she would be entitled to for doing the same job, at the time the qualifying period commenced, had he or she been recruited directly by the hirer – Reg 5(1).

'Pay' is defined in Reg 6(2) as 'any sums payable to a worker of the hirer in connection with the worker's employment, including any fee, bonus, commission, holiday pay or other emolument referable to the employment, whether payable under contract or otherwise'. There are, however, a number of exclusions from the definition, which are set out in Reg 6(3) (see 'Exclusions' below).

1.104 The BIS Guidance stresses that the basic principle underlying Reg 6 is that an agency worker is entitled to 'pay for work done'. This means that he or she can rightfully be excluded from incentives and rewards that properly reflect the long-term relationship between the hirer and its permanent staff. The guidance gives the following examples of what may constitute 'pay':

- basic pay
- overtime payments
- allowances for working shifts or unsocial hours
- risk payments for hazardous duties
- payment for annual leave (any entitlement above the statutory minimum of 5.6 weeks can be added to the hourly or daily rate)
- bonuses or commission payments directly attributable to the amount or quality of the work done by the individual. This might include commission linked to sales or production targets, payments related to quality of personal performance and non-contractual payments which have been paid with such regularity that they have become a matter of custom and practice (see 'Bonuses' below)
- vouchers or stamps that have monetary value and are not provided through 'salary sacrifice schemes' – e.g. luncheon or childcare vouchers (see page 29).

1.105 Some of these entitlements may be subject to qualifying conditions that apply to permanent staff, in which case they will also apply to agency workers. For example, an agency worker may only qualify for overtime payments where he or she has worked in excess of standard hours, not simply by working a shift that permanent staff tend to do on an overtime basis. Others may require a minimum period of service or employment at the time of a payment. For example, there may be a requirement for the agency worker to still be working in the role when a bonus payment is made.

1.106 **Tips.** The BIS Guidance does not deal expressly with whether tips constitute 'pay' for the purposes of the equal treatment principle. It is likely that voluntary tips would constitute pay, whether paid in cash or by card, as these are usually directly attributable to the quality of service provided. However, the situation is less clear where all tips are added to a central 'pot' and then shared among the staff equally, whether by the hirer itself or under a tronc system. If all staff receive the same amount regardless of the quality of the service, the amount attributable to tips received by each worker would arguably not constitute pay. On the other hand, given that the reason the tips are divided up is to recognise the contribution made by all staff, not just front-line waiters, to the quality of the customer's experience, an argument could be made that the share of the tip is, still, directly attributable to the amount or quality of the work done by the individual.

Compulsory service charges raise similar difficulties. Where these are simply imposed without giving the customer any genuine choice in the matter, it is difficult to argue that they are directly attributable to the work done by the individual worker. If, however, the customer is afforded a genuine opportunity to decline to pay a service charge, it could be argued that it does constitute pay, and that the agency worker is entitled to equal treatment in respect of it.

Exclusions. The principles of equal treatment do not apply to pay-related **1.107** benefits that are in some way linked to longer term reward and retention. Reg 6(3) expressly excludes the following payments and rewards from the definition of 'pay':

- occupational sick pay (the AWR do not affect an agency worker's entitlement to statutory sick pay)

- pensions, allowances and gratuities in connection with retirement or loss of office (although agency workers are covered by automatic pension enrolment)

- occupational maternity, paternity and adoption pay (the AWR do not affect an agency worker's statutory entitlements)

- redundancy pay (statutory and contractual)

- payments or rewards linked to financial participation schemes (defined in Reg 6(5) as any scheme offering workers of the hirer a distribution of shares or options, or a share of profits in cash or in shares. This will cover share ownership schemes and phantom share schemes)

- any bonus, incentive payment or reward that is not directly attributable to the amount or quality of the work done by a worker, e.g. to encourage loyalty or reward long-term service (see 'Bonuses' below)

- payments for statutory time off, such as for carrying out trade union duties

- guarantee pay

- advances and employee loans

- expenses (e.g. accommodation or travel expenses)

- any payments that fall outside the employment relationship.

1.108 Crucially, most benefits in kind, such as private health insurance, company car allowances, training allowances and staff discounts, expressly fall outside the scope of 'pay' under the AWR. Reg 6(4) specifies that any monetary value attaching to any payment or benefit in kind given to a worker by the hirer is not 'pay' of the worker. This is subject to one exception covering vouchers or stamps that are of fixed value expressed in monetary terms, and capable of being exchanged for money, goods and/or services (whether on its own or together with other vouchers, stamps or documents, and whether immediately or only after a time). Thus, while luncheon vouchers would constitute pay, other subsidies, such as subsidised gym membership, would not.

According to the BIS Guidance, statutory and contractual notice pay linked to the loss of employment also fall outside the scope of the AWR, as do additional discretionary, non-contractual payments, such as a one-off payment to celebrate a particular event, provided they are not made with such regularity that they have become custom and practice (see page 30).

1.109 *TUC complaint.* The Trades Union Congress (TUC) lodged a formal complaint with the European Commission on 2 September 2013, arguing that the AWR fail to implement the Directive properly into domestic law. The TUC argues, among other things, that the definition of 'pay' in the AWR is inconsistent with the Directive. In the TUC's view, the exclusions in Reg 6(3) mean that the AWR definition of pay is narrower than that used in other UK employment and tax legislation – for example, S.27 of the Employment Rights Act 1996, which defines 'wages' for the purposes of the statutory right not to suffer unauthorised deductions from wages.

The TUC contends that the narrower definition in the AWR, as a derogation from the principle of equal treatment of agency workers, would have required the agreement of the social partners at national level (namely, the TUC and the Confederation of British Industry (CBI)) in order to comply with the Directive. Although the TUC and the CBI agreed that occupational sick pay and occupational pensions should be excluded from the definition, the TUC submits that they did not agree to some of the other exclusions set out in Reg 6(3) – namely, bonuses not directly attributable to the amount or quality of work done (such as attendance allowances, profit-related bonuses and loyalty bonuses); share options; and contractual maternity, paternity and adoption pay. In particular, given the widespread use of profit-related pay, share schemes and incentive schemes by private sector employers, the TUC argues that the exclusion of these forms of remuneration from the scope of the AWR gives rise to significant pay discrimination against agency workers.

Bonuses. Bonus payments, and the extent to which agency workers are entitled **1.110** to such payments, can be a contentious issue. The BIS Guidance emphasises that, while there are many different types of bonus and commission payments, the key question when deciding whether an agency worker qualifying for equal treatment is entitled to any such payment is whether it is 'directly attributable to the amount or quality of the work done by the worker' within the meaning of Reg 6(3) (see page 30). This wording would cover the following payments:

- a commission payment linked to sales

- a bonus payable to all staff who meet specific individual performance targets

- a bonus payable on the basis of individual performance over a given period – say, a year.

By contrast, the following would fall outside the scope of 'pay' and thus the equal treatment principle:

- a bonus reflecting the overall performance of the company, or the part of the organisation where the agency worker has worked, with little or no recognition of individual contribution

- a bonus designed to reward long-term loyalty and service rather than individual performance.

However, where a bonus contains a mixture of individual and company **1.111** performance elements, and the hirer is able to identify the percentage that links to personal performance, that element of the bonus is payable to the agency worker. If the percentage that links to personal performance is not identifiable, it is unclear whether or not the bonus should be included as pay. However, as Reg 6(3) expressly excludes 'any bonus, incentive payment or reward that is not directly attributable to the amount or quality of the work done by a worker', and an unidentifiable part of a bonus is surely 'not directly attributable' to anything in particular, we would argue that it should probably be excluded for the purposes of the equal treatment principle (but see 'Exclusions – TUC complaint' above).

The Guidance stresses that an agency worker should be given the same *opportunity* to achieve a bonus, and be subject to the same criteria, as directly recruited staff. However, this is not to say that there may not be valid reasons for paying the agency worker less than directly recruited staff, or indeed nothing at all. For example, the directly recruited employee's higher bonus may reflect his or her performance over a longer period, whereas the agency worker's bonus might legitimately reflect only the time spent on the assignment. Similarly, an agency worker might not meet minimum eligibility criteria for the payment of a bonus; for example, a service requirement. Indeed, such criteria might well operate to exclude agency workers from hirers' bonus schemes altogether.

1.112 Eligibility for a bonus may be made subject to a worker being in employment on a particular date. Where an agency worker has yet to complete the qualifying period on such a date, there may be uncertainty as to whether or not he or she is eligible. It is best to assume that, once the agency worker has completed the qualifying period, he or she becomes eligible to a bonus backdated to the eligibility date. This will ensure that the agency worker receives the same pay as he or she would be entitled to for doing the same job, at the time the qualifying period commenced, had he or she been recruited directly by the hirer (as in that case he or she would not have been subject to a qualifying period) – Reg 5(1).

1.113 **Performance appraisal systems.** A previous version of the AWR excluded bonus payments that were awarded in the context of a performance appraisal system from the scope of the equal treatment regime. However, these were subsequently included. That said, the BIS Guidance emphasises that this does not mean that hirers must integrate agency workers into their performance management systems for permanent staff (see pages 31–32). Equal treatment is required in terms of the end, not the means. It is thus open to the hirer to adopt a simpler system for tracking an agency worker's performance, including an appraisal system operated in conjunction with the agency or based on the agency's existing performance feedback arrangements. Such a system might, for example, take less account of career development.

However, if the hirer does decide to integrate the agency worker fully into its existing appraisal system, the Guidance states that doing so should not of itself affect the worker's employment status (although clearly this would ultimately be for an employment tribunal to determine). In this regard, it should be noted that some lawyers are advising clients to set out in any relevant documentation that the AWR are the only reason why the agency worker is being included in the appraisal process.

1.114 **'The Swedish derogation'.** There is an important exception to the right to equal treatment set out in Reg 5. Where an agency worker has a permanent contract of employment with the TWA which satisfies certain requirements, and is paid a minimum amount between assignments, he or she is not entitled to parity of pay (although all other rights under the AWR, including equal treatment in respect of working time and annual leave, continue to apply). This is commonly known as 'the Swedish derogation', because the Swedish government advocated its inclusion in the Temporary Agency Workers Directive.

There may well be advantages for the hirer in using this derogation, as it may mean that the hirer is able to pay less in respect of the services of agency workers covered by the derogation. However, this is not universally the case, and the potential benefit of the Swedish derogation will vary from sector to sector. For example, where agency workers are highly skilled or valuable professionals, they may already earn as much or more than comparable permanent employees, and there would therefore be no commercial motivation to avoid the impact of the equal pay provision in the AWR. Furthermore, the derogation carries an increased risk for the TWA in that, as an employee, the agency worker would be entitled to rely on a number of employment protection rights, including unfair dismissal. TWAs would be likely to seek to pass this risk on to the hirer in the form of increased fees or additional warranties, should the hirer insist on the derogation applying.

In order for the Swedish derogation to apply, the permanent contract of **1.115** employment with the TWA must satisfy the detailed requirements of Reg 10. This provides that, to the extent to which it relates to pay, Reg 5 does not have effect in relation to an agency worker who has a permanent contract of employment with a TWA if:

- the contract was entered into before the beginning of the first assignment under that contract, and

- includes terms and conditions in writing relating to –

  - the minimum scale or rate of remuneration or the method of calculating remuneration

  - the location or locations where the agency worker may be expected to work

  - the expected hours of work during any assignment

  - the maximum number of hours of work that the agency worker may be required to work each week during any assignment

  - the minimum number of hours of work per week that may be offered to the agency worker during any assignment, provided that it is at least one hour, and

  - the nature of the work that the agency worker may expect to be offered, including any relevant requirements relating to qualifications or experience – Reg 10(1)(a).

In addition, the contract of employment must contain a statement that the effect of entering into it is that the employee does not, during the currency of the contract, have any entitlement to the rights conferred by Reg 5 in so far as they relate to pay – Reg 10(1)(b).

A further requirement is that during any period under the contract – after the **1.116** end of the first assignment under that contract – in which the agency worker is not working temporarily for and under the supervision and direction of a hirer but is available to do so, the TWA must:

- take reasonable steps to seek suitable work for the agency worker (for work to be 'suitable' the nature of the work and the applicable terms and conditions must be the same as those included in the agency worker's contract of employment – Reg 10(2))

- if suitable work is available, propose the agency worker to a hirer who is offering such work, and

- pay the agency worker a 'minimum amount' of remuneration in respect of that period (see 'Minimum amount' below) – Reg 10(1)(c).

The TWA must not terminate the contract of employment until it has complied with these obligations for an aggregate of not less than four calendar weeks during the contract – Reg 10(1)(d). This means that if there have been fewer than four calendar weeks during the contract when the agency worker has been between assignments, and paid accordingly, the TWA cannot terminate the contract until it has made up the agency worker's remuneration to the value of four calendar weeks' pay (in addition to any contractual entitlement there may be to notice pay), *and* looked for suitable work for the agency worker. In other words, the requirement cannot simply be met by paying the agency worker four weeks' pay in lieu.

1.117 One of the requirements of Reg 10(1)(a) is that the contract must have been entered into 'before the beginning of the first assignment under that contract'. The meaning of this phrase was considered by an employment tribunal in Bray and ors v Monarch Personnel Refuelling (UK) Ltd ET Case No.1801581/12. B and five others were tanker drivers employed by MPR Ltd, an employment agency, on 'zero-hours' contracts (meaning they were paid as and when required for work – see Chapter 5, 'Zero-hours and other "atypical" contracts'). Throughout their employment with MPR Ltd, the tanker drivers had continuously worked for BP plc (a long-standing client of MPR Ltd) on a series of assignments. Anticipating the coming into force of the AWR, BP plc informed MPR Ltd that after 30 November 2011 it would only accept agency workers employed under 'Swedish derogation' contracts. MPR Ltd duly put its drivers on new 'guaranteed-hours' contracts.

The drivers subsequently lodged claims against MPR Ltd under the AWR, contending that the 'guaranteed-hours' contract did not fall within Reg 10 and could not therefore be relied on to deny them pay parity with BP plc's directly recruited employees. In particular, they argued that the 'assignment' they were working on had begun months before the contract was entered into. In other words, the contract of employment had not been 'entered into before the beginning of the first assignment under that contract', as required by Reg 10(1)(a).

1.118 The employment judge disagreed. He considered that 'contract of employment' for the purpose of Reg 10(1) meant the one in force 'at the beginning of the first assignment'. He noted that 'assignment' is defined by Reg 2 as 'a period of time during which an agency worker is supplied... to a hirer to work temporarily for and under the supervision and direction of the hirer'. However, in his view, this did not necessarily mean the entire period during which an agency worker is hired out to a particular client, but could mean a specific and distinct part of that period. Accordingly, the 'first assignment under that contract' began on 1 December 2011. The judge went on to find that all the drivers had entered into the contract before the beginning of the assignment on 1 December and that, as the contract satisfied the other conditions in Reg 10, MPR Ltd could rely on the Swedish derogation.

The judge accepted that the purpose of the AWR is to provide a degree of protection for agency workers and that, as a derogation from the normal method of protection afforded to agency workers by the Regulations, Reg 10 should be interpreted strictly. However, he rejected the claimants' argument that a purposive construction should be adopted in order to restrict the Swedish derogation to situations where agency workers move between hirers, and to prevent it being imposed onto existing work relationships. He observed that Reg 10 establishes an alternative (albeit more limited) method of protecting agency workers' pay to that set out in Reg 5, in that once its more stringent conditions are met, it gives limited security of income even where no work is provided. The judge noted that this was of particular benefit to casual and seasonal agency workers who do not have the relatively stable employment relationship enjoyed by the claimants.

'Minimum amount'. Regulation 10(1)(c)(iii) provides that the TWA must pay **1.119** the agency worker a 'minimum amount of remuneration' between assignments in order for the derogation to apply. That minimum amount is defined in Reg 11 as not less than 50 per cent of the worker's basic pay during the relevant pay reference period or the national minimum wage, whichever is the higher – Reg 11(1) and (3). Only basic pay is taken into account, whether by way of annual salary, payments for actual time worked, or by reference to output or otherwise – Reg 11(4).

A 'pay reference period' is a month or, in the case of a worker who is paid wages by reference to a shorter period (e.g. a week), that period – Reg 11(5). The relevant pay reference period for the purpose of calculating the minimum amount of remuneration is the pay reference period in which the agency worker received the highest level of pay in the 12 weeks preceding the end of the previous assignment (where the assignment lasted for longer than 12 weeks), or during the assignment (where the assignment lasted for 12 or fewer weeks) – Reg 11(2).

TUC complaint. In September 2013 the TUC lodged a formal complaint with **1.120** the European Commission, arguing that the AWR fail to implement the Directive properly into domestic law. Among other things, the complaint contends that Reg 10 fails properly to implement the Swedish derogation, which is set out in Article 5(2). This states that agency workers who are

47

employed on a permanent contract with a TWA and 'continue to be paid' between assignments may be exempted from the right to equal treatment as regards pay.

The TUC argues that the AWR go beyond what is permitted by the Directive in that agency workers employed under the Swedish derogation in Great Britain receive only half their basic pay, or the national minimum wage, between assignments. Evidence gathered by the TUC reveals that agency workers employed on Swedish derogation contracts often experience pay discrimination, with some being paid up to £135 a week less than permanent staff, despite working in the same place and doing the same job. Furthermore, the TUC points out that although the Directive requires agency workers on Swedish derogation contracts to be 'employed on permanent contracts', agencies in Great Britain are only required to pay an agency worker for four weeks between assignments, after which he or she can be sacked.

1.121 Equal treatment: working time and annual leave
Agency workers, like other workers, have certain statutory minimum protections and entitlements under the Working Time Regulations 1998 SI 1998/1833 (WTR) – see 'Other statutory employment rights – working time' below. In addition, once a temporary agency worker has completed the 12-week qualifying period with a hirer, he or she is entitled to the same terms and conditions as those enjoyed by employees recruited directly by the hirer relating to:

- the duration of working time (that is, any period during which an individual is working at the disposal of the employer and carrying out his or her activities or duties or any period during which he or she is receiving work-related training, and any additional period treated as working time under the WTR)

- night work (that is, work between 11 pm and 6 am, unless there is a workforce agreement in place specifying work of not less than seven hours, part of which takes place between midnight and 5 am)

- rest periods and rest breaks (a rest period is a period which is not working time or a rest break or annual leave to which the individual is entitled under the WTR or the contract), and

- annual leave – Regs 5 and 6.

1.122 So, for example, an agency worker may be entitled to an hour's lunch break as opposed to the statutory minimum 20-minute rest break laid down in the WTR, or more generous leave than the statutory entitlement of 5.6 weeks per year. However, the BIS Guidance notes that, as a way of simplifying the administration of the annual leave right, it is possible for entitlement above the statutory

48

minimum to be dealt with as a one-off payment at the end of an assignment or 'rolled up' into the worker's hourly or daily rate (see page 33).

Where a comparable worker is entitled to no more than the statutory entitlements under the WTR, the agency worker's rights will correspond. For example, the Department of Education's non-statutory advice on the application of the AWR to supply teachers, 'Agency Workers Regulations 2010: supply teachers' (March 2014), states that for permanent teachers in schools maintained by an authority in England and Wales there is no specific provision in the School Teachers' Pay and Conditions Document for holidays or annual leave. Thus, agency supply teachers should receive payment for statutory annual leave when they take it, in accordance with the WTR.

What precisely is meant by 'equal treatment' in this context? In Wilson and ors **1.123** v Kelly Services (UK) Ltd ET Case No.2403421/12 an employment tribunal had to decide whether KS Ltd, a recruitment agency that hired out its employees to work as 'operatives', had correctly matched the annual leave entitlement of the hiring company, HPES Ltd, for the purposes of Reg 5. After the AWR came into force, KS Ltd agreed to give the claimants an additional five days' paid annual leave to correspond with the paid annual leave that operatives employed by HPES Ltd were receiving. However, the manner in which the agency operated and calculated this entitlement differed in the following respects:

- the claimants had to accrue annual leave before they could request it, whereas HPES Ltd employees were entitled to request paid annual leave whenever they liked

- KS Ltd calculated holiday pay by averaging out the pay received in the 12 weeks preceding the leave, whereas HPES Ltd calculated holiday pay by reference to the employee's wage on the date the leave was taken.

The employment tribunal held that the accrual system adopted by KS Ltd did not contravene Reg 5. It noted that the arrangement was compatible with the WTR, which impose certain restrictions in relation to the timing of annual leave, and did not prevent the claimants from receiving the additional five days' leave accorded to HPES Ltd employees. However, the tribunal considered that the way in which the agency calculated holiday pay did contravene Reg 5 since it was potentially disadvantageous in the event that the claimants took leave within 12 weeks of receiving a salary increase.

Establishing equal treatment **1.124**
The BIS Guidance confirms that the right to equal treatment applies in respect of terms that would be 'ordinarily included' in the agency worker's contract had he or she been recruited directly by the hirer. The terms will be determined by looking at, among other things, the relevant pay scale or structure, company handbooks, the terms included in contracts as a matter of course, and any

49

relevant collective agreements. There may, for instance, be a 'going rate' for a particular job. There is no need for an agency worker to identify an actual comparator when asserting a right to equal treatment, although the existence of such a person will obviously make it easier to establish a claim (but see 'TUC complaint' below).

In Wilson and ors v Kelly Services (UK) Ltd Case No.2403421/12 an employment tribunal had to decide whether the actual comparators relied upon by the claimants were appropriate. W and three others were employed by a recruitment agency, KS Ltd, to work as 'operatives' for one of its clients, HPES Ltd. They were paid £6.10 per hour plus a 10 per cent shift allowance. Towards the middle of 2011, KS Ltd had discussions with HPES Ltd about terms and conditions with a view to ensuring compliance with the AWR when they came into force on 1 October. KS Ltd was informed by HPES Ltd that as at 1 October any new employee would be paid in accordance with the lowest pay band, namely £12,962 per annum, plus a 20 per cent shift allowance. W and the three other operatives were duly paid that amount by the agency when the Regulations came into force. They brought tribunal claims for breach of Reg 5, based on the fact that on 1 August 2011 HPES Ltd had directly recruited nine operatives from KS Ltd to become its permanent employees at a starting salary of £15,000.

1.125   In the tribunal's view, these nine employees were not appropriate comparators. It noted that pay progression at HPES Ltd depended on 'sustained performance' rather than 'mere experience', and that none of the claimants had been regarded by HPES Ltd as sufficiently valuable to justify permanent employment in August. As there was nothing to indicate that any of the claimants' overall performances had improved since then, the tribunal was not persuaded that, had they been recruited as permanent employees on 1 October 2011, they would have been offered a starting salary of more than £12,962.

The tribunal did note, however, that from 1 November 2011 the salaries of the majority of HPES Ltd's permanent employees – except those with performance issues – had increased to £15,500 to bring them into line with a recently negotiated collective agreement. The tribunal concluded that had any of the claimants been directly recruited by the hiring company, their salaries would also have increased to £15,500 on 1 November since their performance was regarded as satisfactory by HPES Ltd. It followed that, in failing to pay this amount to the claimants (following completion of their 12-week qualifying periods), the agency had breached its obligations under Reg 5.

1.126   **Deemed compliance.** Where the relevant terms and conditions of employees employed by the hirer match those of the agency workers and are consistent with the terms and conditions ordinarily included in the contracts of employees recruited to fill that job, the hirer and the TWA will be *deemed* to be compliant with the Regulations. This is because Reg 5(1) is 'deemed to have been complied with' where there is a comparable employee whose relevant terms and conditions match those of the agency worker and are consistent with the terms the hirer usually gives employees recruited to fill that job – Reg 5(3). The comparator needs to be an employee (not a worker) working for and under the supervision and direction of the hirer, who is – at the time the breach is alleged to have taken place – carrying out the same or broadly similar work to the agency worker, having regard, where relevant, to whether he or she has a similar level of qualification and skills – Reg 5(4)(a). Where there is no comparable employee working or based at the same establishment, the hirer can point to a comparator at a different establishment who satisfies the above requirements, but not to a predecessor – Reg 5(4)(b) and (5). In terms of pay, it is not just basic pay that falls to be compared, but the whole pay package, to the extent that it constitutes 'pay' within the meaning of the AWR – see 'Equal treatment: pay' above.

TUC complaint. In September 2013 the TUC lodged a formal complaint with 1.127 the European Commission arguing that the AWR fail to implement the Directive properly into domestic law. Among other things, the TUC contends that the 'deemed compliance' provision is incompatible with the Directive. In its view, under Reg 5(3) the principle of equal treatment is deemed to be satisfied if there is a comparable employee, doing the same or similar work as the agency worker, who receives the same pay and conditions even if other directly employed workers are paid much more. The TUC considers that the provision enables employers to introduce new lower wage rates, which are paid only to agency workers and a single directly employed individual. The TUC further submits that where there is an actual 'comparable employee', the agency worker is prevented from arguing that if he or she were recruited directly by the hiring company, he or she would have been paid a higher rate of pay. It is argued that this is inconsistent with the Directive, Article 5(1) of which provides that an agency worker's basic working and employment conditions shall be 'at least those that would apply if they had been recruited directly by that undertaking to occupy the same job'. The TUC contends that this wording allows a worker to rely on a purely hypothetical comparator, whereas Reg 5(3) deprives the worker of that possibility where there is a comparable employee on the same pay and conditions.

Some of the TUC's concerns are perhaps met by Reg 5(3)(b), which provides that the relevant terms of the comparable employee must be terms and conditions ordinarily included in the contracts of comparable employees. If the employer introduced a lower rate of pay for agency workers which only applied to a single directly employed individual, that lower rate would arguably not be 'ordinarily included' in the contracts of employment of comparable employees and therefore the Reg 5(3) defence could not be relied on.

Comparison of terms or package. The AWR are unclear as to whether a term- 1.128 by-term approach is appropriate to determine whether or not equal treatment has been provided, or whether the agency worker's package taken as a whole should be compared to that which would apply had he or she been recruited directly for the same job. Presumably, elements relating to pay would have to be treated separately from those relating to working time or annual leave. But should the pay package be taken as a whole, or divided into constituents? The question is important, as a specialist worker's basic rate of pay may well be higher than that of a permanent worker, but other elements, such as bonuses, may be less favourable or not paid at all.

The BIS Guidance is silent on this issue. However, it appears to countenance the possibility that a 'whole package' approach might be taken in that in its summary of what constitutes 'pay' it states that 'basic pay' means 'pay for work done; annual salary usually converted in hourly/daily rate', but then adds: 'NB to this may be added some or all of the other contractual elements below [overtime pay, bonus or incentive payment, holiday pay, vouchers or stamps, and paid time off for ante-natal appointments] and includes shift/unsocial hours/pay and risk payments for hazardous duties' (see page 33). Furthermore, in giving an illustration of the application of the principle of equal treatment for agency workers who work through umbrella companies, the guidance suggests that 'where an umbrella worker receives part of their pay as reimbursement for travel expenses and, for example, where a directly recruited worker or employee would receive £100 per day, the umbrella worker must still receive £100 a day but this can be made up of £80 plus £20 reimbursement of travel expenses' (see page 28). In other words, the Guidance appears to assume that a 'whole package' approach should be taken to determining 'pay'.

1.129 This approach may be supported by comparison with the Part-time Workers (Prevention of Less Favourable Treatment) Regulations 2000 SI 2000/1551. These Regulations specifically require a term-by-term approach, giving part-time workers the right not to be treated less favourably than the employer treats a comparable full-time worker 'as regards the terms of his contract' – Reg 5(1)(a). By contrast, the AWR simply refer to 'pay'. The Part-Time Workers Regulations 2000 are discussed in Chapter 3, 'Part-time workers'.

1.130 Enforcement

A mere suspicion on the part of an agency worker that his or her rights under the AWR have been violated will probably not be enough to found a complaint under the Regulations. As a result, Reg 16 gives agency workers the right to request information from the hirer or TWA in relation to their duties under Regs 5 (equal treatment), 12 (access to collective facilities and amenities) and 13 (right to be informed about and to apply for posts with hirer).

The first step in an equal treatment claim will be for the agency worker to make a written request to the TWA for a written statement containing information relating to the treatment in question – Reg 16(1). Within 28 days of receiving such a request, the TWA must provide a written statement setting out relevant information relating to the basic working conditions in force at the hirer; the factors which the TWA considered when determining the basic working and employment conditions which applied to the agency worker at the time when the alleged breach of Reg 5 is said to have taken place; and, where the TWA is relying on the deemed compliance defence, the basis on which the TWA considered that a person is a comparable employee, along with a description of that person's basic working and employment conditions – Reg 16(2). If the worker has not received the statement within 30 days of the request, he or she may make a written request to the hirer for a written statement containing information about the basic working and employment conditions that are in force – Reg 16(3). The hirer has 28 days within which to provide the statement – Reg 16(4).

A similar right to a written statement from the hirer exists in relation to the **1.131** right to access collective facilities and amenities and to be informed about job vacancies – Reg 16(5) and (6).

Any information provided under Reg 16 is admissible as evidence in any proceedings under the AWR – Reg 16(8). Futhermore, a tribunal can draw any inference it considers it just and equitable to draw (including an inference that the TWA or hirer has infringed the right in question) where there has been a deliberate failure to provide information, or where any written statement supplied is evasive or equivocal – Reg 13(9).

Contracting out   1.132
The restrictions on contracting out in S.203 ERA are extended by Reg 15 to cover the provisions of the AWR, thus preventing an employee from contracting out of his or her rights under the Regulations.

Liability   1.133
Given the tripartite nature of the relationship between agency workers, TWAs and hirers, the question arises as to who should be liable for non-compliance: the TWA or the hirer? The answer is that both may be liable.

Under Reg 14(1), a *TWA* is liable for any breach of Reg 5 to the extent that it is responsible for the infringement. However, there is a potential defence for an agency – see 'Statutory defence for TWAs' below. Where more than one TWA is party to the proceedings, when deciding whether or not each TWA is responsible in full or in part, the tribunal will have regard to the extent to which each was responsible for the determination, or application, of any of the agency worker's basic working and employment conditions – Reg 14(5).

Regulation 14(2) provides that the *hirer* shall also be responsible for any breach **1.134** of Reg 5 to the extent that it is responsible for the infringement. The hirer will also be liable for any breach of Reg 12 (access to collective facilities and amenities) or Reg 13 (right to be informed about and to apply for posts with the hirer) – Reg 14(6).

1.135 **Statutory defence for TWAs.** Liability for breach of Reg 5 will fall on either the TWA or the hirer, depending on who is responsible for the infringement (and the extent to which they are responsible) – Reg 14(1) and 14(2). However, Reg 14(3) provides a defence for the TWA where it can establish that:

- it has obtained, or has taken reasonable steps to obtain, relevant information from the hirer about the basic working and employment conditions in force at the hirer's business and the relevant terms and conditions of comparable employees

- where it has received this information, it has acted reasonably in determining the basic working and employment conditions to which the agency worker would be entitled at the end of the qualifying period, and

- where it is responsible for applying those basic working and employment conditions to the agency worker, it has ensured that the agency worker has been treated accordingly – Reg 14(3).

An employment tribunal had cause to consider the Reg 14(3) defence in Wilson and ors v Kelly Services (UK) Ltd ET Case No.2403421/12, the facts of which are set out under 'Right to equal treatment – appropriate comparator' above. The tribunal found that the TWA, KS Ltd, had breached its obligations in respect of pay under Reg 5 and went on to consider whether it had established the statutory defence afforded by Reg 14(3) – i.e. that it had 'acted reasonably in determining what the agency worker's basic working and employment conditions should be at the end of the qualifying period'. In the tribunal's view, KS Ltd had not done so.

1.136 In the tribunal's view, it was incumbent on KS Ltd to make appropriate enquiries to identify more accurately the basis on which a new recruit employed by the hiring company, HPES Ltd, would be remunerated throughout the qualifying period. By the end of the 12-week qualifying period (which for the purposes of this claim started to run on 1 October 2011, when the AWR came into force), reasonable enquiries would have disclosed to KS Ltd that the basic salaries of 75 per cent of the 'standard terms' operatives employed by HPES Ltd had been increased from 1 November 2011 to £15,500 per annum. On the assumption that HPES Ltd would have informed KS Ltd that there were no performance issues that would have disqualified the claimants from the increase, KS Ltd should reasonably have concluded that all the claimants would have been paid £15,500 per annum from 1 November 2011 had they been recruited by HPES Ltd as permanent employees. As KS Ltd had failed to undertake such reasonable enquiries, it could not rely on the statutory defence.

Protection from detriment and unfair dismissal   1.137

Agency workers have the right not to be subjected to any detriment by, or as a result of, any act or deliberate failure to act of a TWA or hirer on the ground that the worker:

- brought proceedings under the AWR

- gave evidence or information in connection with such proceedings brought by any agency worker

- made a request for a written statement under Reg 16 (see 'Enforcement' above)

- otherwise did anything under the AWR in relation to a TWA, hirer or any other person

- alleged that a TWA or hirer has breached the AWR (unless the allegation was false and made in bad faith)

- refused (or proposed to refuse) to forgo a right conferred by the AWR

or on the ground that the TWA or hirer believes or suspects that the agency worker has done or intends to do any of these things – Reg 17(2), (3) and (4). Liability for breach of Reg 17(2) rests with whichever of the TWA or the hirer was responsible for the act, or failure to act, that the worker contends was to his or her detriment – Reg 14(7).

If the agency worker is an employee, he or she cannot bring a detriment claim under Reg 17(2) if the detriment in question amounts to a dismissal – Reg 17(5). However, such employees can bring claims of automatically unfair dismissal against their employer for any of the reasons listed above – Reg 17(1), (3) and (4) – see IDS Employment law Handbook, 'Unfair Dismissal' (2010), Chapter 10, 'Automatically unfair dismissal'. This is in addition to any 'ordinary' unfair dismissal claims they may be able to bring under the Employment Rights Act 1996 (ERA) – see IDS Employment Law Handbook, 'Unfair Dismissal'.

Furthermore, agency workers who are employees have the right not to be **1.138** dismissed for redundancy for any of the reasons listed above where the circumstances constituting the redundancy applied equally to one or more other employees in the same undertaking who held positions similar to that held by the employee and who have not been dismissed – S.105(1) and (7N) ERA (see IDS Employment Law Handbook, 'Redundancy' (2011), Chapter 8, 'Unfair redundancy', under 'Automatically unfair redundancy').

There is no qualifying service for claims brought under Reg 17 AWR or S.105 ERA.

1.139 **Time limits and remedies**

Claims under the AWR must be brought in the employment tribunals – Reg 18(2)–(3). Claims are subject to the standard three-month time limit, which can be extended where the tribunal considers it just and equitable to do so or to facilitate early conciliation – Reg 18(4)–(7) (see further IDS Employment Law Handbook, 'Employment Tribunal Practice and Procedure' (2014), Chapter 5, 'Time limits').

On upholding a complaint, the remedies available to a tribunal are:

- a declaration as to the rights of the agency worker

- an award of compensation, or

- a recommendation that the agency or hirer takes reasonable action to reduce the adverse effect on the agency worker of any matter to which the complaint relates – Reg 18(8). (If a TWA or hirer fails without reasonable justification to comply with a recommendation, the tribunal may make, or increase, an order of compensation – Reg 18(18).)

1.140 In most cases, compensation – calculated in accordance with Reg 18(10) and (11) – will be the likely remedy, and it is important to note here that, as with discrimination legislation, there is no cap on the amount that can be awarded. There is, however, a *minimum* award of two weeks' pay for breaches of Regs 5 (the right to equal treatment) and 10 (the provision for pay between assignments) and in respect of complaints of detriment under Reg 17(2) relating to those two provisions, unless, taking account of the conduct of the parties, two weeks' pay is not a just and equitable amount, in which case the tribunal can reduce the award as it considers appropriate – Reg 18(12) and (13). Unlike discrimination legislation, the tribunal is not permitted to make an award for injury to feelings – Reg 18(15). An additional award of no more than £5,000 may also be made where the TWA or hirer structured the agency worker's assignments in such a way as to prevent him or her completing his or her qualifying period – Reg 18(14) (see 'Equal treatment: the qualifying period – anti-avoidance provision' above). Where compensation is ordered and there is more than one respondent, the amount payable by each will be such as the tribunal considers just and equitable having regard to the extent of each respondent's responsibility for the breach – Reg 18(9) and (14).

1.141 # Other statutory employment rights

As discussed under 'Rights under the Agency Workers Regulations 2010' above, the Agency Workers Regulations 2010 SI 2010/93 (AWR) provide temporary agency workers with a limited number of rights aimed specifically at them, provided they fall within the scope of the Regulations and have completed the 12-week qualifying period of service, where relevant. However, in addition to these specific rights, agency workers may also be entitled to benefit from other employment protection rights that are of more universal application. In many cases, entitlement will depend on the individual agency worker's employment status, and whether he or she is an 'employee' or 'worker' within the meaning of the applicable legislation. In some cases, however, the legislation is specifically drafted so as to apply to agency workers, regardless of their status.

We discuss the question of employment status under 'Employment status' below. In this section we examine a number of specific UK statutory employment protection rights and consider the tests that apply to determine whether or not agency workers are covered. Such rights include:

- the right to be paid the national minimum wage

- the right not to suffer unlawful deductions from wages

- protection under the whistleblowing provisions

- rights under the Working Time Regulations 1998 SI 1998/1833 to paid annual leave, rest breaks and limits on working time, and protection against detriment for exercising those rights

- protection against discrimination under the Equality Act 2010

- certain maternity and parental rights.

The rights to claim unfair dismissal and to take statutory family leave, together **1.142** with other rights only available to 'employees', are not extended to agency workers except in so far as they can demonstrate that they are employees. This issue is discussed under 'Employment status' below.

National minimum wage   1.143
The right to receive the national minimum wage (NMW) is governed by the National Minimum Wage Act 1998 (NMWA) and the National Minimum Wage Regulations 1999 SI 1999/584. The effect of this legislation is to amend workers' contracts of employment to provide a minimum rate per hour, below which they should not be paid. The standard rate applies to workers aged 21 and over, and there are other rates for young workers and apprentices. These rates are set annually.

As we discuss below, agency workers will generally be entitled to the NMW. It is important to note, however, that the right to equal treatment in terms of pay under the AWR applies *in addition* to the right to the NMW. In other words, where an agency worker is covered by the AWR, he or she will be entitled to receive the same pay that he or she would have received as a direct recruit, and this may exceed the NMW – see under 'Rights under the Agency Workers Regulations 2010 – equal treatment: pay' above.

1.144 An agency worker will be entitled to be paid the NMW where he or she has entered into or works under a contract either with the agency or employment business which supplies him or her ('the agent'), or with the hirer to which he or she is supplied to carry out work ('the principal'), which is:

- a contract of employment, or

- any other contract, whether express or implied and (if it is express) whether oral or in writing, whereby the individual undertakes to do or perform personally any work or services for another party to the contract whose status is not by virtue of the contract that of a client or customer of any profession or business undertaking carried on by the individual – S.54(3) NMWA.

In other words, the first limb of S.54(3) covers employees, and the second covers 'workers', so long as they are not providing services to the agent or principal as client or customer of their own profession or business.

1.145 In some cases agency workers will not fall into either category, usually because they are unable to demonstrate the existence of the necessary contract – see 'Employment status' below for a discussion of the circumstances in which a contract may be implied where there is no express contract. In such cases, S.34 provides that the provisions of the NMWA will still apply, so long as the worker is not providing services to the agent or principal as client or customer of his or her own profession or business. Under S.34, the NMWA has effect *as if* there were a worker's contract between the agency worker and either the agent or the principal, depending on whichever is responsible for paying the agency worker in respect of the work – S.34(2)(a). Normally, it will be clear who is responsible for paying the agency worker and ensuring that the worker is remunerated at a rate not less than the NMW. Where this is not so, S.34(2)(b) provides that the person who *actually* pays the agency worker in respect of the work is the person responsible for paying the NMW.

The EAT considered the application of S.34 in Hurst v Galloway Ltd (t/a G2) EAT 0111/04. In that case H, an actor, had been sent by his agency to attend auditions with different hirers and had not been paid in respect of them. He brought an NMW claim against the agency, alleging that it had breached the NMWA by failing to ensure that he received a fee for attending the auditions. The EAT held that, even though H was self-employed, he was an agency worker for NMW purposes by virtue of S.34 and therefore entitled to be paid at least the NMW. However, as S.34(2)(a) made clear, this entitlement could only be enforced against the hirer (being the person who was responsible for paying him) and not the agent. Accordingly, his claim was dismissed on the ground that it was directed against the wrong respondent.

1.146 It is worth noting that despite acknowledging the employment tribunal's factual finding that the claimant was self-employed, the EAT considered that he was capable of falling within the provisions of the NMWA. While citing most of S.34, it did not cite S.34(1)(c), which provides, in effect, that the section will not apply in circumstances where an individual is working for a person whose status is that of 'a client or customer of any profession or business undertaking carried on by the individual'. Generally, this provision has been considered to exclude all self-employed workers from the scope of entitlement, and certainly many – probably most – self-employed people will not be entitled to the NMW. However, some self-employed people may still fall within the definition of 'worker', and be entitled to the NMW, if they provide the services in question as part of a profession or business undertaking carried on by someone else, rather than providing services to a client pursuant to their own profession or business undertaking. This distinction was clarified by the Court of Appeal in Hospital Medical Group Ltd v Westwood 2013 ICR 415, CA.

For further details of the NMW, see IDS Employment Law Handbook, 'Wages' (2011), Chapter 5, 'The national minimum wage'.

Deductions from wages
1.147

Whereas the right not to be unfairly dismissed contained in the Employment Rights Act 1996 (ERA) applies only to employees, the right not to suffer unlawful deductions from wages, contained in the same Act, applies to a wider category of 'workers'. The definition of worker for this purpose is identical to that in the NMWA, discussed under 'National minimum wage' above. S.230(3) defines a worker as an individual who has entered into or works under (or, where the employment has ceased, has worked under):

- a contract of employment (defined as a 'contract of service or apprenticeship'), or

- any other contract, whether express or implied, and (if express) whether oral or in writing, whereby the individual undertakes to do or perform personally any work or services for another party to the contract whose status is not by virtue of the contract that of a client or customer of any profession or business undertaking carried on by the individual.

This definition potentially covers a wide range of individuals who provide 1.148 personal services under a contract, such as agency workers. However, as discussed under 'National minimum wage' above, it does not extend to self-employed people who are genuinely pursuing a business activity on their own account and providing the work in question for a client or customer of that activity. See 'Employment status' below for a discussion of the circumstances in which a contract may be implied where there is no express contract.

For further details of the right not to suffer unlawful deductions, see IDS Employment Law Handbook, 'Wages' (2011), Chapter 3, 'Protection of wages – 1'.

1.149 Whistleblowing

Section 47B ERA confers a right on workers not to be subjected to any detriment on the ground that they have made a protected disclosure (colloquially known as 'whistleblowing'). (The right in S.103A ERA not to be unfairly dismissed for making a protected disclosure is extended only to employees.)

As indicated under 'Deductions from wages' above, the definition of 'worker' for the purposes of the ERA is contained in S.230(3), and covers an individual who has entered into or works under (or, where the employment has ceased, has worked under):

- a contract of employment (defined as a 'contract of service or apprenticeship'), or

- any other contract, whether express or implied, and (if express) whether oral or in writing, whereby the individual undertakes to do or perform personally any work or services for another party to the contract whose status is not by virtue of the contract that of a client or customer of any profession or business undertaking carried on by the individual.

1.150 While this definition is apt to cover agency workers, there are many who will fall outside its scope because of the complexity of their contractual arrangements. (See 'Employment status' below for a discussion of the circumstances in which a contract may be implied where there is no express contract.) To ensure that such workers are in fact covered by S.47B, S.43K(1)(a) states that, for the purposes of the protected disclosure provisions, the term 'worker' includes an individual who is not covered by S.230(3), if

- he or she is or was introduced or supplied to do work by a third person (i.e. an agency), and

- the terms of his or her engagement are or were in practice substantially determined not by the individual but by the person for whom he works or worked (i.e. the end-user), or by the third person, or by both.

The person who substantially determines or determined the terms on which the agency worker is or was engaged is treated as being the 'employer' for the purposes of the whistleblowing provisions – S.43K(2).

1.151 It is important to note that S.43K covers not only individuals who are *supplied* by an agency, but also those who are simply *introduced* by one. The EAT made this clear in Croke v Hydro Aluminium Worcester Ltd 2007 ICR 1303, EAT, where C provided his services as a consultant engineer through a personal services company, A Ltd. He obtained work via a recruitment agency with HAW Ltd, under an arrangement governed by two contracts: one contract between A Ltd and the agency which stated that A Ltd would provide technical services to the agency, and naming C as the consultant provided to carry out the services, and a second contract between the agency and HAW Ltd for the supply of technical services that mirrored the terms of the first.

After the agency terminated A Ltd's contract, C commenced proceedings in an employment tribunal against HAW Ltd, claiming that the reason for the termination of his service contract was that he had made a protected disclosure to HAW Ltd, and that he had thereby suffered an unlawful detriment contrary to S.47B(1). The tribunal considered that it did not have jurisdiction to hear C's claim as he was not a worker within the meaning of S.230(3): there was no contract between C and HAW Ltd, C was not subject to HAW Ltd's internal disciplinary procedures, and A Ltd could substitute C with another consultant. The tribunal further found that C could not rely on S.43K as this only protects *individuals* whose services are 'supplied' to an end-user by an agency, not companies such as A Ltd.

C appealed to the EAT against the tribunal's decision that he did not fall within **1.152** the extended definition of 'worker' provided for by S.43K. He argued, among other things, that the tribunal had erred in only considering whether the agency had supplied his services, and not whether it had 'introduced' him to HAW Ltd. The EAT agreed that the tribunal had erred in failing to consider whether the agency had introduced C, regardless of whether it had supplied him as an individual or through A Ltd. In the EAT's view, it was apparent from the tribunal's findings that the agency did introduce C to do the work. It had considered HAW Ltd's specific request for engineers and had identified C as an individual who might potentially do that work. Furthermore, it was C's own CV – not a document from the agency offering to provide his services – that was then sent to HAW Ltd, following which C was personally interviewed by the company. It was only after the interview that the agency and HAW Ltd agreed that C would be supplied through A Ltd.

The EAT then considered C's alternative argument that S.43K does apply to protect an individual who supplies his or her labour through a limited company or where there is no direct contractual chain between the individual and the supplier/introducer. C claimed that the tribunal had erred in limiting its consideration to the formal contractual position and should have looked at the realities of the situation. Relying on the Court of Appeal's decision in MHC Consulting Services Ltd v Tansell and anor 2000 ICR 789, CA, which dealt with the construction of the Disability Discrimination Act 1995, he contended that where the purpose of statutory provisions is to provide protection from discrimination or victimisation, it is appropriate to construe those provisions as far as possible to provide protection rather than deny it. The EAT agreed with this argument, although it noted that it had to be cautious before transplanting an approach appropriate to one particular statute directly to another.

Applying this purposive approach to the issue of who supplied C's services, the **1.153** EAT concluded that had the tribunal considered this issue by reference to the realities of the relationship rather than the strict contractual position, it would have concluded that C was supplied to work for HAW Ltd by the agency. C was the consultant named as the employee of the 'service provider' (A Ltd) in the contract between the agency and HAW Ltd whom the agency agreed would provide the services, and he was the one supplied to HAW Ltd to perform the work and for whose work HAW Ltd paid the agency. Moreover, although the service provider was entitled to substitute C, it could do so only where the agency and HAW Ltd had a 'reasonable veto'.

A purposive approach was also adopted in Keppel Seghers UK Ltd v Hinds EAT 0019/14 where the EAT upheld a tribunal's decision that an agency worker who worked through a service company was covered by S.43K. The EAT emphasised that whole purpose of the statutory extension to the definition of 'worker' and 'employer' was to go beyond the normal contractual focus of those terms for statutory purposes in the employment field and did not require the existence of a contract.

1.154 Working Time Regulations 1998
The Working Time Regulations 1998 SI 1998/1833 (WTR) provide 'workers' with the following rights and protections:

- an average 48-hour working week

- daily and weekly rest periods and rest breaks

- paid annual leave

- protections in respect of night work.

These are discussed in depth in IDS Employment Law Handbook, 'Working Time' (2013).

1.155 The definition of 'worker' for the purposes of the WTR is the same as that in S.230(3) ERA and S.54(3) NMWA – see 'Deductions from wages', 'Whistleblowing' and 'National minimum wage' above. Reg 2(1) states that 'worker' means an individual who has entered into or works under (or, where the employment has ceased, worked under):

- a contract of employment, or

- any other contract, whether express or implied and (if it is express) whether oral or in writing, whereby the individual undertakes to do or perform personally any work or services for another party to the contract whose status is not by virtue of the contract that of a client or customer of any profession or business undertaking carried on by the individual.

Agency workers will often fall within this definition. In such cases, the agency is likely to be the employer, as it will normally be the agency that enters into a written contract with the worker. However, the Regulations make special provision in relation to agency workers who are not otherwise regarded as workers.

Regulation 36 applies where an agency worker: **1.156**

- is supplied by an agent to do work for another party ('the principal') under a contract or other arrangement between the agent and the principal

- is not a worker because of the absence of a worker's contract between the individual and the agent or principal, and

- is not a party to a contract under which he or she undertakes to do the work for another party to the contract whose status is, by virtue of the contract, that of a client or customer of any profession or business undertaking carried on by the individual.

Where these conditions are fulfilled, the agency worker is treated as being a worker for the purposes of the WTR and as being employed by whichever of the agent or the principal is responsible for paying him or her, or, if neither is responsible, by whichever in fact pays the agency worker. This formulation is similar to that found in the NMWA – see 'National minimum wage' above.

Practical problems are likely to arise in relation to agency workers who are **1.157** employed by an agent but who receive instructions from the principal on whose premises they work. In this situation, the agency will be responsible for complying with the Regulations, but will have little control over the individual's day-to-day working arrangements. One possible solution may be for the contract between the agency and the principal to stipulate that the principal must ensure, on the agency's behalf, that the limits and entitlements set out in the WTR are complied with and that the appropriate record-keeping obligations are fulfilled. However, the agency, as the employer, would retain ultimate responsibility for ensuring compliance.

Discrimination and equal pay **1.158**

Part 5 of the Equality Act 2010 prohibits discrimination on specified grounds (e.g. race, sex and disability) by employers against existing or prospective employees. The definition of 'employment' is broad – broader than under the Employment Rights Act 1996 (ERA) in the context of the right to claim unfair dismissal – and covers individuals working under a contract of employment, apprentices, and self-employed people working under a contract personally to do work – S.83(2). This definition does not require the same level of mutual obligation required for a classic contract of service. So, for example, in London Borough of Camden v Pegg and ors EAT 0590/11 the EAT held that an agency worker supplied to the Council was employed by the agency, even though she was under no ongoing obligation to accept work offered by the agency. The fact that P owed express contractual duties to the agency whenever she did accept an assignment was enough to satisfy the definition of 'employment' under what is now S.83 EqA.

The definition of employment in S.83(2) also applies to the right to equal pay. However, where an agency worker is employed by the employment business which supplies him or her, consideration will need to be given as to whether or not there is an appropriate comparator. Assuming that the worker is unable to point to a comparator employed by the same employment business at the same hirer, within the meaning of S.79(3) EqA, he or she would have to demonstrate that although the comparator is assigned to work for a different hirer, 'common terms' apply between them, within the meaning of S.79(4). For details of what is meant by 'common terms', see IDS Employment Law Handbook, 'Equal Pay' (2011), Chapter 4, 'Comparators', under '"Same employment" or "single source" – same employment at different establishments'.

1.159 **Discrimination by the principal.** An agency worker who is employed by an agency but who suffers discrimination at the hands of the end-user, or 'principal', to which he or she is supplied to work will not be covered by the definition in S.83(2) unless he or she also has an express or implied contractual relationship with the principal. To counter this, the EqA contains specific provisions prohibiting discrimination against contract workers (such as agency workers) by the principal (though no similar provision applies in respect of the right to equal pay). S.41 EqA provides that a principal must not discriminate against or victimise a contract worker:

- as to the terms on which the principal allows the worker to do the work – S.41(1)(a) and (3)(a)

- by not allowing the worker to do, or to continue to do, the work – S.41(1)(b) and (3)(b)

- in the way the principal affords the worker access, or by not affording the worker access, to opportunities for receiving a benefit, facility or service – S.41(1)(c) and (3)(c)

- by subjecting the worker to any other detriment – S.41(1)(d) and (3)(d).

Section 41(2) further provides that a principal must not, in relation to contract work, harass a contract worker, while S.41(4) states that a duty to make reasonable adjustments applies to a principal (as well as to the employer of a contract worker).

1.160 A 'principal' is a person who makes work available for an individual ('the contract worker') who is:

- employed by another person, and

- supplied by that other person in furtherance of a contract to which the principal is a party (whether or not that other person is a party to it) – S.41(5).

It is clear that there does not need to be a direct contractual relationship between the employer and the principal for the protection to apply. The agency worker could thus be supplied via an intermediary. However, to come within S.41 the individual must have a contract with the agency or employment business which provides the initial link in the supply chain, and this contract must be one of 'employment', within the wide definition set down by S.83(2) EqA. In London Borough of Camden v Pegg and ors (above), for example, P was supplied by one agency (R2) through another agency (R3) to the local authority for whom she worked. The tribunal found that she was a contract worker employed by R2 and that the local authority was her principal within the meaning of what is now S.41. The fact that there was an intermediary (R3) did not affect these conclusions. The EAT agreed and rejected the appeal.

Although there does not need to be a direct contractual relationship between **1.161** the employer and the principal, there must be an unbroken chain of contracts between the two. In MHC Consulting Services Ltd v Tansell and anor 2000 ICR 789, CA, for example, T was a computer specialist who, in order to secure the benefits of limited liability, had chosen to provide his services through the establishment of his own company. He was employed by this company, which contracted with an employment agency, which in turn supplied his services to an insurance company. The Court of Appeal upheld the EAT's decision that T could bring a complaint of disability discrimination against the insurance company. Lord Justice Mummery, delivering the judgment of the Court, thought it irrelevant that there was no direct contractual relationship between the limited company that employed the individual and the insurance company that made the work available. Taking into account the underlying purpose of the discrimination legislation, the Court considered it more probable than not that Parliament had intended to confer protection in these circumstances.

For discussion on the question of whether an agency worker may be employed directly by the principal, see 'Employment status – relationship with the end-user' below.

Discrimination by employment service providers. Where an employment **1.162** agency or business is not an employer within the S.83 EqA definition, it may nonetheless be liable for discrimination against an agency worker in its capacity as an 'employment service provider'. The term 'employment service provider' covers a spectrum of recruitment and supply agencies, including those who provide services 'for finding employment for persons' and 'supplying employers with persons to do work' – see S.56(2) EqA. Under S.55(1), an employment service provider must not discriminate against a person in the arrangements it makes for selecting persons to whom to provide, or to whom to offer to provide, the service; as to the terms on which it offers to provide the service to the person; or by *not* offering to provide the service to the person. It is also unlawful for a service-provider to discriminate in the terms on which it provides the service to a person, by not providing the service to a person, by terminating the provision of the service to a person, or by subjecting a person to any other detriment – S.55(2). For further details, see IDS Employment Law Handbook, 'Discrimination at Work' (2010), Chapter 29, 'Liability of other bodies', under 'Employment service-providers'.

An example:

- **Chappell v Vital Resources Ltd** ET Case No.1301251/07: C, aged 61, responded to VR Ltd's advertisement for electric meter installers. He had over 30 years' relevant experience. Although his application initially received very positive feedback, after he was asked his age, the agency told him that the job was no longer available. It later transpired that jobs were offered to two other applicants who were younger and far less experienced than C. He lodged an employment tribunal claim alleging direct age discrimination. The tribunal held that C had suffered direct discrimination. Material to its conclusion was the fact that the agency could not offer a plausible explanation for why it had offered a formal interview to the two less-experienced candidates but not to C.

1.163 Harassment and victimisation by employment service providers are also prohibited – S.55(3), (4) and (5). However, there are important exceptions permitting service providers to discriminate in certain circumstances – see IDS Employment Law Handbook, 'Discrimination at Work' (2010), Chapter 30, 'General exceptions', under 'Employment services'.

For discussion on the question of whether a particular employment services provider is subject to the duty to make reasonable adjustments in respect of disabled people, see IDS Employment Law Handbook, 'Discrimination at Work' (2010), Chapter 29, 'Liability of other bodies', under 'Employment service-providers – reasonable adjustments'.

1.164 Statutory sick pay

Statutory sick pay (SSP) is payable to employees whose average gross weekly earnings over the previous eight weeks were at or above the lower earnings limit for the payment of national insurance contributions (currently £109 a week). An employee for these purposes is a person who is gainfully employed in Great Britain either under a contract of service or in an office with emoluments chargeable to Schedule E income tax – S.163(1) Social Security Contributions and Benefits Act 1992. The Statutory Sick Pay (General) Regulations 1982 SI 1982/894 provide that, subject to some exceptions, an 'employed earner' for social security purposes is to be treated as an employee – Reg 16.

Thus, agency workers are entitled to SSP as long as they satisfy the other conditions of eligibility. Whoever is responsible for deducting PAYE tax and Class 1 national insurance contributions is liable to pay SSP in these circumstances.

For further details, see IDS Employment Law Handbook, 'Wages' (2011), Chapter 7, 'Statutory sick pay', under 'Qualifying for SSP'.

Maternity and parental rights   1.165

Article 5(1)(a) of the EU Temporary Agency Workers Directive (No.2008/104) requires that the principle of equal treatment in respect of basic working and employment conditions extends to 'the rules in force in the undertaking on protection of pregnant women and nursing mothers'. At the time the Agency Workers Regulations 2010 SI 2010/93 (AWR) came into force, this principle was already partially satisfied by the provisions on pregnancy and maternity discrimination in the Equality Act 2010, as these apply to a broad category of 'worker' – see under 'Discrimination and equal pay' above.

However, to ensure that agency workers were fully protected, Schedule 2 to the AWR inserted new sections into the Employment Rights Act 1996 (ERA), giving pregnant agency workers who have completed the 12-week qualifying period the right to paid time off for ante-natal care and to be suspended from working for a hirer where there are health and safety risks. If a pregnant worker is suspended on health and safely grounds she has the right to be offered alternative work; and if no alternative work exists, to be paid during the suspension by the temporary work agency. These provisions are discussed under 'Time off for ante-natal care' and 'Health and safety measures' below.

Statutory maternity, paternity and adoption leave and pay. Agency workers 1.166 will only be entitled to take statutory maternity, paternity and adoption leave if they are employees within the meaning of S.230(1) ERA. Thus, unless agency workers have an employment contract with the employment business or temporary work agency which places them with a hirer, or are employed by the hirer itself, they will have no right to take – or, importantly, return to the same assignment from – statutory maternity, paternity or adoption leave. However, they may have contractual rights to such leave.

Note that where a worker is not entitled to statutory maternity leave, the 'protected period' during which she will be protected against unfavourable treatment because of pregnancy, or related to pregnancy or childbirth or its consequences, will end two weeks after the end of the pregnancy – S.18(6)(b) EqA (see IDS Employment Law Handbook, 'Maternity and Parental Rights' (2012), Chapter 13, 'Discrimination and equal pay', under 'Direct discrimination – protected period').

1.167 The rights to maternity, paternity and adoption leave are discussed in detail in IDS Employment Law Handbook, 'Maternity and Parental Rights' (2012), Chapter 3, 'Maternity leave'; Chapter 7, 'Paternity leave and pay'; and Chapter 6, 'Adoption leave and pay'. The question of agency workers' employment status is discussed under 'Employment status' below.

Statutory maternity pay (SMP), and the equivalent statutory payments for paternity and adoption leave, are treated slightly differently, with the effect that agency workers may be entitled to receive pay from the agency that supplies them even if they are not entitled to statutory leave. However, in the absence of a statutory entitlement to leave, an agency worker would need to be able to show a contractual right to leave.

1.168 The rights to maternity, paternity and adoption pay are discussed in detail in IDS Employment Law Handbook, 'Maternity and Parental Rights' (2012), Chapter 5, 'Statutory maternity pay'; Chapter 7, 'Paternity leave and pay'; and Chapter 6, 'Adoption leave and pay'.

Note that the AWR exclude 'any payment in respect of maternity, paternity or adoption leave' from agency workers' entitlement to the same basic and working conditions as employees following the 12-week qualifying period – see Reg 6(3)(c). Thus, an agency worker will not be entitled to, for example, maternity pay purely on the basis that under Reg 5 she should be treated – in terms of pay – as if she had been recruited directly. See 'Rights under the Agency Workers Regulations – equal treatment: pay' above.

1.169 **Time off for ante-natal care.** Pregnant agency workers are entitled to be permitted, by both the temporary work agency (TWA) and the hirer, to take paid time off for ante-natal care (unless they are employees and are already entitled to take such time off under Ss.55–57 ERA) – Ss.57ZA–57ZD ERA. However, like the right to equal treatment in respect of basic working and employment conditions generally, the right to time off for ante-natal care applies only after a 12-week qualifying period of service – S.57ZD(1)(a). Furthermore, the right falls away where the agency worker ceases to be covered by the right to equal treatment under the AWR – S.57ZD(1)(b). For details of the qualifying period, see 'Rights under the Agency Workers Regulations 2010 – equal treatment: qualifying period' above.

After the first ante-natal appointment, the agency worker will be permitted to attend further appointments only if, on request, she produces for inspection by the TWA or hirer a certificate from a registered medical practitioner, registered midwife or registered nurse stating that she is pregnant; and an appointment card or some other document showing that the appointment has been made – S.57ZA(2) and (3). She may take time off from any period when, in accordance with the terms under which she works temporarily for and under the supervision and direction of the hirer, she is required to be at work – S.57ZA(4).

However, there is no duty on the hirer or TWA to provide such time off beyond the original intended, or likely, duration of the assignment, whichever is the longer – S.57ZD(2).

An agency worker who is permitted to take time off under S.57ZA is entitled **1.170** to be paid by the TWA for the period of absence at the 'appropriate hourly rate' – S.57ZB(1). This can be set off against any contractual remuneration that may be payable – S.57ZB(5). The appropriate hourly rate is normally calculated by dividing one week's pay by the number of that agency worker's normal weekly working hours with the hirer that are in force on the day when the time off is taken – S.57ZB(2). However, where the number of normal working hours during the assignment differs from week to week or over a longer period, one week's pay is divided instead by the number of normal working hours averaged over a period of 12 weeks ending with the last complete week before the day on which the time off is taken – S.57ZB(3).

An agency worker may complain to an employment tribunal that the TWA or hirer has unreasonably refused to permit her to take time off as required by S.57ZA, or that the TWA has failed to pay the whole or any part of any amount to which she is entitled under S.57ZB – S.57ZC(1) and (2). Such a complaint must be presented within three months beginning with the date of the appointment, or, if not reasonably practicable, within such further period as the tribunal considers reasonable – S.57ZC(3). If the tribunal finds that the TWA or hirer unreasonably refused to permit the agency worker to take time off, it will award her an amount equal to the remuneration to which she would have been entitled under S.57ZB if she had not been refused the time off – S.57ZC(5). It is for the tribunal to decide how much it would be just and equitable for each party to pay, having regard to the extent of their respective responsibility for the infringement – S.57ZB(6). If the complaint is that the TWA has failed to pay the agency worker the whole or part of any amount to which she is entitled under S.57ZB, the tribunal will order the TWA to pay to the agency worker the amount which it finds due to her – S.57ZB(7).

In addition, an agency worker has the right not to be subject to any detriment by any act, or deliberate failure to act, by the TWA or hirer on the ground that the worker exercised (or proposed to exercise) the right to take time off under S.57ZA or received (or sought to receive) remuneration under S.57ZB – Ss.47C(5) and 48(1AA).

Health and safety measures. Employers have a duty under the Management of **1.171** Health and Safety at Work Regulations 1999 SI 1999/3242 ('the 1999 Regulations') to carry out risk assessments in respect of pregnant workers. This duty applies in respect of virtually all workers, including agency workers, and is imposed on both the TWA that directly employs the agency worker and on the hirer for whom the agency worker is temporarily working. For full details, see IDS Employment Law Handbook, 'Maternity and Parental Rights' (2012),

69

Chapter 2, 'Health and safety protection', under 'Risk assessments – duties in respect of temporary and agency workers', and in the section 'Risk assessments', under 'Conducting a risk assessment – temporary and agency workers'.

Once a risk assessment has been carried out, the employer must take measures to reduce or remove any risks identified. In this regard, the AWR inserted specific provisions into the 1999 Regulations requiring hirers to take risk avoidance measures where they engage agency workers via a TWA. These provisions only apply where the agency worker has completed the necessary 12-week qualifying period under the AWR – Reg 18AB (see 'Rights under the Agency Workers Regulations – equal treatment: qualifying period' above).

1.172 Reg 16A provides that where the measures required of the employer would not avoid the risk to the agency worker, the hirer is under a duty to alter the agency worker's working conditions or hours if it would be reasonable to do so. However, if this would not be reasonable, the hirer must inform the TWA of that fact and the agency must then end the supply of the agency worker to the hirer – Reg 16A(2). Where this happens the TWA will come under a duty to offer the agency worker suitable alternative work with another hirer, if available – S.68B ERA. If no alternative work is available, the agency worker has a limited right to be paid remuneration during the remaining period of the engagement that has been brought to an end by virtue of the operation of Reg 16A(2).

Where any risk to an agency worker who is a new or expectant mother relates to infectious or contagious disease, Reg 16A(3) suggests that a hirer does not have to take specific avoidance measures provided that the level of risk within the workplace is no greater than that which the worker may encounter outside it. However, the provision is not entirely clear.

1.173 For full details of the risk avoidance scheme that applies to pregnant workers and new mothers (including agency workers), see IDS Employment Law Handbook, 'Maternity and Parental Rights' (2012), Chapter 2, 'Health and safety protection'.

1.174 Employment status

Establishing the employment status of any worker is important, as this will determine the employment rights and protections to which he or she is entitled. Some rights, such as the right to be paid the national minimum wage and the right to paid annual leave, are accorded to 'workers' (see 'Other statutory employment rights' above), while others, including the right to claim unfair dismissal, the right to receive statutory redundancy pay and the right to take maternity leave, are only available to the narrower category of 'employees'. For these purposes, an 'employee' is an individual who has entered into or works, or worked, under a contract of employment – S.230(1) Employment Rights Act 1996 (ERA). A contract of employment means 'a contract of service or apprenticeship, whether express or implied, and (if it is express) whether oral or in writing' – S.230(2).

However, whether a particular individual falls within the statutory definition of worker and/or employee cannot be conclusively decided by looking at the statutes alone, but rather is determined by applying various common law tests that have been developed by the courts over time. Briefly, in order for a contract of any kind to exist, there must be an offer and acceptance, an intention to create legal relations, and consideration for work done, and the terms must be sufficiently clear and certain to be enforceable – see IDS Employment Law Handbook, 'Contracts of Employment' (2009), Chapter 1, 'Basic requirements', under 'Formation of the contract'. For a contract to amount to an *employment* contract, there must be present at least the essential prerequisites of mutuality of obligation and sufficient control – Montgomery v Johnson Underwood Ltd 2001 ICR 819, CA. Further key requirements are that the individual provides personal service, is sufficiently integrated into the employer's organisation, and is not carrying out the work as part of his or her own business. The relevant considerations are discussed in full in IDS Employment Law Handbook, 'Contracts of Employment' (2009), Chapter 1, 'Basic requirements', under 'Who is an employee?'

Because of the complexity of the typical tripartite agency arrangement, **1.175** identifying the employment status of an agency worker can prove to be particularly difficult. A typical arrangement will involve an employment business entering into a contract with the agency worker to provide him or her with work with a client (the hirer) of the employment business. But the relationship between the employment business and the worker may well continue while the worker carries out that work for the client. For example, the employment business may pay the worker out of a fee received from the client.

Often the written terms of the contract between the employment business and worker stipulate that there may be periods when no work is available, and that the employment business is not obliged to find work for, or to pay, the worker at those times. However, agency working arrangements are not necessarily short term and they can sometimes last for several years and may give the appearance of being no different from a standard employment arrangement, especially where the agency worker works closely alongside permanent employees and the client exercises a considerable degree of control over the agency worker's work.

In none of the relevant legislation – i.e. the Employment Agencies Act 1973 **1.176** ('the 1973 Act'), the Conduct of Employment Agencies and Employment Businesses Regulations 2003 SI 2003/3319 ('the 2003 Regulations') or the Agency Workers Regulations 2010 SI 2010/93 (AWR) – is the status of agency workers clarified for the purposes of employment protection legislation and the matter is left to be decided under the common law tests of status. (This is in contrast to tax and national insurance legislation, which treats temporary agency workers as though they were employees of the employment business for the purposes of determining liability for income tax and national insurance contributions. This, however, has no bearing on their employment status for other purposes.)

Below, we consider how the courts approach the contractual and employment status of agency workers, first in relation to the employment business and then in relation to the end-user to which they are assigned. It should be noted that the courts (and, indeed, the general public) tend to use the term 'employment business' and 'employment agency' interchangeably to mean a business that engages workers under some form of contract and then supplies them to clients as and when required. This is a very different type of arrangement to that carried on by recruitment agencies, which introduce work-seekers to potential employers. In this section we are concerned solely with the former type of business and all references to employment businesses or employment agencies should be read accordingly.

1.177 **Relationship with the employment business**

In most cases there will be no doubt that there is a contract between the employment business and the worker. However, establishing that the contract is one of employment is likely to be problematic, regardless of how long the agency worker has been on the books of a particular employment business, or how long he or she has been assigned to work for a particular hirer.

A specific engagement within the context of a worker's ongoing arrangement with an employment business may give rise to a contract of employment – McMeechan v Secretary of State for Employment 1997 ICR 549, CA. However, it is unlikely that the general relationship between an employment business and an agency worker 'on the books' will give rise to a contract of employment. This is because there is usually no obligation on the employment business to find work for the worker and no obligation on the worker to accept any work that is offered. In Wickens v Champion Employment 1984 ICR 365, EAT, the EAT held that the terms under which agency workers were engaged were quite inconsistent with the normal features of a contract of employment. It particularly stressed the absence of mutual obligations to provide or to do work and the absence of 'the elements of continuity, and care of the employer for the employee, that one associates with a contract of service'. The EAT followed the same approach in Ironmonger v Movefield Ltd (t/a Deering Appointments) 1988 IRLR 461, EAT, despite the worker in that case having worked for a particular company through the same employment business for five years.

1.178 In most cases a specific assignment will give rise to sufficient mutuality of obligation: it is a question of assessing the agency worker's relationship when he or she does in fact turn up for work regardless of the fact that there may be no general obligation on him or her to do so. In Montgomery v Johnson Underwood Ltd 2001 ICR 819, CA, the Court of Appeal stated that 'an offer of work by an employment agency, even at another's workplace, accepted by the individual for remuneration to be paid by the agency, could satisfy the requirement of mutuality of obligation', although clearly each case will turn on its own facts.

It is the issue of control that is more likely to provide the stumbling block for the finding of a contract of employment. This raises particular problems in the context of agency work, as control of the agency worker will often be shared by the employment business and the hirer, although frequently an employment business will exercise very little control over a worker's day-to-day activities. The Court of Appeal in Montgomery held that control lay between the hirer and the agency worker. The claimant was held not to be an employee of the employment business as it had 'little or no control, direction or supervision' over her. The Court doubted that sufficient control could be found in the employment business's right to terminate the worker's service if she failed to meet the hirer's requirements in terms of skill, integrity or reliability.

Similarly, in Dacas v Brook Street Bureau (UK) Ltd 2004 ICR 1437, CA, the **1.179** Court of Appeal agreed with an employment tribunal that a worker was not an employee of an employment business. D was registered as a temporary worker with BSB Ltd, an employment business, which assigned her to work exclusively as a cleaner at a mental health hostel run by Wandsworth Council. D worked exclusively for the Council for over four years until the arrangement was terminated, whereupon she presented an unfair dismissal claim on the basis that she had been the employee of either the Council or BSB Ltd. Relying on Montgomery, the Court of Appeal held that the contract between BSB Ltd and D was not a contract of service. The employment business was under no obligation to provide D with work, and she was under no obligation to accept any work offered. Furthermore, BSB Ltd did not exercise day-to-day control over D or her work – that control had been exercised by the Council. The Court stated that the fact that BSB Ltd agreed to do some things that an employer would normally do (for example, paying wages) did not make it the employer.

The Court of Appeal also held, unanimously, that D did not have a contract of service with BSB Ltd regarding the specific assignment at the mental health hostel. The Court thought that BSB Ltd's role was not that of D's employer, but rather that of an employment business finding suitable work assignments for her and, so far as the Council was concerned, performing the task of staff supplier and administrator of staff services. Furthermore, the Court considered that the real control over the work done by D at the hostel was not exercised by BSB Ltd. Instead the tribunal should have considered the possibility of an implied contract of service between D and the Council (see further 'Relationship with the end-user' below).

1.180 The issue of whether a worker was employed by an employment business also arose in Bunce v Postworth Ltd t/a Skyblue 2005 IRLR 557, CA. In that case, B signed a document confirming that he was entering into a contract for services with the employment business, which was not intended to give rise to a contract of employment. P Ltd was under no obligation to provide work and B under no obligation to accept any. B was allotted 142 assignments before the contract was terminated. The Court of Appeal agreed with the tribunal's analysis that B was not an employee of the employment business because the contract lacked the necessary requirements of control and mutuality of obligation. While the Court accepted the possibility that an overarching 'umbrella' agreement between a worker and an agency could arise, governing individual contracts of employment between the two, it concluded that there was no such arrangement in the instant case.

Similarly, in Secretary of State for Business, Innovation and Skills v Studders and ors EAT 0571/10 the EAT held that agency workers were not employees of the agency through which they obtained assignments. The agreement between the agency and the workers stated that it was not a contract of employment; that no contract existed between assignments; that the agency was not obliged to provide work and the workers were not obliged to accept it; and that either side could terminate an assignment at any time without notice. While the agency exercised a modest degree of control over holidays, it had no day-to-day control over the claimants' work. The EAT concluded that the contract showed no intention to create an employment relationship and that the requirements of mutuality of obligation and control were absent. Although the agency paid tax and national insurance contributions on the basis that the workers were employees, this was a neutral factor because it was a statutory requirement.

1.181 In Consistent Group Ltd v Kalwak and ors 2008 IRLR 505, CA, the Court of Appeal rejected the EAT's approval of a tribunal's finding that there was a contract of employment between workers and an employment business that purported to engage them as self-employed subcontractors. The EAT had held that the employment business, which provided accommodation and transport for the foreign workers, exercised an exceptional level of economic control over them that was sufficient to give rise to a contract of employment, even though it did not manage their day-to-day working activities. Taking a stricter approach, the Court of Appeal held that since there was an express term in the contract between the parties describing the staff as self-employed, a contract of employment could not be implied in direct contradiction unless it was necessary to do so and the express term was properly reasoned to be a sham. However, this stricter approach was subsequently disapproved by the Supreme Court in Autoclenz Ltd v Belcher and ors 2011 ICR 1157, SC, where their Lordships made it clear that it is not necessary for a court to find that the parties had a common intention to misrepresent the true nature of their respective obligations before it is allowed to disregard contractual terms. It is sufficient that those terms do not represent the true agreement between the parties.

The above cases demonstrate that in most situations the relationship between the agency worker and the employment business will not be one of employment, unless there is an express employment contract. There may still be instances where an agency worker can successfully claim to be an employee of the employment business, depending on the circumstances. It will, however, be necessary to show an exceptional level of control over the worker, as was found in Augustin v Total Quality Staff Ltd and anor EAT 0343/07. There, the EAT held that A was employed by TQS Ltd, an employment business, primarily because, while working, he had been under the supervision of H, an employee of TQS Ltd. The EAT went on to hold that A was employed under a series of daily contracts of employment. This was because, while A was not contractually obliged to accept the work offered to him on a daily basis, once he did accept he was then obliged to carry out his duties until that day's shift was completed.

Furthermore, in Russell and ors v 24/7 Support Services Ltd (in liquidation) **1.182** and ors ET Case No.2602005/05 the claimants, who were bank nurses and care workers, were found to be employees of an employment business. Although there was no obligation on the employment business to provide work and the agency workers were not obliged to accept any work offered, the tribunal found that the relationship was properly characterised as one of employment. Key to its decision were the facts that the employment business was obliged to provide training, which workers were obliged to attend, and that it operated what was to all intents and purposes a disciplinary procedure, which could result in a worker being unable to obtain work through the business. However, the tribunal did note that the 'overarching' mutual obligation with regard to training was 'unique' in this type of case.

Relationship with the end-user   1.183

The courts have generally been very reluctant to find that workers supplied by an employment business are employees of the end-user, largely on the basis that where there is no express contract between the worker and the end-user (both, instead, contracting with the employment business), there can be no contract of employment – see, for example, Hewlett Packard Ltd v O'Murphy 2002 IRLR 4, EAT. However, in Franks v Reuters Ltd and anor 2003 ICR 1166, CA, the Court of Appeal held that dealings between an agency worker and an end-user over a period of years were capable of generating an *implied* contractual relationship.

Thus, the length of the relationship between the worker and the end-user may be a relevant factor in determining whether it is an employment relationship. Indeed, in Dacas v Brook Street Bureau (UK) Ltd 2004 ICR 1437, CA, the Court of Appeal expressed the obiter view that employment tribunals must consider the possibility of an implied contract of service needing to be inferred between the worker and the end-user even where there is no express contract between them. Lord Justice Sedley considered it 'simply not credible' that a worker could be employed by nobody after being assigned to the same end-user for a period of a year or more. And in Cable and Wireless plc v Muscat 2006 ICR 975, CA, the Court upheld a tribunal's decision that it was necessary to imply a contract between a contractor and an end-user in order to give it 'business reality', given that the contractor worked under the direction of the end-user's managers, arranged his holidays to suit the end-user, and was described as an 'employee' in company documentation.

1.184 The uncertainty that arose as a result of these cases was largely put to rest by the EAT in James v Greenwich London Borough Council 2007 ICR 577, EAT, where Mr Justice Elias, then President of the EAT, set out a comprehensive formulation of the law on the employee status of agency workers. In that case, J worked for the Council through an employment business. After two years, she switched employment businesses and joined BSPS Ltd for a better rate of pay. She entered into a temporary worker agreement with BSPS Ltd, which provided that her work under the contract with the employment business did not give rise to a contract of employment with either the employment business or the client. Under the agreement between BSPS Ltd and the Council, the employment business was responsible for paying J and J was deemed to be under the supervision, direction and control of the Council for the duration of the assignment. When J brought a claim of unfair dismissal, the tribunal found – applying Dacas v Brook Street Bureau (UK) Ltd (above) – that it could not imply a contract of employment between J and the Council. J did not receive her basic pay from the Council, was not paid any benefits such as sick pay and holiday, was not subject to the Council's disciplinary and grievance procedures, and had ultimately been replaced with another worker provided by the agency. Furthermore, there was no obligation upon J to provide her services to the Council, nor any corresponding obligation on the Council to provide J with work. Since the irreducible minimum of mutual obligation required to support the existence of a contract of employment was absent, it followed that J was not an employee of the Council.

On appeal, the EAT held that the tribunal had been entitled on the facts to decide that there was nothing to justify implying a contract of employment. Elias P observed that, in Dacas, Mummery LJ had encouraged tribunals to consider the possibility of an implied contract between the agency worker and the end-user, but noted that he had gone on to state that a contract would only arise from a 'necessary inference'. This meant that such a contract could only be implied if the contractual test of necessity as set out in Aramis 1989 1 Lloyd's Rep 213, CA, had been satisfied. Elias P also disagreed with Sedley LJ's observations in Dacas with regard to the legal implications of a long-standing arrangement, emphasising that the mere passage of time is not sufficient to give rise to employee status.

Elias P laid down the following guidance to assist tribunals in deciding whether **1.185** to imply an employment contract between an agency worker and an end-user:

- the key issue is whether the way in which the contract is performed is consistent with the agency arrangements, or whether it is only consistent with an implied contract of employment between the worker and the end-user

- the key feature in agency arrangements is not just the fact that the end-user is not paying the wages, but that it cannot insist on the agency providing the particular worker at all

- it will not be necessary to imply a contract between the worker and the end-user when agency arrangements are genuine and accurately represent the relationship between the parties, even if such a contract would also not be inconsistent with the relationship

- it will be rare for an employment contract to be implied where agency arrangements are genuine and, when implemented, accurately represent the actual relationship between the parties. If any such contract is to be implied there must have been, subsequent to the relationship commencing, some words or conduct that entitle the tribunal to conclude that the agency arrangements no longer adequately reflect how the work is actually being performed

- the mere fact that an agency worker has worked for a particular client for a considerable period does not justify the implication of a contract between the two

- it will be more readily open to a tribunal to imply a contract where, as in Cable and Wireless plc v Muscat (above), the agency arrangements are superimposed on an existing contractual relationship between the worker and the end-user.

When the case came before the Court of Appeal (2008 ICR 545), the Court **1.186** agreed with the EAT's approach and confirmed that a tribunal will only be entitled to imply an employment contract between an agency worker and an end-user where it is necessary to do so to give business reality to the situation. In the Court's view, there will be no such necessity where agency arrangements are genuine and accurately represent the relationship between the parties. Interestingly, Mummery LJ (giving the leading judgment) took the opportunity to qualify his own guidance in Dacas v Brook Street Bureau (UK) Ltd (above), holding that 'Dacas is not authority for the proposition that the implication of [an employment contract] is inevitable in a long-term worker agency situation. It only [points] to it as a possibility, the outcome depending on the facts found by the tribunal in the particular case.' Furthermore, in direct contradiction of Sedley LJ's obiter comments in Dacas, the Court stated that an employment contract should not be implied simply because the worker has been engaged with one client for a significant period of time.

Mummery LJ went on to say that there was no conflict between the Court of Appeal's decisions in Dacas and Muscat and the EAT's subsequent decision in James. The Court in Dacas raised the possibility, which had not been considered by the tribunal in that case, that a contract of service might, by necessary inference, be found to exist with the end-user. It did not suggest, however, that such an implication was inevitable. In each case, the question 'must be decided in accordance with common law principles of implied contract and, in some very extreme cases, by exposing sham arrangements'. He also expressly approved the guidance (as set out above) given by the EAT in the instant case.

1.187 Elias P's guidance has subsequently been followed in a number of cases, including Craigie v London Borough of Haringey EAT 0556/06 and Wood Group Engineering (North Sea) Ltd v Robertson EAT 0081/06. In both, the EAT held that it was not necessary to imply a contract of employment between an agency worker and an end-user as their working relationships were adequately explained by express contractual arrangements. Similarly, in Heatherwood and Wexham Park Hospitals NHS Trust v Kulubowila and ors EAT 0633/06 the EAT overturned a tribunal's decision that an agency worker was employed by a hospital trust. Although the facts were consistent with there being an employment relationship, they were equally consistent with there being no employment relationship. An employment contract would not be implied unless the facts were only consistent with there being such a relationship. The fatal factor for the claimant here was his earlier application for a permanent post with the trust. For this reason, the instant case was easily distinguishable from Cable and Wireless plc v Muscat (above), where there had initially been an employment relationship with the end-user. In reaching this decision, the EAT made it clear that the ordinary common law principles applied. For a contract to be implied, it must be reasonably necessary to do so to give business reality to a situation. It would be fatal to the implication of a contract if the parties would have acted as they did in the absence of a contract.

By contrast, in Harlow District Council v O'Mahony and anor EAT 0144/07 the EAT upheld a tribunal's finding that a contract of employment could be implied between the agency worker and the end-user. A number of factors made it necessary to imply such a contract to reflect the reality of the relationship between them: O'M was interviewed by the end-user before he was taken on and was then subject to the control of his supervisor; he had no further contact with the employment business thereafter save that he submitted his timesheets to it and was paid by it; he negotiated a pay rise directly with the end-user; he was subject to the end-user's disciplinary procedures; he needed the end-user's permission to take holidays; and he needed to notify them when he was absent through sickness. In these circumstances it was necessary to imply a contract between O'M and the end-user to explain the employment relationship as it had developed between them. The employment business's role was limited to that of an agent for the end-user, obtaining personnel for it and administering payment to the worker. But in Muschett v HM Prison Service 2010 IRLR 451, CA, the Court of Appeal held that an employment tribunal judge had not erred in finding that a claimant who had been supplied by an employment agency to work for a company was not an employee of that company within the meaning of S.230(1) ERA. The judge's finding that the claimant's status remained at all times that of an agency worker and that it at no point metamorphosed into that of an employee under a contract of employment with the company was unimpeachable on the evidence. The claimant's argument that he would not have performed the extra duties he claimed to have performed except in the belief that he would become a permanent employee was irrelevant. An employment contract cannot be created by the mere, and unilateral, wish of the putative employee.

The Court of Appeal confirmed in Tilson v Alstom Transport 2011 IRLR 169, **1.188** CA, that whether a contract should be implied is ultimately a matter of law and involves an objective analysis of all the relevant circumstances. But the parties' understanding that there is no such contract in place explaining the terms of their relationship, and their inability to reach an agreement on the terms such a contract should contain, are 'extremely powerful factors' militating against any such implication.

In conclusion, the threshold for establishing employment status is high and many claimants will fail in their bids to establish that they are indeed employees. An employment relationship will only be implied between an agency worker and an end-user where it is necessary to give effect to the reality of the relationship between them. In considering whether it is necessary to imply a contract of employment, tribunals will look at all the circumstances of a case. The decision in James means that few agency workers will have the right to claim unfair dismissal against the end-user when their engagement is brought to an end – even if the engagement has lasted for a number of years. As Mummery LJ pointed out in James v Greenwich London Borough Council (above), as long as a tribunal correctly applies the test of 'necessity' in line with Elias P's guidance, agency workers who fail to establish employee status before an employment tribunal are extremely unlikely to succeed on appeal, given the high hurdle imposed by a perversity challenge. There are, of course, instances where an agency worker can successfully claim to be an employee of the agency itself. In such cases, however, it will be necessary to show an exceptional level of control by the agency over the workers.

1.189 Vicarious liability

At common law, an employer is vicariously liable for a tortious act (such as negligence) carried out by an employee in the course of his or her employment. In Dacas v Brook Street Bureau (UK) Ltd 2004 ICR 1437, CA, one of the arguments Lord Justice Sedley employed in support of his view that agency workers on long-term assignments must be employees was that if they were not, any third party who was injured by a tort committed by an agency worker in the course of his or her work would be unable to rely on the doctrine of vicarious liability to bring a claim against the organisation that exercised control over that agency worker.

However – and as the Court of Appeal accepted in Cable and Wireless plc v Muscat 2006 ICR 975, CA – an end-user *may* in certain circumstances acquire vicarious liability for the tortious acts and omissions of an agency worker assigned to it, even if it is not the worker's employer. At common law, an employer may be liable for torts committed by an agency worker in the employment of another, or who is self-employed, if it controls both the work to be done and also the method of performing it. Thus, in Interlink Express Parcels Ltd v Night Trunkers Ltd 2001 EWCA Civ 360, CA, drivers employed by NT Ltd and supplied to IEP Ltd to drive IEP Ltd's vehicles were held to be temporary deemed employees of IEP Ltd.

1.190 Another relevant question is whether the end-user exercises control over the agency worker, so that it can be said that it had a duty to prevent the tortious act or omission taking place. Whether an employee is deemed to be the temporary employee of the end-user of his or her services turns on the facts of the case. The inquiry should focus on the negligent act or omission and the court should ask itself whose duty it was to prevent that act.

This was established in Hawley v Luminar Leisure Ltd and ors 2006 IRLR 817, CA, where the Court of Appeal held that a nightclub owner was vicariously liable for the personal injury caused when a doorman at one of its clubs punched a customer in the face, notwithstanding that the doorman was the employee of a security firm who had supplied his services to the nightclub. It was the nightclub which, if not the general employer in law, acted as if it were in fact the doorman's employer and exercised many of the powers of the general employer, including detailed control over what the doorman did and how he was to do it.

1.191 Nevertheless, proving that the end-user has sufficient control over the agency worker's actions such that liability passes to it will not be easy. In Hawley, there had been an effective and substantial transfer of control and responsibility from the security firm to the nightclub, so it was appropriate that the employee be deemed the temporary employee of the nightclub for the purposes of the

80

doctrine of vicarious liability. By contrast, in Biffa Waste Services Ltd and anor v Maschinenfabrik Ernst Hese GmbH and ors 2008 EWCA Civ 1257, CA, the Court of Appeal held that a contractor did not have sufficient control over the way in which its sub-contractor's employees carried out their work to assume vicarious liability for their negligence in causing a fire. It was important not to confuse supervision with control: in the context of skilled labour, the fact that the contractor supervised the work did not mean that it controlled the workers. In this case, the workers were skilled welders. They had not become part of the contractor's business: their work took place only over a couple of days. Furthermore, four men had been supplied instead of the two whose work had been contracted, but there was no basis on which to distinguish between the two for which the contractor might be liable and the two for which it could not be liable.

2 Fixed-term employees

Scope and coverage of FTE Regulations

Equal treatment

Right to be informed of available vacancies

Right to receive written statement

Unfair dismissal rights

Protection from detriment

Redundancy rights

Successive fixed-term contracts

Enforcement and remedies

Fixed-term employees make up a substantial part of the workforce in Great **2.1** Britain, and indeed Europe. Until fairly recently, however, employment rights were confined to individuals with traditional working arrangements and led to concerns at a European level that fixed-term workers were being less favourably treated than those on open-ended or 'permanent' contracts. These concerns led to the adoption in June 1999 of the EU Fixed-term Work Directive (No.99/70) ('the FTW Directive'), which puts into effect the framework agreement on fixed-term contracts concluded between the social partners and annexed to the Directive. The agreement establishes a general framework for improving the quality of fixed-term work by:

- protecting fixed-term workers from being less favourably treated than those on open-ended or 'permanent' contracts, and

- preventing abuse arising from the use of successive fixed-term employment contracts or relationships.

The Directive was implemented in Great Britain (i.e. England, Scotland and Wales) by the Fixed-term Employees (Prevention of Less Favourable Treatment) Regulations 2002 SI 2002/2034 ('the FTE Regulations'), which came into force on 1 October 2002 – pursuant to S.45 of the Employment Act 2002 (EA). In Northern Ireland, separate (but very similar) Regulations apply – the Fixed-term Employees (Prevention of Less Favourable Treatment) Regulations (Northern Ireland) 2002 SI 2002/298 – enacted under S.46 EA.

In this chapter we begin by considering the scope and coverage of the FTE **2.2** Regulations, before exploring the specific rights afforded to fixed-term

83

employees in more detail: the principle of equal treatment (i.e. the right to be treated no less favourably than permanent employees), and the rights to be informed of available vacancies and to receive a written statement. We then discuss the right not to be unfairly dismissed or be subjected to a detriment on a ground relating to the Regulations before turning to the provisions aimed at preventing abuse arising from the use of successive fixed-term employment contracts. Finally, we look at the enforcement of rights under the Regulations, together with available remedies.

2.3 **Government guidance**. The Department for Business, Innovation and Skills (BIS) has provided some short guidance on 'Fixed-term employment contracts' ('the BIS Guidance'), available on the gov.uk website, to which we refer where relevant. Prior to the launch of the gov.uk website, a more detailed guide was available – 'Fixed-term work – guidance', produced by the old Department for Business, Enterprise and Regulatory Reform (BERR). This guidance can now be found on the National Archives website but it is no longer updated and should therefore be treated with some caution. Nevertheless we do refer to the BERR guidance in this chapter, where relevant, since it is much more detailed than the BIS Guidance and makes a number of useful points.

2.4 ## Scope and coverage of FTE Regulations

The FTE Regulations provide protection to 'fixed-term employees', defined in Reg 1(2) as any 'employee who is employed under a fixed-term contract'. This definition contains two elements: the contract must be a 'fixed-term contract' and the individual concerned must be an 'employee'.

2.5 ### Employment under a 'fixed-term contract'
A 'fixed-term contract' is a contract of employment that, 'in the normal course', will terminate on:

- the expiry of a specific term

- the completion of a particular task, or

- the occurrence or non-occurrence of any other specific event, except the attainment of normal retirement age – Reg 1(2).

This is wider than the previous common law definition, which only applied to contracts whose maximum duration was certain – in other words, the first of the above categories. Now the term 'fixed-term contracts' embraces not only contracts that are stated to be for a fixed term, but also those that are limited by the completion of a task or by a particular event (often referred to as 'task contracts').

84

The statutory definition of 'fixed-term contracts' could cover the following: **2.6**

- 'seasonal' or 'casual' employment contracts that cover a short period or task, e.g. employees at children's summer camps, agricultural workers, or shop assistants working specifically for Christmas or another busy period

- contracts intended specifically to cover for maternity, parental or paternity leave, or sick leave

- contracts that cover peaks in demand and which will expire when demand returns to normal levels

- contracts that will expire when a specific task is complete (e.g. setting up a new data base, painting a house or running a training course).

A contract is still a fixed-term contract even if it can be brought to an end by notice within the term – Allen v National Australia Group Europe Ltd 2004 IRLR 847, EAT. Thus, for example, a provision in a three-year fixed-term contract that it can be terminated by three months' notice on either side does not change its character.

Claims by permanent employees. A permanent employee is defined as an   **2.7** employee who is not employed under a fixed-term contract – Reg 1(2). Self-evidently, the FTE Regulations are not aimed at providing protection to permanent employees. However, it may be possible for a permanent employee to bring a claim under the Regulations where he or she used to be a fixed-term employee and is now suffering discrimination as a result. In Valenza and ors v Autorità Garante della Concorrenza e del Mercato 2013 ICR 373, ECJ, the claimants became permanent employees of AGCM, having been previously employed under successive fixed-term contracts. They complained that AGCM had set their pay at the starting level for permanent employees, without taking account of the service they had accrued as fixed-term employees. The ECJ held that a failure to take into account periods of fixed-term service when assessing pay would contravene the FTW Directive unless it could be objectively justified. The mere fact that the periods of service were completed under fixed-term contracts did not constitute an objective ground. The claimants were entitled to rely upon the Directive despite the fact that the alleged discrimination occurred when they had become permanent workers, since the treatment at issue concerned periods of service completed as fixed-term workers.

It is questionable whether the FTE Regulations specifically provide for a remedy in these circumstances. Reg 1(2) uses the present tense, defining a fixed-term employee as someone who 'is employed' under a fixed-term contract, and there is no separate provision under which a former fixed-term employee who has converted to permanent status can bring a claim before a tribunal. However, since the Valenza decision clearly establishes that such a claim should be available, a purposive interpretation of the Regulations is necessary in order to

85

make this possible. Private sector workers will be able to rely on the principle recently confirmed in EBR Attridge LLP (formerly Attridge Law) and anor v Coleman 2010 ICR 242, EAT, that national courts (including employment tribunals) must interpret provisions of domestic law that are intended to implement a Directive in order to achieve, 'so far as possible', an outcome consistent with the objective pursued by the Directive. To discharge this duty, courts have the flexibility to insert additional wording into domestic legislation. Public sector workers can rely directly on the relevant provisions of a Directive, provided they are sufficiently clear and precise. However, as the FTW Directive does not deal directly with this issue they too will need to rely upon a purposive interpretation of the FTE Regulations.

2.8 'Employees' only

The FTE Regulations apply only to 'employees', not to the wider category of 'workers'. 'Employee' for these purposes is defined in S.45 EA (the enabling provision for the FTE Regulations) as 'an individual who has entered into or works under (or, where the employment has ceased, worked under) a contract of employment' – S.45(6)(a). 'Contract of employment' is, in turn, defined as a 'contract of service or apprenticeship, whether express or implied, and (if it is express) whether oral or in writing' – S.45(6)(b). This definition is identical to that contained in S.230(1) of the Employment Rights Act 1996 (ERA) for the purposes of claiming, for example, unfair dismissal or a redundancy payment. For a detailed discussion of the definition of an employee, see IDS Employment Law Handbook, 'Contracts of Employment' (2009), Chapter 1, 'Basic requirements', under 'Who is an employee?'.

Interestingly, although apprentices are included in the definition of employee found in S.45(6), they are specifically excluded from the scope of the Regulations. This is discussed under 'Classes of employment specifically excluded' below. There are also certain classes of employment that are specifically included within the remit of the Regulations – see 'Classes of employment specifically included' below.

2.9 The Government's decision to limit the scope of the Regulations to employees rather than to extend it to cover all workers has been a controversial one. Arguably, the practical effect of limiting protection to employees is to exclude many of the individuals who are most likely to suffer discrimination because of their fixed-term status; namely, those working on a casual basis who, because of the loose nature of their working arrangements, do not fall within the narrow definition of employee.

In addition to concerns about the practical effect of the statutory limitation, there has been some debate as to whether, in confining the scope of the Regulations to employees, the Government has in fact failed to fully implement the FTW Directive. This is because the Directive applies to all fixed-term workers 'who have an employment contract or employment relationship as defined in law, collective agreements or practice in each Member State' – Clause 2(1). During the House of Commons Standing Committee F debates on the Employment Bill, Alan Johnson, then Minister of State for Employment Relations, rejected the view that in limiting the scope of the Regulations in this way the Government would not be fully implementing the Directive. In particular, he pointed to the fact that a similar interpretation had been given to the almost identical wording used in the EU Parental Leave Directive (No.96/34) when drafting the Maternity and Parental Leave etc Regulations 1999 SI 1999/3312 (Hansard, 21 January 2002 am, col 539).

The case of Del Cerro Alonso v Osakidetza (Servicio Vasco de Salud) 2008 ICR **2.10** 145, ECJ, however, casts some doubt on Mr Johnson's view. The ECJ concluded that the FTW Directive was 'applicable to all workers providing remunerated services in the context of a fixed-term employment relationship linking them to their employer'. The concept of an 'employment contract' under UK law is narrower than the concept of an 'employment relationship' under EU law and it is therefore arguable that the restriction of the FTE to 'employees' could be vulnerable to challenge.

Classes of employment specifically included   2.11
The following classes of employment are specifically included within the scope of the Regulations:

- Crown employment (provided that, having regard to the terms and conditions of the person in question, he or she would be an employee if not in Crown Employment) – Reg 13(1) and (2)(b). Crown employment is defined as 'employment under or for the purposes of a government department or any officer or body exercising on behalf of the Crown functions conferred by a statutory provision' – Reg 13(2)(a)

- employment by a territorial, auxiliary or volunteer reserve association under the Reserve Forces Act 1996 – Reg 14(1)(b)

- employment as a member of the House of Lords or House of Commons staff – Regs 15 and 16

- service as a police officer (including a special constable) or police cadet – Reg 17(1). A police officer or police cadet is treated as being employed by the chief officer of police (or, in Scotland, the chief constable); the person who has the direction and control of the body of constables or cadets in question; or, in the case of a constable or other person who has been seconded to the National Crime Agency, that Agency in respect of actions taken by, or on behalf of, it – Reg 17(1A) and (2).

2.12 Classes of employment specifically excluded

There are also a number of specific exclusions from the scope of the Regulations. These are as follows:

- employees working under contracts of apprenticeship, or under apprenticeship agreements (governed by the Apprenticeships, Skills, Children and Learning Act 2009) – Reg 20. (Apprenticeships are discussed in detail in Chapter 6, 'Apprentices')

- agency workers – Reg 19 (see 'Agency workers' below)

- people employed on training schemes supported by the Government or an Institution of the European Community – Reg 18(1). To fall within this exclusion, the training system in question must be specifically designed to provide training or work experience for the purpose of seeking or obtaining work

- people employed on work experience placements of one year or less that they are required to attend as part of a higher education course – Reg 18(2). In England and Wales a 'higher education course' is defined in Schedule 6 to the Education Reform Act 1988 and includes undergraduate, postgraduate and teacher training courses

- serving members of the armed forces – Reg 14(1)(a).

2.13 In Hudson v Department for Work and Pensions 2013 ICR 329, CA, the Court of Appeal, by a majority, held that the exclusion from the FTE Regulations of employees on Government training schemes applies not only in respect of schemes on which employees are employed at the time they seek to rely on the Regulations, but also in respect of those on which they were previously employed. Accordingly, the majority held that an employee's previous employment on a series of fixed-term training schemes did not count towards the four years of continuous employment required for her to achieve permanent employment status under Reg 8. This provision is considered further under 'Successive fixed-term contracts' below.

2.14 **Agency workers.** An agency worker is defined as 'any person who is supplied by an employment business to do work for another person under a contract or other arrangements made between the employment business and the other person' – Reg 19. 'Employment business' means 'the business... of supplying persons in the employment of the person carrying on the business, to act for, and under the control of, other persons in any capacity' – Reg 19(3). The BIS Guidance explains that this means, in essence, that workers don't count as fixed-term employees if they have a contract with an agency, rather than the company they are working for. The ECJ in Della Rocca v Poste Italiane SpA 2013 3 CMLR 15, ECJ, confirmed that the exclusion of agency workers is compatible with the FTW Directive. It held that the Directive does not apply to the relationship between a temporary work agency and an employment agency, or to the relationship between the worker and the end-user. Thus it could not be relied on to establish a permanent employment relationship between an agency worker and an end-user.

Note, however, that agency workers are given separate protection under the Agency Workers Regulations 2010 SI 2010/93. The rights of agency workers are discussed in detail in Chapter 1, 'Agency workers'.

Statutory sick pay. The FTE Regulations do apply to agency workers in one **2.15** important respect: entitlement to statutory sick pay. Before the FTE Regulations came into force, employees who were on contracts of less than three months were excluded from entitlement to statutory sick pay (SSP) by para (2)(b) of Schedule 11 to the Social Security Contributions and Benefits Act 1992 (SSCBA). That exclusion was repealed in respect of fixed-term employees in 2002 by Reg 11 of the FTE Regulations and, following the case of Revenue and Customs Commissioners v Thorn Baker Ltd and ors 2008 ICR 46, CA (which held that the exclusion still applied to agency workers whose contracts were for a specified period of less than three months), in respect of agency workers in 2008 – see Reg 19(1) (as amended by the Fixed-term Employees (Prevention of Less Favourable Treatment) (Amendment) Regulations 2008 SI 2008/2776).

Fixed-term employees working abroad 2.16
The FTE Regulations are silent as to their territorial scope. However, in Ashbourne v Department for Education and Skills EAT 0123/07 the EAT held that the House of Lords' decision in Lawson v Serco Ltd and other cases 2006 ICR 250, HL, on the territorial scope of unfair dismissal claims under the ERA applied equally to the Regulations. In Lawson, Lord Hoffmann stated that, as a general principle, employees are only able to claim unfair dismissal in Great Britain if they are 'employed in Great Britain'. He added that employees working wholly abroad may satisfy the test in certain limited circumstances – for example, where they are able to show strong connections with Great Britain and British employment law.

Employees working abroad who fail to satisfy the Lawson test may seek to argue that the principle established in Bleuse v MBT Transport Ltd and anor 2008 ICR 488, EAT, applies to allow them to bring a claim under the Regulations. That case held that the Lawson test ought to be modified in its application to UK law where necessary to give effect to directly effective rights derived from EU law. The Bleuse principle was endorsed by the Court of Appeal in Secretary of State for Children, Schools and Families v Fletcher and another case 2010 ICR 815, CA (an unfair dismissal case). There, the Court accepted that the principle of effectiveness in EU law required that the implied territorial limitation in domestic law on the right not to be unfairly

89

dismissed should be modified to permit such a claim where that was necessary for the vindication of a right derived from EU law – in that case, the FTE Regulations. Otherwise, F's EU-derived right to a permanent contract would be denied if he could be dismissed on the basis that he was employed on a fixed-term contract that had expired, as in such a situation he would have no remedy for unfair dismissal. (The circumstances in which a fixed-term employee becomes entitled to permanent status are discussed under 'Successive fixed-term contracts' below.)

2.17 The Bleuse principle was also applied by the Court of Appeal in Ministry of Defence v Wallis 2011 ICR 617, CA (a sex discrimination case). However, when the Fletcher case subsequently came before the Supreme Court, where it was decided on other grounds, Baroness Hale cast some doubt on the Bleuse principle. Although sympathetic to the principle, she put forward the obiter view that its correctness was open to some doubt and that, had she been required to decide the point, a reference to the European Court of Justice would have been necessary – Secretary of State for Children, Schools and Families v Fletcher and another case 2011 ICR 495, SC. Therefore, it cannot be said that the Bleuse principle is an established legal doctrine, although there is certainly some strong judicial support for it.

For further discussion of the case law relating to territorial jurisdiction, see IDS Employment Law Handbook, 'Employment Tribunal Practice and Procedure' (2014), Chapter 1, 'Tribunals' jurisdiction', under 'Limits to tribunals' jurisdiction – territorial jurisdiction'.

2.18 Employer's liability for employees and agents
For the purposes of the FTE Regulations, an employer is treated as liable for anything done by an employee in the course of his or her employment, whether or not it was done with the employer's knowledge – Reg 12(1). However, under Reg 12(3) the employer has a defence if it can prove that it took such steps as were reasonably practicable to prevent the employee from 'doing that act, or doing, in the course of his employment, acts of that description'.

An employer is also treated as liable for anything done by a person acting as agent for the employer with the employer's authority – Reg 12(2).

2.19 For the purposes of Reg 12, the secondment of any constable or other person to the National Crime Agency to serve as a member of its staff will be treated as employment by the Agency (and not as employment by any other person), and anything done by a person so seconded in the performance, or purported performance, of his or her functions will be treated as done in the course of that employment – Reg 17(1B).

Equal treatment

2.20

At the heart of the FTW Directive is the principle of equal treatment. Clause 4 provides that 'in respect of employment conditions, fixed-term workers shall not be treated in a less favourable manner than comparable permanent workers solely because they have a fixed-term contract or relation unless different treatment is justified on objective grounds'. This principle is reflected in Reg 3 of the FTE Regulations, which provides that fixed-term employees have the right not to be treated less favourably than comparable permanent employees because they are fixed-term, unless the different treatment can be objectively justified. This is similar to the concept of direct discrimination under the Equality Act 2010 (EqA), i.e. less favourable treatment of an individual because of a protected characteristic – S.13(1) EqA. However, an important distinction is that, unlike under the EqA, it is possible for employers to objectively justify less favourable treatment under the FTE Regulations.

Note that permanent employees do not have the converse right to be treated no less favourably than fixed-term employees under the Regulations. It is therefore theoretically possible for an employer to treat fixed-term employees *more* favourably than permanent employees, provided of course that this does not infringe another employment right such as the right not to be treated less favourably on the grounds of sex, race or disability.

Less favourable treatment

2.21

Under Reg 3 of the FTE Regulations a fixed-term employee has the right 'not to be treated by his employer less favourably than the employer treats a comparable permanent employee':

- as regards contractual terms, or

- by being subjected to any other detriment by any act, or deliberate failure to act, of the employer – Reg 3(1).

In particular, the fixed-term employee should not be treated less favourably in relation to:

- any period of service qualification relating to any particular condition of service (see 'Period of service qualifications' below)

- the opportunity to receive training, or

- the opportunity to secure any permanent position in the establishment (see 'Opportunity to secure permanent position' below) – Reg 3(2).

The non-renewal of a fixed-term contract does not, of itself, amount to less **2.22** favourable treatment. In Webley v Department for Work and Pensions 2005 ICR 577, CA, the claimant's only complaint was that her fixed-term contract had not been renewed after 51 weeks' employment. The Court of Appeal upheld an employment tribunal's decision that this did not give rise to a claim under the Regulations. The Court observed that fixed-term contracts are not outlawed by legislation. That being so, and since it is the essence of a fixed-term contract that it comes to an end at the expiry of the fixed term, the Court held that the termination of a fixed-term contract by the effluxion of time cannot, in itself, constitute less favourable treatment under the Regulations, and nor can an employer's failure to convert a fixed-term contract into a permanent contract. Note, however, that an employee whose contract is being renewed after four years of continuous (fixed-term) employment has the right to be treated as a permanent employee, unless the use of a further fixed-term contract is objectively justified – Reg 8. This is discussed under 'Successive fixed-term employees' below.

2.23 **Pay and pensions.** It is important to note that the FTE Regulations cover less favourable treatment relating to pay and pensions. The Government at the time took the view – subsequently found to be erroneous – that the Directive did not apply to pay or pensions. However, the original public consultation revealed that significant pay disparities existed in the UK between permanent employees and those on fixed-term contracts and that in some sectors such as education, health and social work this had had a disproportionate impact on female employees. Therefore, both Ss.45 and 46 of the EA and the Regulations themselves were drafted to cover discrimination against fixed-term employees in relation to all terms and conditions including pay and pensions. This means that paying a fixed-term employee less money than a comparable permanent employee can constitute less favourable treatment.

The Government's view that the Directive does not apply to pay and pensions was rebutted by the ECJ in Del Cerro Alonso v Osakidetza (Servicio Vasco de Salud) 2008 ICR 145, ECJ, where it confirmed that the prohibition of less favourable treatment in Clause 4(1) *does* cover pay. Member States intervening in the case, including the UK, argued that it did not, because the Directive was adopted by the Council of the European Union under the procedure contained in Article 139 of the EC Treaty – now Article 155 of the Treaty on the Functioning of the European Union (TFEU). Article 139 authorises the adoption of Directives dealing with the matters listed in Article 137 of the EC Treaty (now Article 153 TFEU). However, Article 137(6) (now Article 153(5)) specifically excludes pay from these matters. The Member States also relied on the ECJ's judgments in Dellas v Premier Ministre 2006 IRLR 225, ECJ, and Vorel v Nemocnice eský Krumlov (Case C-437/05), ECJ, where the ECJ stated that the EU Working Time Directive (No.93/104) (now the EU Working Time Directive (No.2003/88)) could not apply to workers' pay for on-call time because of Article 137(5).

In answer to this argument, the ECJ in Del Cerro held that while the fixing of **2.24** the level of wages is excluded from the European harmonisation process, this did not mean that the exception in Article 137(6) should be extended to any question involving any sort of link with pay: if so, some of the areas listed in Article 137(1) as targets for social policy, such as working conditions, would be deprived of much of their substance. In this case, the exception did not prevent a fixed-term worker from relying on the principle of non-discrimination in the Directive to seek the benefit of a condition reserved to permanent workers, even though application of that principle would have an effect on pay. Such an approach was not inconsistent with the decisions in Dellas and Vorel.

Pension schemes. While the Regulations require employers to offer access to **2.25** occupational pension schemes to fixed-term employees on the same basis as comparable permanent employees (unless different treatment is objectively justified), they do not require employers to offer special alternative benefits – such as contributions to a private pension scheme – to fixed-term employees who choose not to join a company pension scheme, unless this option is offered to comparable permanent employees. Where a waiting period to join an occupational pension scheme applies to permanent employees, the same period should apply to fixed-term employees, unless a longer period is objectively justified.

Contractual terms. A fixed-term employee has the right not to be treated less **2.26** favourably as regards the terms of his or her contract – Reg 3(1)(a). A term-by-term approach is required when considering less favourable treatment in this context – Hart and ors v Secretary of State for Education and Skills ET Case No.2304973/04. Therefore, an employer cannot avoid a finding that a particular term is less favourable on the ground that the overall package of benefits enjoyed by a claimant and comparator are equivalent. An employee's benefits package can only be looked at in the round when an employer seeks to justify any less favourable treatment on objective grounds – see 'Objective justification – contractual terms' below.

'Any other detriment'. A fixed-term employee has the right not to be treated **2.27** less favourably by being subjected to 'any other detriment' – Reg 3(1)(b). Although the term 'detriment' is widely used in discrimination legislation, there is no statutory definition in the Regulations or elsewhere. However, the appeal courts have frequently been called upon to consider its boundaries, primarily in the context of discrimination law under the EqA (and the legislation that preceded it). This jurisprudence is fully discussed in IDS Employment Law Handbook, 'Discrimination at Work' (2010), Chapter 25, 'Discrimination during employment', under 'Any other detriment – meaning of detriment'.

The meaning of 'detriment' in Reg 3(1)(b) of the FTE Regulations was considered by the EAT in Coutts and Co plc and anor v Cure and anor 2005 ICR 1098, EAT. The case concerned the non-payment of a bonus to fixed-term employees, which the claimants alleged amounted to less favourable treatment

93

contrary to the Regulations. Before the employment tribunal a question arose as to whether C and F had presented their claims in time. In order to answer this question, the tribunal had to ascertain what the 'detriment' was and when it took place. In its view, the less favourable treatment or detriment was not an announcement made about the bonuses in April 2001. Neither claimant had suffered a detriment as a result of that announcement, because they had not been employed as fixed-term workers at that time, and because it had amounted to no more than a statement of the company's general intention to make bonus payments. The tribunal considered that the bonus payments were not finalised until a memorandum of 13 November 2002, which stated that fixed-term employees would be excluded from payment. It was at this point that any acts of less favourable treatment (or detriment) would have occurred, and thus it was from this date that the three-month time limit started to run. Although the claims, which were presented on 10 and 17 March 2003, were outside the three-month time limit, the tribunal exercised its discretion under Reg 7(3) to allow them to proceed.

2.28 The employer appealed to the EAT, arguing that the detriment occurred in April 2001, when it had announced that a bonus would be paid. Since that announcement took place before the Regulations came into force on 1 October 2001, no cause of action arose. The EAT noted that the complaints concerned a detriment which took the form of a one-off act, and not a deliberate failure to act or a series of similar acts or failures to act. The EAT also stated that, unlike a claim of less favourable treatment in relation to a contractual term, detriment claims must show both less favourable treatment and a detriment. On the issue of what amounts to a detriment, the EAT applied the approach of the House of Lords in Shamoon v Chief Constable of the Royal Ulster Constabulary 2003 ICR 337, HL, that a detriment occurs when 'a reasonable worker would or might take the view that he had thereby been disadvantaged in the circumstances in which he had thereafter to work'.

The EAT went on to hold that the tribunal had correctly decided that the date of the detriment was 13 November 2002, and not April 2001. In reaching this decision the tribunal had found that the employer's approach to the bonus differed between April 2001 and November 2002. The 2002 announcement was not a reiteration of the 2001 decision – the announcement in April 2001 was conditional and insufficiently detailed. It required further clarification, including details regarding eligibility, which were subsequently provided in the memorandum of 13 November 2002.

2.29 The tribunal had also decided that thereafter nothing remained to be done prior to the bonus payments being electronically transferred into the bank accounts of eligible employees on 18 December 2002. It had therefore correctly rejected the contention that this was the date of detriment, which would have meant that both claimants' complaints were in time. Since the employer had not sought to challenge the tribunal's subsequent decision to exercise its discretion to extend time under Reg 7(3), the EAT dismissed its appeal on this issue.

Period of service qualifications. Regulation 3(2)(a) expressly provides that **2.30** any period of service qualification relating to any particular conditions of employment must be the same for fixed-term employees (except where different periods are justified on objective grounds). This reflects Clause 4 of the FTW Directive. For example, if permanent employees get an extra five days' paid holiday after one year's service, fixed-term employees should get the same increase in holiday after this period, unless there is an objective reason for their serving a longer qualifying period.

Note that in order to qualify for many *statutory rights* (such as unfair dismissal and redundancy payments), it is necessary for an employee to have acquired a minimum period of continuous employment, calculated according to the rules set out in Chapter 1 of Part XIV of the ERA (Ss.210–219). Under these provisions, employment under successive fixed-term contracts with the same employer will be continuous employment, so long as there is no gap that breaks continuity between the contracts – see further 'Successive fixed-term contracts – continuous employment' below. For full details of the statutory rules governing continuity of employment, see IDS Employment Law Handbook, 'Continuity of Employment' (2012).

Any provision that disregards periods of service on fixed-term contracts for **2.31** the purposes of determining length of service is likely to amount to less favourable treatment under the FTW Directive, unless it can be objectively justified – Valenza and ors v Autorità Garante della Concorrenza e del Mercato 2013 ICR 373, ECJ. There, the ECJ held that disregarding prior periods of fixed-term service when determining the length of service (and thereby the pay level) of civil servants who had obtained permanent status, without taking account of any other circumstances, would be disproportionate and therefore not objectively justified.

The ECJ in Valenza was considering an Italian law that dealt with accrued service as opposed to continuity of employment. In the UK, as explained above, periods of service on fixed-term contracts count towards an employee's continuous service provided the continuity provisions are satisfied, so any benefit based on statutory continuity is unlikely to breach the Directive. Where, however, an employer provides a contractual benefit on the basis of 'length of service' defined by reference to the contract, it will need to ensure that the contractual definition does not disregard periods on fixed-term contracts, unless either the work done under such contracts is not comparable or it can objectively justify excluding such periods.

Redundancy. The right to equal treatment under Reg 3 means that fixed-term **2.32** employees should not be selected for redundancy purely because they are on

95

fixed-term contracts, unless this can be objectively justified. This is discussed further under 'Redundancy rights – redundancy selection' below. Similarly, fixed-term employees should receive the same level of redundancy payments that comparable permanent employees receive, unless different treatment is objectively justified. This is discussed under 'Redundancy rights – contractual redundancy pay' below.

2.33 **Opportunity to secure permanent position.** The Regulations specifically provide that the right not to be treated less favourably includes the right not to be treated less favourably in relation to the opportunity to secure any permanent position in the establishment – Reg 3(2)(c). Any difference between the availability of internal vacancies to fixed-term and to permanent staff must be objectively justified. To ensure that a fixed-term employee is able to exercise the right conferred by Reg 3(2)(c), he or she also has the right to be informed of any available vacancies in the establishment by the employers – Reg 3(6). This is discussed under 'Right to be informed of available vacancies' below.

2.34 **Comparable employees**
In order to determine whether a fixed-term employee has been treated less favourably, it is necessary to compare the way in which he or she has been treated with the treatment accorded to a 'comparable permanent employee' – Reg 3(1). The term 'permanent employee' is defined in Reg 1(2) as any 'employee who is not employed under a fixed-term contract'. The meaning of 'fixed-term contract' is discussed under 'Scope and coverage of FTE Regulations – employment under a "fixed-term contract"' above.

'Comparable employees' are dealt with in Reg 2, which sets out three criteria to be applied when determining the appropriate comparator. These require that – at the time the allegedly discriminatory treatment takes place – both employees must be:

- employed by the same employer

- engaged in the same or broadly similar work, and

- work at the same establishment.

All three must be met in order for Reg 2 to be satisfied.

2.35 **Same employer.** The first criterion set out in Reg 2 is that both employees must be employed by the same employer – Reg 2(1)(a)(i). As the current BIS Guidance makes clear, this means that a fixed-term employee cannot compare conditions with an employee at an associated employer's establishment. According to S.231 ERA, 'any two employers shall be treated as associated if (a) one is a company of which the other (directly or indirectly) has control, or (b) both are companies of which a third person (directly or indirectly) has control'.

Same or broadly similar work. The second criterion set out in Reg 2 is that **2.36** both employees must be 'engaged in the same or broadly similar work having regard, where relevant, to whether they have a similar level of qualification and skills' – Reg 2(1)(a)(ii). The original language in the draft version of the Regulations allowed employers to consider whether fixed-term employees and comparable permanent employees had a similar level of qualification, skills and experience. However, after consultation, the Government removed the word 'experience', as the FTW Directive does not allow for experience to be taken into account.

In Hart and ors v Secretary of State for Education and Skills ET Case No.2304973/04 an employment tribunal stressed that a restrictive interpretation of the word 'broadly' would undermine the legislation's purpose. A claimant must establish broad similarity in the nature and subject matter of the work, as well as approximate equivalence in the level of expertise and responsibility involved. Applying this approach, the tribunal held that the jobs under comparison were broadly similar despite the fact that one was more operational and the other had a higher policy content: the essential function, to advise, was the same.

It is worth noting that the wording of Reg 2(1)(a)(ii) FTE Regulations is **2.37** virtually identical to that in Reg 2(4)(a)(ii) of the Part-time Workers (Prevention of Less Favourable Treatment) Regulations 2000 SI 2000/1551, except the latter provision *does* contain the word 'experience'. In Matthews and ors v Kent and Medway Towns Fire Authority and ors 2006 ICR 365, HL, the House of Lords gave some guidance of the meaning of 'same or broadly similar' work under the 2000 Regulations, which will undoubtedly also be relevant when considering the concept under the FTE Regulations. Their Lordships stated that in assessing the question of 'same or broadly similar' work, particular weight should be given to the extent to which the work of the two groups is in fact the same and the importance of that work to the enterprise as a whole. Otherwise there is a risk of giving too much weight to differences which are the almost inevitable result of one worker being full time and another working less than full time. The House of Lords went on to provide the following guidance:

- the work done by the part-timers and full-timers – including the similarities and differences between that work – must be looked at as a whole

- the extent to which the work performed by the two groups is 'exactly the same' is of great importance

- if the two groups spend a lot of time carrying out the 'core activity of the enterprise', their work is likely to be broadly similar regardless of any additional tasks that full-timers are required to perform

- differences in the level of qualification, skills and experience are only relevant where they impact upon work that the part-timers actually carry out.

97

2.38 As noted above, the Matthews case – which is fully discussed in Chapter 3, 'Part-time workers', under 'Less favourable treatment – comparing treatment' – is likely to be highly relevant when considering the question of 'same or broadly similar' work under the FTE Regulations. Indeed, in Nisbet and anor v GMB Union ET Case No.2502453/12 an employment tribunal followed the House of Lords' guidance when considering whether fixed-term employees and their comparators were engaged in broadly similar work. The claimants were employed by the GMB as Learning Organisers under fixed-term contracts which only entitled them to statutory redundancy pay if they were made redundant. By contrast, Organising Officers employed under permanent contracts were entitled to enhanced redundancy pay. When considering whether the claimants and the Organising Officers were engaged in 'broadly similar work', the tribunal observed that the main responsibility of both was to recruit new members for the union. This responsibility was explicit in the Organising Officer's job descriptions and, although not recorded in the claimants' job descriptions, it was key to their role in practice. In this regard, the tribunal noted that the focus had to be on what the claimants did in practice, not what was set down in their job description. Neither post required any formal qualifications but negotiation and communication skills were key to both.

The tribunal observed that there were also some material differences. The Organising Officers did not have the responsibility of recruiting Union Learning Representatives, negotiating learning agreements and persuading employers to set up learning centres. The Learning Organisers did not have the responsibility of negotiating pay, representing members in grievance and disciplinary hearings, submitting collective agreements or generally organising the members. However, following the approach of their Lordships in Matthews, the tribunal concluded that – looking at the two jobs as a whole, taking into account both similarities and differences – the work of the claimants and their comparators was broadly similar. The tribunal attached particular weight to the fact that recruitment was the core function of both jobs and to the importance of that activity to the union. Although there were also material differences between the two jobs, they were outweighed by the similarities.

2.39 **Same establishment.** A fixed-term employee must also work or be based at the same establishment as the comparable permanent employee – Reg 2(1)(b). Where there is no comparable employee working or based at the same establishment who satisfies the first two requirements, the comparison may be made with an employee who works or is based at a different establishment and satisfies those requirements – Reg 2(1)(b). However, an employee is not a comparable permanent employee if his or her employment has ceased – Reg 2(2).

Essentially, this means that there must be a real comparator within the employer's organisation at the time the allegedly discriminatory treatment takes place and that, unlike in other areas of discrimination law, a hypothetical comparison is not permissible. Where there is no appropriate comparator at the fixed-term employee's workplace, and the employer has more than one workplace, comparison can be made with an appropriate permanent employee at another workplace.

Choice of comparator. Where a fixed-term employee does the same work as **2.40** several permanent employees whose contractual terms are different, the fixed-term employee may have to select which one to use as a comparator. However, the chances of the claim of equal treatment being successful will depend, in large part, on the employee selecting an appropriate comparator. To maximise his or her chances of success, it may be prudent for the employee to cite a number of comparators in the alternative when submitting a claim under the Regulations.

Many commentators have noted that the definition of comparable employees in the Regulations could present a difficult hurdle for fixed-term employees seeking to bring claims of less favourable treatment. As suggested above, if the fixed-term employee chooses the wrong comparator, his or her claim could fail. Moreover, as mentioned under 'Same establishment' above, fixed-term employees must choose an actual comparator and cannot rely on a hypothetical one. The strictness of the definition of 'comparable permanent employee' means that a fixed-term employee may be unable to find an appropriate comparator, with the result that his or her claim will fail before it gets off the ground.

The Trades Union Congress (TUC) has been particularly critical of the scope of **2.41** Reg 2. In its objections to the proposed definition of 'comparator' made in response to the Government consultation on the draft Regulations, it noted that a substantial proportion of temporary workers would have problems finding comparators under the Regulations. It also argued that the problem of identifying a permanent comparator is likely to disproportionately affect fixed-term employees working in sectors where there is a high concentration of temporary workers, such as higher education or the hotel and catering trade. The TUC recommended that where fixed-term workers cannot establish a comparator in the same employment, they should be allowed a choice of opting for a comparison in accordance with an applicable collective agreement, with a worker in the same occupation or industrial sector, or with a hypothetical comparator. However, the Government did not take up these suggestions.

Treatment on ground that employee is fixed-term employee   2.42
It is not sufficient for a fixed-term employee simply to show that he or she has been treated less favourably than a comparable permanent employee. The reason for that treatment is crucial. Under Reg 3(3)(a) the employee will only succeed where the less favourable treatment was 'on the ground that the employee is a fixed-term employee'. It follows that the employee's claim will fail where the employer can show that the reason for treating the employee less favourably was some other factor.

99

There is considerable overlap here with the provisions of Reg 2(1)(a) defining a comparable permanent employee (see 'Comparable employees' above). Where an employer is able to show some other reason for treating the employee less favourably than a comparator – for example, level of qualification or skills, or a difference in the work – then it is quite possible that the tribunal will also find that the employee's chosen comparator is not a comparable permanent employee under Reg 2. The employee's claim would therefore fail on both counts.

2.43 In Williams v Carmarthenshire County Council ET Case No.1603253/12 W succeeded in proving that the less favourable treatment she had suffered was on the ground of her fixed-term status. The Council had reallocated the bulk of her responsibilities and duties to a permanent employee, L, upon the latter's return from secondment. An employment tribunal observed that W had not been appointed to cover L's post while on secondment. Their posts were entirely separate. W was, however, a comparable employee. She was engaged in broadly similar work to W and had a similar level of qualification and skills. The tribunal found that the treatment was on the ground that W was a fixed-term employee. L's workload had substantially reduced upon her return from secondment and the Council felt that it had a duty to prefer L over W purely because L was a permanent employee. This was not a basis upon which the Council could objectively justify less favourable treatment and therefore the tribunal upheld W's claim under Reg 3.

In Clitheroe v Canal and River Trust ET Case No.1805771/13, by contrast, the employee failed to establish that the employer's treatment of him was due to his fixed-term status. From March 2007 until November 2012 C was employed as a lock-keeper under a series of fixed-term contracts with breaks in between. His contracts tended to begin in February/March and end in October/November. Until February 2013, employees received enhanced payments for working bank holidays. However, the Trust decided to end this arrangement for new employees from February 2013 onwards. C's new fixed-term contract with the Trust did not begin until after February 2013 and he therefore did not receive enhanced pay for working bank holidays. He complained that he was being subjected to the detriment of not being paid the enhanced payment because he was a fixed-term employee. An employment tribunal dismissed his claim, holding (among other things) that the reason for C not being paid the enhanced payment was not that he was employed on a fixed-term contract, but that his employment under that contract did not begin until after February 2013.

2.44 The fact that the less favourable treatment applies to *all* non-permanent employees does not mean that it cannot be on the ground of fixed-term status. In Coutts and Co plc and anor v Cure and anor 2005 ICR 1098, EAT, the EAT dismissed the employer's submission that C and F had not been treated less favourably on the ground of being fixed-term employees because the exclusion from the bonus applied to all non-permanent employees, of which they were only one category. It held that once a fixed-term employee is found to have suffered less favourable treatment because of his or her fixed-term status, it is irrelevant whether the employer discriminates against other employees who may or may not be protected, under either the Regulations or another piece of anti-discrimination legislation. The EAT noted that the correct approach to Reg 3(3) was not to analyse the issue as a matter of causation, but rather to apply a subjective test and ask why the alleged discriminator acted as he or she did. This mirrored the approach taken by the House of Lords (in respect of a victimisation claim brought under the Race Relations Act 1976) in Chief Constable of West Yorkshire Police v Khan 2001 ICR 1065, HL.

Right to receive written statement. Under Reg 5, fixed-term employees may **2.45** submit a request in writing to the employer for a written statement of the reasons for the less favourable treatment. This applies to all the rights provided for in Reg 3, including the right not to be treated less favourably. The employer must provide such a statement within 21 days of the request – Reg 5(1). A tribunal may draw any inference that it considers just and equitable from an employer's omission to provide a statement – Reg 5(3). For further details, see 'Right to receive written statement' below.

Burden of proof. The burden of proof is on the employer to identify the ground **2.46** for the less favourable treatment or detriment – Reg 7(6). As noted by the employment tribunal in Nisbet and anor v GMB Union ET Case No.2502453/12, this means that there is an inference that the treatment in question is on the ground of an employee's fixed-term status, which can be displaced if the employer provides satisfactory evidence of some other reason.

Objective justification   2.47
Even if the reason for the less favourable treatment is that the employee is on a fixed-term contract, the treatment will not be unlawful if it is 'justified on objective grounds' – Reg 3(3)(b). This mirrors the wording of Clause 4(1) of the FTW Directive, which provides that, 'in respect of employment conditions, fixed-term workers shall not be treated in a less favourable manner than comparable permanent workers solely because they have a fixed-term contract or relation unless different treatment is justified on objective grounds'.

There is no definition of objective justification in the Directive, although its meaning was considered by the ECJ in Del Cerro Alonso v Osakidetza (Servicio Vasco de Salud) 2008 ICR 145, ECJ. There the Court held that the unequal treatment at issue must be justified by 'precise and concrete factors, characterising the employment condition to which it relates, in the specific context in which it occurs and on the basis of objective and transparent criteria'. Therefore, a difference in treatment between fixed-term and permanent workers could not be justified on the basis of a 'general abstract national norm, such as a law or collective agreement'.

───────────────────────────────────── **101**

2.48 Moreover, the ECJ held that in order for objective justification to be made out the unequal treatment must '[respond] to a genuine need, [be] appropriate for achieving the objective pursued and [be] necessary for that purpose'. This is reminiscent of the test set out in the relevant EU equality Directives in the context of indirect discrimination, which provide that a provision, criterion or practice will be indirectly discriminatory unless it 'is objectively justified by a legitimate aim and the means of achieving that aim are appropriate and necessary'. Case law relating to objective justification under these Directives will therefore be relevant when considering objective justification under the FTE Regulations. For further details, see IDS Employment Law Handbook, 'Discrimination at Work' (2012), Chapter 17, 'Indirect discrimination: objective justification'.

2.49 **Contractual terms.** Although objective justification is not defined in the Regulations, Reg 4 states that where a fixed-term employee is treated less favourably as regards any term of his or her contract, that treatment will be regarded as justified on objective grounds if the terms of the fixed-term employee's contract, taken as a whole, are at least as favourable as the terms of the comparable employee's contract. It is questionable whether this approach accords with the concept of 'objective justification' under the Fixed-term Directive, as defined by the ECJ in Del Cerro Alonso v Osakidetza (Servicio Vasco de Salud) (above), but putting that question to one side for a moment, this means that where the less favourable treatment in question relates to a contractual term, there are two key ways in which an employer can objectively justify the treatment under the Regulations:

- first, by showing that there is an objective reason for not giving the fixed-term employee a particular benefit or for giving him or her the benefit on inferior terms – Reg 3(3)(b). In considering whether such an objective reason exists, an employment tribunal should adopt the approach set out in Del Cerro, or

- secondly, by showing that the value of the fixed-term employee's total package of terms and conditions is at least equal to the value of the comparable permanent employee's total package of terms and conditions.

2.50 Note that the second form of objective justification – i.e. the total package approach – is only available to the employer if the less favourable treatment in question *relates to a contractual term*. Where the benefit at issue is non-contractual, the employer cannot rely upon the fact that an employee's total package of terms and conditions may be more beneficial – Reg 4.

2.51 *Objective reason.* The test under Reg 3(3)(b) essentially reflects the traditional test for objective justification, as established by the various EU equality Directives and ECJ case law. As the previous BERR guidance indicated, a comparison should be made on a term-by-term basis: every individual term of a fixed-term employee's employment package should be exactly the same – or, if appropriate, the same on a pro rata basis – as the equivalent term of the comparable permanent employee's package, and any difference in terms must be objectively justified. A similar term-by-term approach operates in respect of the sex equality clause under S.66 EqA for the purposes of equal pay – see IDS Employment Law Handbook, 'Equal Pay' (2011), Chapter 2, 'Right to equal pay', under 'The sex equality clause – term-by-term comparison'.

Total package. Under Reg 4, where a fixed-term employee is treated less **2.52** favourably as regards a term of his or her contract, this will be taken to be justified if the contractual terms, *taken as a whole*, are at least as favourable as those of the comparator. This means that an employer can show that less favourable treatment of a fixed-term employee is objectively justified by showing that the value of the fixed-term employee's total package of terms and conditions is at least equal to the value of that of the comparable permanent employee.

This 'total package' approach is in contrast to the approach taken in equal pay and other areas of discrimination law and it is questionable whether it accords with the FTW Directive. According to Lord Sainsbury of Turville, the Government decided to provide for two different methods of objective justification to give employers flexibility, as consultation showed that some employers preferred the package approach, while others did not. He noted that 'there will sometimes be a very good reason why a particular benefit is not given to a fixed-term member of staff; it would be time-consuming and irrelevant to make a tribunal consider every aspect of employees' employment packages in all cases' – House of Lords Grand Committee, 11 April 2002, col CWH518. However, not all respondents to the consultation were in favour of the flexibility offered by the two different routes of objective justification. In its response to the Government consultation on the draft Regulations, the TUC stated its opposition to the use of the package approach, arguing that it has no precedent in discrimination law and would be complicated for tribunals to assess. Furthermore, the fact that the total package approach only applies to less favourable *contractual* terms could lead to protracted disputes about whether or not the benefit at issue is contractual.

The package approach means that employers will be able to balance a less **2.53** favourable condition against a more favourable one, so long as the fixed-term employee's overall employment package is not less favourable than that of the comparable permanent employee. There is nothing about the operation of the package approach in the current BIS Guidance but the previous BERR guidance dealt with it in some detail. That guidance stated that employers would not be prevented from paying higher upfront rewards in return for reduced benefits elsewhere. For example, an employer who wishes to restrict fixed-term employees' access to a company pension scheme may do so provided the employees are adequately compensated in some other way; for example, by

103

receiving additional pay. In appraising an employee's total package of benefits, the value of the benefits should be assessed on their objective monetary worth, rather than on the value the employer or the employee perceives them to have. Another example given in the BERR guidance is of a fixed-term employee who is paid £20,800 per year (£400 per week), which is the same as a comparable permanent employee, but gets three days' fewer paid holiday a year. To ensure that the fixed-term employee's overall employment package is not less favourable, his or her annual salary is increased to £20,970. The extra £170 represents the value of three days' holiday pay (worked out as annual salary divided by 365).

The BERR guidance made it clear that employers can still show that there is an objective reason for not giving a particular benefit if they choose to use a package approach. Employers do not have to make up for the value of a missing benefit if they can show an objective reason for not giving it. According to the guidance, when a package approach is used, it will be objectively justified for a fixed-term employee to have a less favourable overall package than a comparable permanent employee if the difference consists of one or more terms that it is objectively justified not to give the fixed-term employee.

2.54 Right to be informed of available vacancies

As noted under 'Equal treatment – less favourable treatment' above, the Regulations specifically provide that the right not to be treated less favourably contained in Reg 3(1) includes the right not to be treated less favourably in relation to the opportunity to secure any permanent position in the establishment – Reg 3(2)(c). To ensure that a fixed-term employee is able to exercise the right conferred by Reg 3(2)(c), he or she also has the right to be informed by the employer of any available vacancies in the establishment – Reg 3(6). An employee will be taken to have been 'informed by his [or her] employer' only if the vacancy is contained in an advertisement that the employee has a reasonable opportunity of reading in the course of his or her employment, or the employee is given reasonable notification of the vacancy in some other way – Reg 3(7). It is therefore advisable for employers to inform fixed-term employees of vacancies in the same way and at the same time as permanent employees.

Although there is nothing in the BIS Guidance about this, the previous BERR guidance stated that it will usually be sufficient to display a vacancy notice in a place where all employees would be expected to see it or e-mail the vacancy list to all employees – both permanent and fixed-term. However, everything will depend on the particular circumstances of the case. In Williams v Carmarthenshire County Council ET Case No.1603253/12, for example, an employment tribunal held that the employer had failed to satisfy the requirements of Reg 3(6) and (7) by advertising permanent posts on its intranet. This was because W was at the time off work sick and did not have access to the intranet at home.

While an employee who claims that he or she has been treated less favourably **2.55** under Reg 3(1) in relation to securing permanent employment may bring a general claim of less favourable treatment and cite the failure to inform as evidence of this, Reg 3(6) provides a specific free-standing right that can itself be the subject of tribunal proceedings. This means that, even if the employee does not feel that he or she has been discriminated against in the selection procedure for a permanent post, the fact that he or she was not informed of it could give rise to an action – Reg 7(1). The time limit for bringing such a claim is three months commencing with the date – or, if more than one, the last date – on which other individuals, whether or not employees of the employer, were informed of the vacancy – Reg 7(2)(b). For further information on enforcement of this right and available remedies, see 'Enforcement and remedies' below.

Right to receive written statement 2.56

Under Reg 5, fixed-term employees who consider that their employer may have treated them in a manner which infringes any right conferred by Reg 3 may submit a request in writing to the employer for a written statement of the reasons for the treatment. The right to receive a written statement applies to all the rights provided for in Reg 3; that is, the right not to be treated less favourably and the right to receive information about permanent vacancies (see 'Equal treatment' and 'Right to be informed of available vacancies' above). The employer must provide such a statement within 21 days of the request – Reg 5(1).

There is nothing in the BIS Guidance on the right to receive a written statement. However, the previous BERR guidance stated that an employer's statement should set out the reasons for the difference in treatment or, if appropriate, that there has been no less favourable treatment. If an employer is using the package approach to justify any different treatment, the statement should explain this. (The package approach is explained under 'Equal treatment – objective justification' above.)

Clearly, employers will need to take great care when drafting written reasons. **2.57** According to the BERR guidance, they should view the request for a written statement as an opportunity to clarify why a fixed-term employee receives particular treatment. The intention behind Reg 5 is not to enable fixed-term employees to discover what pay and benefits their colleagues are receiving.

The employer's statement is admissible in evidence in any proceedings under the Regulations – Reg 5(2). An employer's failure to supply such a statement has no direct legal effect in itself. However, if separate proceedings are brought under the Regulations, a tribunal may draw any inference that it considers just and equitable (including an inference that the employer is in breach of the Regulations) if it appears that the employer deliberately and without reasonable excuse omitted to provide a statement, or that the written statement is evasive

105

or equivocal – Reg 5(3). This provision is similar to S.38 EqA, which provides that a court or tribunal may draw an inference of discrimination from an employer's failure to answer an employee's question or from an evasive or equivocal answer – see IDS Employment Law Handbook, 'Discrimination at Work' (2010), Chapter 33, 'Proving discrimination', under 'Requesting information and disclosure of evidence'.

2.58 **Right to receive written statement under ERA**
The right to receive a written statement under the FTE Regulations does not apply where the less favourable treatment in question consists of the dismissal of the employee and the employee is entitled to a written statement of reasons for the dismissal under S.92 ERA – Reg 5(4).

An employee's right under S.92 ERA arises in any of the following circumstances:

- where an employer gives notice of dismissal – S.92(1)(a)

- where an employer dismisses without notice – S.92(1)(b), or

- where the employee is employed under a limited-term contract and the contract terminates by virtue of the limiting event without being renewed under the same contract – S.92(1)(c). As explained under 'Unfair dismissal rights – definition of dismissal' below, a 'limited-term contract' under the ERA is the equivalent of a fixed-term contract under the FTE Regulations.

2.59 If S.92 does not apply, a fixed-term employee who considers that his or her dismissal amounts to less favourable treatment under the Regulations will be entitled to receive a written statement under Reg 5. As a general rule, S.92 does not assist employees who have less than two years' continuous service on the effective date of termination (EDT) of the employment contract – S.92(3).

An employer is under no obligation to provide a written statement unless a request has been made by the employee – S.92(2). This is subject to S.92(4) and (4A) which provides that, where an employee is dismissed while pregnant or during ordinary or additional maternity or adoption leave, he or she is entitled to receive written reasons without having to make a request. For full details of the right to a written statement of reasons for dismissal under S.92, see IDS Employment Law Handbook, 'Unfair Dismissal' (2010), Chapter 21, 'Written reasons for dismissal'.

2.60 # Unfair dismissal rights

The FTE Regulations made several changes to unfair dismissal law, giving fixed-term employees greater protection upon termination of their employment. Not least, the Regulations created a new category of dismissal for the purposes of claiming unfair dismissal and statutory redundancy pay – see 'Definition of dismissal' and 'Redundancy rights – statutory redundancy pay' below. The Regulations also introduced new rights protecting employees from dismissal on certain grounds related to their fixed-term status – see 'Automatically unfair dismissal' below.

It is important to note that the regular qualifying periods apply in the same way as they apply to permanent employees. Thus, in order to make a claim for 'ordinary' unfair dismissal, a fixed-term employee must have at least two years' continuous service. This is determined in accordance with the rules governing continuous employment set out in Ss.210–219 ERA – see 'Successive fixed-term contracts – continuous employment' below. For full details of the statutory rules governing continuity of employment, see IDS Employment Law Handbook, 'Continuity of Employment' (2012).

As with permanent employees, it must be shown that a fixed-term employee **2.61** claiming unfair dismissal has been dismissed unfairly. This is touched upon under 'Reasonableness of dismissal' below. However, for full details of the right not to be unfairly dismissed, see IDS Employment Law Handbook, 'Unfair Dismissal' (2010).

Definition of dismissal   2.62

An employee who wishes to claim unfair dismissal must first show that he or she has been dismissed within the meaning of S.95 ERA. This states that an employee will be treated as dismissed if:

- his or her contract of employment is terminated by the employer with or without notice – S.95(1)(a)

- he or she is employed under a limited-term contract and the contract expires by virtue of the limiting event without being renewed under the same terms – S.95(1)(b), or

- he or she has been constructively dismissed – S.95(1)(c). A constructive dismissal occurs when an employee resigns, with or without notice, because of a repudiatory breach of contract by the employer.

There is also a dismissal where an employee under notice of dismissal from the employer resigns on a date earlier than the date on which the employer's notice is due to expire – S.95(2).

A 'limited-term contract' under S.95(1)(a) is the equivalent of a fixed-term **2.63** contract under the Regulations. It is defined as a contract that:

- is not intended to be permanent, and

- contains a provision that it will terminate by virtue of a limiting event – S.235(2A) ERA.

107

A 'limiting event' is:

- in the case of a contract for a fixed term, the expiry of the term

- in the case of a contract made in contemplation of the performance of a specific task, the performance of that task, and

- in the case of a contract which provides for its termination on the occurrence of an event (or the failure of an event to occur), the occurrence of the event (or the failure of the event to occur).

2.64 Thus, where an employee's fixed-term contract expires without being renewed, this amounts to a dismissal. This is the case even if the employee knew at the outset that it would not be renewed or that it was unlikely to be renewed – Nottinghamshire County Council v Lee 1980 ICR 635, CA. Similarly, the expiry of a task contract on completion of the task (or event) in question amounts to a dismissal. The effective date of termination for a limited-term contract which terminates by virtue of the limiting event without being renewed means the date on which the termination takes effect – S.97(1)(c).

2.65 **Non-renewal by mutual consent.** Despite the fact that the wording of S.95(1)(b) appears to cover all non-renewals of limited-term contracts, whether instigated by the employer, by the employee or by agreement, it seems that the non-renewal of a limited-term contract by mutual consent will not amount to a dismissal. In Manson and Johnston v (1) University of Strathclyde (2) Automated Microscopy Systems Ltd EAT 356/87, for example, M and J, two research fellows, agreed to the non-renewal of their fixed-term contracts with the university because they wanted to take up jobs with a company set up for the commercial exploitation of their research. The EAT was not prepared to view the non-renewal as a dismissal but rather as a termination by mutual agreement (thus barring the two from claiming redundancy payments from the university). The Appeal Tribunal was swayed by the fact that there was no redundancy situation and that M and J could have stayed in the employ of the university had they wished, i.e. they were not put under any pressure to leave. In Thames Television Ltd v Wallis 1979 IRLR 136, EAT, on the other hand, a researcher who had been employed on a series of fixed-term contracts was held to have been dismissed when her contract was not renewed – the fact that she had received an ex gratia payment because of that non-renewal did not mean that the contract was terminated by mutual agreement.

2.66 **Expiry of apprenticeship.** There are some limited-term contracts which by their very nature cannot be renewed; for example, contracts of apprenticeship or training. In North East Coast Shiprepairers Ltd v Secretary of State for Employment 1978 ICR 755, EAT, an apprentice's contract expired and he was not taken on as a journeyman fitter. The EAT held that the contract of apprenticeship was strictly a one-off contract that was incapable of being renewed, since engagement as a journeyman would have been under a completely new contract. The dismissal was due to the expiry of the contract of apprenticeship and the apprentice was not therefore entitled to a redundancy payment. This is reflected in the FTE Regulations, which specifically exclude those working under a contract of apprenticeship from their scope – Reg 20 (see 'Scope and coverage of FTE Regulations – "employees" only' above). Note, however, that if an apprentice is kept on for a short time after the end of his or her apprenticeship, any subsequent dismissal may be unfair – Primary Fluid Power Ltd v Brislen EAT 0611/04. For these purposes, employment under a contract of apprenticeship will count when determining whether an employee has the requisite continuous employment to bring a claim. The Brislen case is discussed further under 'Reason for dismissal – some other substantial reason' below.

Reason for dismissal   2.67

An employer wishing to defend an unfair dismissal claim must show that the reason for dismissal amounts to one of the potentially fair reasons set out in S.98(1) and (2) ERA. These are: capability, conduct, redundancy, restriction imposed by law or 'some other substantial reason' of a kind such as to justify the dismissal (SOSR). Where the expiry of a limited-term contract is concerned, the two most common reasons relied upon by employers are:

- SOSR, or

- redundancy.

These are discussed in more detail below.

Note that where the dismissal is for a reason listed in Reg 6 of the FTE Regulations, it will be automatically unfair – i.e. unfair without any consideration of reasonableness. This is discussed under 'Automatically unfair dismissal' below.

The expiry of a limited-term contract is not in itself a potentially fair reason for **2.68** dismissal. An employer must show either that the expiry amounts to SOSR or that it is by reason of redundancy. In Tansell v Henley College Coventry 2013 IRLR 174, EAT, an employment tribunal dismissed T's claim for unfair dismissal, holding that the reason for his dismissal was the expiry of the fixed term and that the process by which the contract came to an end was entirely legitimate and fair. Allowing T's appeal, the EAT noted that the non-renewal of a fixed-term contract was a dismissal by virtue of S.95(1)(b). In other words, the expiry of T's contract was the dismissal itself, not the reason for it. The tribunal had erred by eliding the mode of dismissal with the reason for dismissal. The reason must be one of those listed in S.98(2) or some other substantial reason, and the tribunal must decide whether the reason relied on by the employer is among those listed.

Although the tribunal had expressly rejected T's alleged reasons for his dismissal, it did not follow that it should be taken as having accepted the

109

college's submission that redundancy was the reason for dismissal. If that were the case it was, in the EAT's view, 'extraordinary that the tribunal did not say that it was accepting that reason in express terms'. The tribunal did not recount or even summarise the statutory definition of redundancy, and nor did it apply that definition or give any reasons why it found that there was a genuine redundancy. If it had accepted that the reason for dismissal was redundancy it would, the EAT held, have at least done that much. This was not to take an unduly technical approach. According to the EAT, the reason for dismissal should 'virtually leap from the page, such is its significance'.

2.69 **Some other substantial reason.** It is well established that the expiry of a limited-term contract can be a substantial reason for dismissal. However, this will not automatically be the case. In Terry v East Sussex County Council 1976 ICR 536, EAT, the EAT said that the expiry of a fixed-term contract could be SOSR for a dismissal but it was still up to the employer to show what the reason was and establish that it was substantial. If the expiry of a limited-term contract was automatically SOSR for dismissal, employers could hide behind pleas of SOSR simply by calling a contract limited-term when the real reason for termination was something else altogether.

In Fay v North Yorkshire County Council 1986 ICR 133, CA, the Court of Appeal clarified the circumstances in which the expiry of a limited-term contract can amount to SOSR: it must be shown that the contract was adopted for a genuine purpose, which was known to the employee, and that that purpose had ceased to be applicable. F, a teacher, was employed under four successive fixed-term contracts and when her last contract was not renewed she brought an unfair dismissal claim. The tribunal ruled that her dismissal was for SOSR and reasonable. The Court of Appeal upheld this. The tribunal had been entitled to conclude that the short-term contracts under which F had been successively employed were the ordinary kind of fixed-term contract and were for the genuine purpose of covering a period of temporary absence. The purpose of the contract had been brought to F's attention and, when that purpose came to an end and the post was filled by someone else, the short-term contract was not renewed.

2.70 Employers are expected to show clear evidence of a substantial reason for dismissal due to the expiry of a limited-term contract, as the following cases demonstrate:

- **Primary Fluid Power Ltd v Brislen** EAT 0611/04: the EAT upheld a tribunal's decision that the dismissal of an apprentice three months after the conclusion of his fixed-term apprenticeship was unfair. On 3 July 2000, B started a three-year apprenticeship with PFP Ltd and this required him to work at PFP Ltd's premises as well as studying at college. By the time of the end of his apprenticeship in July 2003 he was still engaged on a City and Guilds course and had also started an NVQ Level 3 course. B's statement of terms and conditions of employment was varied on 21 July 2003 and signed by a senior manager to indicate that 'a successful probation/induction has been served'. PFP Ltd dismissed B on 25 November because there was no permanent position for him and B claimed unfair dismissal. PFP Ltd argued that B's employment had terminated at the end of his fixed-term apprenticeship, and this had been prolonged until the end of November when it had learned that the City and Guilds course was completed and B had started on the NVQ Level 3. It argued that the dismissal was for SOSR. The tribunal held that the contract made it clear that the apprenticeship came to an end in July 2003. There was no evidence to suggest that there was a consensual extension of the apprenticeship to November to take account of the courses B was undertaking. PFP Ltd tried to argue that it had a genuine and reasonable belief, albeit a mistaken one, that the fixed-term apprenticeship ended in November. But the EAT noted that PFP Ltd had in its possession all the relevant contractual documents and it could have clarified the position in July but did not do so

* **West Midlands Regional Health Authority v Guirguis** EAT 567/77: G's fixed-term contract as a locum consultant radiologist was not renewed because the regional health officer thought it an undesirable policy to employ locums. However, locums were often employed for a longer period than G had been employed for. The employer had therefore failed to show that it had any policy, let alone a policy which amounted to a substantial reason for G's dismissal. Thus it failed to establish a potentially fair reason for dismissal.

Where an employee is engaged in order to cover for another employee who is, **2.71** or will be, absent because of pregnancy, childbirth, adoption leave, additional paternity leave, or medical or maternity suspension, his or her dismissal upon the resumption of work by the original employee will be treated as being for SOSR – S.106(1) ERA. This is discussed further under 'Temporary cover' below.

SOSR dismissals are discussed in detail in IDS Employment Law Handbook, 'Unfair Dismissal' (2010), Chapter 8, 'Some other substantial reason'.

Redundancy. Depending on the circumstances, the expiry and non-renewal of **2.72** a fixed-term contract may be by reason of redundancy, rather than SOSR. Redundancy is defined in S.139(1) ERA and the definition applies to both claims for redundancy payments and unfair dismissal claims. Under S.139(1) an employee is dismissed by reason of redundancy if, among other things, his or her dismissal is wholly or mainly attributable to the fact that:

* the employer has ceased or intends to cease to carry on the business for the purposes of which the employee was employed, or

* the requirements of business for employees to carry out work of a particular kind have ceased or diminished or are expected to cease or diminish.

111

In Pfaffinger v City of Liverpool Community College and another case 1997 ICR 142, EAT, the claimants were lecturers who had been employed for many years on a series of fixed-term contracts, each of which was for a single academic term. When the employer tried to renegotiate the terms of the contracts the claimants brought claims for redundancy payments. The EAT noted that the combined effect of the definition of 'dismissal' and the definition of a 'redundancy situation' is that, where an employee is employed on a succession of fixed-term contracts, the employee may be dismissed for redundancy on the expiration of each contract. The EAT concluded that the claimants were dismissed when their fixed-term contracts expired at the end of the academic term and that the reason for the dismissals was redundancy, in that the employer had no need for part-time lecturers to carry out the function of part-time lecturing during the vacation. (Note that the fact that the claimants may have had continuity of employment throughout the series of fixed-term contracts for other statutory purposes did not prevent the expiry of each fixed-term contract being by reason of redundancy.) This case is discussed further under 'Redundancy rights – statutory redundancy pay' below.

2.73 By contrast, in Shrewsbury and Telford Hospital NHS Trust v Lairikyengbam 2010 ICR 66, EAT, a locum consultant cardiologist who was employed on a series of fixed-term contracts was not dismissed for redundancy when his contract was not extended. There remained a requirement for the work of a consultant cardiologist on the expiry of L's contract: the position of locum consultant was essentially the same as the substantive consultant post for which L had unsuccessfully applied.

It makes no difference that the employee knows in advance that the contract is unlikely to be renewed because the work is diminishing. If the reason for non-renewal is a reduction in the need for employees to do work of a particular kind, then non-renewal is a dismissal for redundancy – Nottinghamshire County Council v Lee 1980 ICR 635, CA.

Redundancy dismissals are discussed in detail in IDS Employment Law Handbook, 'Redundancy' (2008), Chapter 8, 'Unfair redundancy'.

2.74 **Temporary cover.** The non-renewal of a temporary contract to cover for an absent employee – for example, one who is suffering long-term illness – does not fall within the definition of redundancy. If the absent employee later decides not to return, thus creating a job vacancy, and the temporary employee is not offered the post, dismissal is still not for redundancy but may be for SOSR – Whaite v Dumfries and Galloway Regional Council EAT 223/92. Similarly, where the limited-term contract is to replace an employee who is away on secondment, the return of the seconded employee will be the reason for dismissal, not redundancy – Greater Glasgow Health Board v Lamont EATS 0019/12. In that case, it was accepted that the job in question was only ever a 'single employee job', so that there was no question of any diminution in the employer's requirement for employees to carry out work of a particular kind within the meaning of S.139 ERA.

Indeed, where an employee is engaged in order to cover for another employee who is, or will be, absent because of pregnancy, childbirth, adoption leave, additional paternity leave, or medical or maternity suspension, S.106(1) provides that his or her dismissal upon the resumption of work by the original employee will be treated as being for SOSR. However, S.106(1) will only apply where the employer informed the employee on his or her engagement, in clear and unambiguous language, that the employment would be terminated on the return of the permanent employee – Victoria and Albert Museum v Durrant 2011 IRLR 290, EAT. In that case, which concerned maternity leave cover, the EAT also observed that where another reason for dismissal exists (such as redundancy), S.106 will not always displace that reason in favour of SOSR. That will only happen where there is no other reason for dismissal than to facilitate the return to work of the woman from maternity leave. For example, if an employee is 'bumped' out of a post so as to accommodate somebody whose post had disappeared, and the bumped employee is then given work covering for somebody on maternity leave and subsequently dismissed on her return, that employee might still be dismissed for redundancy. A detailed discussion of S.106 can be found in IDS Employment Law Handbook, 'Maternity and Parental Rights' (2012), Chapter 14, 'Replacement employees', under 'Less favourable treatment – dismissal of replacement'.

Reasonableness of dismissal   2.75

Once an employer has shown a potentially fair reason for dismissal, the tribunal must go on to decide whether the dismissal for that reason was fair or unfair. Below, we consider some issues that may be relevant to the question of reasonableness in the context of fixed-term contracts.

Purpose of contract not communicated to employee. Termination of a 2.76 limited-term employment contract may be unfair if the purpose of that contract was not communicated to the employee. In Adams v Coventry University ET Case No.1303464/07 A was initially employed by the university on a temporary contract. At the end of September 2005 she was offered a permanent job by the local Council, at which point the university offered her improved conditions in order to retain her services. A was left with the impression that she was to become a permanent employee, although on 10 October she accepted a fixed-term contract for one year. The contract was further extended, but A was dismissed after the person whose job she had been covering returned to work from maternity leave. The tribunal upheld A's claim for unfair dismissal. She had not been told that she was being employed only to cover an absent employee – the temporary contract she was offered did not mirror the maternity absence and she was never told that it did. She was offered it because the university wanted to persuade her to stay at a time when she had been offered a permanent

113

job elsewhere. There were further extensions to her contract without any reference to the extensions covering maternity absence. The university should also have done more to look for suitable alternative employment.

2.77 **Failure to consider suitable alternative employment.** The failure to look for suitable alternative employment was also a consideration in Rochdale Metropolitan Borough Council v Jentas EAT 494/01, where J, a temporary employee, was repeatedly re-engaged on a series of one-month contracts for a period of 20 months. When her final contract came to an end, her employment terminated. A tribunal found that there was SOSR for the decision not to renew her contract but that the dismissal was unfair because the employer had not considered whether suitable temporary work was available in another department. J had a substantial period of service, had moved from position to position, and had sought to obtain a permanent position with the employer. The EAT upheld this decision, while commenting that it was a 'one-off case on particular facts'.

Where a permanent position is created to replace a temporary post, the employer may be expected to help the temporary incumbent apply for the permanent post. Two examples:

- **Gavin v Home Office Immigration and Nationality Directorate** ET Case No.1802566/01: G was unsuccessful in his application for the permanent post, which was filled by an external candidate. Although a Council order providing that permanent posts could only be filled by open competition established SOSR for the non-renewal of G's fixed-term contract, the tribunal held that the employer should have done more than simply tell G of the vacancy in a casual phone call. He should have been pointed in the right direction and told of the application procedure

- **Darbyshire v Governing Body of All Saints CE Primary School** ET Case No.2405746/05: D was employed as a teacher on a temporary fixed-term contract from 1 September 2004 to 31 August 2005 or the return of the post holder from maternity leave, whichever was the sooner. There were no problems over her abilities during the year and she made it clear to the head teacher on a number of occasions that she would like to remain at the school should the teacher on maternity leave decide not to return. Early in July 2005 a teaching assistant in the school told the head teacher that she would like to apply for the post if the teacher did not return. The head teacher approached the governing body, who agreed the appointment. D was informed of the appointment on 12 July and her employment terminated on 31 August. A tribunal found that D had been unfairly dismissed. It was unreasonable for the school not to have given D the opportunity to be considered for the post or to take any steps to consult her before giving the post to another person. Had the governing body been made aware of D's

114

wish to remain at the school it would have given serious consideration to her superior qualifications.

The FTE Regulations give employees on fixed-term contracts the right to be **2.78** informed by their employer of all available vacancies within the establishment in which they work – Reg 3(6) (see 'Right to be informed of available vacancies' above). It is likely that a failure by the employer to comply with this duty will be a factor in the consideration of the fairness of any dismissal. In addition, as noted under 'Equal treatment – less favourable treatment' above, the Regulations specifically provide that the right not to be treated less favourably contained in Reg 3(1) includes the right not to be treated less favourably in relation to the opportunity to secure any permanent position in the establishment – Reg 3(2)(c).

Acas Code of Practice. Note that the Acas Code of Practice on Disciplinary **2.79** and Grievance Procedures (2009) – which is taken into account by tribunals in determining the procedural fairness of most dismissals and, if breached, may lead to an adjustment in compensation – states that it does not apply to the non-renewal of fixed-term contracts. The Acas Code will, however, apply to dismissals before the expiry of the fixed term, because of, for example, misconduct or capability (see immediately below).

One element of a fair procedure is the right to appeal – see paragraph 25 of the Code. It is, however, worth mentioning in this regard, that where an employee on a fixed-term contract is dismissed before the expiry of the fixed term, but succeeds in having the dismissal overturned on appeal, the appeal does no more than reinstate the original contract. If the appeal takes place after the end of the fixed term, it does not, without more, extend the contract beyond the date on which it would have expired – Prakash v Wolverhampton City Council EAT 0140/06.

The provisions of the Acas Code are discussed in depth in IDS Employment Law Supplement, 'Disciplinary and Grievance Procedures' (2009).

Misconduct or capability. An employer is entitled to dismiss an employee for **2.80** misconduct or capability before the expiry of the fixed term, provided it acts reasonably and follows a fair procedure. A fair procedure will generally involve an employer issuing warnings and giving the employee an opportunity to improve. In Stolt Offshore Ltd v Fraser EATS 0041/02 SO Ltd employed F on a series of fixed-term contracts of 12 months' duration each. The first contract ran for the calendar year 1999, and there were subsequent contracts for the years 2000 and 2001. In each case, formal contracts were not signed until well into the relevant periods. In November 1999 F was given a final written warning, which was confirmed by letter dated 24 January 2000. The final warning was to be in force for 24 months. Upon further misconduct in 2001, F's contract was terminated by SO Ltd, which maintained that the final written warning was still in force. F brought a claim of unfair dismissal before a tribunal.

115

The tribunal majority found that it was 'nonsensical' of the company to put a 24-month warning in place when F's contract of employment was to last for only 12 months. According to the majority, while SO Ltd had the discretion to issue a final written warning lasting 24 months, it was incumbent upon the company, as a reasonable employer, to draw F's attention to this on giving him a new contract in 2000. As it did not do so, the final written warning did not apply to the new contract and it was not reasonable for SO Ltd to have regard to the warning when disciplining F in 2001. Accordingly, F's dismissal was unfair.

2.81 On appeal the EAT held that there was no inconsistency between the existence of a 12-month fixed-term employment contract and the issuing of a warning to last for a period longer than that, provided there is power in the original contract to make such an order. No one disputed that there was such power in the original contract. Thus, the remaining matter for the EAT to consider was whether the renewal contract had to make reference to the existing warning for that warning to continue to be effective. In the EAT's opinion, the tribunal majority's position went too far. S.95(1)(b) ERA provides that the non-renewal of a fixed-term contract constitutes a dismissal for the purposes of unfair dismissal law (see 'Definition of dismissal' above). One result of this section, according to the EAT, was to entitle an employer to assume that when a fixed-term contract is renewed, it contains aspects of the previous contract that are still relevant without needing to be restated in express terms. As such, it was appropriate for F's final written warning to remain in effect for its full 24-month duration, and there was no need for SO Ltd to advise F of its continuing effect. The tribunal, therefore, should have taken into account the continuing existence of the final written warning when considering whether SO Ltd's actions were within the band of reasonable responses. Applying this understanding of the law, the EAT reviewed the uncontested facts and found that the only conclusion the tribunal could reasonably have come to was that SO Ltd's decision to dismiss F was within the band of reasonable responses and that, therefore, F's dismissal was fair. Accordingly, the appeal was allowed.

Capability and misconduct dismissals are discussed in detail in IDS Employment Law Handbook, 'Unfair Dismissal' (2010), Chapter 4, 'Capability and qualifications', and Chapter 6, 'Conduct'.

2.82 **Automatically unfair dismissal**
By virtue of Reg 6(1) and (3) of the Regulations, a dismissal will be automatically unfair (i.e. unfair without any consideration of reasonableness) where the reason, or principal reason, for the dismissal is that the employee has done, or the employer believes or suspects that the employee has done or intends to do, any of the following:

- brought proceedings against the employer under the FTE Regulations

116

- requested from the employer a written statement of reasons for less favourable treatment under Reg 5 (see 'Right to receive written statement' above) or written confirmation that his or her contract is to be viewed as permanent under Reg 9 (see 'Successive fixed-term contracts – written statements' below)

- given evidence or information in connection with proceedings brought by any employee under the Regulations

- otherwise done anything under the Regulations in relation to the employer or any other person

- alleged that the employer has infringed the Regulations (unless the allegation was false or not made in good faith – Reg 6(4))

- refused (or proposed to refuse) to forgo a right conferred by the Regulations

- declined to sign a workforce agreement for the purposes of the Regulations (see 'Successive fixed-term contracts – collective modification of the rules' below)

- performed (or proposed to perform) any functions or activities of a workforce representative or candidate (see 'Successive fixed-term contracts – collective modification of the rules' below).

2.83 A fixed-term employee who believes that his or her dismissal is automatically unfair under Reg 6 should bring the claim under Part X of the ERA. Note that the two-year qualifying period in S.108 ERA which is normally applicable to unfair dismissal does not apply to Reg 6 dismissals – para 3(11), Sch 2.

It is worth mentioning here that an employee also has the right not to be subjected to any detriment (short of dismissal) by any act, or deliberate failure to act, of the employer on any of the grounds listed above – Reg 6(2). This is discussed further under 'Protection from detriment' below.

2.84 **Automatically unfair redundancy.** Section 105 ERA – which governs automatically unfair redundancy – provides, inter alia, that an employee who is dismissed will be regarded as automatically unfairly dismissed if:

- the reason (or, if more than one, the principal reason) for the dismissal is that the employee was redundant

- the circumstances constituting the redundancy applied equally to one or more other employees in the same undertaking who held positions similar to that held by the employee and who have not been dismissed by the employer, and

- the reason (or, if more than one, the principal reason) for which the employee was selected for dismissal was one specified in Reg 6(3) of the Regulations (i.e. for one of the reasons listed immediately above) – S.105(1) and (7F).

2.85 The employee will lose his or her right to claim unfair dismissal under S.105 where the reason (or principal reason) for redundancy selection is that the employee has alleged that the employer infringed the Regulations (or that the employer believes or suspects that the employee has done so or intends to do so) and the allegation was false and not made in good faith – S.105(7F) and Reg 6(4).

Automatically unfair redundancy under S.105 is discussed in detail in IDS Employment Law Handbook, 'Redundancy' (2008), Chapter 8, 'Unfair redundancy', under 'Automatically unfair dismissal'.

2.86 Protection from detriment

An employee has the right not to be subjected to any detriment by any act, or deliberate failure to act, of the employer on any of the grounds listed in Reg 6(3) – Reg 6(2). These are the same grounds that apply for automatically unfair dismissal under Reg 6(1) – see 'Unfair dismissal rights – automatically unfair dismissal' above. This provision does not cover detriment that amounts to a dismissal – Reg 6(5). The meaning of 'detriment' is considered under 'Equal treatment – less favourable treatment' above, in the context of less favourable treatment under Reg 3(1). Note, however, that in contrast with detriment under Reg 3(1), there is no need under Reg 6(2) for the employee to show less favourable treatment with a comparator and the defence of objective justification is not available.

As with automatically unfair dismissal, an employee will lose his or her right not to be subjected to a detriment under the Regulations where he or she has alleged that the employer infringed the Regulations (or that the employer believes or suspects that the employee has done so or intends to do so) and the allegation was false and not made in good faith – Reg 6(4).

2.87 A fixed-term employee who believes his or her right not to be subjected to a detriment has been breached may bring a complaint to a tribunal – Reg 7(1). Unlike unfair dismissal claims, the claim should be brought under the Regulations and not under the ERA – see 'Enforcement and remedies' below for a discussion on the enforcement of this and other rights under the Regulations.

2.88 Redundancy rights

The right for fixed-term employees not to be treated less favourably than comparable permanent employees (discussed under 'Equal treatment' above) is likely to have a major impact both on the choice of redundancy selection criteria and on the redundancy pay package. In this section we highlight those aspects of the redundancy scheme that are of particular relevance to fixed-term employee status. For a full discussion of the law, see IDS Employment Law Handbook, 'Redundancy' (2011).

Statutory redundancy pay 2.89

When an employee's fixed-term contract expires without being renewed, this amounts to a dismissal for the purposes of claiming unfair dismissal rights and statutory redundancy pay under the ERA – Ss.95(1)(b), 136(1)((b) and 235(2A) ERA. This applies to contracts that are stated to be for a fixed term and to those that are limited by the completion of a task or by a particular event (together known as 'limited-term' contracts under the ERA). The same definition of dismissal also applies for the purpose of claiming unfair dismissal under S.95(1)(b) and is fully discussed under 'Unfair dismissal rights – definition of dismissal' above.

When does entitlement to statutory redundancy pay arise? The regular **2.90** qualifying periods apply in the same way as they apply to permanent employees. Thus, in order to claim redundancy benefits, a fixed-term employee must have at least two years' continuous service, assessed in accordance with the rules governing continuous employment set out in Ss.210–219 ERA (discussed under 'Successive fixed-term contracts – continuous employment' below). Secondly, as with permanent employees, it must be shown that a fixed-term employee claiming redundancy pay has been dismissed by reason of redundancy – see the section 'Unfair dismissal rights' above, under 'Reason for dismissal – redundancy'. Full details of the right to a redundancy payment can be found in IDS Employment Law Handbooks, 'Redundancy' (2008), Chapter 6, 'Redundancy payments'.

In Pfaffinger v City of Liverpool Community College and another case 1997 ICR 142, EAT, the EAT held that where an employee is employed on a succession of fixed-term contracts, he or she may be dismissed for redundancy on the expiration of each contract, provided that on each occasion a redundancy situation exists. Although S.212(3)(b) acted to preserve continuity of employment in these cases (see 'Successive fixed-term contracts – continuous employment' below), it did not have the effect of preventing the expiration of a fixed-term contract from being a dismissal or preventing there being a redundancy situation.

The effect of the EAT's decision is that employees who work under a series of **2.91** fixed-term contracts may become entitled to a statutory redundancy payment in relation to the expiry of any contract after they have completed two years' service. Receipt of a redundancy payment does not break continuity for the purpose of, for example, unfair dismissal claims. However, under S.214(2) continuity is broken for the purpose of determining qualifying service for redundancy. This means that, once employees have received a statutory

119

redundancy payment, they have to accrue a further two years' service before being entitled to another. This case is discussed further under 'Unfair dismissal rights – reason for dismissal' above.

2.92 **Waiver of statutory redundancy pay.** The general rule is that any provision attempting to exclude an employee's rights under the statutory redundancy scheme or to preclude his or her right to claim a redundancy payment in a tribunal is void – S.203(1) ERA. Unlike many employment rights, it is not possible to use a settlement agreement or an Acas-conciliated agreement to exclude the right to a redundancy payment. S.197 ERA used to allow fixed-term employees to sign a written agreement waiving rights to a statutory redundancy payment upon the expiry and non-renewal of a contract for a fixed term of two years or more. However, this provision was repealed by para 3(15) of Schedule 2 to the FTE Regulations and, subject to the transitional provisions mentioned below, it is now only possible for employees to 'opt out' of the redundancy payments scheme by way of collective agreement combined with an exemption order – S.157 ERA. (For further details, see IDS Employment Law Handbook, 'Redundancy' (2008), Chapter 5, 'Qualifications and exclusions', under 'Contracting out – collective contracting out'.) Therefore, any waivers inserted into contracts agreed, renewed or extended after the Regulations came into effect on 1 October 2002 will be invalid, and fixed-term employees whose contracts expire and are not renewed by reason of redundancy will have a right to a statutory redundancy payment if they have been continuously employed for two years or more.

Although this means that fixed-term employees cannot be excluded from the statutory redundancy scheme, it is important to note that fixed-term employees may be excluded from *contractual* schemes if such exclusion can be objectively justified. This is discussed further under 'Contractual redundancy pay' below.

2.93 Note that there was some confusion in the past as to the validity of existing waivers in fixed-term contracts extended for less than two years. S.197(5) ERA provided that a waiver of redundancy pay rights under a fixed-term contract lapsed automatically at the end of the fixed term. If the contract was then renewed, a further agreement to exclude redundancy payments had to be made if the waiver was to continue to operate. However, S.197(5) was unclear as to whether the renewed term had to be for two years or more in order for the new waiver clause to be valid. S.197 has now been repealed, so the issue is only of relevance to fixed-term contracts to which the transitional provisions apply (see below).

2.94 *Transitional provisions.* The repeal of S.197 was not retroactive and transitional provisions contained in para 5 of Schedule 2 state that any existing waiver shall have effect where the 'relevant date' under S.145 ERA (i.e. the termination date) falls on or after 1 October 2002 and both of the following conditions are satisfied:

- the contract was entered into before 1 October 2002 and has not been renewed since or – where there have been one or more renewals – the only or most recent renewal was agreed before that date, *and*

- the agreement to exclude any right to a redundancy payment was entered into and took effect before 1 October 2002.

Obviously, with the effluxion of time these transitional provisions have become increasingly irrelevant and the vast majority of fixed-term employees with two or more years of continuous employment are now covered by the statutory scheme.

Contractual redundancy pay 2.95

As we saw under 'Equal treatment' above, fixed-term employees have the right not to be treated less favourably than comparable permanent employees on the ground of their fixed-term status, unless the different treatment can be objectively justified – Reg 3. This means that fixed-term employees should receive the same level of redundancy payments as comparable permanent employees, unless different payments are objectively justified. An employer may be able to demonstrate objective justification for any difference in treatment if the fixed-term employee did not expect his or her employment to last longer than the term of the first contract.

In Nisbet and anor v GMB Union ET Case No.2502453/12 an employment tribunal held that the employer's exclusion of fixed-term employees from an enhanced redundancy scheme was not objectively justified. The main justification put forward by the GMB Union was that although it had engaged the claimants to work as Learning Officers on a union learning project, the project (including the claimants' salaries) was paid for by the Union Learning Fund (ULF). The ULF was only prepared to fund the salaries of those working on the project, not redundancy payments. In the tribunal's view, the GMB's argument would have been a powerful one had its part in the learning project been purely nominal, and had the claimants only been employed by the union for convenience. That, however, was not the position. The GMB had entered into the project for the benefit that it would gain. In addition it had agreed to make some contribution towards the running costs. It was plainly part of the agreement that the union would meet any redundancy costs. Indeed, the union had been prepared to make statutory redundancy payments to the claimants. There was no evidence to show that the union's contribution to the overall costs would have been disproportionate if the enhanced redundancy payments had been made to the claimants.

The second purported justification was that the GMB had a policy of not making **2.96** permanent employees redundant. Accordingly, the policy for enhanced redundancy payments was a 'fallback provision' which was designed to give some comfort to employees but which was unlikely in practice to result in any

121

payments. Where, on the other hand, employees were recruited on fixed-term contracts for specific projects, the likelihood that redundancy payments would be due was considerably greater. The union referred to the BERR guidance, which stated that where 'companies have special redundancy schemes to compensate permanent employees for the unexpected loss of their jobs and these companies generally employ fixed-term employees on fixed-term contracts with no reasonable expectation of a renewal, it may be possible to justify excluding fixed-term employees from the contractual redundancy payments scheme'.

The tribunal observed that this Guidance has no statutory force. However, it could see a possible objective justification in cases where a project is expected to last for a year or two with no expectation of continued employment beyond that period. In the instant case, by contrast, the project had been running for several years by the time the final contracts were entered into. One of the claimants, N, had been employed for nearly eight years, presumably with several renewals of his contract. The tribunal noted that the traditional reasons for redundancy payments are to reward the employee for past service and to cushion the employee for a period against the loss of his or her employment. Those considerations apply with particular force to a fairly long-serving employee such as N. The tribunal therefore concluded that the less favourable treatment was not justified on objective grounds.

2.97 Redundancy selection

The right to equal treatment under Reg 3 (see 'Equal treatment' above) means that fixed-term employees should not be selected for redundancy purely because they are on fixed-term contracts, unless this can be objectively justified. However, where a fixed-term employee has been brought in specifically to complete particular tasks or to cover for a peak in demand, it is likely that an employer could objectively justify selecting him or her for redundancy at the end of the contract.

Where length of service is the main criterion for redundancy selection, the same criteria should apply to fixed-term employees as apply to comparable permanent employees, unless differences are objectively justified. According to the BERR guidance, it is acceptable if the effect of a 'last in, first out' policy is that more fixed-term than permanent employees are made redundant, as long as the policy is applied consistently.

2.98 As noted under 'Equal treatment' above, it is not unlawful under the FTE Regulations to treat fixed-term employees more favourably than permanent employees. However, a redundancy selection exercise that favours fixed-term employees could well be unreasonable under S.98(4) ERA. An example:

- **Davies v JCB Transmission** ET Case No.2901458/08: JCB employed a number of workers on contracts which stated that they were on a temporary appointment of uncertain duration, they were employed to cover peaks in demand, and the contract would expire when demand reduced. By 2008 the company suffered a downturn in demand and decided to implement redundancies. It put all employees, permanent and those on temporary contracts, into one pool for selection. An employment tribunal found that it was unreasonable to include the fixed-term employees in the same pool for selection as permanent employees. The fixed-term contracts were determinable upon the occurrence of a specific event – a downturn in demand – and JCB would not have faced a successful claim of treating the fixed-term employees less favourably by terminating their contracts because demand had reduced.

Unfair dismissal   2.99
Dismissal for redundancy where the employee is selected for dismissal on one of the grounds listed in Reg 6(3) is automatically unfair – see 'Unfair dismissal rights – automatically unfair dismissal' above. This right is entirely distinct from the right to claim ordinary unfair dismissal under S.98 ERA where a fixed-term contract expires and is not renewed by reason of redundancy – see the section 'Unfair dismissal' above, under 'Reason for dismissal – redundancy'.

Collective redundancy   2.100
Employers are required to inform and consult the workforce when they propose to dismiss as redundant 20 or more employees at one establishment within a period of 90 days or less – S.188 Trade Union and Labour Relations (Consolidation) Act 1992 (TULR(C)A). Previously, only fixed-term contracts of three months or less were specifically exempted from these collective consultation obligations. However, S.282 TULR(C)A has been amended so that all fixed-term contracts which have reached their agreed termination point are now expressly excluded. Therefore, the dismissal of employees at the end of their fixed-term contracts will not count towards the 20-employee threshold which triggers the duty to consult under S.188. Acas guidance on 'How to manage collective redundancies' confirms that this is the case even if the expiry of the fixed-term contract occurs within the same 90-day period as the proposed collective redundancies.

Prior to this amendment, the extent to which fixed-term contracts were included within the collective consultation regime depended upon whether or not the reason for the expiry of the fixed-term contract related to the individual concerned – University and College Union v University of Stirling 2014 IRLR 287, Ct Sess (Inner House). In that case, the Inner House of the Court of Session noted that the definition of 'redundancy dismissal' for collective consultation purposes is 'dismissal for a reason not related to the individual concerned or for a number of reasons all of which are not so related' – S.195(1) TULR(C)A. The Court suggested that if an employer engages a large number of workers on fixed-term contracts and then dismisses them according to the demands of its

123

business, this would not relate to the individual concerned. On the other hand, where an employee enters into a fixed-term contract on a voluntary basis for specific reasons, such as a particular research project or to cover a period of maternity leave, the fact that the employee has entered into such a contract would be a matter related to the individual.

2.101 The effect of this decision is rather limited since, as noted above, the TULR(C)A has now been amended to exclude the expiry of fixed-term contracts from the collective consultation obligations. The EAT in that case had reached a more wide-ranging conclusion than the Court of Session, holding that dismissal on expiry of a fixed-term contract is always for a reason related to the individual concerned and thus never for redundancy under the TULR(C)A. The Government decided to put this decision on a statutory footing and introduced an amendment to S.282 TULR(C)A with effect from 6 April 2013. S.282(2) now provides that expiring fixed-term contracts are expressly excluded from the collective consultation rules set out in Ss.188–198 TULR(C)A unless the fixed-term employment in question is terminated by reason of redundancy before the expiry of the term, the completion of the task or the occurrence or non-occurrence of the event specified in the contract. Thus, as a general rule – and despite the Court of Session's more nuanced approach – the expiry of fixed-term contracts will not count towards the threshold of 20 dismissals for triggering collective consultation obligations. However, the Court of Session's reasoning may still be relevant when deciding whether other types of contract have been terminated for a reason related to the individual concerned.

It is important to note that the S.282 exemption does not apply to fixed-term contracts that are ended prematurely (i.e. before the intended expiry of the contract term). Employers should therefore be wary of disregarding fixed-term employees as a matter of course when determining whether proposed dismissals are likely to reach the threshold for collective consultation: it is only those fixed-term contracts which would expire during the relevant 90-day period that can safely be disregarded.

The collective consultation regime is discussed in IDS Employment Law Handbook, 'Redundancy' (2008), Chapter 12, 'Collective redundancies'.

2.102 Successive fixed-term contracts

It is not uncommon for employers to use successive fixed-term contracts as an alternative to permanent employment. However, this practice can deny employees certain rights that they would be entitled to if they were employed on a permanent basis. As a result, the FTW Directive aims to limit the use of successive fixed-term employment contracts by requiring Member States to introduce 'one or more of the following measures:

(a) objective reasons justifying the renewal of such contracts or relationships;

(b) a maximum total duration of successive fixed-term employment contracts or relationships;

(c) the number of renewals of such contracts or relationships' – Clause 5.

In this section we consider the provisions contained in the FTE Regulations aimed at implementing this requirement.

Gaining permanent status 2.103

Regulation 8 of the FTE Regulations states that an employee on a fixed-term contract will be regarded as a permanent employee if *all* the following circumstances apply:

- the employee is currently employed under a fixed-term contract and that contract has previously been renewed, or the employee has previously been employed on a fixed-term contract before the start of the current contract – Reg 8(1)

- the employee has been continuously employed under fixed-term contracts for four years or more – Reg 8(2)(a) (see 'Continuous employment' below)

- at the time of the most recent renewal – or, where the contract has not been renewed, at the time that the contract was entered into – employment under a fixed-term contract was not justified on objective grounds – Reg 8(2)(b) (see 'Objective justification' below).

By virtue of Reg 1(2) a 'renewal' includes an extension.

Where the above conditions apply, the provisions in the contract that restrict its duration will cease to have effect and the contract will be regarded for all purposes as being a contract of indefinite duration. The date from which the fixed-term employee becomes a permanent employee is whichever is the later of the date on which the current contract was entered into or last renewed, or the date on which the employee acquired four years' continuous service – Reg 8(3).

There is no limit on the duration of the first contract for the purposes of Reg 8. **2.104** This means that an initial fixed-term contract could be for a term of four years or more without falling foul of this provision. However, where a first fixed-term contract lasts for four years or more and is then renewed, the second contract will be regarded as permanent, unless the use of a further fixed-term contract can be objectively justified.

One consequence of Reg 8 is that the provisions of Ss.86–91 of the Employment Rights Act 1996 (ERA) will apply. These provide for minimum periods of notice, based on length of service, which automatically apply unless longer periods are contractually agreed – for further details see IDS Employment Law Handbook, 'Contracts of Employment' (2009), Chapter 8, 'Termination by dismissal', under 'Express dismissal – dismissal with notice'.

2.105 Note that it is possible for an individual's fixed-term contract to become a contract for an indefinite period by virtue of the notice provisions in S.86 ERA. S.86(4) provides that where an individual is employed under a contract for a fixed term of one month or less and has been employed for three months or more, his or her contract is to have effect as though it were for an indefinite period. However, given that the section requires that the contract must be for a 'term certain' of one month or less, it is unlikely that it applies to task contracts, i.e. contracts that expire on the completion of a task or the occurrence or non-occurrence of an event rather than on a specified date. The wording of this provision has not been changed by the Regulations despite the extension of the definition of dismissal in the ERA to include task contracts – see 'Unfair dismissal rights – definition of dismissal' above.

An employee who considers that by virtue of Reg 8 he or she is a permanent employee may make an application to an employment tribunal for a declaration to that effect – Reg 9(5). However, an application can only be made under this provision if:

- the employee is employed by the employer at the time he or she makes the application, and

- the employee has previously requested a written statement from the employer under Reg 9(1) confirming that the employee is now a permanent employee (see 'Written statements' below) and the employer has either failed to provide such a statement or has made a statement giving reasons why the contract remains fixed-term – Reg 9(6).

2.106 Continuous employment

The limitation on successive fixed-term contracts only applies where the employee has been continuously employed under fixed-term contracts for four years or more – Reg 8(2)(a). This means that the employee must have been continuously employed for four years or more either under his or her current fixed-term contract (at the time of its renewal or extension) or under that contract taken together with the fixed-term contracts he or she was previously employed under. However, any period of continuous employment prior to 10 July 2002 does not count towards the four-year period – Reg 8(4). This means that for the purposes of calculating the four-year period of continuous employment, a fixed-term employee's service does not begin to run until that date.

For the purposes of Reg 8, continuity of employment is determined in accordance with the rules governing continuous employment set out in Ss.210–219 ERA – Reg 8(4). Under those rules only weeks governed by a contract of employment count – S.212(1). This can pose particular problems for fixed-term employees who are often employed to cover one-off short-term staff shortages or in sectors where breaks occur between contracts; for example, in the tourist industry or the education sector. Gaps of less than a week in length between the expiration of one fixed-term contract and the beginning of another will not break continuity of employment. However, gaps of more than a week will do so unless they can be shown to fall within one of the exceptions found in S.212(3). These include where the break amounts to a temporary cessation of work (S.212(3)(b)) or an 'arrangement or custom' (S.212(3)(c)).

Note that the Court of Appeal in Hudson v Department for Work and Pensions **2.107** 2013 ICR 329, CA, ruled that Reg 18(1) – which excludes work on a Government training or work experience scheme from the scope of the Regulations – meant that any periods (whether still ongoing or in the past) during which an employee was employed on a Government training scheme did not count towards the four-year period. This led to the conclusion that the claimant, despite having four years' continuous employment under the ERA, was not employed on a permanent contract.

The rules governing the continuity of employment under the ERA are discussed in detail in IDS Employment Law Handbook, 'Continuity of Employment' (2012). Below we focus on those aspects of the rules that are of particular relevance to fixed-term employment.

Temporary cessation of work. The temporary cessation of work exception in **2.108** S.212(3)(b) ERA is the one most frequently relied upon by fixed-term employees for the purpose of showing that continuity of employment has been preserved between the expiry of one fixed-term contract and the start of another – in particular where employees are employed on a series of fixed-term contracts as a result of seasonal work or work tied in to school or college terms.

In Ford v Warwickshire County Council 1983 ICR 273, HL, Lord Diplock made some obiter comments regarding the meaning of 'temporary'. He equated the term with 'transient' or 'lasting only a relatively short time'. However, in Flack and ors v Kodak Ltd 1986 ICR 775, CA, the Court of Appeal expressed some unease with Lord Diplock's obiter remarks. Lord Justice Parker stressed that 'temporary' should not be viewed as meaning 'very short' but should be considered relatively. He said that a nine-month cessation could hardly be regarded as very short, but if an employee has been employed for 11 years a nine-month cessation may still be regarded as merely temporary, particularly if there was evidence that it was intended to be so. Lord Justice Woolf commented that the word 'temporary' is not used in the sense of something that is not permanent, since otherwise in every case where employment has been resumed after a dismissal on account of a cessation of work, that provision would apply to preserve continuity.

The meaning of 'work' under S.212(3)(b) was examined by the EAT in North **2.109** Yorkshire County Council and anor v Laws EAT 1376/95. L was a teacher who had been employed until 31 December 1992 on full-time fixed-term contracts.

127

From 6 January 1993 to 23 July 1993 she was employed on a fixed-term contract to cover P's maternity leave. P returned to work in September 1993. From 1 September 1993 the claimant was employed on two fixed-term contracts at another school until her dismissal in July 1995. The question at issue was whether the period between 23 July 1993 and 1 September 1993 broke the claimant's continuity. The employer argued that there had been no cessation of work, so that S.212(3)(b) could not apply to preserve continuity. It maintained that there was work available, in the sense of work under a contract of employment. P was employed throughout the period of the summer break. This, it argued, demonstrated that work was available, albeit that it was available to P rather than to L. The EAT conceded that it found the point difficult but in the end it rejected the employer's argument. The word 'work' in S.212(3)(b) means the actual performance of duties and not 'employment' or 'being employed under a contract of employment'. In this sense there was no work available during the summer holidays since there had been a cessation of actual duties. Accordingly, there was a temporary cessation of work within the meaning of S.212(3)(b) and the claimant's continuity was preserved.

It should be noted that predictable and regular cessations are covered by S.212(3)(b), as well as unpredictable ones. It seems, however, that the method of assessing whether or not continuity has been broken differs depending upon whether the gaps are regular or unpredictable.

2.110 *Regular gaps in employment.* In Ford v Warwickshire County Council (above) Lord Diplock commented that in considering employment under a series of fixed-term contracts with gaps in between, continuity would only be broken if, when 'looking backwards from the date of the expiry of the fixed-term contract on which the employee's claim is based, there is to be found between one fixed-term contract and its immediate predecessor an interval that cannot be characterised as short [relative] to the combined duration of the two fixed-term contracts'. That case concerned a teacher employed for eight years under a succession of fixed-term contracts that expired every year at the start of the summer holidays.

It seems, however, that the strict mathematical approach advocated by Lord Diplock only applies if the gaps in employment are predictable and regular, not where they are unpredictable and irregular – Flack and ors v Kodak Ltd 1986 ICR 775, CA (see 'Unpredictable gaps in employment' below).

2.111 An example of the type of regular employment to which the mathematical approach was appropriate can be found in Sillars v Charrington Fuels Ltd 1989 ICR 475, CA. In that case S had worked for 15 years as an HGV driver delivering fuel during the winter months. He was employed from around October each year until around May. S's employment had followed a fairly regular pattern, with the period of employment each year varying between 21 and 32 weeks. His last two periods of employment had been for 30 weeks and

27 weeks. When S's employment came to a permanent end in 1986 and he claimed unfair dismissal and a redundancy payment, the employer argued that he did not have the requisite continuous employment because of his absence from work during the summer months. S argued that these breaks were due to temporary cessations of work, so that continuity was preserved. He maintained that the fact that it was the intention of both employee and employer that the work would resume again before the next winter and that seasonal workers kept the same payroll number, overalls and lockers from season to season pointed to the cessations being temporary and not permanent. The tribunal compared the periods when the employee was absent with the periods when he was working and concluded that, since the absences were not relatively short, there was no temporary cessation of work.

On appeal to the EAT, S argued that the tribunal had applied the wrong test and, in the light of the Flack decision, should instead have considered all the circumstances of the employment, including the fact that it was the intention of the parties that the employee return to work each autumn. The EAT rejected that argument, however, saying that the Court of Appeal in Flack had not rejected the mathematical approach for cases where there was a regular pattern of absence. On further appeal, the EAT's decision was upheld. The Court of Appeal held that 'temporary' had to be construed as a relatively short period of time and, whichever period was looked at in this case, the employee had only ever been employed for approximately half of each year. The fact that a cessation is not permanent does not mean that it is 'temporary'.

When using the mathematical approach, tribunals should ensure that the **2.112** periods of work and of absence are correctly compared with each other. In Berwick Salmon Fisheries Co Ltd v Rutherford and ors 1991 IRLR 203, EAT, the claimants were fishermen engaged on a seasonal basis. Normally the season ran from February to September but in 1986 and 1987 it did not start until April. In December 1987 the employer sold the business and the fishermen claimed redundancy payments. When considering whether the fishermen's employment was continuous, a tribunal contrasted the most recent absence of 29 weeks with the sum of the two surrounding periods of work – which totalled 46 weeks in all. The EAT held that the tribunal had erred in its approach. It had counted two periods of employment but only one period of absence, even though each period of employment was followed by a period of absence. On looking at the facts correctly, it could be seen that in the last two years the employees had spent more time out of work than in. The breaks of employment did not therefore constitute temporary cessations of work within the meaning of S.212(3)(b) and continuity was not preserved.

Unpredictable gaps in employment. In Flack and ors v Kodak Ltd (above) – a **2.113** case involving employment which fluctuated according to seasonal needs on an intermittent and irregular basis – an employment tribunal followed the method

129

advocated by Lord Diplock in Ford v Warwickshire County Council (above). It worked backwards from the employees' final dismissal dates, looked at each gap in employment and expressed its length as a percentage of the lengths of the periods of employment on either side. In each case it found at least one gap that was substantial in percentage terms and it concluded that those gaps, which all fell within the last two years of employment, broke continuity so that none of the claimants qualified for a redundancy payment when their department was closed down.

The Court of Appeal unanimously agreed with the EAT that the tribunal had applied the wrong test. The Ford case had been one of fixed-term contracts with a completely regular pattern of employment. In the instant case, by contrast, the claimants had been employed at irregular intervals over a period of between three and 11 years. To qualify for redundancy payments they had to show two years' continuous employment ending with the final dismissal, but all had periods of absence during those two years, as well as during their earlier employment. It was agreed by both sides that these absences were because of a cessation of work: the only question at issue was whether the cessations were 'temporary'.

2.114 Moreover, it had been conceded at the outset of the Ford case that the breaks involved were 'temporary' and Lord Diplock's remarks were obiter – i.e. not an essential part of the decision. The right test when there has been an irregular pattern of intermittent employment is to look at all the circumstances in the light of the whole history of employment, as stipulated by the House of Lords in Fitzgerald v Hall, Russell and Co Ltd 1970 AC 984, HL. Sir John Donaldson MR gave an instructive example. An employee works continuously for ten years, then business falls off. He is absent because of a cessation of work for one week, works again for another week, then is laid off because of a cessation of work for four weeks, then works a final week and is dismissed on account of redundancy. The four-week absence is 200 per cent of the two one-week periods on either side and on the strict mathematical approach adopted by the tribunal it could not be regarded as temporary and would break continuity. Sir John thought that such a result would be 'an obvious nonsense': no tribunal that looked at a four-week break in the context of the complete employment history of over ten years would be likely to regard it as anything but temporary.

An example of the type of irregular employment to which the comments of the Court of Appeal in the Flack case were relevant is Corkhill v North Sea Ferries EAT 275/91. In that case the employee was a merchant seaman employed on board ferries first by P&O and then by NSF, an associated employer. The work was seasonal, with business dropping off in the winter. The employee started work with P&O in 1984, working for periods of between three and 19 months with gaps of varying lengths in between. In 1989 he transferred to NSF. He worked for nine months, had a break of approximately three months, and then worked for another five months before he resigned. A tribunal, when considering whether he had continuous service from 1984, decided that it should disregard his service with P&O on the ground that 'that employment has now ceased and only the subsequent employment by [NSF] is relevant here'. It held that the three-month period broke the employee's continuity. However, on appeal, the EAT ruled that the tribunal had been wrong to disregard the earlier period of employment. It noted the decisions in the Fitzgerald and Flack cases and held that the employee's employment with P&O was not irrelevant to the issue of temporary cessation, where the whole pattern of employment needs to be examined.

Arrangement or custom. As noted above, continuity can be preserved by **2.115** 'arrangement or custom' under S.212(3)(c) ERA. Theoretically there is no limit to the period of absence that can qualify under this provision, although the length of the absence may affect a tribunal's assessment of whether the employee continued to be regarded as continuing in employment despite the fact that the contract of employment has been terminated.

Section 212(3)(c) has been relied on by teachers employed on fixed-term contracts, who have argued that there is a custom that employment is regarded as being continuous during summer vacations following the termination of their contracts at the end of the summer term and the start of new contracts at the beginning of the autumn term. The EAT considered this matter in ILEA v Rowe EAT 158/81 and was at least prepared to allow that, where there is a succession of fixed-term contracts and everyone anticipates that renewal will take place, a custom within the terms of S.212(3)(c) could be established. However, it is generally the case that, whenever the issue of continuity arises in the context of teaching, the matter is decided on the basis of whether there has been a 'temporary cessation of work' under S.212(3)(b) in accordance with Ford v Warwickshire County Council (above).

In Clitheroe v Canal and River Trust ET Case No.1805771/13 an employment **2.116** tribunal held that a fixed-term employee had failed to establish a custom whereby continuity was preserved between contracts. C was employed as a lock-keeper under a series of fixed-term contracts between March 2007 and November 2012. His contracts tended to begin in February/March and end in October/November. In the tribunal's view, there was no arrangement or custom whereby continuity was preserved between contracts, only a hope that in the following year there would be work which would be offered when the need to increase the number of lock-keepers arose in the spring.

Is Reg 8(2)(a) compatible with the Directive? In its response to the **2.117** Government's consultation on the draft FTE Regulations in April 2002, the TUC raised concerns about the effect of the four-year continuous employment requirement on the ability of fixed-term employees to qualify for permanent status under Reg 8. The TUC expressed the view that unscrupulous employers

131

could seek to avoid their duties under the Regulations by ensuring that fixed-term employees had gaps between successive contracts preventing them from satisfying the four years' continuous employment requirement. However, the TUC's recommendation that the four-year period should be reduced to two years or less was not taken up by the Government.

To compound the TUC's concerns, it has been held that in determining whether S.212(3)(b) applies, it is irrelevant that the employer may have been pursuing a deliberate policy of ensuring that its employees did not accrue sufficient service to qualify for employment rights – Booth and ors v United States of America 1999 IRLR 16, EAT. In Harding v Department of Employment ET Case No.42000/95 H was employed on a series of fixed-term contracts but had one break of approximately five months. A tribunal held that there was no temporary cessation of work as there was work available but it had not been allocated to H. The fact that the employer had deliberately not offered the work to H so as to ensure that she did not accrue continuous employment did not assist her.

2.118 However, these decisions must be thrown into doubt in light of the ECJ's decision in Adeneler v Ellinikos Organismos Galaktos 2006 IRLR 716, ECJ. At issue in that case were provisions of Greek law which provided for the conversion of successive fixed-term contracts into a contract of permanent duration. Presidential Decree No.81/2003 provided that 'successive' fixed-term contracts aimed at covering the fixed and permanent needs of the employer, and whose total duration amounted to two years, would automatically be converted into contracts of indefinite duration. However, contracts were to be regarded as 'successive' for this purpose only if they were separated by a period of not longer than 20 days.

The claimants challenged the compatibility of this definition of 'successive contracts' with the FTW Directive. The ECJ noted that although the definition of 'successive' in this context had been left to Member States to determine under national law, this margin of appreciation was not unlimited and must not compromise the objective that the Directive strives to achieve. Because the definition of 'successive' was key to the Directive's effectiveness, a restrictive definition would compromise its aims – for example, an employer could easily circumvent the rule simply by leaving the requisite length of time between contracts. The Decree was therefore incompatible with the Directive.

2.119 Although this case focuses on specific provisions of Greek law, the ECJ's decision that the exclusion of fixed-term contracts separated by more than 20 working days from the provisions allowing for automatic conversion into permanent contracts was incompatible with the Directive may be relevant to UK law. As noted above, the automatic conversion provisions of the FTE Regulations depend on the employee being able to show four years' continuous employment under fixed-term contracts, calculated in accordance with the rules set out in Ss.210–219 ERA. Under those rules, a week during which a contract of employment does not subsist breaks continuity. Although there are numerous exceptions to that rule – for example, where the break is a temporary cessation of work (see 'Temporary cessation of work' above) or where there is a custom or arrangement which preserves continuity (see 'Arrangement or custom' above) – these exceptions tend to be restrictive in their ambit. As a result, fixed-term employees may find themselves unable to bridge continuity between successive contracts and therefore be denied permanent status at the end of the four-year period. Such employees might well argue that, in the light of the ECJ's ruling in Adeneler, the continuity rules are too restrictive to comply with the FTW Directive.

Objective justification   2.120

Under Reg 8(2) a fixed-term contract can be renewed beyond the four-year period where this is justified on objective grounds. In keeping with the concept of objective justification in other areas of discrimination law, the use of a further fixed-term contract should be:

- aimed at achieving a legitimate objective; for example, a legitimate business objective

- necessary to achieve that objective, and

- an appropriate way to achieve that objective.

Although the assessment of the objective reason put forward must refer to the renewal of the most recent employment contract entered into, the existence, number and cumulative duration of successive contracts of that type concluded in the past with the same employer may be relevant in the context of that overall assessment – Kücük v Land Nordrhein-Westfalen 2012 ICR 682, ECJ.

Unsurprisingly, the ECJ in Adeneler v Ellinikos Organismos Galaktos (above) **2.121** held that the fact that national legislation authorises the use of successive fixed-term contracts is not in itself objective justification. 'Objective reasons' meant precise and concrete circumstances characterising a given activity which, in that context, justify the use of such contracts. The authorisation of the use of fixed-term contracts in a general and abstract manner by statute (in that case, a Greek Presidential Decree) without specific justification does not meet those criteria.

In Duncombe v Secretary of State for Children, Schools and Families 2011 ICR 495, SC, the Supreme Court gave some useful guidance on the issue of objective justification under the FTE Regulations. The claimants were employed by the Secretary of State to work as teachers in a European School (i.e. a school established by the EU and Member States for the education of the children of staff working in EU institutions) – F in the UK and D in Germany. Teaching posts in European Schools are usually subject to a maximum of nine years'

133

duration under the Staff Regulations made by the Governors of the European Schools in 1996 (the Nine Year Rule). Under those Regulations, teachers are employed on an initial two-year probationary period, which can be followed by a contract of three years, then a final contract of four years. In exceptional cases, an extension of one further year may be granted. In most Member States, the teachers are permanent employees of the state and return to work in their home countries at the end of their secondment to a European School. However, since teachers in the UK are generally employed by local education authorities or by the governing body of the school in which they work, the Nine Year Rule presents a problem for the UK Government in so far as the Secretary of State has to employ teachers specifically to work in the European Schools and on fixed-term contracts which reflect the Nine Year Rule. As a result, there is no work for these teachers to return to once their secondment to the European Schools is over.

2.122 Baroness Hale, giving the leading judgment in the Supreme Court, began by noting that the teachers' claims were in fact about the Nine Year Rule itself, not the three- or four-year periods which comprise it. In other words, they were complaining about the fixed-term nature of their employment rather than about the use of successive fixed-term contracts that make up that employment. She observed that the FTE Regulations and the Directive are only concerned with the prevention of discrimination against workers on fixed-term contracts and the abuse of successive fixed-term contracts. Employing people on single fixed-term contracts, she noted, does not offend against either the Regulations or the Directive, and had the claimants been employed on a single fixed-term contract of nine years, they would have had no complaint. As a result, it was not the Nine Year Rule which had to be justified, but the use of the latest fixed-term contract bringing the employment up to nine years.

In Baroness Hale's view, the use of a fixed-term contract in these circumstances could be 'readily justified' by the existence of the Nine Year Rule. The teachers were employed to do a particular job which could only last for nine years. As a result, the Secretary of State could not foist them on the schools for a longer period. Furthermore, the teachers could not be employed to do any alternative work because there was none available. Baroness Hale went on to say that there was also no question of the Staff Regulations trumping the Directive. She took the view that there was no inconsistency between them, since those Regulations were concerned with the duration of a secondment to a European School, not the duration of employment. It followed that the case of Adeneler v Ellinikos Organismos Galaktos (above), in which the ECJ held that a Greek national law which conflicted with the Directive did not amount to objective justification for the purposes of the Directive, was not relevant.

2.123 **Temporary cover.** The need to cover staff shortages may in principle constitute an objective reason justifying the continued use of fixed-term contracts, even if temporary cover is required on an ongoing basis. This was confirmed by the ECJ in Kücük v Land Nordrhein-Westfalen (above), which observed that where an employer has a large workforce, it is inevitable that temporary replacements will frequently be necessary due to employees being on sick, parental, maternity or other leave. In these circumstances the temporary replacement of employees could constitute an objective reason under Clause 5(1)(a) of the Directive justifying the use of successive fixed-term contracts. According to the Court, this conclusion was all the more compelling where, as in the case before it, national legislation justifying the renewal of fixed-term contracts also pursued recognised social policy objectives. Indeed, previous ECJ case law had held that the concept of 'objective reason' in Clause 5(1)(a) encompasses the pursuance of social policy objectives, which include pregnancy and maternity protection and reconciling professional and family obligations – objectives met by using successive fixed-term contracts to provide temporary cover.

However, the ECJ also emphasised that the renewal of fixed-term contracts in order to cover the need for permanent staff (as opposed to the need for replacement staff) is not justified under Clause 5(1)(a). The renewal of successive fixed-term contracts must be intended to cover temporary, as opposed to permanent, needs. But the ECJ stressed that the mere fact that the need to cover temporary personnel shortages could be met by hiring permanent staff – even where those shortages are recurring or even permanent – did not mean that an employer who uses successive fixed-term contracts is acting in an abusive manner contrary to Clause 5(1). To hold that that provision requires the moving of a fixed-term worker onto a permanent contract where an employer has a permanent need for replacement staff would go beyond the objectives of the Directive and would disregard the discretion left to Member States in implementing it into national law.

Collective modification. As the BERR guidance pointed out, it is possible for **2.124** employers and employees' representatives to agree objective reasons as part of a collective or workforce agreement (see 'Collective modification of the rules' below). For example, the employers and union or other representatives of professional sports people, actors or other employees who work in sectors where it is traditional to work on fixed-term contracts may agree, in a collective or workplace agreement, that the nature of the profession or work should be regarded as an objective reason for continued employment on fixed-term contracts.

Unfavourable changes to terms and conditions 2.125
In Huet v Université de Bretagne Occidentale Westfalen 2012 ICR 694, ECJ, the ECJ held that when providing for the automatic conversion of a fixed-term employment contract into an employment contract of indefinite duration, Member States must ensure that this does not result in any material amendments to the clauses of the previous contract in a way that is, overall, unfavourable to

the person concerned. They are not, however, obliged to ensure that the permanent contract reproduces in identical terms the principal clauses set out in the previous contract.

The Huet decision is likely to have limited impact in the UK since, as mentioned above, Reg 8 of the FTE Regulations states that an employee on a fixed-term contract will automatically be regarded as a permanent employee if, among other things, he or she has been employed on fixed-term contracts for over four years. The mechanism by which it achieves this is to provide, in Reg 8(2), that the provision of the fixed-term contract that restricts its duration will be of no effect. The consequence is that the formerly fixed-term employee becomes a permanent employee on exactly the same terms and conditions as before – the only difference between the two contracts is the absence of a term limiting its duration.

2.126 Collective modification of the rules

Under Reg 8(5) of the FTE Regulations the successive fixed-term contracts provisions set out in Reg 8(1)–(3) can be modified by way of a collective or workforce agreement in order 'to prevent abuse arising from the use of successive fixed-term contracts'. Such an agreement can relate to any employee or particular description of employees and can specify one or more of the following:

- a maximum total period for which the employee or employees may be continuously employed on a fixed-term contract or on successive fixed-term contracts – Reg 8(5)(a). (This in effect allows for a variation, up or down, of the four-year continuous employment requirement)

- the maximum number of successive fixed-term contracts and/or renewals which may validly be used before the employee is regarded as permanent – Reg 8(5)(b)

- the grounds upon which the use or renewal of a fixed-term contract may be objectively justified – Reg 8(5)(c).

Regulation 8(5) gives employers and employees the option of entering into a collective or workforce agreement in order to provide an alternative to the statutory scheme. However, as that provision makes clear, any agreement made pursuant to Reg 8(5) must also be aimed at preventing abuse arising from the use of successive fixed-term contracts. What is unclear, though, is whether this is a statutory requirement, in the sense that an otherwise valid agreement made under Reg 8(5) would be rendered invalid if it was apparent from its terms that it was significantly less effective at preventing such abuse when compared to the statutory scheme.

2.127 Collective agreements. A 'collective agreement' is defined by Reg 1(2) as a 'collective agreement within the meaning of S.178 of the Trade Union and Labour Relations (Consolidation) Act 1992. S.178(1) provides that a collective agreement is 'any agreement or arrangement made by or on behalf of one or more trade unions and one or more employers or employers' associations'.

The trade union parties to any agreement must be independent within the meaning of S.5 TULR(C)A – Reg 1(2). This means that they must not be under the domination or control of an employer and must not be liable to interference by an employer (arising out of the provision of financial or material support or by any other means) tending towards such control.

Workforce agreements. A workforce agreement provides a non-union means **2.128** of varying the provisions on successive fixed-term contracts. It is defined in Reg 1(2) as an agreement between an employer and its employees or their representatives in respect of which the conditions set out in Schedule 1 to the Regulation are satisfied. It is important to note that employees whose terms and conditions are provided for to *any extent* in a collective agreement cannot also be covered by a workforce agreement. This is because the provisions concerning workforce agreements apply only in respect of 'relevant members of the workforce', and such members are defined in para 2 of Schedule 1 to the FTE Regulations as 'all of the employees employed by a particular employer, excluding any employee whose terms and conditions of employment are provided for, wholly or in part, in a collective agreement'.

Under para 1 of Schedule 1 there are a number of criteria that must be satisfied if the workforce agreement is to be valid. The agreement must:

- be in writing
- have effect for a specified period that does not exceed five years
- apply either to all relevant members of the workforce or to all relevant members of the workforce who belong to a particular group
- be signed by the representatives of the workforce or representatives of the particular group of employees to which the agreement applies (excluding, in either case, any representative who is not a relevant member of the workforce on the date on which the agreement is first made available for signature).

Note that in the case of an employer who employs 20 or fewer employees on **2.129** the date when the agreement is first made available for signature, the agreement may be signed by a majority of all the employees employed by the employer.

Before the agreement is made available for signature, the employer must provide all the employees to whom it is intended to apply with copies of the text of the agreement and such guidance as those employees might reasonably require in order to understand the agreement fully.

The option of reaching an agreement with a particular group of employees is aimed at modifications in relation to particular sites, departments or categories

137

of employee. Where an agreement relates to a 'particular group', this means 'the relevant members of a workforce who undertake a particular function, work at a particular workplace or belong to a particular department or unit within their employer's business' – para 2, Sch 1.

2.130 *Employee representatives.* As noted above, a workforce agreement must be signed by representatives of the workforce or of a particular group of employees, except where the employer employs 20 or fewer employees, in which case the agreement can be signed instead by a majority of the employees. Under para 2 of Schedule 1 'representatives of the workforce' are defined as 'employees duly elected to represent the relevant members of the workforce', while 'representatives of the group' are defined as 'employees duly elected to represent the members of a particular group'. The requirements relating to the election of representatives are set out in para 3 of Schedule 1. They are that:

- the number of representatives to be elected is determined by the employer

- the candidates for election must be relevant members of the workforce, and the candidates for election as representatives of a group must be members of that group

- no employee who is eligible as a candidate should be unreasonably excluded from standing

- all the relevant members of the workforce or group must be entitled to vote

- the employees entitled to vote must be able to vote for as many candidates as there are representatives to be elected, and

- the election must be conducted so as to secure that, so far as is reasonably practicable, those voting do so in secret, and the votes given at the election are fairly and accurately counted.

Employees who are representatives of members of the workforce for the purposes of Schedule 1 or who stand for election have the right not to suffer a dismissal or detriment as a result – Reg 6(1), (2) and (3)(a)(viii) (see 'Unfair dismissal rights – automatically unfair dismissal' and 'Protection from detriment' above for further details).

2.131 *Employee's refusal to sign a workforce agreement.* Under Reg 6(1) and (3)(a)(vii) of the Regulations a dismissal will be automatically unfair where the reason, or principal reason, for the dismissal is that the employee has declined to sign a workforce agreement for the purpose of modifying the Reg 8 provisions (see 'Unfair dismissal rights – automatically unfair dismissal' above). Similarly, an employee has the right not to be subjected to any detriment by any act, or deliberate failure to act, of the employer on the ground that he or she has declined to sign a workforce agreement – Reg 6(2) and (3)(a)(vii) (see 'Protection from detriment' above for further details).

Written statements
2.132

A fixed-term employee who considers that by virtue of Reg 8 he or she is a permanent employee may request in writing from the employer a written statement confirming that this is the case. The employer must then, within 21 days of the request, provide written confirmation that the employee's contract is to be regarded as permanent or, alternatively, provide a statement giving reasons why his or her contract remains fixed term – Reg 9(1). If the reasons given by the employer as to why the employee's contract remains fixed term include an assertion that there are objectively justifiable grounds for the use or renewal of a fixed-term contract, the employer must provide a statement of those grounds – Reg 9(2).

Under Reg 9(3) a written statement provided by an employer under Reg 9 is admissible as evidence in any proceedings before a court, an employment tribunal and the Inland Revenue Commissioners (now Her Majesty's Revenue and Customs). It should be noted that this rule applies to any proceedings, and not just to proceedings under the Regulations (unlike a written statement of reasons for less favourable treatment under Reg 5 – see 'Right to receive written statement' above). If it appears to the court or tribunal in any proceedings that the employer has deliberately and without reasonable excuse omitted to provide a statement, or has given a statement that is evasive or equivocal, the court or tribunal may draw any inference which it considers just and equitable for it to draw – Reg 9(4).

Enforcement and remedies
2.133

Some of the rights accorded to fixed-term employees – like the right to claim unfair dismissal – are enforced under the ERA. Others – including the right not to be treated less favourably and the right not to suffer a detriment – are enforced under the FTE Regulations themselves. In most cases, however, the first step a fixed-term employee should take is to ask his or her employer for a written statement, regardless of the type of claim he or she may subsequently pursue.

Under Reg 5, a fixed-term employee who considers that his or her employer may have treated him or her less favourably than a permanent employee contrary to Reg 3 may submit a request in writing to the employer for a written statement of the reasons for the treatment. In addition, where an individual considers that by virtue of Reg 8 he or she is a permanent employee, he or she may request in writing a written statement confirming that this is the case – Reg 9. Indeed, an individual who wishes to apply for a declaration under Reg 9(5) that he or she is a permanent employee *must* first apply for a written statement under Reg 9(1).

A Reg 5 written statement is admissible in evidence in any proceedings under 2.134 the Regulations – Reg 5(2). A Reg 9 written statement is admissible in *any*

139

proceedings, i.e. not just proceedings under the Regulations. An employer's failure to supply a written statement has no direct legal effect in itself. However, a tribunal may draw any inference that it considers just and equitable if it appears that the employer deliberately and without reasonable excuse omitted to provide a statement, or that the written statement is evasive or equivocal – Regs 5(3) and 9(4). For further details, see 'Right to receive written statement' and 'Gaining permanent status – written statements' above.

Written statements of the reasons for dismissal are governed by S.92 ERA and are discussed in IDS Employment Law Handbook, 'Unfair Dismissal' (2010), Chapter 21, 'Written reasons for dismissal'.

2.135 Tribunal complaints

Under the Regulations a fixed-term employee may present a complaint to an employment tribunal that he or she has:

- suffered less favourable treatment contrary to Reg 3(1)

- not been informed of available vacancies under Reg 3(6)

- suffered a detriment contrary to Reg 6(2) – Reg 7(1).

In respect of the right not to be treated less favourably under Reg 3(1), a fixed-term employee can complain that he or she has been treated less favourably with regard to the terms of his or her contract or by being subjected to any other detriment by any act, or deliberate failure to act, of the employer. Reg 3(6) also gives fixed-term employees a free-standing right to be informed of available vacancies. Unlike the right to receive a written statement, this right can be the subject of tribunal proceedings in itself. Thus, even if the employee does not feel that he or she has been discriminated against in the selection procedure for a permanent post, the fact that he or she was not informed of it could give rise to an action.

2.136 A tribunal also has jurisdiction under Reg 9(5) to make a declaration to the effect that an employee's fixed-term contract should be treated as a contract of indefinite duration pursuant to Reg 8. An employee seeking such a declaration must request a written statement from the employer under Reg 9(1) asking for confirmation that the contract is permanent prior to bringing a claim before the tribunal – for further details, see 'Gaining the status of a permanent employee' above.

Note that unfair dismissal complaints made in respect of Reg 6(1) should be brought under Part X of the ERA. Claims for redundancy payments should be bought under Part XI of the ERA. Remedies for unfair dismissal are explained in IDS Employment Law Handbook, 'Unfair Dismissal' (2010), Chapter 14, 'Remedies', while redundancy payments are discussed in IDS Employment Law Handbook, 'Redundancy' (2011), Chapter 6, 'Redundancy payments'.

Time limit for bringing a claim. Complaints under Reg 7 must be made within 2.137 three months of the date of the less favourable treatment or detriment, or, where an act (or failure to act) is part of a series of similar acts (or failures to act) comprising the less favourable treatment or detriment, the last of them – Reg 7(2)(a). In the case of a complaint that the employee was not informed of an available vacancy under Reg 3(6), the complaint must be presented within three months of the date (or last date) on which other individuals (whether or not employees) were informed of the vacancy – Reg 7(2)(b). A tribunal may hear a claim presented out of time where, in all the circumstances of the case, it considers that it is just and equitable to do so – Reg 7(3).

For the purpose of calculating the date of the less favourable treatment or detriment:

- where a term in a contract is less favourable, the treatment will be regarded as taking place on each day of the period during which the term is less favourable – Reg 7(4)(a), and

- a deliberate failure to act will be treated as done when it was decided on – Reg 7(4)(b). In the absence of evidence to the contrary, an employer will be taken to decide not to act when it does an act inconsistent with doing the failed act or, if it has done no such inconsistent act, when the period expires within which it might reasonably have been expected to have done the failed act if it were to be done – Reg 7(5).

Note that the early conciliation rules apply to claims made under the FTE 2.138 Regulations. This means that special provisions apply to extend the time limits in Reg 7(2) in order to facilitate early conciliation under the auspices of Acas before a claim is submitted to the tribunal – Reg 7A. For details of the early conciliation scheme, see IDS Employment Law Handbook, 'Employment Tribunal Practice and Procedure' (2014), Chapter 3, 'Conciliation, settlements and ADR', under 'Early conciliation', and Chapter 5, 'Time limits', under 'Extension of time limit under early conciliation rules'.

Burden of proof. Once an employee has presented a complaint under Reg 3(1) 2.139 or Reg 6(2) to a tribunal, the burden of proof is on the employer to identify the ground for the less favourable treatment or detriment – Reg 7(6). As noted by an employment tribunal in Nisbet and anor v GMB Union ET Case No.2502453/12, this means that there is an inference that the treatment in question is on the ground of an employee's fixed-term status, which can be displaced by the employer if there is satisfactory evidence of some other reason.

Remedies
2.140
Where an employment tribunal finds that a complaint made under Reg 7 is well founded, it has the power to take any of the following steps that it considers just and equitable:

141

- make a declaration as to the rights of the employee and the employer in relation to the matters to which the complaint relates – Reg 7(7)(a)

- order the employer to pay compensation to the employee – Reg 7(7)(b)

- recommend that the employer take reasonable action within a specified time to obviate or reduce any adverse effect suffered by the employee – Reg 7(7)(c).

Where an employer fails, without reasonable justification, to comply with a recommendation made under Reg 7(7)(c), the tribunal may, if it thinks it just and equitable to do so, increase the amount of compensation ordered under Reg 7(7)(b) or, if no order has been made under that provision, make such an order – Reg 7(13).

2.141 **Amount of compensation.** The amount of compensation to be awarded under Reg 7(7)(b) will be such that the tribunal considers just and equitable in all the circumstances having regard to the infringement complained of and any loss attributable to that infringement – Reg 7(8). That loss will include any reasonable expenses and any benefit the employee might reasonably be expected to have had but for the infringement – Reg 7(9). There is no statutory cap on the amount of compensation that can be awarded but the usual rules on mitigation of loss and contributory conduct apply – Reg 7(11) and (12) – for details, see IDS Employment Law Handbook, 'Unfair Dismissal' (2010), Chapter 18, 'Compensatory awards: adjustments and reductions', under 'Failure to mitigate losses' and 'Contributory conduct'.

Regulation 7(10) provides that no award can be made for injury to feelings arising out of less favourable treatment under Reg 3. This contrasts with the position in respect of discrimination under the Equality Act 2010 (see IDS Employment Law Handbook, 'Discrimination at Work' (2010), Chapter 36, 'Compensation: heads of damage – injury to feelings', under 'Mitigation of loss') but reflects the position under the Part-time Workers (Prevention of Less Favourable Treatment) Regulations 2000 SI 2000/1551 – see Chapter 3, 'Part-time workers', under 'Enforcement and remedies – remedies and compensation'. It seems that compensation for detriment under Reg 6 *can* include an award for injury to feelings (since it is not specifically excluded).

2.142 **Contracting out**

By virtue of S.203(1) ERA, any provision in an agreement, whether or not it is contained in a contract of employment, purporting to exclude or limit the operation of any provision of the ERA or to preclude anybody from complaining to an employment tribunal is void. S.203(2) ERA sets out a number of exceptions to the general restriction on contracting out, the two most important of which are where the parties have entered into an Acas-conciliated agreement to settle a claim under S.203(2)(e), or where the parties have entered into a settlement agreement in accordance with S.203(2)(f) – see IDS Employment

Law Handbook, 'Employment Tribunal Practice and Procedure' (2014), Chapter 3, 'Conciliation, settlements and ADR', under 'Prohibition against contracting out of statutory rights', for further details.

Regulation 10 extends the application of S.203 to the FTE Regulations so that a fixed-term employee may not contract out of his or her rights under the Regulations except in accordance with the exceptions set out in S.203(2). It should be noted, however, that the Regulations do allow for the modification of the provisions relating to successive fixed-term contracts in Reg 8. Specifically, Reg 8(5) allows for the modification of the application of Reg 8(1)–(3) (which sets out the circumstances in which a fixed-term contract can be regarded as permanent) by way of a collective agreement or workforce agreement – see 'Gaining the status of a permanent employee – collective modification of the rules' above.

Acas conciliation   2.143
The Acas conciliation scheme contained in S.18 of the Employment Tribunals Act 1996 (ETA) applies to the following claims:

- the right of a fixed-term employee not to be treated less favourably on the ground of his or her fixed-term status – Reg 3(1) (see 'Equal treatment' above)

- the right of a fixed-term employee to be informed by his or her employer of available vacancies – Reg 3(6) (see 'Right to be informed of available vacancies' above)

- the right of a fixed-term employee not to suffer a detriment in relation to fixed-term employment – Reg 6(2) (see 'Protection from detriment' above)

- the right of an employee employed under successive fixed-term contracts to receive a written statement of variation that he or she is now a permanent employee – Reg 9 (see 'Gaining the status of a permanent employee' above).

Accordingly, Acas's powers and duties to attempt to conciliate employment disputes (including under the early conciliation scheme) will apply where the above rights are claimed. For further details, see IDS Employment Law Handbook, 'Employment Tribunal Practice and Procedure' (2014), Chapter 3, 'Conciliation, settlements and ADR'.

Appeals to EAT   2.144
The EAT's main jurisdiction for determining appeals from the decisions of employment tribunals is contained in S.21(1) ETA. That provision allows appeals to the EAT on any question of law arising from a decision of, or arising in any proceedings before, an employment tribunal under the FTE Regulations.

3 Part-time workers

According to statistics published by the Office of National Statistics for **3.1** January–March 2014, over eight million people work part time in the UK: nearly a quarter of the total workforce. A considerable majority of these deliberately choose to work part time, suggesting that part-time working should be viewed primarily as a form of flexible working adopted by workers needing to combine other responsibilities or activities, such as caring or studying, with work. However, in some cases work is offered on a part-time basis by employers to suit their own purposes; for example, in order to make financial savings or to cover peaks and troughs in demand.

Although part-time working basically involves the worker working fewer hours than full-time colleagues, the term can encompass a variety of different working patterns, including short days or weeks, job-sharing, term-time working, evening or weekend work, and casual or supply work. Similarly, part-time patterns may be adopted by a variety of types of 'worker', including employees, agency workers and the self-employed. While this chapter focuses on the rights and protections afforded to part-time workers on the basis of their part-time status, it should be borne in mind that the full extent of particular workers' employment rights and protections will depend primarily on their employment status.

The prevalence of part-time working today makes it hard to comprehend the **3.2** extent to which employment law and working practices used to cater primarily for work patterns traditionally associated with full-time employment. Part-time workers were frequently denied pro rata benefits and service-related benefits, and suffered lower rates of basic pay. Furthermore, until 1995, most employment protection legislation contained qualifying thresholds that excluded many part-time workers. These thresholds were abolished following

145

the House of Lords' decision in R v Secretary of State for Employment ex parte Equal Opportunities Commission and anor 1994 ICR 317, HL, that they were in breach of European sex equality law.

Indeed, until the implementation of the EU Part-time Work Directive (No.97/81) ('the PTW Directive') by the UK Government in 2000, part-timers sought to address their differential treatment primarily through recourse to the laws on sex discrimination and equal pay. This was on the basis that since most part-time workers are women, discriminatory treatment of part-time workers is likely to amount to indirect sex discrimination and/or breach the principle of equal pay for equal work, unless such treatment can be objectively justified. However, the laws on indirect sex discrimination and equal pay are complex and require part-time workers to show that there has been gender-based bias in the treatment received. To address this, the PTW Directive, extended to the UK by EU Directive (No.98/23), was adopted. This implements the Framework Agreement on part-time work concluded between European cross-industry organisations, which is annexed to the Directive and which aims to secure parity of treatment between part-time workers and their full-time counterparts on a gender-neutral basis. The Directive was implemented in the UK by the Part-time Workers (Prevention of Less Favourable Treatment) Regulations 2000 SI 2000/1551 ('the PTW Regulations'). These Regulations are the primary means for tackling discrimination against part-time workers and are the main focus of this chapter.

3.3 Scope of PTW Regulations

The core right contained in the PTW Regulations – the right not to be treated less favourably than a comparable full-time worker – applies to 'part-time workers' – Reg 5. However, the right not to be automatically dismissed found in Reg 7 is available only to part-time *employees* – see 'Unfair dismissal and unlawful detriment' below. In this section we discuss what is meant by a 'part-time worker' and 'part-time employee' under the PTW Regulations, and explain which groups of workers are specifically excluded from their scope.

3.4 What is a part-time worker?
The PTW Regulations define a part-time worker as a worker who is

- paid wholly or in part by reference to the time he or she works, and

- having regard to the custom and practice of the employer in relation to workers employed by the worker's employer under the same type of contract, is not identifiable as a full-time worker – Reg 2(2).

By contrast, a full-time worker is a person who is 'paid wholly or in part by reference to the time he works and, having regard to the custom and practice of the employer in relation to workers employed by the worker's employer

146

under the same type of contract, *is* identifiable as a full-time worker' (our stress) – Reg 2(1).

The first element of the definition of a part-time worker in Reg 2(2) indicates **3.5** that only those who are paid at least partly by reference to time worked are covered by the PTW Regulations. Therefore, a worker who is paid entirely on a piece-work basis, or as various stages of a project are fulfilled, will not be covered by the PTW Regulations, even if he or she works on fewer days or for shorter hours than others in the same workplace. This may exclude a number of seasonal or casual labourers. However, so long as at least one element of such a worker's pay reflects the time he or she has worked, he or she will constitute a 'part-time worker' and potentially fall within the protection of the Regulations.

The second element of the definition reflects the fact that whether or not someone works part time can only be determined relative to what it means to work 'full time'. In turn, what amounts to 'full-time' work is dependent upon the particular organisation or role in which the work is undertaken, as different jobs may have different expectations of what it is to work full time. Many jobs will adopt a traditional interpretation of 'full time', meaning working seven or eight hours a day for five days a week. By contrast, a full-time teacher in a maintained school is required to be available for work for 195 days in any school year, and for a maximum of 1,265 hours, including teaching and non-teaching time (School Teachers' Pay and Conditions Document).

In order to reflect such differences, the PTW Regulations define as 'part time' a worker who is not 'full time' in the context of the particular employer's custom and practice and the *type of contract* on which the worker is engaged – Reg 2(1).

'Same type of contract'. Regulation 2(3) provides some guidance as to what is **3.6** meant by the 'same type of contract' by reference to which a worker may be identified as full-time or part-time. The effect of this provision is that the following types of worker are to be regarded as distinct from one another and as being employed on *different* types of contract (i.e. *not* on the same type of contract):

- employees employed under a contract that is not a contract of apprenticeship – Reg 2(3)(a)

- employees employed under a contract of apprenticeship – Reg 2(3)(b)

- workers (who are not employees) – Reg 2(3)(c)

- 'any other description of worker that it is reasonable for the employer to treat differently from other workers on the ground that workers of that description have a different type of contract' – Reg 2(3)(d).

For example, in determining whether an employee (who is not on a contract of apprenticeship) is a part-time worker, he or she should be compared to

147

other employees (not on a contract of apprenticeship) of the employer who are identifiable as full-time workers. If he or she works for fewer days or hours than those 'full-time' employees, then he or she will be a 'part-time worker' (and, indeed, a part-time employee) for the purposes of the PTW Regulations. It is irrelevant what days or hours are worked by full-time employees on contracts of apprenticeship, or by full-time workers who do not have employee status.

3.7 Likewise, a worker who is not an employee should be compared to other workers of the employer who are not employees and who are identifiable as full-time. If that worker works for fewer days or hours than such full-time workers, he or she will be a part-time worker for the purposes of the PTW Regulations. It is irrelevant what days or hours are worked by full-time *employees* of the employer.

The last category listed in Reg 2(3) – 'any other description of worker that it is reasonable for the employer to treat differently from other workers on the ground that workers of that description have a different type of contract' – was considered by the House of Lords in Matthews and ors v Kent and Medway Towns Fire Authority and ors 2006 ICR 365, HL. This concerned a test case brought by 'retained' part-time firefighters who claimed that they had been treated less favourably than their full-time colleagues with regard to their terms and conditions of employment. Retained firefighters usually have other jobs, but spend time on call for operational duties in order to respond to peaks in demand.

3.8 The employment tribunal considered whether the two groups were employed under 'the same type of contract' as defined by Reg 2(3), in the context of determining whether or not the two groups were comparable for the purposes of the retained firefighters' claim. It noted that both groups appeared to be employed under contracts of employment falling within Reg 2(3)(a). However, despite there being a 'high degree of commonality' between the terms and conditions of the two groups, there were also significant differences. For example, the full-timers worked a 'very structured shift system of 42 hours per week with overtime', whereas the part-timers, aside from committing themselves to a weekly attendance of two to three hours for training and drill, were simply on call for between 84 and 156 hours a week. The tribunal concluded that, owing to the 'ad hoc demand-led nature' of the part-time role, the retained firefighters were 'a very special, anomalous, atypical and possibly unique group of employees' falling within what is now Reg 2(3)(d). It followed that they were to be regarded as workers whom it was reasonable for the employer to treat differently from the full-time firefighters on the ground that they had a 'different type of contract'.

However, when the case reached the House of Lords, a majority of their Lordships accepted the retained firefighters' argument that the types of contract listed in Reg 2(3) are mutually exclusive categories of working relationship.

Since, like the full-time firefighters, the retained firefighters were working under a contract of employment within the meaning of Reg 2(3)(a), they could not also be working under a 'different type of contract' within what is now Reg 2(3)(d). According to Baroness Hale, this is simply the final category on the list. It 'expressly refers to "any other description of worker" which in any ordinary use of language means "any description of worker other than those described in the preceding paragraphs"'. Accordingly, since both the retained and full-time firefighters worked under a contract falling within Reg 2(3)(a), the majority concluded that they worked under the 'same type of contract'.

Note that the Matthews case was decided in the context of determining whether **3.9** the claimants could properly compare their treatment with that of the full-time firefighters for the purposes of their claim of less favourable treatment under Reg 5, not of determining whether the retained firefighters were 'part-time' within the meaning of Reg 2(2). Thus, their Lordships' reasoning was influenced by the need not to undermine the purpose of the PTW Directive in bringing about equal treatment – see the section 'Less favourable treatment' below, under 'What is less favourable treatment? – comparable full-time worker'. However, it would be nonsensical for Reg 2(3) to be interpreted in one way for the purpose of determining whether someone is a part-time worker, and in another for the purpose of determining who is a comparable full-time worker, so their conclusion still applies in this context.

Worker/employee. For the purposes of the PTW Regulations, an 'employee' is **3.10** someone who has entered into or works or worked under a contract of employment – Reg 1(2). A 'worker' means someone who has entered into or works or worked under:

- a contract of employment, or

- any other contract, whether express (oral or in writing) or implied, whereby he or she 'undertakes to do or perform personally any work or services for another party to the contract whose status is not by virtue of the contract that of a client or customer of any profession or business undertaking carried on by the individual' – Reg 1(2).

This definition excludes many self-employed workers, where the contract on which they are relying is part of a business carried out on their own account.

The scope of Reg 1(2) was considered by the Supreme Court in Ministry of **3.11** Justice (formerly Department for Constitutional Affairs) v O'Brien 2013 ICR 499, SC, in the context of judicial office holders. In that case (which is also discussed under 'Exclusions – judicial office holders' below), O worked as a Recorder – a daily fee-paid, part-time judge – from 1978 until his retirement, on his 65th birthday, in 2005. At that time he requested a retirement pension calculated as a proportion of that to which a full-time Circuit Judge would be entitled if he or she had retired on the same date. The Department for

149

Constitutional Affairs – now the Ministry of Justice (MoJ) – rejected his request since, under the Judicial Pensions Act 1981 and the Judicial Pensions and Retirement Act 1993, fee-paid judges had no entitlement to a pension on retirement.

One of the issues the case raised was whether or not O was a 'worker'. The Supreme Court noted that although a Recorder holds an office marked by a high degree of independence of judgement, and is not subject to the directions of any superior authority as to the way in which he or she performs the function of judging, nevertheless that judicial office partakes of most of the characteristics of employment. However, it preferred not to express a concluded view on whether judges are 'workers', given that the question of whether judges are covered by the PTW Regulations is bound up with issues of EU law. It therefore asked the European Court of Justice to clarify if national law can determine whether judges are 'workers' within the meaning of Clause 2(1) of the Framework Agreement (annexed to the PTW Directive), or if 'worker' is an autonomous concept of European law. Clause 2(1) states that the Framework Agreement applies to 'part-time workers who have an employment contract or employment relationship as defined by the law, collective agreement or practice in force in each Member State'.

3.12 The European Court of Justice (ECJ) (in O'Brien v Ministry of Justice 2012 ICR 955, ECJ) held that there is no single definition of 'worker' in EU law and that the PTW Directive clearly allows Member States to interpret 'worker' in accordance with national law. However, Member States' discretion is not unlimited, and any definition must respect the effectiveness of the Directive and the general principles of EU law. Thus, Member States may not apply rules that jeopardise a Directive's objectives or deprive it of effectiveness. In particular, they may not remove, at will, certain categories of people from its protection.

In the ECJ's view, the fact that judges are office holders under national law is insufficient reason in itself to deprive them of the protection of the Directive. Judges may only be excluded if their relationship with the MoJ is, by its nature, substantially different from an employment relationship between an employer and a worker. This would be a matter for the Supreme Court to assess, bearing in mind the differentiation between workers and self-employed people. The ECJ pointed to various relevant factors in this regard, including the way judges are appointed and removed; the way their work is organised; the fact that they are expected to work during defined periods (albeit with more flexibility to manage their time than members of other professions); and their entitlement to sick pay, maternity and paternity pay, and other benefits. The ECJ noted that treating judges as workers in no way undermines the independence of the judiciary, or the right of Member States to provide that the judiciary has a particular status.

When the case returned to the Supreme Court, the Court confirmed its **3.13** provisional view that Recorders are 'workers'. There were clear differences between the position of a Recorder and that of a self-employed person: Recorders do public service work; they are expected to observe the terms and conditions of their appointment and to work defined times and periods; and, during service, they are entitled to the same benefits as full-time judges. These facts made it clear that Recorders are not free agents, able to work as and when they choose. For example, O had to explain, and apologise for, his failure to achieve the required number of sittings in two consecutive years, and the fact that he was a self-employed barrister merely underlined the different character of his commitment to the public service when he undertook the office of Recorder. Thus, the Court held that Recorders are in an employment relationship for the purposes of Clause 2(1) of the Framework Agreement and must therefore be treated as 'workers' under the PTW Regulations.

Parliamentary staff. Special provisions extend the scope of the PTW Regulations **3.14** to Parliamentary staff. Under Reg 14, any person who is employed under a worker's contract with the Corporate Officer of the House of Lords is covered. Similarly, under Reg 15 any person who was appointed by the House of Commons Commission, or who is a member of the Speaker's personal staff, will be protected.

Crown employment and armed forces. Persons in Crown employment are also **3.15** covered – Reg 12. For these purposes, references to an 'employee' and a 'worker' are to be construed as references to those in Crown employment to whom those definitions are 'appropriate'; and references to an employee's contract or that of a worker are to be construed as references to the terms of employment of those in Crown employment to whom those definitions are appropriate – Reg 12(3). By virtue of Reg 13, the Regulations also apply to the armed forces to a large extent, although this is subject to some limitations and exceptions – see 'Exceptions – armed forces' below.

Police service. The provisions relating to the police service are more **3.16** complicated. Those appointed to the office of constable or as a police cadet are to be treated as employed (under a contract of employment) by the 'relevant officer' (usually the chief officer of police) – Reg 16(1) and (2). However, constables seconded to the National Crime Agency (NCA) are to be treated as employed by the NCA – Reg 16(1A) and (1B). (Note that this regulation is particularly confusing in that although Reg 16(4) states that the 'relevant officer, as defined by paragraph (3), shall be treated as a corporation sole', paragraph (3) does not exist. This is presumably a drafting error; the reference should be to paragraph (2).)

Two part-time contracts. In Hudson v University of Oxford 2007 EWCA Civ **3.17** 336, CA, the Court of Appeal held that a worker was entitled to bring a claim under the PTW Regulations where he was employed under two part-time contracts but claimed that he was treated less favourably than a full-time worker doing the same work because he was paid less. H submitted that even though he was a part-time worker under two separate contracts, there was no reason in principle why the comparison should not be between a part-time worker doing two jobs and a full-time worker doing both jobs together. The Court of Appeal thought that it was at least arguable that, where an employee has two part-time contracts with the same employer and is performing contractual duties which are in practice so closely related that it would be difficult to say at a given moment whether he or she was performing his or her duties under one or the other contract or both, it would be necessary to have regard to both part-time contracts simultaneously in considering whether he or she has been treated less favourably. However, the success of such a claim would depend on the facts. In any event, it is envisaged that such circumstances will rarely arise in practice.

3.18 Exclusions

Not all part-time workers are protected by the PTW Regulations. The Regulations purport to exclude two categories of worker: certain members of the armed forces and holders of judicial office who are remunerated on a daily fee-paid basis.

3.19 Armed forces. The general rule is that the provisions of the PTW Regulations (other than the right to claim unfair dismissal under Reg 7(1)) apply to service as a member of the armed forces and to employment by a territorial, auxiliary and volunteer reserve association – Reg 13(1). However, a member of the armed forces may not bring a complaint to an employment tribunal without first making the complaint to an officer under the 'service redress procedures', and even then he or she may not start tribunal proceedings if he or she has withdrawn the complaint under the service redress procedures, or is to be treated as having withdrawn it under Reg 13(4) – Reg 13(3).

There is one exception to the general rule. Reg 13(2) provides that the PTW Regulations do not have effect in relation to service as a member of the reserve forces in so far as that service consists in undertaking training obligations under Ss.38, 40 or 41 of the Reserve Forces Act 1980, under S.22 of the Reserve Forces Act 1996 (RFA), or pursuant to regulations made under S.4 RFA; or consists in undertaking voluntary training or duties under S.27 RFA.

3.20 This exclusion was applied in R (Manson) v Ministry of Defence 2006 ICR 355, CA. M, a major in the Territorial Army, complained that he had been denied a pension by the Ministry of Defence in respect of his service, and that this infringed the PTW Regulations. However, an employment tribunal held that M's service was excluded by Reg 13(2) because, in so far as his service exceeded the 16 days' training a year required of him, it was with his consent or was done on a voluntary basis and so fell within S.22 or S.27 RFA. The tribunal refused to consider M's argument that the Reg 13(2) exclusion was incompatible with the PTW Directive on the ground that this issue had been raised too late, and the Court of Appeal declined to interfere with its decision.

Judicial office holders. Claimants have had more success in challenging the **3.21** blanket exclusion of judicial office holders remunerated on a daily fee-paid basis from the scope of the PTW Regulations – see Reg 17. In Ministry of Justice (formerly Department for Constitutional Affairs) v O'Brien 2013 ICR 499, SC (also discussed in the section 'What is a part-time worker?' above, under 'Worker/employee – are fee-paid judges workers?'), O worked as a Recorder – a daily fee-paid, part-time judge – until his retirement. He complained to an employment tribunal that the policy preventing part-time judges paid on a daily fee basis from receiving a judicial pension was unjustifiable less favourable treatment in breach of Reg 5 of the PTW Regulations. Although Reg 17 prevents judges remunerated on a daily fee basis from bringing a claim, O argued that this was incompatible with the PTW Directive.

As discussed above, the Supreme Court held that Recorders were 'workers' under the Regulations and in an employment relationship for the purposes of Clause 2(1) of the Framework Agreement. Given this conclusion, the exclusion in Reg 17 would only remain valid if the Ministry of Justice (MoJ) could justify on objective grounds treating Recorders differently to full-time judges with regard to access to the retirement pension scheme. The Court noted that the MoJ had not previously had a justification for the policy: its rationale for excluding fee-paid part-time judges was simply to save costs, which could not, by itself, constitute justification. This did not prevent the MoJ from advancing a different and better justification for maintaining the policy now, but the Court observed that greater respect is likely to be given to a policy which was carefully thought through by reference to the relevant principles at the time it was adopted. As Lord Justice Mummery pointed out in R (on the application of Elias) v Secretary of State for Defence 2006 IRLR 934, CA – a Court of Appeal case on justification of indirect discrimination – it would be difficult to justify the proportionality of the means chosen to carry out the aims if the alternatives were not examined or the necessary evidence gathered at the time.

The Court considered the aims now put forward by the MoJ to justify the **3.22** blanket exclusion: to fairly distribute the state's resources to fund judicial pensions (by supporting full-timers who make a greater contribution to the working of the justice system and who do not have other opportunities of providing for their retirement); to recruit a sufficiently high number of good quality candidates to salaried judicial office; and to keep the cost of judicial pensions affordable and sustainable. The Court accepted that, with regard to the first aim, it may be legitimate for an employer to operate a scheme that gives greater reward to those who are thought to need it the most, or who make a greater contribution. However, as the Advocate General had made clear when

153

giving her Opinion to the ECJ in this case (in O'Brien v Ministry of Justice 2012 ICR 955, ECJ), the unequal treatment of different classes of employees must be justified by the existence of precise, concrete factors, characterising the employment condition concerned in its specific context and on the basis of objective and transparent criteria, and here there were no precise and transparent criteria for assessing either need or contributions. Some part-timers require protecting as much as, if not more than, full-timers. Nor had it been shown that fee-paid part-timers, as a class, contribute less to the justice system than full-timers, as a class. In any event, the proper approach to differential contributions would be to make special payments for extra responsibilities. The argument also failed to take into account the benefits of having a cadre of fee-paid part-timers who could be flexibly deployed to meet fluctuations in demand.

Moving on to the two remaining aims, the Court did not doubt that recruiting a high quality judiciary was a legitimate aim, but it applied to the part-time judiciary as much as to the full-timers. Nor had it been shown that denying a pension to the part-timers had a significant effect upon the recruitment of full-timers. The Court further accepted that the ECJ's decision in Jørgensen v Foreningen af Speciallaeger and anor 2000 IRLR 726, ECJ, showed that while measures intended to ensure sound management of public expenditure may be justified, this would not extend to deliberately discriminating against part-time workers in order to save money. While the state may decide for itself how much it will spend on its justice system, the choices it makes must be consistent with the fundamental principles of equal treatment and non-discrimination – principles which could not depend on how much money the state had at a particular time and how it allocated it. Such an argument would not avail a private employer, and should similarly not avail the state in its capacity as employer. In the instant case, the MoJ's arguments amounted to nothing more than the fact that if Recorders got a pension then the pension of Circuit Judges would have to be reduced – a purely budgetary consideration which could not justify discrimination. Thus, the Court concluded that, as no objective justification had been shown for the difference in treatment, O was entitled to a pension on terms equivalent with a Circuit Judge but on a pro rata basis.

3.23 The upshot of the Supreme Court's decision in O'Brien is that Reg 17 is effectively redundant. Indeed, in response to this case and related decisions, the MoJ issued a statement on 17 June 2014 to the effect that it would implement a fee-paid Judicial Pension Scheme for fee-paid service from 7 April 2000 to 31 March 2015 for eligible fee-paid judicial office holders, to mirror the current scheme under the Judicial Pensions and Retirement Act 1993. A new Judicial Pension Scheme 2015, to apply to both fee-paid and salaried judicial office holders, is due to commence on 1 April 2015, following consultation in respect of the implementing regulations.

Less favourable treatment 3.24

The core right conferred by the PTW Regulations is the right for part-time workers not to be treated by their employer less favourably than the employer treats comparable full-time workers, either:

- as regards the terms of their employment contract – Reg 5(1)(a), or

- by being subjected to any other detriment by any act, or deliberate failure to act, of the employer – Reg 5(1)(b),

where the reason for the treatment is that the worker is a part-time worker, and the treatment is not justified on objective grounds – Reg 5(2).

In Hendrickson Europe Ltd v Pipe EAT 0272/02 the EAT held that an employment tribunal considering whether a breach of Reg 5 has occurred must answer the following four key questions:

- what is the treatment complained of?

- is that treatment less favourable?

- is that less favourable treatment on the ground that the worker is part-time?

- if so, is the less favourable treatment justified?

What treatment is covered? 3.25

Regulation 5(1) gives part-time workers a right not to be treated less favourably than a comparable full-time worker as regards contractual terms, or by being subjected to 'any other detriment', but otherwise does not explicitly define what sort of treatment might fall within its scope. The Framework Agreement (annexed to the PTW Directive) simply states that part-time workers should not be treated less favourably than comparable full-time workers 'in respect of employment conditions' – Clause 4(1).

The Government's online guide to 'Part-time workers' rights' (at www.gov.uk) suggests that part-time workers should receive the same treatment as full-time workers in respect of:

- pay rates

- sick pay, maternity, paternity and adoption leave and pay

- pension opportunities and benefits

- holidays

- training and career development

- selection for promotion and transfer

- redundancy selection

155

● opportunities for career breaks.

3.26 However, this is a non-exhaustive list and other forms of treatment may also come within the scope of Reg 5(1). For example, a part-time worker could bring a detriment claim under Reg 5(1)(b) in respect of his or her dismissal – Hendrickson Europe Ltd v Pipe (above).

Note that where a claimant has been subjected to less favourable treatment in more than one respect, at least in detriment cases under Reg 5(1)(b), tribunals should look at what has happened in its full context. Thus, in Hendrickson (above), the less favourable treatment in question incorporated 'the continued pressure on [the claimant] to work full time, that she would have to work full time if she wished to remain in employment, the selection for redundancy process devised by the employers as it applied to [her] (which meant that her dismissal became inevitable), and finally her dismissal'.

3.27 **Pro rata principle.** In determining whether a part-time worker has been treated less favourably than a comparable full-time worker, the 'pro rata principle' must be applied, unless it is inappropriate – Reg 5(3). This means that, where a comparable full-time worker receives a particular level of pay or benefit, a part-time worker is entitled to receive no less than the proportion of that pay or other benefit which reflects the number of hours that he or she works – Reg 1(2). For example, if a comparable full-time worker works five days a week and earns £20,000 a year, a part-time worker who works three days a week should earn no less than £12,000 a year.

However, where a part-time worker has been subjected to a detriment, such as being selected for redundancy on the ground of his or her part-time status, it would clearly be 'inappropriate' to apply the pro rata principle in determining whether there has been less favourable treatment. Nor would it be appropriate to pro-rate the provision of safety equipment, such as a protective helmet – see the opinion of the Advocate General in Österreichischer Gewerkschaftsbund v Verband Österreichischer Banken und Bankiers (Case C-476/12), ECJ.

3.28 Quantifiable pay and benefits, such as entitlements to bonuses, bank holidays and annual leave, are normally susceptible to a pro rata calculation. However, depending on how the entitlement is calculated, there may be no need to apply the pro rata principle, because proportionality is 'built in'. Consider the following examples (the last two of which are taken from the archived 2008 Department for Business, Enterprise and Regulatory Reform (BERR) guide, 'Part-time workers: The law and best practice – a detailed guide for employers and part-timers' (URN 02/1710) ('the BERR guide')):

● where annual leave is calculated in weeks, and a part-time worker works a proportion of each week, the part-time worker should be entitled to the same number of weeks' leave as a comparable full-time worker. However, he or she will receive fewer *days'* leave overall, as he or she works for only a proportion of each week

- a retailer allows its workers a career break of up to two years. The qualifying period for the break is three years. A part-time worker is entitled to a two-year break under the same conditions as a full-time worker

- a health authority provides its workers with four weeks' extra paid maternity leave, on top of their statutory entitlement. A part-time worker who works 20 hours a week will be entitled to the full four weeks in extra paid maternity leave.

Where possible, other benefits, such as health insurance, subsidised mortgages, **3.29** staff discounts and company cars, should be provided to part-time workers pro rata. Where this is not possible, employers will need to consider whether or not they can objectively justify withholding such benefits from part-time workers (see 'Justifying less favourable treatment' below). Alternatively, the whole benefit could be provided, or the pro rata financial equivalent, or the employer might pay a proportion of an annual insurance premium, leaving it to the worker to fund the rest.

Three examples (from the BERR guide):

- a finance company provides staff mortgages at a reduced rate of interest for all staff, both full-time and part-time. The same preferential rate of interest applies regardless of hours worked, and likewise the same multiplier to determine the mortgage advance

- as part of its package of benefits a company provides workers with new company cars every two years. It calculates that the benefit to part-time workers, many of whom work less than 50 per cent of normal hours, would be disproportionate to the cost of providing the car. Instead, it calculates the financial value of the benefit and provides part-time workers with a pro rata amount towards their travel expenses

- a post as a health visitor requires considerable driving, and hence a car is attached to the job. Two job-sharers share the car in order to fulfil their duties, each using the car on the days that they work.

In James and ors v Great North Eastern Railways EAT 0496/04 (also discussed **3.30** under 'Overtime' below) the EAT gave some guidance on the application of the pro rata principle set out in Reg 1(2). The fundamental purpose of this principle, stated the EAT, is to enable a valid comparison to be made between the remuneration of a part-time worker and that of his or her full-time counterpart, in order to identify any less favourable treatment and its extent. A tribunal addressing itself to Reg 5 should always consider whether it is appropriate to adopt the pro rata principle in the case before it and, if it is appropriate, how it should be applied.

In the James case, part-time workers complained of less favourable treatment where their full-time comparators, who were contractually obliged to work an average of 40 hours per week, were paid at a basic rate for the first 35 hours worked in a week, and at a rate of one and a quarter times the basic rate for the remaining five hours, owing to an 'additional hours allowance'. The part-time workers, however, were paid at the basic rate in respect of all their contractual hours. The EAT considered that in making a comparison between the two, the pro rata principle should be applied to the wages of the part-time claimants and their full-time counterparts as a whole. In its view, the claimants' proposed method of applying the principle to the additional hours allowance in isolation from their basic pay would not lead to a valid comparison, but would result in the claimants effectively 'claiming to be paid at a much higher hourly rate than their full-time counterparts'.

3.31 The EAT provided a calculation to illustrate the effect of the different methods of payment adopted by G Ltd in respect of full- and part-timers. Assuming a basic rate of pay of £10 per hour, a full-timer working his or her contractual hours would, taking the additional hours allowance into account, receive a weekly wage of £412.50 at an overall hourly rate of £10.31. In contrast, a comparable part-timer working 30 contractual hours per week would receive a weekly wage of £300 at an overall hourly rate of £10. The true difference in pay, in this illustration, would be £0.31 per hour.

3.32 **Pay.** Clearly, a right to be treated no less favourably in respect of the terms of the contract of employment encompasses a right to the same basic hourly rate of pay. In addition, a part-time worker may be entitled to enhanced rates of pay in special circumstances, where these apply to a comparable full-time worker. Consider the following examples (from the BERR guide):

- where an employer awards a Christmas bonus, part-time workers should be entitled to receive a pro-rated amount, according to the number of hours they work (see 'Pro rata principle' above)

- where working early and late shifts attracts time-and-a-half pay for full-time workers, part-time workers should also receive time-and-a-half pay for working those shifts. Note, however, that Reg 5 does not entitle part-time workers to overtime as soon as they work in excess of their normal working hours (see 'Overtime' below)

- a part-time care assistant should receive the same unsocial hours payment for working between midnight and 6 am as a comparable full-time colleague.

In O'Brien v Ministry of Justice ET Case No.4102933/13 an employment tribunal held that a fee-paid employment judge was treated less favourably than a comparable full-time salaried employment judge in respect of fee payments for decision-writing. O, a fee-paid employment judge, complained about the system under which she was paid fees for decision-writing. Under that system, where a decision could not be written up on the same day as a hearing, a fee-paid judge could claim a quarter of a day's sitting fee for writing-up time lasting three and a half hours or less, and half a day's sitting fee for writing-up time lasting over three and a half hours. However, salaried employment judges were afforded time during normal working hours for decision-writing, which was paid as part of their salary. O claimed that the system resulted in her being paid less for writing-up than a salaried employment judge, which amounted to less favourable treatment than a comparable full-time worker contrary to Reg 5(1). The Ministry of Justice argued that it rounded up fees for writing-up in some cases and rounded them down in others, so that, overall, fee-paid employment judges were paid in full for their time spent writing decisions.

The employment tribunal noted that the system for paying a decision-writing **3.33** fee to fee-paid employment judges appeared 'to be lacking in principle and rationale'. However, the question was not whether the system was fair but whether it was comparable between fee-paid and salaried employment judges. The tribunal found that the Ministry of Justice was unable to produce empirical evidence to support its 'averaging' defence. Furthermore, the tribunal found that fee-paid judges are not in fact paid in full because the most that a fee-paid employment judge can receive for a full day's decision-writing is a half day's fee. In contrast, a salaried judge receives his or her salary for such a day. Thus, the tribunal found that the Ministry of Justice had treated O less favourably than a comparable full-time salaried employment judge in respect of her right to a fee for decision-writing. The treatment was on the ground that O was a part-time worker because only fee-paid judges were subjected to the fee payment system.

Overtime. By virtue of Reg 5(4), a part-time worker must be paid the same **3.34** overtime rates as a full-time worker, but he or she does not become entitled to overtime pay until he or she has worked the same number of hours that a full-time worker must work in order to become so entitled. However, a practice of only offering available overtime to full-time workers may discriminate against part-time workers under the general principle in Reg 5(1).

The BERR guide gives the following example:

- a hotel, in which full-timers work five eight-hour days per week, hits a busy period in the run up to Christmas. It asks all its staff to work extra hours. A part-time worker who normally works 9–12 agrees to work 9–2. She receives her normal hourly rate of pay, with no overtime payment, for the additional hours. The same applies to a second part-time worker who normally works two days a week, and agrees to work four. A third part-time worker normally works three days a week, and agrees to work for five days and one evening. She receives her normal pay rate for the extra two days, but receives an overtime payment for the extra evening.

159

3.35 In some cases it may not be entirely clear whether a particular allowance amounts to an overtime payment. This was the issue in James and ors v Great North Eastern Railways EAT 0496/04 (also discussed under 'Pro rata principle' above). GNER's full-time workers were contractually obliged to work an average of 40 hours per week, calculated over an eight-week cycle. They were also required, on occasion, to work overtime. For the first 35 hours worked in a week, the workers were paid at a basic rate. Their pay for the remaining five contractual hours was paid at a rate of one and a quarter times the basic rate, owing to an 'additional hours allowance'. Time worked in excess of the 40 contractual hours was also paid at one and a quarter times the basic rate. Similarly, part-time workers were contractually obliged to work a set average number of hours per week. Unlike the full-time workers, however, they were paid at the basic rate in respect of all their contractual hours, receiving no additional hours allowance. Furthermore, their overtime was also paid at the basic rate, unless they exceeded 35 hours' work in a week, at which point any further hours worked were paid at the rate of one and a quarter times the basic rate.

J and two other part-time workers brought claims before an employment tribunal, alleging that GNER's payment structure discriminated against them contrary to the PTW Regulations. The tribunal dismissed their claims. In its view, the additional hours allowance amounted to an overtime payment and thus fell within the Reg 5(4) exception to the principle of discrimination. The tribunal referred to the allowance as an 'incentive' for the full-time workers to turn up to work in excess of 35 hours per week. However, on appeal the EAT noted that the exception contained in Reg 5(4) only applies where a part-time worker is treated less favourably in respect of *overtime* he or she has worked. In the EAT's view, this case did not involve such a scenario. The additional hours allowance in question was payable to full-time workers in respect of a proportion of their *normal* contractual hours. It followed that the alleged less favourable treatment stemmed from the fact that part-timers, who were not entitled to the allowance, were paid less than full-timers in respect of the contractual hours that they worked. Contrary to the tribunal's findings, the part-time workers' claims were not, in any way, based on overtime payments and therefore Reg 5(4) did not bite upon the claims.

3.36 **Pensions.** According to the ECJ, the term 'employment conditions' in Clause 4(1) of the Framework Agreement (annexed to the PTW Directive) covers pensions which depend on an employment relationship between worker and employer, but excludes statutory social security pensions, which are determined less by that relationship than by considerations of social policy – Istituto nazionale della previdenza sociale v Bruno and anor (C-395/08 and another), ECJ.

This means that employers must not treat part-time workers less favourably in terms of access to pension schemes and contributions, unless less favourable treatment can be objectively justified.

Holidays and holiday pay. Where a part-time worker works regular hours **3.37** each week, and holiday entitlement is expressed in weeks, his or her entitlement will be the same as that of a full-time worker. This is because the value of a week's holiday in terms of days or hours will naturally vary according to the length of a worker's normal working week. Accordingly, while a part-time worker is entitled to the same number of weeks' leave as a full-time worker, the entitlement expressed in terms of days will be less. For example, a worker who works half time, or 2.5 days a week, has the same entitlement to statutory annual leave as a worker who works five days a week – 5.6 weeks. However, this corresponds to half the number of days that the full-time worker may take: 14 working days a year.

However, where a part-time worker works irregular weeks, it will be more appropriate to calculate his or her holiday entitlement on a daily (or even hourly) basis pro rata to the full-time equivalent. See IDS Employment Supplement, 'Holiday Rights' (2008), Chapter 1, 'Right to annual leave', under 'Calculating leave entitlement – irregular working patterns' for assistance.

In Zentralbetriebsrat der Landeskrankenhäuser Tirols v Land Tirol 2010 IRLR **3.38** 631, ECJ, the European Court held that a right to paid annual leave accumulated during a period of full-time employment, and which the worker had not yet had the opportunity to exercise, could not be reduced pro rata upon the worker changing to part-time employment. Such a reduction was precluded by the EU Working Time Directive (No.2003/88) and the Framework Agreement on part-time work (annexed to the PTW Directive). Nor was it compatible with EU law to oblige a worker in that position to take the outstanding leave on a reduced level of holiday pay.

Bank and public holidays. The position regarding bank and public holidays **3.39** can give rise to some confusion. The basic principle is that part-time workers should not be treated less favourably than comparable full-time workers in respect of a contractual entitlement to bank and public holidays. As most bank holidays fall on a Monday, part-time workers who work regular days but not on Mondays are likely to be at a disadvantage. In most cases, an appropriate way of removing such disadvantage is to give all workers a pro rata entitlement to bank and public holidays, and/or days off in lieu, according to the hours they work.

In some cases, part-time workers who do work on Mondays will in fact be better off than comparable full-time workers, in terms of the proportion of bank and public holidays they are entitled to. If so, the employer may require such part-time workers to 'pay back' their holiday excess in the interests of fairness. However, full-time workers have no right to be treated no less favourably than part-time workers, so giving part-time workers more than their fair share of bank and public holidays would not breach the PTW Regulations.

3.40 A claimant alleging less favourable treatment in respect of bank and public holidays must be able to establish that the treatment was on the ground that he or she is a part-time worker – see 'Reason for less favourable treatment' below. In McMenemy v Capita Business Services Ltd 2007 IRLR 400, Ct Sess (Inner House), the Court of Session considered that even though a part-time worker was entitled to proportionately fewer bank and public holidays than full-time workers, there was no less favourable treatment because the reason for the difference was not the worker's part-time status. M worked part time for C Ltd in a call centre which operated seven days a week. All the call centre employees – whether part- or full-time – were subject to an identical term in their employment contracts providing that they were only entitled to the benefit of public holidays where these fell 'on [their] normal working day'. M worked on Wednesdays, Thursdays and Fridays, and therefore did not get time off on, or time in lieu of, public holidays that fell on Mondays. He brought a claim before an employment tribunal alleging that he had received less favourable treatment than a comparable full-time worker contrary to Reg 5.

The tribunal found that M had suffered a detriment compared with full-time members of his team because he did not receive time off for public holidays that fell on Mondays. However, it found that the reason for M's treatment had not been his part-time status, noting that a full-time worker could equally lose out on time off for public holidays where he or she worked only five of the seven days on which the call centre was open. The tribunal noted that in the year prior to M's claim, his line manager, K – who then worked Tuesdays to Saturdays – had also been told that he was only entitled to time off for public holidays where they fell on a day he normally worked.

3.41 The EAT and the Court of Session both upheld the tribunal's decision. The Court of Session thought that it was clear on the facts, and in particular the employer's policy on public holidays, that the reason the claimant suffered less favourable treatment than a comparable full-time worker was that he had agreed that he would not work on Mondays. If a full-time colleague of the claimant worked a fixed shift from Tuesday to Saturday, he or she would not receive the benefit of statutory holidays which fell on Mondays either. Conversely, if the claimant or any other part-time worker worked on Mondays they would receive the benefit of Monday public holidays in exactly the same way as full-time employees.

Unusually in this case the employer operated seven days a week, so that a number of full-time employees who worked over the weekends also missed out on public holidays. Such a situation could also act to the benefit of part-timers – for example, a part-timer working Monday to Wednesday would be in an advantageous position compared to a full-time worker who worked Tuesday to Saturday, since the part-time worker would receive all the benefits of the Monday public holidays whereas the full-time worker would receive none. But had the employer in the McMenemy case operated only between Monday and Friday, the normal working days of the full-time employees would by definition have included public holidays, and so it would have been arguable that the policy in respect of part-timers who did not work on public holidays was in breach of the PTW Regulations. When considering the reason why the part-time worker suffered the less favourable treatment, it would be impossible to find a full-time comparator who lost out on public holidays. In these circumstances the employer might find it difficult to argue that the reason the part-time employee did not get public holidays was simply that he or she did not work on those days, since it would be impossible to separate the fact of not working on certain days from the fact of being part time.

Access to training. Part-time workers should not be denied access to training **3.42** on the basis of their part-time status. It is worth observing that training courses are unlikely to be susceptible to the pro rata principle, and thus providing no less favourable treatment in terms of training may involve allowing part-time workers proportionally *more* time to attend training, with respect to their hours worked, than full-time workers. However, where the time and expense spent on training is disproportionate to the hours worked by a part-time worker, the employer may be able to objectively justify reducing the part-time worker's access to training – see 'Justifying less favourable treatment' below.

The BERR guide advises that it is best practice for employers to arrange training so as to ensure that it is conveniently located and timed for part-time workers, unless this is not possible. It gives the following example:

- a media company employs ten part-time and ten full-time staff. The company provides IT training for its staff. The course consists of two full days of training. This arrangement would make it difficult for its part-time workers to attend since they work mornings only. After a request from the company, the trainer agrees to offer the course as four mornings.

Redundancy selection. Employers may fairly dismiss for redundancy where **3.43** the requirements of the business for employees to carry out work of a particular kind, or for employees to carry out work of a particular kind in the place where they are employed, have ceased or diminished – S.139(1)(b) Employment Rights Act 1996. Where the requirements for employees to carry out particular work have diminished, but not sufficiently to lose a full-time post, an employer may be tempted simply to make a part-time worker redundant. However, this may constitute a detriment under Reg 5 unless the selection can be objectively justified.

Two case examples:

- **McGuinness v North Estates Ltd** ET Case No.2400578/08: a tribunal found that a part-time administrator was selected for redundancy because she worked part time. Another administrator who worked part time was also made redundant, whereas a full-time employee doing similar work was retained, and there was no evidence that the employer had considered retaining the part-time employees

- **Clarke v Brookside (1998) Ltd t/a Nottingham Volkswagen and anor** ET Case Nos.2600301/09 and another: C was employed as a fleet sales executive. Following a period of maternity leave she worked for three days a week. In April 2008 B Ltd recruited a new fleet sales manager to whom C was to report. The tribunal accepted C's evidence that he made comments about her being the 'part-time department' and 'a baby machine'. Following a downturn in business C was informed in October 2008 that she was at risk of redundancy. As she was pregnant she asked if she could bring forward her maternity leave and take a year's leave to give the market time to recover, but B Ltd rejected that proposal and she was dismissed as redundant later that month. A tribunal found that C was discriminated against on grounds of her gender and part-time working arrangement.

3.44 However, in Vij-Solanki v IDT Global Ltd ET Case Nos.2203531/08 and another V's claim of less favourable treatment on the ground of part-time status was rejected. In June 2008 V's employer had to make redundancies and V, who worked three days a week, was selected. She claimed, among other things, that in being selected for redundancy and dismissed she had been less favourably treated than her full-time colleagues. However, the tribunal found that apart from a remark that V did not show the same 'commitment' as the others in her pool, there was nothing in the selection exercise which could have led it to believe that V's status as a part-time worker was the reason for her treatment. The employer had demonstrated its willingness to accommodate flexible or part-time working in agreeing to V's two requests to reduce or change her hours following periods of maternity leave. The tribunal was satisfied, notwithstanding the comment regarding her commitment, that V's selection for redundancy was because she scored lower than her colleagues, and that there was no evidence that her scores were tainted by her part-time status. It noted that in fact it would have suited the employer's 'budgetary imperatives' better to have selected a full-time worker rather than V for redundancy.

3.45 **No need to exercise term in question.** It could be argued that there can be no less favourable treatment in respect of a term that has not yet been exercised. However, the EAT gave short shrift to an employer's contention to this effect in Sharma v Manchester City Council 2008 ICR 623, EAT. There the employer argued that Reg 5(1) does not allow an employee to challenge a less favourable term itself, but only to complain about treatment which is less favourable, and that therefore the mere existence of a less favourable term which has not been implemented in any way did not constitute less favourable treatment. However, the EAT held that it was open to a part-time worker to challenge the terms of his or her contract whether or not they have had any immediate practical impact upon him or her. It had 'no doubt' that a person is being treated less favourably as regards the terms of his or her contract if those contractual terms are less favourable. A part-time worker does not have to wait until the term is triggered to his or her detriment before he or she can commence proceedings.

In the EAT's view, the PTW Regulations make this clear in that, among other things, Reg 8(4)(a) provides that less favourable treatment with regard to contract terms shall be regarded as taking place on each day of the period in which the term is less favourable. Furthermore, one of the remedies available to employment tribunals under the PTW Regulations is to declare the rights of the claimant. In the EAT's view, that is plainly appropriate where less favourable terms have been imposed but not yet implemented. Thus, it was plainly possible for the mere existence of the term to constitute grounds for complaint.

Comparing treatment   3.46

The right under Reg 5 is the right to be treated no less favourably than a 'comparable full-time worker' – Reg 5(1). As discussed under 'What treatment is covered? – pro rata principle' above, in considering whether a part-time worker has been treated less favourably, the pro rata principle must be applied, where it is appropriate.

Regulation 2(4) sets out the criteria for establishing who is a comparable full-time worker in relation to a particular part-time worker. The effect of this provision is that a part-time worker can compare his or her position with that of a full-time worker if, at the time when the treatment that is alleged to be less favourable to the part-time worker takes place:

- both workers are employed by the *same employer* under the *same type of contract* (see 'Same employer and same type of contract' below)

- both workers are engaged in the *same or broadly similar work*, having regard, where relevant, to whether they have a similar level of qualification, skills and experience (see 'Same or broadly similar work' below); and

- the full-time worker works or is based at the *same establishment* as the part-time worker.

However, if there is no full-time worker working or based at the same **3.47** establishment as the part-time worker, the part-time worker may compare his or her treatment with that of a full-time worker who works or is based at a different establishment, provided that the full-time worker satisfies the first two requirements above.

The wording of Reg 2(4) reflects that of Clause 3(2) of the Framework Agreement (annexed to the PTW Directive), which provides that a comparable full-time worker is 'a full-time worker in the same establishment having the same type of employment contract or relationship, who is engaged in the same or a similar work/occupation, due regard being given to other considerations which may include seniority and qualification/skills'.

A concession by the employer that a claimant has been unlawfully discriminated against on the ground of his or her part-time status necessarily involves an acceptance that he or she has been treated less favourably than a comparable full-time worker – Royal Mail Group plc v Lynch EAT 0426/03. In such circumstances the claimant will have no need to identify such a comparator.

3.48 **Same employer and same type of contract.** The part-time worker must be employed by the same employer as his or her comparator. There is no provision for comparison with a worker employed by an associated employer.

The requirement for a comparator to be employed by the same employer on the same type of contract may mean that some part-time workers who are employed on unique types of contract are simply unable to demonstrate less favourable treatment. This may be a particular problem for workers on 'zero-hours' contracts. The ECJ recognised this in Wippel v Peek and Cloppenburg GmbH and Co KG 2005 ICR 1604, ECJ, where the Court found that there was no full-time worker in the establishment with the same type of contract or employment relationship as W for the purposes of the comparison required by the PTW Directive. A part-time worker such as W – who worked according to need, was paid by the hour only for the hours actually worked and who could choose to refuse work – could not compare herself with a full-time worker who was required to work a fixed number of hours a week for a fixed salary and who did not have the option of refusing the work. It followed that a contract such as W's, under which work was offered according to need and which did not provide for the length of weekly working time or for the organisation of working time, did not offend the Directive.

3.49 The PTW Regulations provide some guidance as to what is meant by being employed under the same type of contract by spelling out four categories of worker/employee who are to be regarded as being employed under *different* types of contract (vis-à-vis one another). As explained in the section 'Scope of PTW Regulations' above, under 'What is a part-time worker? – worker/employee', these are:

- employees employed under a contract that is not a contract of apprenticeship – Reg 2(3)(a)

- employees employed under a contract of apprenticeship – Reg 2(3)(b)

- workers (who are not employees) – Reg 2(3)(c), and

- 'any other description of worker that it is reasonable for the employer to treat differently from other workers on the ground that workers of that description have a different type of contract' – Reg 2(3)(d).

For example, a part-time employee (who is not on a contract of apprenticeship) can compare his or her treatment to that of a full-time employee (not on a contract of apprenticeship), because they are both on the same type of contract. However, he or she cannot compare his or her treatment with that meted out to a full-time employee on a contract of apprenticeship, or to a full-time worker who does not have employee status, because they are on different types of contract. Likewise, a part-time worker who is not an employee can compare his or her treatment to that of a full-time worker who is not an employee. However, he or she cannot compare his or her treatment with that of a full-time employee.

As discussed above, the House of Lords considered the meaning of the phrase **3.50** 'same type of contract' in Matthews and ors v Kent and Medway Towns Fire Authority and ors 2006 ICR 365, HL, and concluded that the four categories listed in Reg 2(3) are mutually exclusive. In that case, a number of 'retained' part-time firefighters argued that they had been treated less favourably than their full-time counterparts by being denied access to the Fireman's Pension Scheme, in respect of the arrangements for sick pay and with regard to increased pay for additional responsibilities.

The employment tribunal considered whether the retained firefighters could compare themselves with full-time firefighters for the purposes of their claim under the PTW Regulations. One issue was whether the two groups were employed under 'the same type of contract' for the purposes of Reg 2(4). The tribunal noted that both groups appeared to be employed under contracts of employment falling within Reg 2(3)(a). However, despite there being a 'high degree of commonality' between the terms and conditions of the two groups, there were also significant differences. For example, the full-timers worked a very structured shift system of 42 hours per week with overtime, whereas the part-timers, aside from committing themselves to a weekly attendance of two to three hours for training and drill, were simply on call for between 84 and 156 hours a week. The tribunal concluded that, owing to the 'ad hoc demand-led nature' of the part-time role, the retained firefighters were 'a very special, anomalous, atypical and possibly unique group of employees' falling within what is now Reg 2(3)(d). It followed that they were to be regarded as workers whom it was reasonable for the employer to treat differently from the full-time firefighters on the ground that they had a 'different type of contract'.

When the case reached the House of Lords, the retained firefighters argued that **3.51** the types of contract listed in Reg 2(3) were mutually exclusive. Since, like the full-time firefighters, they were working under a contract of employment within the meaning of Reg 2(3)(a), they could not also be working under a 'different type of contract' within what is now Reg 2(3)(d). The majority of the House of Lords (Lord Mance dissenting) accepted this argument. Baroness Hale stated that Reg 2(3) sets out a number of mutually exclusive 'categories of working relationship, within which part-time and full-time workers are to be regarded as

167

comparable but between which they are not'. Reg 2(3)(d) is simply the final category on the list. According to Baroness Hale, it 'expressly refers to "any other description of worker" which in any ordinary use of language means "any description of worker other than those described in the preceding paragraphs"'. Accordingly, since both the retained and full-time firefighters worked under a contract falling within Reg 2(3)(a), the majority concluded that they worked under the 'same type of contract' for the purposes of Reg 2(4)(a)(i).

Baroness Hale pointed out that the above construction accords with the purpose of Reg 2, which is designed simply 'to provide a threshold to require the comparison between full- and part-time workers to take place'. Overcoming the hurdle of Reg 2 then paves the way for 'a sensible appreciation of what is and is not less favourable treatment' under Reg 5, and for consideration of whether any differences in treatment are objectively justified. Furthermore, Baroness Hale explained, 'part-time employment is inevitably different from full-time employment in a number of ways, yet the purpose of the [PTW Regulations] is to secure that it is treated equitably'. If the 'threshold of comparability' under Reg 2 were to be high, the Regulations, contrary to their purpose, would 'only apply in the most straightforward of situations'.

3.52 Lord Hope agreed, adding that 'an over-precise view as to what makes one type of contract different from another would tend to undermine the purpose' of the EU legislation to which the PTW Regulations give effect. He drew analogies with the concepts of 'a type of person or a type of car', explaining that, although there are many variations and differences within each type, there is 'something that brings them all together within the same category'. In Lord Hope's view, Reg 2(3) adopts this approach to a 'type of contract'. It does 'not suggest that a contract can be treated as being of a different type from another just because the terms and conditions that it lays down are different'.

The primary outcome of this aspect of their Lordships' decision is that where a part-time worker is an employee not on a contract of apprenticeship, he or she is on the 'same type of contract' as *any* full-time employee not on a contract of apprenticeship also employed by the employer for the purposes of a Reg 5 claim. It does not matter if the contracts appear to be of very different types (although note that to be a 'comparable full-time worker' the full-time employee must also be engaged in the same or broadly similar work as the part-time employee – see 'Same or broadly similar work' below).

3.53 The question then arises: in what circumstances would a worker fall within the Reg 2(3)(d) category? Possibly, an employer might rely on this category to justify treating agency workers, or workers (not employees) on fixed-term contracts, differently from directly recruited permanent workers. However, treating temporary agency workers less favourably after a 12-week qualifying period would itself fall foul of the Agency Workers Regulations 2010 SI 2010/93 (see Chapter 1, 'Agency workers', under 'Rights under the Agency Workers

Regulations – equal treatment: the basic principle'). It is likely that the main use of Reg 2(3)(d) will be to enable employers to treat casual or seasonal labour, and workers on zero-hours contracts, differently from the rest of the workforce, without incurring liability under the Regulations.

Same or broadly similar work. In order to be comparable for the purposes of **3.54** a Reg 5 claim, the part-time worker and his or her comparator must also be engaged in the 'same or broadly similar work', having regard, where relevant, to whether they have a similar level of qualification, skills and experience – Reg 2(4)(a)(ii). In assessing whether work is the same or broadly similar, particular weight should be given to the extent to which the work of the two groups is in fact the same and the importance of that work to the enterprise as a whole – Matthews and ors v Kent and Medway Towns Fire Authority and ors (above). Otherwise there is a risk of giving too much weight to differences which are the almost inevitable result of one worker being full-time and the other working less than full time.

In that case (discussed under 'Same employer and same type of contract' above), the majority of the House of Lords (Baroness Hale, Lord Hope and Lord Nicholls) held that the tribunal had erred in finding that the part-timers and the full-timers were not engaged in 'broadly similar work'. The tribunal had noted that 'at the scene of the fire the actual job function carried out by all attending is essentially the same'. However, the full-timers had 'measurable additional job functions', such as carrying out community fire safety work. Also, there were different entry standards, probationary standards and training for the two groups, leading the tribunal to find that there were material differences in their 'level of qualification and skills'.

According to their Lordships, the tribunal had made the mistake of treating its **3.55** task under Reg 2(4)(a)(ii) as similar to that required by S.1(4) of the Equal Pay Act 1970 (since repealed and superseded by S.65(2) and (3) of the Equality Act 2010 (EqA)). However, there is an important difference between the two tests. S.1(4) EqPA provided that a woman was employed on like work with a man if their work was 'of the same or a broadly similar nature, and the differences (if any) between… the things they do are not of practical importance in relation to terms and conditions of employment'. Reg 2(4)(a)(ii), on the other hand, contains no reference to 'differences of practical importance'. Thus, although the work done by part-timers and full-timers must be looked at as a whole, the key question under Reg 2(4)(a)(ii) is not whether the work of the two groups is different, but whether it is 'broadly similar'. This technical point is important since the part-time working rules invite 'a comparison between two types of worker whose work will almost inevitably be different to some extent'. The tribunal had assessed the differences between the two groups as having 'high', 'medium' or 'low' importance. However, having addressed the differences, Lord Hope pointed out, it 'did not assess the weight that ought to be

169

given to the similarities'. It failed to address properly the question posed by Reg 2(4)(a)(ii) of whether, notwithstanding its finding that the full-time firefighters had measurable additional job functions, the work in which the two groups was engaged was 'broadly similar'.

According to Baroness Hale, two matters of great importance under Reg 2(4)(a)(ii) are the extent to which the work performed by the two groups in question is 'exactly the same', and the extent to which this shared work is important to the enterprise as a whole. Where full-timers and part-timers spend much of their time on the core activity of the enterprise the fact that the full-timers perform additional tasks would not prevent the work of the two groups being regarded as 'the same or broadly similar'. The tribunal had acknowledged that the work of the retained firefighters and the full-time firefighters at 'the fire ground' was the same. However, it 'failed to acknowledge the centrality of that work to the enterprise of the Fire Brigade as a whole'. Furthermore, at no stage did it suggest that there was any qualitative difference between the firefighting work performed by the two groups. Largely, the tribunal's reference to the higher qualifications and skills of the full-time workers related to the additional activities that they were called upon to carry out, and not to the core activity of fighting fires.

3.56 On remission, the employment tribunal in Matthews found that the retained firefighters did indeed carry out the same or broadly similar work to the full-time firefighters, in that both groups carried out the same central duties – Matthews and ors v Kent and Medway Town Fire Authority and ors ET Case No.6100000/01.

3.57 **Hypothetical comparator?** Unlike discrimination claims, there is no provision for a comparison to be made with a hypothetical comparator. This was made clear by the EAT in Carl v University of Sheffield 2009 ICR 1286, EAT. C was a part-time lecturer who taught shorthand at the University. She brought a claim under the PTW Regulations, alleging that she had been treated less favourably than a named comparator, M, who worked under a full-time university teacher's contract, in that M was paid for preparation time and she was not. Alternatively, C argued that she had been paid less pro rata than a hypothetical comparator; that is, a 'generic teacher' on a full-time university teacher's contract. She also claimed that she had been treated less favourably in relation to training.

The employment tribunal concluded that C, a part-time teacher of shorthand to NVQ3 level, was not doing 'broadly similar' work to M, a full-time teacher of sociology up to PhD level. M had skills and experience 'way beyond' that of C, and her contribution was both vocational and academic while C's teaching was purely vocational. It followed that M was not a true comparator under the Regulations. The tribunal did, however, find that C could compare herself to a hypothetical comparator but concluded that, in the circumstances, there had been no less favourable treatment.

C appealed to the EAT, and the University cross-appealed against the tribunal's **3.58** finding that C could rely on a hypothetical comparator. The EAT agreed with the University that C was not entitled to compare herself to a hypothetical comparator. In reaching this decision, the EAT noted that it is well established that in a complaint of direct sex or race discrimination, for example, a claimant can use an actual or hypothetical comparator. Under what is now S.13 EqA, 'a person (A) discriminates against another (B) if, because of a protected characteristic [e.g. sex or race], A treats B less favourably than A treats *or would treat* others' (our stress). However, in an equal pay claim (under what is now Chapter 3 of Part 5 of the EqA), the comparison must be made with an actual male comparator, not a hypothetical male. Unlike S.13, the 'or would' wording does not appear in the equal pay provisions. Nor does this formula appear in the definition of comparable full-time workers in the PTW Regulations. The EAT also noted that there are two specific and exceptional categories for which the Regulations permit a hypothetical comparator under Regs 3(2) and 4(2), both involving workers changing from full time to part time. This suggested that hypothetical comparators were not permitted in all other circumstances.

The EAT accepted that national law should be interpreted, so far as possible, to **3.59** achieve the result sought by EU legislation. However, it did not accept that the Framework Agreement (annexed to the PTW Directive) requires that a hypothetical comparator be made available. In Wippel v Peek and Cloppenburg GmbH and Co KG 2005 ICR 1604, ECJ, where the European Court rejected a part-time worker's claim for want of an appropriate full-time comparator, there was no attempt by the Court to construct a hypothetical comparator with whom the claimant could compare herself. Furthermore, in McMenemy v Capita Business Services Ltd 2006 IRLR 761, EAT, a different division of the EAT had suggested that in the light of Wippel, a hypothetical comparator was not appropriate in determining whether a part-time worker had been treated less favourably under the PTW Regulations (although when McMenemy reached the Court of Session, that Court observed that it would be appropriate to consider a hypothetical comparator when determining the reason why the part-time worker was less favourably treated – see McMenemy v Capita Business Services Ltd 2007 IRLR 400, Ct Sess (Inner House)). The EAT agreed with this interpretation. It accordingly allowed the University's cross-appeal on this issue, and C's claim failed because of the absence of an actual full-time comparator.

Self-comparison. Where a full-time worker becomes a part-time worker, **3.60** either seamlessly or following a period of absence not exceeding 12 months, Regs 3 and 4 allow him or her to compare his or her treatment with the way in which he or she was treated as a full-time worker. This is in addition to the

171

right to compare his or her treatment with that of a comparable full-time worker in the normal way.

3.61 *Full-time worker moving directly to part-time work.* Regulation 3 applies to a worker who was previously a full-time worker (as defined by Reg 2(1) – see 'Scope of PTW Regulations – what is a part-time worker?' above) and, following the termination or variation of his or her contract, continues to work under a new or varied contract – whether it is of the same type or not – that requires a lower number of weekly hours of work – Reg 3(1). In these circumstances the worker can rely on Reg 5 as if there were a comparable full-time worker employed under the terms that applied to him or her immediately before the variation or termination – Reg 3(2).

Note that Reg 3 does *not* require the new or varied contract to be of the same type as the old one. (Indeed, Reg 3 does not, explicitly, require the new or varied contract to be with the same employer, although it could be argued that the requirement that the worker 'continues to work' under a new or varied contract assumes this.) This means that where, for example, an *employee's* full-time contract ends and he or she is taken on as a *worker* on fewer weekly hours, he or she may compare his or her new contractual terms with those he or she enjoyed as an employee. If, for example, the hourly rate of pay for workers is less than for employees, he or she may argue that this constitutes less favourable treatment for the purposes of Reg 5. Nevertheless, for a claim to succeed, it also needs to be established that the less favourable treatment was on the ground that the worker was a part-time worker, and that it was not justified on objective grounds – Reg 5(2). See 'Reason for less favourable treatment' and 'Justifying less favourable treatment' below.

3.62 *Full-time worker returning to part-time work after period of absence.* Regulation 4 covers the situation where a full-time worker:

- returns to work for the same employer after a period of absence of less than 12 months (regardless of whether the absence was as a result of a termination of the worker's contract)

- to the same job or to a job at the same level but for fewer weekly hours than before – Reg 4(1).

3.63 The new contract may be a different contract or a varied contract but, as in Reg 3, need not be of the same type as the old contract.

In these circumstances, the worker may rely on Reg 5 as if there were a comparable full-time worker employed under the terms that applied to him or her immediately before the variation or termination – Reg 4(2)(a). Where, however, it is shown that, had the returning worker continued to work under the original full-time contract, a variation would have been made to its term during the period of absence, the appropriate comparison would be with the varied contract – Reg 4(2)(b).

Although Reg 4 is probably most likely to be used where a worker is switching from full- to part-time working on a return from maternity leave, it can be used after any type of absence, including an absence following the termination of the worker's previous contract.

'Term-by-term' or 'package' comparison? It is not entirely clear whether an **3.64** employment tribunal should adopt a 'term-by-term' approach or consider all terms in the round when comparing a part-time worker's terms of employment with that of a comparable full-time worker. In Matthews and ors v Kent and Medway Towns Fire Authority and ors 2006 ICR 365, HL, the Fire Authority argued that the two sets of contracts should be looked at in the round, with more favourable elements in the part-timers' package being offset against the less favourable elements. Baroness Hale did not 'wish to rule out the possibility that, in certain cases, a less favourable term might be so well balanced by a more favourable one that it could not be said that the part-timers were treated less favourably overall'. Nor was it impossible that 'more favourable treatment on one point might supply justification for less favourable treatment on another'. On the facts of the case, however, she found it difficult to see how the differently structured pay packages of the two groups could justify the part-timers' exclusion from the pension scheme, or the different way of calculating sick pay which the tribunal had found to be less favourable.

It is tempting to draw comparisons with the law on equal pay. The 'equality clause' implied into every contract of employment by S.66 EqA operates in respect of each individual term of the contract: it does not treat all the terms relating to pay as generic. This was made clear by the House of Lords in Hayward v Cammell Laird Shipbuilders Ltd 1988 ICR 464, HL, where it rejected the employer's argument that any less favourable terms in a claimant's contract could be counterbalanced by other more favourable terms. S.1(2)(c) of the Equal Pay Act 1970 (now Ss.65 and 66 EqA, read together) stated that 'if any term of the woman's contract is or becomes less favourable to the woman than a term of a similar kind in the contract under which [the] man is employed, that term of the woman's contract shall be treated as so modified as not to be less favourable'. In their Lordships' view, 'term' referred to a distinct provision or part of a contract, and thus a woman was entitled not to be treated less favourably than a man under each individual provision of her contract, regardless of whether her contract as a whole could be said to be not less favourable than his.

However, this language is not replicated in the PTW Regulations. Instead, **3.65** Reg 5(1)(a) gives a part-time worker the right not to be treated less favourably 'as regards the terms of his [or her] contract'. Furthermore, the Framework Agreement (annexed to the PTW Directive) states that part-time workers

173

should not be treated in a less favourable manner 'in respect of employment conditions' – Clause 4(1). Thus, in an appropriate case, it would be open for an employer to argue that even though a part-time worker received less favourable treatment in respect of one contractual term, the fact that he or she received more favourable treatment in respect of a closely allied term meant that he or she was not less favourably treated 'as regards the terms of his [or her] contract'.

Nevertheless, for practical reasons, a tribunal may find it easier to look at each contractual term separately, and only consider whether one may be offset against another when determining whether the less favourable treatment may be justified – see 'Justifying less favourable treatment' below.

3.66 Reason for less favourable treatment

Even if a part-time worker can demonstrate that he or she has been treated less favourably than a comparable full-time worker under Reg 5(1), his or her claim will not succeed unless the treatment was 'on the ground that [he or she] is a part-time worker' – Reg 5(2)(a). A finding as to the reason for the treatment should only be made once the tribunal has decided that the worker has been treated less favourably under Reg 5(1) – Calder v Secretary of State for Work and Pensions EAT 0512/08. It is for the employer to identify the ground for the less favourable treatment or detriment – Reg 8(6).

It appears that even if a tribunal does not consider the matter with precision, its decision may still stand if it is reasonably clear from its statements that it understood what reason was operating on the mind of the employer. In Hendrickson Europe Ltd v Pipe EAT 0272/02 P worked part-time as an accounting assistant, alongside three full-time employees. HE Ltd told her that it had decided to reduce the number of accounting assistants to three full-time employees only, and that if she wished to remain employed she would have to return to full-time work. P was unable to commit to full-time work and was dismissed by reason of redundancy. An employment tribunal upheld her claim under the PTW Regulations and one of the issues before the EAT was whether the tribunal had sufficiently analysed whether the treatment was on the ground that P worked part time. The EAT referred to the tribunal's reasoning that P had been dismissed purely because she would work only 32.5 rather than 37.5 hours. Furthermore, the EAT considered that the tribunal's finding that H Ltd had selected P for redundancy on account of her part-time status could not be viewed as perverse, because P was told that if she wanted to stay in employment, she would have to become a full-time worker. The EAT noted that it was 'difficult to see how one of the purposes of the... Regulations should not be to endeavour to protect part-time workers from such pressure'.

3.67 H Ltd argued that, in determining this critical issue, the tribunal should have considered case law requiring it to take into account the employer's reason for the less favourable treatment. The EAT thought that, although it was not expressly covered in the tribunal's decision, it was reasonably clear that the tribunal understood what was operating in the mind of the employer at the time. Furthermore, in deciding whether the less favourable treatment was on the ground that P worked part time, the tribunal was entitled to view the treatment in its full context, incorporating the ongoing pressure on P to revert to full-time work, the redundancy selection process that had made her dismissal inevitable, and the dismissal itself.

Determining reason for treatment. The wording of Reg 5(2)(a) reflects the **3.68** wording of the old discrimination legislation, which required claimants to show that they had been treated less favourably 'on grounds of' or 'on the ground of' a particular characteristic (see, for example, S.3A of the Disability Discrimination Act 1995 and S.1 of the Sex Discrimination Act 1975). The EqA, which replaced these pieces of legislation, has slightly different wording and requires a claimant alleging direct discrimination to show that he or she has received less favourable treatment 'because of' a protected characteristic. However, the meaning is the same.

Thus, tribunals determining whether a part-time worker has been treated less favourably 'on the ground that' he or she is a part-time worker have sought assistance from discrimination case law. In Gibson v Scottish Ambulance Service EATS 0052/04, for example, G, a part-time employee of the Scottish Ambulance Service, was required to be on stand-by for an average of 56 hours a week. In contrast, a comparable full-time worker based at a different station was required to be on stand-by for an average of only 35 hours a week. G commenced proceedings against his employer, alleging discrimination under Reg 5.

In determining whether G's less favourable treatment was on the ground that **3.69** he was a part-time worker, the tribunal applied two different tests in turn to the facts. The first – the 'but for' test – was adopted by the House of Lords in James v Eastleigh Borough Council 1990 ICR 554, HL. This required the tribunal to ask itself whether G would have received the same treatment as his comparator 'but for' his part-time status. The majority of the tribunal found that, had G been a full-time worker, he would still have been required to be on stand-by for more hours than his comparator. The ratio between workers' rostered and stand-by hours varied from area to area, according to demand. G was required to be on stand-by for a considerable number of hours more than his comparator because they worked at different stations, which had different demands.

The tribunal then applied the 'by reason that' test favoured by the House of Lords in Chief Constable of West Yorkshire Police v Khan 2001 ICR 1065, HL. In Khan, a case brought under the victimisation provisions of the Race Relations Act 1976, their Lordships rejected the 'but for' test, holding that a tribunal must examine the reason or motive, conscious or subconscious, for the less favourable treatment in question. The tribunal in this case, therefore, considered whether the requirement that G work a higher ratio of stand-by to rostered

175

hours than his full-time comparator was 'by reason that' he was a part-time worker. It determined that the employer had been motivated by a number of factors, including G's part-time status, though its primary motivation was the level of demand at the respective stations.

3.70 When the case reached the EAT, the Appeal Tribunal considered that the appropriate test for determining the ground for less favourable treatment was the 'by reason that' test in Khan. The ratio between workers' rostered and stand-by hours varied from area to area, according to demand. G was required to be on stand-by for a considerable number of hours more than his comparator because they worked at different stations, which had different demands. In the majority view of the EAT, the tribunal had been correct to investigate the employer's reason or motivation for requiring G to work the ratio of stand-by to rostered hours, which is what gave rise to the detriment.

In Sharma v Manchester City Council 2008 ICR 623, EAT, a case involving a term in part-time workers' contracts which allowed their employer to reduce their working hours, the EAT found it unnecessary to express a view on whether the tribunal should have adopted a 'but for' or 'reason why' test, as it allowed the workers' appeal on other grounds (see 'Sole reason?' below). However, the EAT did express the view that it was not open to the employer to argue that, although 'but for' their part-time status the claimants would not have been less favourably treated, the 'real reason' for the treatment was that their contracts included a term allowing a reduction in hours. It would make a mockery of the PTW Regulations if an employer could successfully argue that differentiating between part-timers and full-timers on the basis of the very term that was alleged to be the source of the less favourable treatment did not constitute discrimination. By analogy, this would potentially allow an employer who, for example, does not pay sick pay to part-timers but does so to full-timers to argue that the reason is due to a difference in their respective contracts of employment rather than part-time status.

3.71 Sole reason? There has been considerable disagreement over whether Reg 5(2)(a) requires a part-time worker to show that his or her part-time status was the *sole* reason for the treatment complained of, or whether it is sufficient for it to simply be one of the reasons for that treatment. The position in England and Wales is that for a claim to succeed under the PTW Regulations, part-time work must be the effective and predominant cause of the less favourable treatment complained of, but need not be the only cause – Carl v University of Sheffield 2009 ICR 1286, EAT. However, in Scotland, the EAT and the Court of Session have held that in order to fall within Reg 5(2)(a), less favourable treatment must be on the *sole* ground of part-time status – Gibson v Scottish Ambulance Service EATS 0052/04 and McMenemy v Capita Business Services Ltd 2007 IRLR 400, Ct Sess (Inner House).

The facts of Gibson are set out above (see 'Determining reason for treatment'). The employment tribunal in that case accepted that the employer had subjected G to a detriment within the meaning of Reg 5(1)(b), but rejected his claim that the treatment was 'on the ground' of his status as a part-time worker. In coming to this decision, the tribunal referred to Clause 4 of the Framework Agreement (annexed to the PTW Directive), which states that part-time workers shall not be treated less favourably than comparable full-time workers solely because they work part time. The tribunal noted that the word 'solely' does not appear in Reg 5(2)(a) of the PTW Regulations, but stated that the Regulations should, so far as possible, be interpreted and applied to give effect to the purpose of the Directive. Taking Clause 4 into account, the tribunal felt that, in order to fall within Reg 5(2)(a), less favourable treatment must be on the sole ground of part-time status.

Looking at the facts of the case, the tribunal found that the employer had been **3.72** motivated by a number of factors, including G's part-time status. However, the employer's primary motivation was the level of demand at the respective ambulance stations. Thus, G's part-time status was not the sole reason for the less favourable treatment. On appeal, the majority of the Scottish EAT upheld the tribunal's decision to dismiss G's claim.

However, the EAT in Sharma v Manchester City Council 2008 ICR 623, EAT, took a different view. S was one of a group of part-time lecturers employed in the Council's adult education service. There were three categories of part-time lecturers: those on 'fractional' contracts, who would work a minimum number of hours each week and receive benefits pro rata to full-timers, but could work extra hours and receive pay at a set rate; 'established' part-timers, whose hours of work could be varied year on year, but who benefited from a contractual term guaranteeing at least one third of the previous year's hours; and 'non-established' part-timers, who had not yet passed the probationary period but were otherwise subject to the same terms as the 'established' workers.

In 2006, the Council decided to cut the amount of adult education. It accordingly **3.73** opted to exercise the term allowing it to reduce the established part-timers' hours. S complained that the reduction was unlawful and amounted to redundancy, but her grievance was rejected. She appealed, arguing that the reduction was contrary to Reg 5, but the appeal also failed. S and eight part-time colleagues then brought claims under the PTW Regulations to an employment tribunal. They claimed that their contractual terms were less favourable, since full-time contracts contained no term permitting a reduction in hours, and also that the decision to reduce their hours was less favourable treatment on the basis of their part-time status. The Council contended that the decision to reduce hours was not taken solely because of the workers' part-time status, citing the fact that the fractional and non-established part-timers had not had their hours reduced. It was simply because of the term in the established

177

part-timers' contracts expressly allowing a reduction in hours that the Council had acted as it did. The tribunal considered that it was bound by Gibson and concluded that part-time status was not the sole reason for the less favourable treatment. However, it noted that if it was wrong about this, such treatment was not justified on objective grounds.

S appealed. The EAT's view was that the construction applied to Reg 5(2) in Gibson v Scottish Ambulance Service (above) – that part-time status had to be the sole reason for the less favourable treatment – was not legitimate. The reference in Clause 4 of the Framework Agreement to 'solely' was simply intended to focus upon the fact that in order to be covered, less favourable treatment of a part-timer must be because of part-time status, and not for some independent reason. The EAT cited the example of an employer choosing to discriminate against all part-timers over the age of 30. In such circumstances, it could be said that there were two reasons for the less favourable treatment – being a part-timer and being over 30 – and it was not credible that the Directive was not intended to outlaw such behaviour. In any event, it was open to a Member State to give more favourable protection than the Directive afforded. The EAT therefore concluded that, once it is found that a part-timer has been treated less favourably than a comparable full-timer, and that being part time was one of the reasons for the treatment, the protection of the PTW Regulations will be engaged. It followed that the Council could not defend the claim by showing that the reason for the claimants' treatment was not just that they were part-timers, but that they were part-timers of a particular category.

3.74 It is worth noting, however, that neither the tribunal nor the EAT in Sharma appear to have had their attention drawn to the fact that Gibson was subsequently applied by the Court of Session in McMenemy v Capita Business Services Ltd (above). Decisions of the Court of Session, while not binding on the English EAT, are of great persuasive authority. McMenemy concerned a policy in relation to time off for public holidays. C Ltd operated a call centre seven days a week. All the call centre employees – whether part- or full-time – were subject to an identical term in their employment contract providing that they were only entitled to the benefit of public holidays where these fell 'on [their] normal working day'. M worked part time on Wednesdays, Thursdays and Fridays, and therefore did not get time off or time off in lieu of public holidays that fell on Mondays. He argued that this constituted less favourable treatment on the ground of his part-time status. However, the Court of Session agreed with the EAT that the part-time worker had to establish that the employer treated him or her less favourably on the sole ground that he or she was a part-time worker, applying Gibson v Scottish Ambulance Service (above). The distinction was not between full-time and part-time workers but between those who worked on Mondays and those who did not, and so M's claim failed.

Despite the decision of the Court of Session in McMenemy, the EAT followed the reasoning adopted in Sharma v Manchester City Council (above) in the subsequent case of Carl v University of Sheffield 2009 ICR 1286, EAT, the facts of which are discussed under 'Hypothetical comparator' above. The employment tribunal in that case relied on Gibson in concluding that, as C's part-time status was not the sole reason for the less favourable treatment, any difference in treatment with regard to training was not on the ground of her part-time status within the meaning of Reg 5(2)(a). C appealed, arguing that the tribunal's self-direction based on Gibson was flawed. Having considered the conflicting case law, the EAT observed that while it was not strictly bound by any of the previous authorities, it agreed with the approach taken in Sharma. Domestic legislation must provide the protection required by the PTW Directive but is not limited to such protection. Less favourable treatment 'on the ground' of part-time status must be defined in the same way as the similar expression used in the Sex Discrimination Act 1975 (since repealed and superseded by the EqA). The EAT therefore concluded that, for a claim to succeed under the PTW Regulations, part-time work must be the effective and predominant cause of the less favourable treatment complained of, but need not be the only cause.

Justifying less favourable treatment   3.75
Even where a part-time worker can show that he or she has been treated less favourably than a comparable full-time worker, and that this treatment was on the ground that he or she is a part-time worker, his or her claim will fail if the employer is able to justify the less favourable treatment on objective grounds – Reg 5(2)(b).

Neither the PTW Regulations nor the PTW Directive give guidance as to what might amount to objective justification of a provision that discriminates against part-time workers. However, it is likely that the same principles apply in this context as apply in the context of indirect discrimination and equal pay under the EqA given that, although different wording is used in the Regulations, all three provisions derive from European law.

The Government's online guide to 'Part-time workers' rights' (at www.gov.uk) 3.76
suggests that objective justification involves an employer showing that there is 'a good reason' to treat part-time workers differently, such as not providing health insurance for part-time employees because the costs involved are disproportionate to the benefits to which part-timers are entitled. More helpfully, the archived 2008 BERR guide, 'Part-time workers: The law and best practice – a detailed guide for employers and part-timers' (URN 02/1710), states that less favourable treatment will only be justified on objective grounds if it can be shown that the treatment is:

•   to achieve a legitimate business objective

179

- necessary to achieve that objective, and

- an appropriate way of achieving that objective.

Such guidance has no legal force but its approach – which imports the test of objective justification in the context of indirect discrimination – accords with that taken by the European Court of Justice. In Österreichischer Gewerkschaftsbund v Verband Österreichischer Banken und Bankiers (Case C-476/12), ECJ, the Advocate General followed a European decision on equal pay when opining that, in the context of considering whether less favourable treatment of a part-time worker is justified, a national court must consider whether a measure chosen corresponds to a real need, is appropriate with a view to achieving the objective pursued and is necessary to that end. Mere generalisations will not be sufficient to justify a difference in treatment and the avoidance of increased costs is not a reason that will objectively justify indirect discrimination.

3.77 The EAT also implicitly approved a tribunal's approach to justification based on the Berr guidance in Tyson v Concurrent Systems Incorporated Ltd EAT 0028/03. It agreed with the claimant that a tribunal, having decided that it would test justification against the three requirements set out above, 'sufficiently and properly concluded in favour of the employers in respect of the first of those three criteria, i.e. that there was a genuine business objective'. However, it had erred in failing to give any reasons for its conclusions that it was necessary for the employer to achieve that objective by acting as it did, and that acting as it did was an appropriate way to achieve that objective.

Thus, cases on objective justification in the context of indirect discrimination and equal pay are likely to be relevant when assessing justification under the PTW Regulations. For a detailed discussion of justification in these contexts, see IDS Employment Law Handbook, 'Equal Pay' (2011), Chapter 8, 'Material factor defence', under 'Showing objective justification'; and IDS Employment Law Handbook, 'Discrimination at Work' (2012), Chapter 17, 'Indirect discrimination: objective justification', under 'Background and overview', 'Legitimate aim', and 'Proportionality'.

3.78 An example of treatment that was found to be not justified under the PTW Regulations:

- **Hendrickson Europe Ltd v Pipe** EAT 0272/02: P worked part time as an accounting assistant, alongside three full-time employees. HE Ltd told her that it had decided to reduce the number of accounting assistants to three full-time employees only, and that if she wished to remain employed she would have to return to full-time work. P was unable to do this, although she offered to increase her hours to 32.5 per week, which would have meant that she worked only five hours less than the full-time workers. However, HE Ltd insisted that P's continued employment was conditional on her reverting to full-time duties and, as P was unable to meet this condition, she was dismissed by reason of redundancy. An employment tribunal found that this was less favourable treatment that was not objectively justified, and the EAT upheld its decision. The tribunal had been well aware of the objective test and had considered carefully how to apply it to the particular facts. It recognised that it was for the employer to make the commercial decision that it was overstaffed and that three accounting assistants were needed instead of four, but the tribunal was entitled to look at all the circumstances, including that P was a part-time worker who, if her offer had been put into the equation, would have been only five hours short of full-time service.

Right to written statement

3.79

A worker who considers that he or she is being treated in a way that infringes his or her rights under Reg 5 of the PTW Regulations (less favourable treatment of part-time workers) may request in writing from the employer a written statement giving particulars of the reasons for the treatment – Reg 6(1). The statement, which must be provided by the employer within 21 days of the request, is admissible as evidence in any proceedings under the PTW Regulations – Reg 6(1) and (2).

If a tribunal finds that:

- the employer deliberately, and without reasonable excuse, failed to provide a written statement, or

- the written statement is 'evasive or equivocal',

it may draw any inference which it considers it just and equitable to draw, including an inference that the employer has infringed the right in question – Reg 6(3).

The right to a written statement under Reg 6 does not apply if the treatment in **3.80** question consists of the dismissal of an employee and the employee is entitled to a written statement of reasons for his or her dismissal under S.92 of the Employment Rights Act 1996 – Reg 6(4). Written statements of the reason for dismissal are explained in IDS Employment Law Handbook, 'Unfair Dismissal' (2010), Chapter 21, 'Written reasons for dismissal'.

Unfair dismissal and unlawful detriment

3.81

Regulation 7 of the PTW Regulations provides protection for workers who are dismissed or subjected to a detriment for enforcing, or seeking to enforce, their rights under the Regulations.

181

3.82 Unfair dismissal. Regulation 7(1) provides that an *employee* will be treated as having been unfairly dismissed if the reason (or principal reason) for his or her dismissal is that he or she has:

- brought proceedings against the employer under the PTW Regulations

- requested from his or her employer a written statement of reasons under Reg 6

- given evidence or information in connection with such proceedings brought by any worker

- done anything else under the PTW Regulations in relation to the employer or any other person

- alleged that the employer had infringed the PTW Regulations (except where the allegation made by the employee is false and not made in good faith – Reg 7(4))

- refused (or proposed to refuse) to forgo a right conferred on him or her by the PTW Regulations – Reg 7(3)(a).

Reg 7(1) also applies where the reason (or principal reason) for the dismissal is that the employer believes or suspects that the employee has done or intends to do any of the above – Reg 7(3)(b).

3.83 A dismissal that falls foul of Reg 7(1) is automatically unfair and, unlike 'ordinary' unfair dismissal, the tribunal is not required to consider the reasonableness of the decision to dismiss. Moreover, the two-year qualifying service requirement for the right to claim unfair dismissal does not apply – S.108 Employment Rights Act 1996 (ERA). Note, however, that only employees can claim unfair dismissal under Reg 7(1). Other types of worker must bring their claim as an unlawful detriment claim under Reg 7(2) – see 'Unlawful detriment' below.

A dismissal contrary to Reg 7(1) is governed by the provisions of Part X of the ERA. For a detailed consideration of the law, see IDS Employment Law Handbook, 'Unfair Dismissal' (2010).

3.84 Unlawful detriment. Workers have the right not to be subjected to any detriment by any act, or any deliberate failure to act, by their employer done on one of the grounds listed in Reg 7(3) (see 'Unfair dismissal' above) – Reg 7(2). Where, for example, a part-time worker is excluded from company meetings because he or she alleged in a previous meeting that he or she was being paid less, proportionately, than a full-time colleague, he or she will be able to bring a claim under Reg 7(2).

An *employee* who is dismissed cannot bring a detriment claim under Reg 7(2) in respect of that dismissal – Reg 7(5). Instead, he or she should bring an unfair dismissal claim under Reg 7(1) (see 'Unfair dismissal' above). A worker who is not an employee, on the other hand, can bring a detriment claim under Reg 7(2) if he or she is dismissed.

The enforcement provisions governing Reg 7(2) are discussed under 'Enforcement and remedies' below.

Enforcement and remedies   3.85

A worker can complain to an employment tribunal that his or her employer has infringed either (or both) of the following rights:

- the right under Reg 5 not to be treated less favourably than a comparable full-time worker, in respect of contractual terms or by being subjected to any other detriment

- the right under Reg 7(2) not to be subjected to a detriment in connection with rights under the PTW Regulations (unless the alleged detriment is the dismissal of an employee) – Reg 8(1).

As explained under 'Unfair dismissal and unlawful detriment – unfair dismissal' above, a complaint by an employee of unfair dismissal contrary to Reg 7(1) should be prosecuted under Part X of the ERA. However, employees and workers alike can claim to have been subjected to a detriment under Reg 5, in the form of their dismissal, in addition to any unfair dismissal/unlawful detriment claim they may be entitled to bring by virtue of Reg 7.

Note that although Reg 6 provides workers with an additional right under the **3.86** PTW Regulations – the right to receive a written statement of reasons for less favourable treatment – this right cannot of itself form the basis of a complaint to an employment tribunal. Rather, a tribunal which is already hearing proceedings under the Regulations may draw an inference from an employer's deliberate failure, without reasonable excuse, to supply a written statement, or from the fact that a written statement is evasive or equivocal – Reg 6(3). Such an inference may, for example, be that the employer has infringed the right not to be treated less favourably, but a tribunal is at liberty to draw any inference it considers just and equitable to draw (or to draw none at all). See further 'Right to written statement' above.

Time limits   3.87

An employment tribunal cannot hear a complaint under Reg 8 unless it is brought before the end of the period of three months (six months for members of the armed forces) beginning with the date of the less favourable treatment or detriment to which the complaint relates – Reg 8(2). However, tribunals retain a discretion to hear any claim under the PTW Regulations that is brought out of time if, in all the circumstances of the case, they consider that it is 'just and equitable' to do so – Reg 8(3). The 'just and equitable' formula is the same as that applicable to out-of-time discrimination claims under S.123(1)(b) EqA and is discussed in detail in IDS Employment Law Handbook, 'Employment Tribunal Practice and Procedure' (2014), Chapter 5, 'Time limits', under '"Just and equitable" extension'.

Note that time stops running while any Acas-facilitated pre-claim conciliation takes place – Reg 8(2A) and 8A (see IDS Employment Law Handbook, 'Employment Tribunal Practice and Procedure' (2014), Chapter 3, 'Conciliation, settlements and ADR', under 'Early conciliation', and Chapter 5, 'Time limits', under 'Extension of time limit under early conciliation rules'). The discretion to extend time where it is just and equitable to do so under Reg 8(3) applies to the new extended time limit in these circumstances – Reg 8A(4).

3.88 **Calculating date of less favourable treatment or detriment.** Except in those cases where the less favourable treatment under Reg 5, or detriment under Reg 7, constitutes a one-off act, it may be unclear when time starts to run for the purposes of the statutory time limits. In these circumstances, the following rules apply:

- where the less favourable treatment complained of under Reg 5 or the detriment complained of under Reg 7(2) consists of detriment in the form of a series of acts or failures to act, time starts to run from the last of those acts or failures to act – Reg 8(2)

- where a term in a contract is less favourable, the treatment is deemed to take place on each day of the period during which the term is less favourable – Reg 8(4)(a). This is subject to Reg 8(4)(b), which applies where the claimant is comparing his or her treatment with his or her own previous treatment as a full-time worker under Regs 3 or 4 (see the section 'Less favourable treatment' above, under 'Comparing treatment – self-comparison'). Under Reg 8(4)(b) where the claimant –

  - moved directly from full-time to part-time work in accordance with Reg 3, the less favourable treatment is treated as occurring on, and only on, the first day on which the claimant worked under the new or varied contract

  - returned to part-time work after a period of absence, prior to which he or she worked full time, the less favourable treatment is treated as occurring on, and only on, the day on which the claimant returned – Reg 8(4)(b)

- a deliberate failure to act under either Reg 5 or Reg 7(2) is treated as done 'when it was decided on' – Reg 8(4)(c). Unless there is evidence to the contrary, a person decides not to act either when he or she does an act inconsistent with doing the failed act, or, if there is no such inconsistent act, when the period expires within which he or she might reasonably have been expected to have done the failed act if it was to be done – Reg 8(5).

Remedies and compensation   3.89

Where an employment tribunal finds that a complaint under the PTW Regulations is well founded it can take such of the following steps as it considers just and equitable:

- make a declaration as to the respective rights of the claimant and employer

- order an award of compensation

- recommend that the employer take, within a specified period, action appearing to the tribunal to be reasonable, in all the circumstances of the case, for the purpose of obviating or reducing the adverse effect on the complainant of any matter to which the complaint relates – Reg 8(7).

If the tribunal makes a recommendation but the employer fails, without reasonable justification, to comply with it the tribunal may, if it thinks it just and equitable to do so, make an award of compensation – Reg 8(14). Or, if it has already awarded compensation, increase the amount.

Compensation. Where a tribunal considers that it is just and equitable to   3.90
award compensation, the amount should be whatever the tribunal considers to be just and equitable in all the circumstances, having regard to:

- the infringement to which the complaint relates, and

- any loss which is attributable to the infringement (subject to the claimant's duty to mitigate such loss – Reg 8(12)) – Reg 8(9).

Losses include any expenses reasonably incurred by the claimant in consequence of the infringement of his or her rights under the PTW Regulations, as well as the loss of any benefit which he or she might reasonably be expected to have had but for the infringement – Reg 8(10). Note, however, that in Ministry of Justice v O'Brien 2014 ICR 773, EAT, the EAT held that the calculation of the amount of pension to which a retired part-time judge was entitled under the PTW Directive and the PTW Regulations should take into account only his period of service since the UK was obliged to bring the Directive into force – on 7 April 2000 – and not any earlier period of service when discrimination against part-time workers had not been rendered unlawful under the Directive.

A tribunal must reduce the award of compensation by whatever proportion it   3.91
considers just and equitable where it finds that the act, or failure to act, to which the complaint relates was to any extent caused or contributed to by the claimant's actions – Reg 8(13). This is commonly referred to as 'contributory conduct' or 'contributory fault' and applies in the same way as it applies to compensatory awards for unfair dismissal. For a comprehensive discussion, see IDS Employment Law Handbook, 'Unfair Dismissal' (2010), Chapter 18, 'Compensatory awards: adjustments and reductions', under 'Contributory conduct'.

Compensation in respect of less favourable treatment under Reg 5 must not include an award for injury to feelings – Reg 8(11). A claimant would therefore be well advised to consider whether he or she was in a position to bring a complaint of indirect sex discrimination in addition to the claim under the PTW Regulations – see 'Discrimination and equal pay' below.

3.92 Contracting out

The general rule is that nobody can contract out of their rights and obligations under the PTW Regulations: any purported agreement to this effect will be void, whether or not it is contained in a contract of employment – Reg 9 (which states that S.203 ERA applies in relation to the PTW Regulations as if they were contained in that Act).

Section 203 ERA contains restrictions on contracting out, but also expressly provides exceptions to this general rule in respect of settlements reached under the auspices of an Acas conciliator, and settlement agreements. In addition, a settlement recorded by the tribunal may effectively bar a claim, as the claimant will be prevented or 'estopped' from bringing another claim in respect of the same facts or issues, unless the decision to dismiss is successfully reviewed or appealed. For more detail on estoppel, see IDS Employment Law Handbook, 'Employment Tribunal Practice and Procedure' (2014), Chapter 2, 'Tribunals' jurisdiction', under 'Relitigation: res judicata and abuse of process'.

3.93 Conciliation

There is an exception to the general rule against contracting out of the PTW Regulations where an Acas conciliator has taken action and an agreement has been reached that the employee will refrain from instituting or continuing with a complaint – S.203(2)(e) ERA. The agreement will be binding if the conciliator has 'taken action' under S.18A, S.18B or S.18C of the Employment Tribunals Act 1996. These sections refer to Acas's powers and duties to attempt to conciliate employment disputes, including under the 'early conciliation' scheme.

For further details of conciliated settlements, see IDS Employment Law Handbook, 'Employment Tribunal Practice and Procedure' (2014), Chapter 3, 'Conciliation, settlements and ADR', under 'Early conciliation', 'Prohibition against contracting out of statutory rights' and 'Acas-conciliated (COT3) agreements'.

3.94 Settlement agreements

Settlement agreements represent another exception to the general rule in S.203(1) that individuals cannot contract out of rights under the PTW Regulations. By virtue of S.203(2)(f)(ii), S.203(1) does not apply where a settlement agreement is entered into, thereby making it possible for parties to settle an employment dispute between themselves without the intervention of an Acas conciliator.

In order to be binding, however, such agreements must:

- be in writing

- relate to the particular proceedings

- only be made where the worker has received advice from a relevant (and fully insured) independent adviser (as defined in S.203(3A)–(4)) as to the terms and effect of the proposed agreement and in particular its effect on his or her ability to pursue his or her rights before a tribunal

- identify the adviser, and

- state that the conditions regulating settlement agreements have been satisfied – S.203(3).

The terms of S.203(3) will be strictly enforced by tribunals and a failure to **3.95** comply with any of the above requirements is likely to render the agreement void. For further details of settlement agreements, see IDS Employment Law Handbook, 'Employment Tribunal Practice and Procedure' (2014), Chapter 3, 'Conciliation, settlements and ADR', under 'Settlement agreements'.

Discrimination and equal pay claims 3.96

Prior to the introduction of the PTW Regulations, part-time workers who suffered discriminatory treatment on the ground of their part-time status had to rely on the discrimination legislation for a remedy, in particular on the Equal Pay Act 1970 and the Sex Discrimination Act 1975 (both since repealed and superseded by the EqA). The rationale for such claims was that since most part-time workers were (and continue to be) women, the unequal treatment of such workers was likely to affect far more women than men. Therefore, unless a clear and objective explanation was provided, the discriminatory treatment of part-time workers was likely to amount to indirect sex discrimination and/or breach the principle of equal pay for equal work.

Although the introduction of the PTW Regulations largely eliminated the need to bring discrimination claims, in practice, part-time claimants often bring claims under the PTW Regulations and the EqA in the alternative. Indeed, where a claimant wishes to obtain an award for injury to feelings, he or she will need to claim under the EqA because this head of compensation is not available under the PTW Regulations – see 'Enforcement and remedies – remedies and compensation', above. However, as the evidential burden in a claim under the PTW Regulations is usually lighter, he or she is likely to pursue a Reg 5 claim as well.

3.97 The EqA is likely to have most impact today in relation to claims brought in response to a refusal to allow part-time working. This is because the PTW Regulations do not provide a 'right' to work part time, but simply provide protection to those who already work part time. Thus, a woman who is refused work on a part-time basis on a return from maternity leave, or to care for a dependent relative, might well claim indirect discrimination on the ground of her sex, on the basis that women are more likely to undertake caring responsibilities and therefore need to work part time. Similarly, a person with ME who is not allowed to reduce his or her working hours could claim indirect discrimination on the ground of his or her disability, or that the employer has failed in its duty to make reasonable adjustments.

Discrimination claims that flow from such refusals are discussed in Chapter 4, 'Flexible working', under 'Discrimination claims'. Here we offer a brief overview of the law on indirect discrimination and equal pay to the extent that these are potentially relevant to existing part-time workers. The law on indirect discrimination and on equal pay is fully explored in IDS Employment Law Handbook, 'Discrimination at Work' (2012), Chapter 16, 'Indirect discrimination: proving disadvantage', and Chapter 17, 'Indirect discrimination: objective justification'; and in IDS Employment Law Handbook, 'Equal Pay' (2011). The duty to make reasonable adjustments is explained in IDS Employment Law Handbook, 'Discrimination at Work' (2012), Chapter 21, 'Failure to make reasonable adjustments'.

3.98 Indirect discrimination

Indirect discrimination occurs when a person (A) applies to another (B) a provision, criterion or practice ('PCP') that is discriminatory in relation to a relevant protected characteristic of B's (such as his or her sex or disability) – S.19(1) EqA. A PCP has this effect if the following four criteria are met:

- A applies, or would apply, the PCP to persons with whom B does not share the relevant protected characteristic

- the PCP puts, or would put, persons with whom B shares the characteristic at a particular disadvantage when compared with persons with whom B does not share the characteristic

- the PCP puts, or would put, B at that disadvantage, and

- A cannot show that the PCP is a proportionate means of achieving a legitimate aim (the 'objective justification' defence – see 'Objective justification' below) – S.19(2).

The burden of proof lies with the claimant to establish the first, second and third criteria – Dziedziak v Future Electronics Ltd EAT 0271/11. If the claimant succeeds, it falls to the employer ('A') to justify the application of the PCP.

It is clear that imposing a requirement to work full time constitutes a PCP – **3.99** Mitchell v David Evans Agricultural Ltd EAT 0083/06. By extension, where a benefit, such as health insurance, is provided only to full-time employees, this effectively amounts to a PCP that employees must work full time in order to receive that benefit. Even where such a requirement is applied to all employees, it would clearly put a part-time worker at a particular disadvantage. Some examples of requirements that have been held to amount to a PCP for the purposes of claiming indirect sex discrimination, and which might affect part-time workers:

- a requirement to work night shifts as part of a rolling shift system – Danso v 1SC Guarding Ltd ET Case No.3301845/09

- a requirement to work until 7 pm one evening a week – Brondel v Viscount Environmental Ltd and ors ET Case No.1805311/10

- a requirement to work during core hours, which included 2.30–5 pm – Glass v Newsquest (North East) Ltd ET Case No.2508468/04

- a requirement to work at least 25 hours a week in the office – Giles v Cornelia Care Homes ET Case No.3100720/05

- a demand that teaching staff in a school take on extra-curricular activities – Briggs v North Eastern Education and Library Board 1990 IRLR 181, NICA.

Where a PCP is shown to exist, the part-time worker must then prove that he or she is disadvantaged by the PCP and establish that other people who share a protected characteristic with him or her also work on a part-time basis, and are thereby also put at a particular disadvantage by the PCP as compared with people who do not share the same protected characteristic. Typically, such claims are brought by female part-time workers on the basis of the protected characteristic of their sex. In many cases, such workers will be able to demonstrate relatively easily that the particular disadvantage they face is shared by other workers who are also female on the basis that it is 'common knowledge' that women have greater childcare responsibilities than men, and thus are more likely to work part time – Chief Constable of West Midlands Police v Blackburn and anor 2008 ICR 505, EAT.

In many cases the main area of dispute is whether the employer can objectively justify the PCP by showing that it is 'a proportionate means of achieving a legitimate aim' – S.19(2). This is discussed under 'Objective justification' below.

Equal pay
3.100
The equal pay provisions in the EqA make it unlawful for an employer to discriminate between men and women in relation to the terms of their contracts of employment. These provisions cover all contractual terms and conditions, not just pay.

The EqA works by implying a 'sex equality clause' into every employee's contract, enabling him or her to bring a tribunal claim where he or she is treated less favourably than a comparable employee of the opposite sex in relation to a contractual term – S.66. However, for a successful equal pay claim, a number of hurdles need to be overcome. Assuming, for simplicity's sake, that the claimant is a female part-time employee, she will need to show that she is employed on 'like work' with the male comparator who is treated more favourably than herself, on 'work rated as equivalent' to his under a job evaluation study, or on 'work of equal value' to his – S.65. If this is established, it is then up to the employer to show that the difference between the two cases is genuinely due to a material factor that is not the difference of sex – S.69 (see 'Objective justification' below). If the difference is not objectively justified, then the claimant's contract is modified so that none of the terms in her contract are less favourable than those of her comparator (on a pro rata basis). This may be done by amending an existing term of her contract so that it corresponds to that in the contract of the comparator, or by inserting a new term into her contract if it is included in the comparator's contract but not in hers – S.66(2)(a) and (b).

3.101 Given the complexity of these provisions and the expense of bringing an equal pay claim, part-time workers who consider that they have been less favourably treated are generally advised to use the PTW Regulations to enforce their rights wherever possible. However, there are some situations in which equal pay law may continue to be relevant. For example, a part-time worker can compare his or her treatment only with a full-time comparator under the PTW Regulations. Under equal pay law, the requirement for a comparator is that he or she must be of the opposite sex, but there is no requirement that he or she work full time. Thus, it would be possible under the equal pay provisions for a female part-time worker to compare her terms and conditions with those of a male worker who may not himself work on a full-time basis, but perhaps works more days or hours than the female worker.

Furthermore, under equal pay law, the sex equality clause operates in respect of each individual term of the contract: it does not treat all terms as a package. This means that less favourable terms in a claimant's contract may not be counterbalanced by more favourable terms – Hayward v Cammell Laird Shipbuilders Ltd 1988 ICR 464, HL. By contrast, the PTW Regulations appear to permit some sort of balancing process, whether at the stage of determining whether there has been less favourable treatment or at the stage of objective justification – see the section 'Less favourable treatment' above, under 'Comparing terms – "term-by-term" or "package" comparison?'. If this is correct, a part-time worker whose contractual terms are less favourable in respect of one element, but more favourable in respect of others, may prefer to bring an equal pay claim to avoid the risk of off-setting. For greater detail, see IDS Employment Law Handbook, 'Equal Pay' (2011), Chapter 2, 'Right to equal pay'.

Objective justification   3.102
The EqA offers employers potential 'escape routes' in respect of indirect discrimination and equal pay claims.

Indirect discrimination. An employer will have a defence to an indirect 3.103 discrimination claim where it can show that its application of a PCP was a 'proportionate means of achieving a legitimate aim' – S.19(2)(d). A wide range of explanations could constitute a legitimate aim. For example, a client's need for a business's services at a particular time may be a legitimate aim that potentially justifies a requirement that staff of that business work full time. However, cost considerations, by themselves, may not be sufficient to amount to a legitimate aim. A common rationale for not providing certain benefits – such as health insurance – to part-time workers is that they cannot be provided on a pro rata basis, and that the cost would be disproportionate to the benefits the part-time worker would be entitled to. Indeed, the Government's online guide to 'Part-time workers' rights' (at www.gov.uk) uses this as an example of when less favourable treatment under the PTW Regulations may be justified. It suggests that in such a case the employer 'may come up with an alternative like asking the part-time worker to make a contribution to the extra cost'. However, while costs savings can indeed justify indirect discrimination, as the law currently stands they can only do so if combined with other factors. Thus, coming up with an alternative may be essential to avoid a finding of discrimination. The 'cost plus' issue is complex and falls outside the scope of this Handbook. However, it is discussed at length in IDS Employment Law Handbook, 'Discrimination at Work' (2012), Chapter 17, 'Indirect discrimination: objective justification', under 'Legitimate aim – costs'.

Once a legitimate aim has been identified, consideration must be given as to whether the discriminatory treatment is a 'proportionate' means of achieving that aim. This involves striking an objective balance between the discriminatory effect of the PCP and the reasonable needs (i.e. the legitimate aim) of the party who applies it – Hampson v Department of Education and Science 1989 ICR 179, CA.

Equal pay. In equal pay cases, the employer can objectively justify unequal 3.104 treatment by explaining the difference by reference to a 'material factor' that does not involve treating the claimant less favourably than the comparator because of her sex. If the employee can show that the 'material factor' is 'tainted' by indirect sex discrimination, then the employer can still rely on it, but only if it can demonstrate that imposing the difference:

- corresponds to a real need on the part of the business

- is an appropriate method of achieving that objective, and

- is necessary in order to achieve that objective – Bilka-Kaufhaus GmbH v Weber von Hartz 1987 ICR 110, ECJ.

191

This is a complex area of law which is examined in depth in IDS Employment Law Handbook, 'Equal Pay' (2011), Chapter 8, 'Material factor defence'.

3.105 # Opportunity to work part time

The PTW Regulations only apply to workers who already work part time. They are aimed at providing rights for part-time workers and at protecting part-time workers from being treated less favourably than full-time workers. They do not give workers a right to change from full-time to part-time work (or vice versa). The right to request such a change is governed by the right to request flexible working, which is discussed in Chapter 4, 'Flexible working'.

However, protecting rights of part-time workers is only one element of the PTW Directive. Clause 1 of the Framework Agreement on part-time work (which is annexed to the Directive and which the Directive implements) states that its purpose is not only to remove discrimination against part-time workers and improve the quality of part-time work, but 'to facilitate the development of part-time work on a voluntary basis and to contribute to the flexible organisation of working time in a manner which takes into account the needs of employers and workers'.

3.106 Clause 5, entitled 'Opportunities for part-time work', expands upon this, providing among other things that:

- Member States and their social partners should, having consulted together, 'identify and review obstacles of a legal or administrative nature which may limit the opportunities for part-time work and, where appropriate, eliminate them' – Clause 5(1)

- a worker's refusal to transfer from full-time to part-time work or vice versa should not itself constitute a valid reason for termination of employment – Clause 5(2), and

- employers should, as far as possible, give consideration to requests by workers to transfer from full-time to part-time work where this becomes available, and to 'measures to facilitate access to part-time work at all levels of the enterprise, including skilled and managerial positions, and, where appropriate, to facilitate access by part-time workers to vocational training to enhance career opportunities and occupational mobility' – Clause 5(3).

The rules requiring employers to consider flexible working requests largely fulfil these requirements, which are clearly aimed at bringing about a culture in which part-time working is seen as acceptable and opportunities to work part time are provided more widely. But in Mascellani v Ministero della Giustizia (Case C-221/13), ECJ, an official of the Italian Ministry of Justice argued that the Framework Agreement went further than this.

In that case M worked part time until, in 2011, the Italian Government **3.107** introduced laws that had the effect of revoking her part-time working arrangements and she was instructed to work full-time hours, spread over six days a week. M sought a declaration that her part-time employment could not be converted into a full-time employment relationship against her wishes, arguing that the conversion was unlawful under the Directive. The Italian Court referred questions to the ECJ for a preliminary ruling on the effect of Clause 5(2) and on whether it precluded a law whereby an employer could convert a part-time employment relationship into a full-time one without the worker's consent.

The Advocate General noted that the language of Clause 5(2) did not seem to grant workers an 'unquestionable right' to refuse conversion of the employment relationship. This provides, in its entirety: 'A worker's refusal to transfer from full-time to part-time work or vice versa should not in itself constitute a valid reason for termination of employment, without prejudice to termination in accordance with national law, collective agreements and practice, for other reasons such as may arise from the operational requirements of the establishment concerned.' In the Advocate General's view, not only was this wording vague, but the power to terminate an employment relationship due to operational requirements seemed to negate the idea of any substantive protection. It was hard to see how the use of the term 'should not' in Clause 5 could give rise to a legally binding obligation. Furthermore, the purpose of the clause – as laid out in Clause 1 – was to contribute to the flexible organisation of working time in a way that took into account the needs not only of workers, but also of employers. Nor did the Advocate General consider that a risk of having to change over to full-time work gave rise to discrimination under any other part of the Framework Agreement, such as the principle of no less favourable treatment.

The ECJ itself has yet to rule on this case. If its decision accords with the opinion of the Advocate General, it will be difficult to argue that Clause 5 of the Framework Agreement is anything more than aspirational in character.

4 Flexible working

Flexible working can cover a wide range of work patterns, including part-time, **4.1** flexitime and homeworking. Under Part 8A of the Employment Rights Act 1996 (ERA), employees have the right to request flexible working by applying for a change in their terms and conditions of employment. The right used to apply solely to parents and carers. However, upon taking office in May 2010, the Coalition Government made it a central plank of its equalities agenda to allow more people to benefit. The right has duly been extended to all employees who have completed 26 weeks' service – see Ss.131–133 of the Children and Families Act 2014 and the Flexible Working Regulations 2014 SI 2014/1398. In addition, the Flexible Working (Procedural Requirements) Regulations 2002 SI 2002/3207 have been repealed, thus removing the detailed statutory procedure for considering requests. Now employers are simply required to consider requests in a 'reasonable manner', a duty underpinned by a statutory Code of Practice on 'Handling requests to work flexibly in a reasonable manner', produced by Acas. The key legislative changes are discussed under 'Right to request flexible working' below. The remainder of the chapter examines the legislative provisions in more detail and considers the effect of unfair dismissal, detriment and discrimination law in this area.

The new rules apply to a flexible working application made on or after 30 June 2014. However, the old rules will continue to apply to a flexible working application made before that date – Reg 2 Flexible Working Regulations. In addition, the changes apply to workplaces in Great Britain only (i.e. England, Scotland and Wales). While a separate consultation on extending the right to request flexible working in Northern Ireland also received a positive public response, legislation to effect this (the Work and Families Bill) was only

195

introduced in the Northern Ireland Assembly on 28 April 2014. Unlike the rest of Great Britain, there is no intention to make any changes to the right-to-request procedure in Northern Ireland.

4.2 Right to request flexible working

The right to request flexible working was introduced in April 2003 – following recommendations made by the independent Work and Parents Taskforce set up by the then Secretary of State for Trade and Industry – to help parents balance their work and family life. The recommendations came in the wake of a consultation on the 'Work and Parents: Competiveness and Choice' Green Paper, which revealed that flexible working was the single biggest issue for parents.

The right was given statutory force by S.47 of the Employment Act 2002 (EA), which inserted new Part 8A (comprising Ss.80F–80I) into the ERA. Much of the detail was, however, contained in the Flexible Working (Eligibility, Complaints and Remedies) Regulations 2002 SI 2002/3236 ('the Eligibility Regulations'), together with the Flexible Working (Procedural Requirements) Regulations 2002 SI 2002/3207 ('the Procedural Regulations'). The right – initially restricted to parents of children under the age of six and parents of disabled children under the age of 18 – was extended to carers of adult dependants in April 2007 by S.12(2) of the Work and Families Act 2006. Two years later, the age limit for non-disabled children was raised to 16 via an amendment to the Eligibility Regulations.

4.3 Upon taking office in May 2010, the Coalition Government made it a central plank of its equalities agenda to introduce the right to request flexible working for all employees ('The Coalition: our programme for government', May 2010). Taking the view that the introduction of the right had been a resounding success, it reasoned that an extension to all would bring further benefits: employees would be able to balance their work and personal responsibilities and employers would be able to retain experienced and skilled staff, thus increasing overall levels of participation in the labour market. Above all, the proposed extension would challenge the prevailing misconception that non-traditional working arrangements are the preserve of parents and carers – particularly women – and effect a cultural change to make flexible working practices the norm.

The proposal was put out for public consultation as part of the Consultation on Modern Workplaces (URN 11/699), which ran for 12 weeks from May to August 2011. The responses, which were published in November 2012, showed widespread public support for an extension of the right to request flexible working to all. They also solidified the Government's view that changes were needed to the existing statutory procedure for considering employees' requests, which some respondents criticised as 'unduly prescriptive' and 'inflexible'.

Children and Families Act 2014 4.4

The legislative vehicle for making the relevant changes was the Children and Families Act 2014 (CFA), coupled with the Flexible Working Regulations 2014 SI 2014/1398 ('the Flexible Working Regulations'). The Flexible Working Regulations revoked the Eligibility Regulations, thereby removing the stipulation that the statutory right to request flexible working is only available to parents of children under 17 (18 if the child is disabled) or to carers of adults. S.80G ERA was also amended so as to remove the requirement on employers to follow the detailed statutory procedure set out in the Procedural Regulations when considering flexible working requests. Instead, employers are under a duty to deal with flexible working requests in a 'reasonable manner' – S.80G(1)(a) ERA. This duty is underpinned by a statutory Code of Practice drawn up by Acas – see 'Acas Code of Practice' below. The old statutory procedure for considering requests is briefly outlined under 'Handling requests for flexible working' below. Interestingly, the Procedural Regulations have yet to be revoked, although presumably they soon will be, given that they no longer apply to requests made after 30 June 2014.

Key changes. In summary, the key changes to the flexible working rules are 4.5 as follows:

- the removal of the requirement to be a carer

- the repeal of the statutory procedure for considering a request

- the introduction of a new duty on employers to consider requests in a 'reasonable manner'

- the removal of the right to be accompanied to a meeting to discuss the request

- the removal of the express requirement to hold an appeal hearing where the request has been rejected

- the introduction of an overall time limit that a request must be considered within three months of receipt.

Monitoring and review. Section 134 CFA provides that the changes made to 4.6 the flexible working scheme must be reviewed within seven years of coming into force and that the Secretary of State must publish the conclusions of the review, which must state, among other things, whether the objectives behind the changes have been achieved. According to the Modern Workplaces Impact Assessment (published in March 2014), the review date is planned for April 2019.

Acas Code of Practice and Guide 4.7

Acas has produced a statutory Code of Practice on 'Handling in a reasonable manner requests to work flexibly' ('the Acas Code') under S.199 of the Trade Union and Labour Relations (Consolidation) Act 1992 (TULR(C)A). The Code

197

must be taken into account by employment tribunals where it is relevant to a question arising in the proceedings – S.207(2) TULR(C)A.

As explained under 'Handling flexible working requests' below, the Code supplements the basic statutory duty on employers to consider requests reasonably. The Code's recommendations are not compulsory, but set out best practice. For example, it recommends that employers provide a right of appeal even though this is no longer a legal obligation. What is reasonable will depend on the circumstances of individual cases and the employer's resources: it may well be unreasonable for an employer with 50 employees not to hold an appeal, while it is less so for a small employer with three staff. The Code is supplemented by a non-statutory good practice guide, 'The right to request flexible working: an Acas guide' ('the Acas guide').

4.8 Who has right to request flexible working?

The statutory right to request flexible working is set out in S.80F ERA. While the pool of eligible employees has been considerably widened, in that the right is no longer restricted to employees who have parental or caring responsibilities, it does not apply to everyone. Two important qualifying conditions still apply: the person making the request must be an *employee*, and must have been employed for at least *26 consecutive weeks* – Reg 3 Flexible Working Regulations.

The removal of the requirement that an employee must have parental or caring responsibilities to make a flexible working request means that employees will be able to apply for flexible working regardless of the reason for the request. In other words, someone who wishes to work reduced hours to have a better work-life balance will be entitled to apply for flexible working in the same way as someone who wants to work fewer hours in order to fit in the school run. This extension is also likely to benefit parents and carers such as grandparents and other relatives or friends who will be able to put in a flexible working application in order to help out with childcare. The reason why the employee is seeking the contractual change is nevertheless likely to remain important, particularly where the employer receives multiple flexible working requests simultaneously and is unable to grant all of them – see 'Handling flexible working requests – prioritising competing requests' below.

4.9 Employees only

As under the old regime, the right to request flexible working only applies to 'employees' and not the wider category of 'worker'. 'Employee' is defined by S.230(1) ERA as 'an individual who has entered into or works under (or, where the employment has ceased, worked under) a contract of employment'. 'Contract of employment' is, in turn, defined as a 'contract of service or apprenticeship, whether express or implied, and (if it is express) whether oral or in writing' – S.230(2). For a detailed discussion of the definition of 'employee', see IDS Employment Law Handbook, 'Contracts of Employment' (2009), Chapter 1, 'Basic requirements', under 'Who is an employee?'.

Excluded categories of employee. Some types of employee are specifically **4.10** excluded from the right to request flexible working. These are:

- agency workers – S.80F(8)(a) ERA makes it clear that agency workers are not qualifying employees for the purposes of S.80F and are therefore excluded from the right to request. This is subject to one exception, which applies to agency workers who are returning to work from a period of parental leave (for which see IDS Employment Law Handbook, 'Maternity and Parental Rights' (2009), Chapter 9, 'Parental leave'). An 'agency worker' is defined as someone who is 'supplied by a person ("the agent") to do work for another ("the principal") under a contract or other arrangement made between the agent and the principal' – S.80F(8)(b). The Government's stated reason for excluding agency workers was that the company in which an agency worker is placed will have approached the agency to provide a specific service without an expectation of having to adjust their working patterns as a result – see para 128 of the Explanatory Notes to the Employment Act 2002 (EA). (Note that nothing in the Agency Workers Regulations 2010 SI 2010/93 has altered this situation – see Chapter 1, 'Agency workers', for full details of these Regulations)

- members of the armed forces – S.192 (read with para 16, Sch 2) ERA

- share fishermen and women – S.199(2) ERA. Note, however, that seafarers employed on ships registered under S.8 of the Merchant Shipping Act 1995 are covered provided that the ship is registered as belonging to a port in Great Britain, that under his or her contract of employment the employee does not work wholly outside Great Britain, and that he or she is ordinarily resident in Great Britain – S.199(7) and (8)

- 'employee shareholders' (within the meaning of S.205A ERA) – S.205(2)(b) (see Chapter 7, 'Employee shareholders').

Crown employees are covered – S.191 ERA, as are parliamentary staff – Ss.194 and 195 ERA.

26 weeks' continuous service   4.11

As under the previous regime, employees must be employed for at least 26 consecutive weeks with the employer before they are entitled to exercise the right to request flexible working – Reg 3 Flexible Working Regulations. In its Modern Workplaces consultation, the Government stated that it had considered removing this requirement, primarily to enable those who need flexibility from the start to enter the labour market. In the end, however, it decided against making the right to request flexible working a 'day one' right, taking the view that the service requirement gave employers certainty as to the terms and conditions on which they hire employees. It also took the view that giving the right to new starters could be counterproductive as some of these employees might have to leave jobs, having wrongly assumed that their working patterns could be changed once they started work. For these reasons, the 26 weeks' continuous service requirement remains in place. The Government has, however, committed to working with private sector employers to encourage them to offer flexible working at the recruitment stage.

According to the Explanatory Note that accompanies the Flexible Working Regulations, continuous employment is to be computed in accordance with Chapter 1 of Part 14 of the ERA – for full details see IDS Employment Law Handbook, 'Continuity of Employment' (2012).

4.12 Multiple requests

If an employee has already made an application under S.80F, he or she cannot make a further application to the same employer for a period of 12 months beginning with the date on which the previous application was made (see 'Making flexible working request – date of request' below) – S.80F(4). This applies whether the employee applied for a permanent or temporary change in terms and conditions, and whether the application was accepted or rejected. Note, however, that if the employee's application is not made in accordance with the statutory procedure, S.80F(4) does not apply and he or she is free to submit another application immediately – see 'Handling flexible working requests – breach of procedure by employee' below.

The Government briefly entertained the idea of allowing more than one flexible working request to be made under the statutory procedure in any 12-month period where the employee's first request relates to a contract variation that is expected to last for less than a year. It believed that this would address the situation where the employee needs to work flexibly on a short-term basis, such as where he or she is caring for someone with a terminal illness or wants to undertake a course of study. 67 per cent of respondents to the consultation agreed that the 'one-request-per-year' restriction should go. However, the Government ultimately decided to retain the restriction, taking the view that the legislation does not actually *prohibit* requests for a temporary contractual change and that most employers will allow such changes if the situation arises – see further 'Scope of right to request flexible working – temporary changes' below.

4.13 Neither the ERA nor the Regulations provide a definition of 'same employer' and it is therefore unclear how S.80F(4) operates where there has been a transfer of the business covered by the Transfer of Undertakings (Protection of Employment) Regulations 2006 SI 2006/264. Presumably an employee whose contract of employment is transferred under those Regulations may be entitled to submit a new flexible working request following the transfer notwithstanding the fact that he or she had already made a request in the preceding 12 months. The employee could simply argue that as a result of the transfer the 'same employer' no longer employs him or her.

Requests by non-qualifying employees 4.14

One problem employers often have to face is how to deal with requests from employees who are not entitled to make requests for flexible working under the statutory scheme, such as employees without the necessary 26 weeks' continuous service or employees who have already made a request within the previous 12 months. Although an employer is not obliged to consider such requests in accordance with the statutory procedure, there may be benefits in so doing. Since the right operates independently of existing employment law rights, an employee whose flexible working request is rejected could, depending on the circumstances, bring a discrimination claim if the reason for the employee's request relates to a protected characteristic – see 'Discrimination claims' below. For instance, a woman who is seeking flexible working to care for her children could bring a claim for indirect sex discrimination. The fact that, for example, the employer followed a reasonable procedure, held meetings to consider the request and provided solid business reasons for rejecting it might help in establishing a defence of objective justification – see 'Discrimination claims – indirect discrimination' below.

Scope of right to request flexible working 4.15

The right to request flexible working means the right to apply for a change in terms and conditions of employment relating to:

- the hours the employee is required to work

- the times the employee is required to work

- where, as between his or her home and a place of business of the employer, the employee is required to work, or

- such other aspect of the employee's terms and conditions as may be specified in regulations – S.80F(1)(a).

It is important to dispel the misconception that the rules give employees the right to work flexibly. An employment tribunal can only interfere with an employer's decision to refuse an application for flexible working if the employer failed to deal with the flexible working application in a reasonable manner or based its decision on an invalid business reason or on incorrect facts – see 'Handling requests for flexible working – grounds upon which employer can refuse request' below. Under the statutory scheme an employee cannot force an employer to acquiesce to a flexible working request. The

201

procedure merely affords the employee the right to make a request and have it considered seriously, and the penalty for breach is an award of compensation rather than an order enforcing the request – see 'Enforcement and remedies – remedies' below.

4.16 Types of flexible working

The terms and conditions listed in S.80(F)(1)(a) could cover a wide range of work patterns. The Modern Workplaces consultation provided the following examples:

- part-time working: employees are contracted to work less than normal full-time hours

- flexitime: employees work a standard core time but can vary their start, finish and break times each day within agreed limits

- compressed hours: employees work their total number of contracted weekly hours in fewer than the usual number of working days each week by working longer individual days. Often a five-day week is compressed into four days

- homeworking: employees work all or part of their contracted hours from home

- annualised hours: employees average out working time across the year so they work a set number of hours per year rather than per week. Normally, they are split into core hours that are worked each week and unallocated hours that can be used for peaks in demand

- term-time working: employees' work follows school term patterns. They work as normal during term-time. During school holidays they do not go to work but are still employed

- structured time off in lieu: employees work longer hours during busy periods and take an equivalent amount of time off (with pay) at a less busy time. There may be limits on the number of hours individuals can build up and when they can take time off

- job-sharing: two employees work part time (which could be part-day, part-week or part-year) and share the duties and responsibilities of a full-time position

- varied-hours working or time banking: prospective employees advertise which hours they are available to work for the day and employers employ them for short periods of time to manage specific pieces of work, such as covering a telephone help-line. For example, an individual might be employed between 6 pm and 9 pm on a Tuesday evening.

Temporary changes   4.17

An employee can apply for temporary, as well as permanent, changes under S.80F(1)(a) ERA. The Acas guide states that if employees are only looking for an informal change for a short period to their working hours or conditions – for instance, to cope with a bereavement or to pursue a short course of study – the employer may wish to consider allowing them to revert back to their old conditions after a specified period (e.g. three months) or after the occurrence of a specific event (e.g. the end of a course of study). Employees should be aware, however, that they do not have a statutory right to request another contractual variation until 12 months after the previous application was made – see 'Who has right to request flexible working? – multiple requests' above.

The Government briefly entertained the idea of introducing a right to make more than one flexible working request under the statutory procedure in any 12-month period where the employee initially applies for a contract variation that is expected to last for less than a year. It believed that this would address the situation where the employee needs to work flexibly on a short-term basis, such as where he or she is caring for someone with a terminal illness or wants to undertake a course of study. 67 per cent of respondents to the consultation agreed that the 'one-request-per-year' restriction should go. However, the Government ultimately decided to retain the restriction, taking the view that the legislation does not actually *prohibit* requests for a temporary contractual change and that most employers will allow such changes if the situation arises.

Making flexible working request   4.18

When making a flexible working request an employee must submit an application to the employer:

- stating that it is an application for a change in terms and conditions under S.80F ERA

- specifying the change applied for and the date on which it is proposed the change should become effective (failure to include this date will invalidate an application – see Hussain v Consumer Credit Counselling ET Case No.1804305/04), and

- explaining what effect, if any, the employee thinks the change would have on the employer and how, in his or her opinion, any such effect might be dealt with – S.80F(2).

In addition, the application must be in writing, be dated, and state whether a previous application has been made by the employee to the employer and, if so, when – Reg 4(b) and (c) Flexible Working Regulations.

Interestingly, there is no requirement for the application to state the reason why 4.19
the request for a change in terms and conditions is being made. In this regard,

203

it is worth noting that the Government specifically rejected an amendment to the Employment Bill (before it became the Employment Act 2002) that would have obliged an employee to state in his or her application the reason he or she needed a change in terms and conditions. It was felt that such a provision would require parents (the then sole beneficiaries of the right) to explain their personal circumstances to employers and force employers to get involved in reviewing the personal details of employees' lives (Alan Johnson, House of Commons Standing Committee F, 24 January 2002 pm, col.624). Therefore, even under the original statutory provisions, employees did not have to provide the reason for the request (although they did have to explain their relationship with the child or adult dependant in question to show that they met the then qualifying conditions).

In theory, therefore, an employer's decision could (and should) be made without the employer knowing the reason for the request, the focus being solely on whether or not the employer's business can accommodate it – see 'Handling requests for flexible working – grounds upon which employer can refuse request' below. That said, if an employee's reason relates to one of the protected characteristics set out in the Equality Act 2010, it then becomes highly relevant since it means that any refusal could potentially be discriminatory – see 'Discrimination claims' below. Therefore, if there is limited availability of flexible working and/or 'competing' requests, it will undoubtedly be reasonable for the employer to enquire into the reason, in order to help it to make a decision under the flexible working provisions and to avoid discrimination. In addition, the employee may wish to put the reason in the application, even though not obliged to do so, since this may bolster his or her request, particularly if it relates to a protected characteristic. However, if the employer subsequently discovers that the employee lied and never intended to use the flexible working pattern for the stipulated purpose, it may take disciplinary action – see further para 123 of the Explanatory Notes to the Employment Act 2002.

4.20 Date of request

The date the application is made is important because an employee cannot make a further application to the same employer for a period of 12 months beginning with that date – see 'Who has the right to request flexible working? – multiple requests' above. According to Reg 5(1) of the Flexible Working Regulations, an application is made on the date it is received by the employer. Reg 5(2) goes on to provide that, unless the contrary is proved, any such application is taken to have been received:

- if sent by post, on the day on which it would have been delivered in the ordinary course of post

- if delivered personally, on the day of delivery.

204

Special conditions apply where an application is sent by electronic transmission. Such an application is taken to be received on the day of transmission (unless the contrary is proved), provided the employer has:

- agreed that the application can be sent by electronic transmission

- specified an electronic address to which the application can be sent, and

- specified the electronic form to be used by the employee – Reg 5(2)(a) and 5(3).

Breach of procedure by employee   4.21
A failure by the employee to follow the correct procedure when making his or her request may afford the employer a defence to any eventual employment tribunal claim under S.80H – see 'Enforcement and remedies' below. An example:

- **Hussain v Consumer Credit Counselling** ET Case No.1804305/04: the claimant, a father of three children aged between two and ten, made a request for flexible working so that he could arrive home early enough to spend some time with his children before they went to bed. He asked for his work pattern to be adjusted so that he would work from 8 am to 4 pm, Mondays to Thursdays. His request was declined on the ground of detrimental effect on ability to meet customer demand and he brought a claim under S.80H. The employment tribunal held that it had no jurisdiction to hear H's claim since his application did not constitute a request for the purposes of S.80F. Not only had H failed to specify the date on which he wanted the change to take effect, but he had also neglected to explain what effect the proposed change would have on his employer. This was fatal to his claim.

However, this could amount to a hollow victory, since the employee could simply resubmit a new flexible working request and force the employer to go through the whole statutory procedure again. This is because S.80F(4), which prevents an employee from making a flexible working request to the same employer within 12 months of the last request, does not operate where that request was not made in accordance with the statutory procedure – see 'Scope and coverage of right to request – multiple requests' above.

If an employee fails to provide all the information required, it would be prudent **4.22** for the employer to inform the employee of this, explain what has been omitted, and ask him or her to resubmit the application once complete. Employers should be aware that an employee whose flexible working request is rejected or ignored simply because it has not been made in accordance with the statutory procedure might have a claim for indirect discrimination, depending on whether the reason for the employee's request relates to a protected characteristic (see 'Discrimination claims' below).

205

4.23 Handling flexible working requests

The procedural requirements governing flexible working requests have been simplified under the new rules. Employers were previously expected to follow the detailed statutory procedure set out in the Procedural Regulations when considering flexible working requests. Now they are simply required to deal with the application in a 'reasonable manner' and notify the employee of the decision on the application, including any appeal, within three months of the date of the application.

Although the Procedural Regulations still apply to requests made before 30 June, they will very quickly become redundant. In brief, under the pre-30 June procedure, each step of the process – i.e. the meeting to discuss the application, the decision and the appeal meeting if the application is refused – is prescribed, as is the time limit within which it must be completed. The employer must hold a meeting with the employee to discuss the application within 28 days of receiving the application and the employer's decision must be notified to the employee no later than 14 days after the meeting. If the application is refused, the employee must exercise his or her right to appeal within 14 days after the date on which notice of the decision was given. Again, any appeal hearing must be held within 14 days after the employee's notice of appeal is given and the employer's decision on the appeal must be communicated to the employee no later than 14 days after the appeal meeting. The Procedural Regulations allow a maximum of three months for the completion of these steps, unless the employer and employee agree an extension to any of the time limits. Full details of the old procedure can be found in IDS Employment Law Handbook, 'Maternity and Parental Rights' (2009), Chapter 11, 'Flexible working', under 'Employers' duties in respect of requests – procedure for considering requests'.

Interestingly, the Procedural Regulations have yet to be revoked (unlike the Eligibility Regulations), although presumably they will be once the old rules are no longer of any relevance.

4.24 Procedure for considering requests

From 30 June 2014, employers are no longer required to follow the statutory procedure set out in the Procedural Regulations. Instead, they are under a duty to consider requests reasonably and within a reasonable period of time. S.80G(1) ERA provides that an employer's obligations in relation to a flexible working application are twofold:

- first, to deal with the application in a 'reasonable manner'; and

- secondly, to notify the employee of the decision on the application, including any appeal, within three months of the date of the application.

206

The Acas Code sets out the basic requirements of a reasonable procedure in relation to flexible working requests, recommending that employers adopt the following basic steps upon receiving a flexible working request:

- discuss the request with the employee
- consider the request carefully, and
- deal with the request promptly.

Despite the reduced statutory requirements, the Code retains much of the same **4.25** procedure (albeit in simplified form). It should be remembered, however, that these recommendations are not mandatory (although breach of the Code can be taken into account by an employment tribunal when deciding liability). At only two pages long, the Code's brevity as to what constitutes a 'reasonable' procedure for the purposes of S.80G is intentional. This reflects the Government's desire to introduce a more informal process to make it as easy as possible for employers to adopt flexible working in their workplaces, preferably by enabling them to utilise their own existing HR processes in dealing with requests.

Discussing the request

4.26

The Acas Code recommends that, upon receiving the request, the employer should arrange to talk with the employee as soon as possible. The employer should discuss the request with the employee in private to find out exactly what changes are being sought and how they might benefit both the employee and the business. While no longer a legal requirement, the Acas guide recommends that the discussion take place at a time and a location that is convenient to both employer and employee. If the initial date for the discussion cannot be kept, another date should be arranged. If the employee fails to attend the meeting and the rearranged meeting without good reason, the employer can treat the application as withdrawn – see 'Withdrawn requests' below. No meeting is needed if the employer intends to approve the request.

Employees no longer have a statutory right to be accompanied by a work colleague or trade union representative at the meeting with the employer. However, both the Code and the guide recommend that the employer allow the employee to be accompanied if he or she so wishes. In its response to the consultation on the draft Code, Acas stated that it considers this to be 'in the interests of good employment relations' and 'particularly helpful when, for example, an employee lacks confidence or where English is not their first language'.

Deciding the request

4.27

Once the employer has met with the employee, it must consider the request carefully. The Acas Code states that a 'reasonable' consideration of the request requires the employer to weigh up the benefits of the requested changes in

207

working conditions for both employer and employee against any adverse business impact of implementing the changes. Any adverse business impact must mirror one or more of the permissible business reasons for refusing a flexible working request contained in the legislation – see 'Grounds upon which employer can refuse request' below. Once the employer has made its decision, it must inform the employee, preferably in writing. The employer may decide to accept the request, reject it, or to accept it in a modified form.

As noted under 'Scope of the right to request flexible working' above, the flexible working provisions do not give employees any substantive rights to have their flexible working requests granted, however meritorious. They merely have the right to have the matter considered, in accordance with the requirements set down in Ss.80F–80I ERA, and for the employer's refusal to be for a valid business reason.

4.28 **Grounds upon which employer can refuse request**

The employer can only refuse the employee's flexible working request for a valid business reason. There are eight such reasons, which are set out in the legislation. They are:

- burden of additional costs
- detrimental effect on ability to meet customer demand
- inability to reorganise work among existing staff
- inability to recruit additional staff
- detrimental impact on quality
- detrimental impact on performance
- insufficiency of work during the periods the employee proposes to work
- planned structural changes – S.80G(1)(b) ERA.

The Acas guide gives practical examples on when each of these reasons may apply. It also notes that, when determining whether a business reason applies, employers should be aware of their obligations under the Equality Act 2010 and not inadvertently discriminate against an employee who has a protected characteristic. For example, a flexible working arrangement could be a reasonable adjustment for a disabled employee – see further 'Discrimination claims – disabled employees' below.

4.29 The Acas Code simply advises that, when refusing an application, the employer should put the decision in writing. This is a change from the previous regime, which required the employer to set out in writing the grounds on which the application was refused and to provide a sufficient explanation as to why those grounds applied. This level of detail is no longer required under the new procedure.

208

Time limits for dealing with request

4.30

While the old statutory procedure imposed strict time limits for each step of the procedure, the Acas Code simply states that employers should deal 'promptly' with requests. This is circumscribed by S.80G(1)(aa) ERA, which provides that the employer 'shall notify the employee of the decision on the application within the decision period'. The 'decision period' is (a) the period of three months beginning with the date on which the application is made, or (b) such longer period as may be agreed by the employer and the employee – S.80G(1B).

Section 80G(1A) goes on to clarify that, if the employer allows the employee to appeal against a decision to reject the application, the reference to the 'decision on the application' in S.80G(1)(aa) is a reference to a decision on the appeal or, if more than one appeal is allowed, the decision on the final appeal. Read together with Reg 5 of the Flexible Working Regulations (discussed under 'Making flexible working request – date of request' above), this means that all requests, including any appeals, must be considered and decided upon within three months of receipt of the application. This time limit may, however, be extended by agreement between the employer and the employee, provided the extension is agreed within six months of receipt of the application – Ss.80G(1B)(b) and 80G(1C).

The upshot of these provisions is that the employer must have concluded the 4.31 process of dealing with a flexible working request within three months of receiving the application, which is the same time limit that applied under the old procedure. That said, as employers may omit the appeal process altogether, they potentially have more time under the new procedure (namely, a total of three months) to discuss the application with the employee and to rule on it. And employers are no longer bound by strict time limits in respect of each separate step of the procedure. It is thus left to each employer to decide, for example, how much time should pass between receipt of the application and the meeting to discuss it with the employee or how soon after the meeting it should notify the employee of its decision. The legislation merely provides that the end date of the entire procedure must not extend beyond three months of the request being made. That said, an employer who puts off dealing with a flexible working request to the very last minute may run the risk of a tribunal finding that it did not deal with the request in a 'reasonable manner' as required by S.80G(1)(a).

Withdrawn requests

4.32

Where a request for flexible working has been withdrawn, the employer is no longer under a duty to consider it. S.80G(1D) provides that an employer can treat an application as withdrawn if the employee without good reason has failed to attend:

209

- two consecutive meetings arranged by the employer in order to discuss the flexible working application, or

- two consecutive meetings arranged by the employer to discuss the appeal against its rejection (if an appeal has been allowed)

and the employer has notified the employee that it has decided to treat that conduct as a withdrawal of the application.

4.33 This provision only applies if an employee has failed to attend the *same type* of meeting more than once. Thus where an employee fails to attend an initial application meeting without reasonable cause (but does subsequently attend such a meeting) and then fails to attend an appeal meeting without reasonable cause, the employer is not entitled to treat the application as withdrawn under S.80G(1D).

(Note that the employer is no longer entitled to treat an application as withdrawn where the employee without reasonable cause has refused to give the employer information that is required by the employer in order to assess whether the contract variation should be agreed.)

4.34 Prioritising competing requests

As the right to request flexible working is now available to all eligible employees, it is likely that employers will at some point receive multiple, competing requests from two or more employees. Where an employer is unable to accommodate all the requests, the question will arise whether the employer should give preference to requests from certain groups of employees, such as parents and carers. During consultation, the Government stated that formally prioritising certain groups of employees would be counterproductive, as this would reinforce the perception that flexible working is primarily for parents and carers and would not promote a culture where it is a legitimate ambition for all employees. However, the Government also accepted that some employers might wish to take employees' personal circumstances into account if they have to prioritise between competing requests. It therefore decided that employers would not be required to prioritise competing requests according to a particular hierarchy of concerns (for example, childcare or care commitments) but would be allowed to take account of any other factors they considered relevant in the event that they had to choose between requests. Where an employer does prioritise, it still has to show that it could not accommodate all the requests for business reasons.

This compromise is unlikely to allay fears among employers that they could potentially leave themselves open to allegations of discrimination where they prioritise some requests over others – see 'Discrimination claims – "competing" requests' below. There is also the possibility that an employee could claim unfair constructive dismissal where the employer rejects his or her request but accepts that of another employee – see 'Detriment and unfair dismissal rights' below.

210

The Acas Code has little to say on how to deal with competing requests, simply **4.35** stating that an employer must not discriminate against an employee when considering a flexible working request. The Acas guide points out that when employers receive more than one request, they are not required to make value judgements about the most deserving. An employer should consider each case on its merits, looking at the business case and the possible impact of refusing a request. It further advises that, before coming to a decision, the employer might want to discuss the changes sought with the affected employees and see if there is room for adjustment or compromise. It even goes so far as to suggest that where this is not possible and an employer is truly unable to distinguish between the requests, it could get the agreement of the employees concerned to consider some form of random selection. Another option, as suggested in the Government's response to the consultation, would be to agree an informal flexible working arrangement or a trial period with a view to reviewing the arrangement at some point in the future. Whatever route the employer takes, it would be sensible to have a flexible working policy in place so that employees know how requests will be decided.

Importantly, the guide states that requests should be considered in the order they are received and that, having considered and approved the first request, the employer should remember that the business context has now changed and can be taken into account when considering the second request against the business reasons set out in S.80G(1)(b) ERA.

Implementing flexible working **4.36**

Any changes to an employee's terms and conditions of employment will be permanent, unless the employer and the employee agree otherwise. For example, an employee who needs to change his or her hours of work for a set period may apply for a temporary change. So long as the employer agrees to it, the employee's hours of work will revert back to the original hours of work at the end of the period.

The Acas guide states that if employees are only looking for an informal change for a short period to their working hours or conditions – for instance, to cope with a bereavement or to pursue a short course of study – the employer may wish to consider allowing them to revert back to their old conditions after a specified period (e.g. three months) or after the occurrence of a specific event (e.g. the end of a course of study). However, employees need to be aware that they do not have a statutory right to request another contractual variation until 12 months after the previous application was made – see 'Who has the right to request flexible working? – multiple requests' above.

There is no statutory provision allowing for the affected employee's benefits to **4.37** be reduced pro rata if he or she is begins working reduced hours under the new

211

flexible arrangement. The Government's position (as stated before the right to request flexible working was introduced in April 2003) is that the consequences of changes to an employee's terms and conditions will be provided for in the employee's contract, either expressly or by implication – Lord Sainsbury, House of Lords Grand Committee, 22 April 2002, col.CWH535. Thus, for example, if a contract provides for benefits when certain criteria are met, an employee will have to meet those criteria under his or her new working arrangements in order to receive them. Similarly, if a contract stipulates an hourly rate of pay, less wages will be due if fewer hours are worked. However, a reduction in the hourly rate itself is likely to be unlawful unless there has been a valid contractual variation.

In Valentine v Medico Legal Professionals Ltd ET Case No.3201634/13 V was employed by MLP Ltd as an administrative assistant from July 2011. Her hours of work were 9 am to 5 pm, Monday to Friday. She took maternity leave between April 2013 and January 2014 and on her return to work she made an application for flexible working and it was agreed that she would work 10.30 am to 2.30 pm Tuesday to Thursday. When she received her payslip at the end of January she discovered that her hourly salary had been reduced. The company's response was that as she was now in a different role, she was not entitled to the same rate of pay as before. An employment tribunal found that V's duties continued to be the same and her role had not changed. There was an agreement that V would work flexibly upon her return to work but that did not provide a reason for altering her hourly rate of pay. It held that the reduction in pay amounted to direct sex discrimination.

4.38 Enforcement and remedies

An employee whose application for flexible working has been rejected can make a complaint to an employment tribunal within the applicable time limit. Where the complaint is successful, the tribunal must make a declaration to that effect and can make an order requiring the employer to reconsider the employee's application or award compensation.

4.39 Grounds for complaint

An employee who makes an application under S.80F can present a complaint to an employment tribunal on the ground that:

- the employer failed to consider the flexible working application in a 'reasonable manner' in accordance with S.80G(1)(a) ERA – S.80H(1)(a) (see '"Reasonable manner"' below)

- the employer failed to notify the employee of the decision on the application, including any appeal, within three months of the date of the application in accordance with S.80G(aa) – S.80H(1)(a)

- the application was refused on a ground that is not a valid business reason under S.80G(1)(b) ERA – S.80H(1)(a) (see 'Handling flexible working requests – grounds upon which employer can refuse request' above)

- the decision was based on incorrect facts – S.80H(1)(b) (see 'Incorrect facts' below), or

- the employer sought to treat the employee's flexible working request as withdrawn under S.80G(1D) without having good grounds for doing so – S.80H(1)(c) (see 'Application treated as withdrawn' below).

A complaint under the first four grounds cannot be made: **4.40**

- in respect of an application that has been disposed of by agreement or withdrawn – S.80H(2), and

- until the employer –

  - has notified the employee of its decision on the application – S.80H(3)(a)

  - where an appeal is allowed, has notified the employee of its decision on the appeal or final appeal (if there is more than one) – S.80H(3)(a) and 80H(3A), or

  - where the employer fails to notify the employee of its decision on the application or (where applicable) appeal, at the end of the decision period (which is the period of three months beginning with the date on which the application was made or such longer period as agreed by the employer and the employee – S.80G(1B)) – S.80H(3)(b).

A complaint under S.80H(1)(c) may be made as soon as the employer has notified the employee that it has decided to treat the application as having been withdrawn – S.80H(3C).

'Reasonable manner'. The new duty on employers to deal with applications in **4.41** a 'reasonable manner' may provide greater scope for challenge than was previously available. However, even under the old rules employers were expected to show some evidence that they had considered a flexible working request seriously. Two examples:

- **Mehaffy v Dunnes Stores (UK) Ltd** ET Case No.1308076/03: following a period of maternity leave, M made a request to work flexibly in order to spend more time at home with her son. The company rejected her request on three grounds: negative impact on performance, negative impact on quality, and additional costs. When her appeal was also rejected, M complained to a tribunal, claiming that the company had failed to comply with its obligations under S.80F ERA because it had failed to give genuine consideration to her request. Taking into account the company's mindset, which was that all managers had to work full time, and the fact that it had no written

213

policy to deal with flexible working requests, the tribunal agreed, finding that the company had closed its mind to the possibility of M working part time. It was, in the tribunal's view, 'reluctantly paying lip-service to working through the flexible work provisions... without any genuine commitment to considering the claimant's proposals'

- **Holder v Mamas and Papas Ltd** ET Case No.1100916/10: H began working in January 2008 as deputy store manager. She went on maternity leave in January 2009 and in November 2009 had an informal meeting with the company to discuss her return to work. She wanted to return on a part-time basis and submitted a flexible working application on 18 December saying she wanted to work 24 hours a week. The employer refused the request, saying that it would be unable to redistribute H's management responsibilities to other members of the team and it would be extremely difficult to recruit a part-time deputy manager. Following the rejection of her appeal, H resigned and brought a claim under S.80H ERA. Upholding that claim, the employment tribunal ruled that the company's reasons for refusing the request were unfounded, since the evidence showed that it had been able to redistribute H's work during her maternity leave and had allowed another manager to work part time. The tribunal was satisfied that the employer's refusal stemmed from an established and entrenched opposition to part-time working or job-sharing among management staff.

4.42 While the duty to consider requests reasonably may shore up the scope for challenge in this area, it is unlikely that tribunals will minutely scrutinise an employer's rationale for refusing such an application, and still less substitute their view as to the feasibility and/or commercial viability of flexible working for that of the employer. However, even where an employee's claim under S.80H fails it may still be possible to bring a discrimination claim – see 'Discrimination claims' below. For example, in Webster v Princes Soft Drinks ET Case No.1803942/04 an employment tribunal declined to give its view as to whether the employer had evaluated each of the issues identified in S.80G, as to do so would have involved second-guessing a management decision. However, the same tribunal found that the refusal amounted to indirect sex discrimination.

4.43 **Incorrect facts.** One of the grounds on which an employee can bring a flexible working complaint under S.80H is where the employer's decision to reject the application was based on incorrect facts. This ground was considered by the EAT in Commotion Ltd v Rutty 2006 ICR 290, EAT, where R, a warehouse assistant, requested a variation of her working pattern in order to care for her granddaughter. The request was rejected on the basis that C Ltd wanted to have a uniform working day, and that shortening R's hours would have a negative impact on the overall warehouse performance and strain resources. The employment tribunal noted that the employer had explained the refusal to permit R to work flexibly by relying on 'detrimental impact on performance', the business ground set out in S.80G(1)(b)(vi). However, it held that C Ltd had failed to make out a legitimate reason for the refusal as the reasons it gave were 'outdated… off the cuff and made without research'. No evidence had been put forward to show that working as a part-time warehouse assistant was not feasible.

On appeal, C Ltd argued that the tribunal had engaged in an objective assessment of the reasons for refusal. The EAT disagreed. It held that: '[I]n order for the tribunal to establish whether or not the decision by the employer to reject the application was based on incorrect facts, the tribunal must examine the evidence as to the circumstances surrounding the situation to which the application gave rise. In doing so, the tribunal are entitled to enquire into what would have been the effect of granting the application. Could it have been coped with without disruption? What did other staff feel about it? Could they make up the time? and matters of that type. We do not propose to go exhaustively through the matters at which a tribunal might wish to look, but if the tribunal were to look at such matters in order to test whether the assertion made by the employer was factually correct, that would not be any misuse of their powers and they would not be committing an error of law.' In R's case, no evidence had been put forward to support the assertion that part-time working as a warehouse assistant was not feasible, and so the tribunal had not erred in finding that assertion to be incorrect.

Application treated as withdrawn. Section 80H(1)(c) ERA is a new provision 4.44 and entitles an employee to bring a complaint where the employer has treated his or her flexible working request as withdrawn without having good grounds for doing so. The circumstances in which an employer may treat an application as being withdrawn are discussed under 'Handling flexible working requests – withdrawn requests' above. Previously, S.80H(2) expressly prohibited an employee from bringing any complaint to an employment tribunal in respect of a flexible working application that had been disposed of by agreement or withdrawn. However, it has now been amended to provide that no complaint *under S.80H(1)(a) or (b)* (i.e. the first four grounds listed under 'Enforcement and remedies' above) may be made in respect of an application which has been disposed of by agreement or withdrawn.

Time limits

4.45

A complaint to an employment tribunal must be brought:

- within three months of the relevant date, i.e. the date on which the employee may make a complaint (see 'Grounds for complaint' above), or

- within such further period as the tribunal considers reasonable where it is satisfied that it was not reasonably practicable for the complaint to have been brought within the three-month period – S.80H(5).

215

For a detailed discussion of time limits and the circumstances in which an extension of time may be granted, see IDS Employment Law Handbook, 'Employment Tribunal Practice and Procedure' (2014), Chapter 5, 'Time limits'.

4.46 Remedies

Section 80I ERA sets out the remedies available for a breach of the right to request flexible working. Where a tribunal finds that a complaint under S.80H is well founded, it must make a declaration to that effect and may:

- make an order requiring the employer to reconsider the employee's application for flexible working – S.80I(1)(a). Note that where a tribunal makes such an order, S.80G (which governs an employer's duties in relation to flexible working applications) applies as if the application had been made on the date of the order – S.80I(4))

- make an award of compensation to be paid by the employer to the employee – S.80I(1)(b).

4.47 The amount of compensation will be such amount as the tribunal considers just and equitable in all the circumstances of the case – S.80I(2). However, this cannot exceed eight weeks' pay – Reg 6 Flexible Working Regulations. The amount of a week's pay is subject to the upper limit specified in S.227 ERA (currently £464 as from 6 April 2014) – para 47(2), Sch 7 Employment Act 2002. Therefore, the maximum amount of compensation that a tribunal can award under S.80I at present is £3,712.

According to the Explanatory Notes to the EA, in deciding the amount of compensation to be awarded, a tribunal should take into account the behaviour of the employer (e.g. whether it has lied) and of the employee (e.g. his or her willingness to consider acceptable alternatives) – see para 140.

4.48 Three examples of how employment tribunals have approached the question of what amounts to 'just and equitable' compensation in the context of flexible working complaints:

- **British Airways plc v Starmer** 2005 IRLR 862, EAT: the employment tribunal noted that, while BA had not provided a business ground in its initial refusal of S's flexible working request, it had acted promptly to rectify its mistake by sending out a more detailed notice of refusal a few days later. As a result, the tribunal concluded that S was not effectively prejudiced by the breach and that it was just and equitable to limit the award to one week's pay. This decision was confirmed by the EAT on appeal

- **Coxon v Landesbank Baden-Wurttemberg** ET Case No.2203702/04: the employment tribunal held that an employer had 'patently failed' to observe the requirements set out in the (now repealed) Procedural Regulations and, as a result, was minded to make the maximum award of eight weeks.

However, in view of the fact that, had serious consideration been given to C's request to work flexibly, it would have been rejected by any reasonable employer, the tribunal decided that it would be just and equitable to reduce the award to six weeks' compensation

- **Watton v RBS Insurance Services Ltd** ET Case No.2803908/10: an employment tribunal found that RBS had been late in responding to W's request for flexible working. However, RBS had accepted that its response was slow and had given W a sincere apology. There had been no factual errors in the refusal of the flexible working request, and eight reasons had been given, all of which were valid within the terms of S.80G(1). Furthermore, RBS had done its best to accommodate W's wishes. The tribunal therefore held that it would not exercise its discretion to order RBS to reconsider the request, particularly since W had become embittered during the process. However, it did order RBS to pay W two weeks' pay by way of compensation for its failure to deal with his request in time.

The remedies available under S.80I are not mutually exclusive – where **4.49** appropriate, an employment tribunal may award compensation as well as making an order for reconsideration. In Snelling v Tates Ltd t/a Spar ET Case No.1502720/03, for example, S, who had sole responsibility for her three-year-old daughter, made an application to work flexibly. The employer had trained area managers in the provisions relating to flexible working but the relevant area manager was not available to deal with S's request and, accordingly, the matter had to be handled by a store manager. S's application was rejected and she complained to a tribunal, alleging breaches of the Procedural Regulations, including a failure to hold a meeting within 28 days of the day she made the application and to inform her of a decision within 14 days thereafter. Upholding her claim, the tribunal ordered the employer to reconsider S's request and pay compensation of £500. This, it believed, recognised the balance between the employer's failure to deal properly with S's claim and its difficulties in handling the new legislation.

Alternative Dispute Resolution
4.50

The Acas guide suggests that the quickest and most effective way for an employee to resolve a dispute over flexible working is in the workplace and that effective workplace communication, including mediation, can help secure agreement. Indeed, since 6 May 2014, anyone wishing to present a flexible working claim under S.80H ERA to an employment tribunal must first contact Acas and be offered early conciliation – see S.18A of the Employment Tribunals Act 1996. The early conciliation rules are discussed in detail in IDS Employment Law Handbook, 'Employment Tribunal Practice and Procedure' (2014), Chapter 3, 'Conciliation, settlements and ADR', under 'Early conciliation'. Suffice to say here that the prospective claimant starts the process by either sending an early conciliation form to Acas or telephoning Acas directly, and

Acas will then contact the parties to see if the dispute can be resolved through conciliation. If the parties do not want to take up the offer of conciliation, or conciliation ends without an agreement having been reached, Acas will issue a certificate to the claimant, who can then present his or her claim to the tribunal. In order to facilitate early conciliation, special provisions allow for the extension of the time limit for presenting a claim – see IDS Employment Law Handbook, 'Employment Tribunal Practice and Procedure' (2014), Chapter 5, 'Time limits', under 'Extension of time limit under early conciliation rules'.

Furthermore, the parties to a flexible working dispute case can use the Acas Arbitration Scheme to settle their differences, rather than making a complaint to an employment tribunal. The purpose of the scheme, which only applies to unfair dismissal and flexible working claims, is to allow the parties to discuss the dispute without having to attend an employment tribunal, which can be legalistic, costly and time-consuming. Since the scheme is entirely voluntary, both parties must agree to the dispute going to arbitration. The arbitrator's decision is final and an employee who decides to use the scheme must waive his or her right to present a complaint to a tribunal. The remedies that an arbitrator can award are no different to those available in tribunal proceedings.

4.51 Where the employee claims that the employer has also breached other employment rights, it will not be possible for the claim to be heard under the Acas scheme. Details of the scheme can be found in IDS Employment Law Handbook, 'Employment Tribunal Practice and Procedure' (2014), Chapter 3, 'Conciliation, settlements and ADR', under 'Arbitration'.

4.52 Detriment and unfair dismissal rights

Special unlawful detriment and unfair dismissal provisions exist that are designed to prevent people from being penalised for exercising their right to request flexible working. These sit alongside the ordinary right not to be unfairly dismissed contained in S.98 ERA that applies to all employees with two or more years of continuous employment – see IDS Employment Law Handbook, 'Unfair Dismissal' (2010).

4.53 Unlawful detriment

Section 47E ERA provides that an employee has the right not to be subjected to any detriment by any act, or deliberate failure to act, by his or her employer done on the ground that the employee:

- made (or proposed to make) an application under S.80F ERA

- brought proceedings against the employer under S.80H, or

- alleged the existence of any circumstance which would constitute a ground for bringing such proceedings.

This section does not apply, however, where the detriment in question amounts to a dismissal – S.47E(2) ERA.

An employee who believes that he or she has been subjected to a detriment can **4.54** present a claim under S.48(1) ERA (having first contacted Acas with a view to early conciliation – see 'Enforcement and remedies – alternative dispute resolution' above). It is for the employer to show the ground on which any act, or deliberate failure to act, was done – S.48(2). Claims are subject to the standard three-month time limit, which can be extended where the tribunal considers it just and equitable to do so or to facilitate early conciliation – S.48(3) (see further IDS Employment Law Handbook, 'Employment Tribunal Practice and Procedure' (2014), Chapter 5, 'Time limits').

Where a tribunal finds a complaint well founded it must make a declaration to that effect and can make an award of compensation – S.49(1). The amount of compensation will be such as the tribunal considers just and equitable in all the circumstances having regard to the infringement and any loss suffered by the claimant as a result – S.49(2).

Unfair dismissal
4.55

Employees who are dismissed in the context of making a request to vary their contractual terms to allow for flexible working are protected from unfair dismissal, as explained below. The rights discussed in this section sit alongside the ordinary right not to be unfairly dismissed contained in S.98 ERA that applies to all employees with two or more years of continuous employment – see IDS Employment Law Handbook, 'Unfair Dismissal' (2010).

Automatically unfair dismissal. Section 104C ERA provides that an employee **4.56** who is dismissed shall be regarded as unfairly dismissed if the reason (or, if more than one, the principal reason) for the dismissal is that the employee:

- made (or proposed to make) an application under S.80F

- brought proceedings against the employer under S.80H, or

- alleged the existence of any circumstance which would constitute a ground for bringing such proceedings.

Thus, the dismissal of an employee for a reason related to his or her application for flexible working will be 'automatically unfair' and the question of reasonableness will not arise. There is no qualifying period of service (see S.108(3)(gi)) or upper age limit for claiming automatically unfair dismissal under S.104C.

In Russell v Holden and Co LLP ET Case No.1102737/12 R was employed by **4.57** H and Co LLP, a firm of solicitors, as a legal secretary. From September 2010 she worked for 20 hours a week, at varying times between Monday and Friday, depending on the firm's needs. She informed her employer that she was pregnant

219

in May 2011, began her maternity leave in November and was due to return on 27 August 2012. She contacted the firm on 7 August asking whether she could return to work for 15 hours a week. The firm asked her to delay her return until 1 October and said it would discuss her working pattern nearer the time. On 21 September she received the notification of redundancies and on 27 September was called to a consultation meeting where she was told that if she could not commit to working her contracted hours it was likely that she would be selected for redundancy. R became very upset and tearful in the meeting, although she said that, at a push, she could return to work 20 hours a week. It was agreed that her return to work would be delayed until the conclusion of the redundancy process. R scored less than her colleagues in the redundancy pool and she was dismissed for redundancy. An employment tribunal upheld her claim of automatically unfair dismissal by reason of having made a flexible working request. While accepting that there was a genuine redundancy situation at the relevant time, it did not accept that that was the reason for R's dismissal. Upon careful consideration, the tribunal found that the real reason was the request she had made for flexible working.

4.58 **Dismissal for asserting a statutory right.** If an employee is dismissed because he or she has tried to exercise the right to request flexible working, he or she may also be able to claim to have been dismissed for asserting a statutory right. Under S.104 ERA an employee's dismissal will be automatically unfair if the reason or principal reason for the dismissal was that:

- the employee brought proceedings against the employer to enforce a relevant statutory right, or

- the employee alleged that the employer had infringed a relevant statutory right.

It is immaterial whether the employee actually has the statutory right in question or whether it has been infringed, but the employee's claim to the right must be made in good faith – S.104(2). Furthermore, it is sufficient that the employee made it reasonably clear to the employer what the right claimed to have been infringed was; it is not necessary actually to specify the right in question – S.104(3).

4.59 A claim under S.104 was made in Horn v Quinn Walker Security Ltd ET Case No.2505740/03. H had been exchanging his morning shifts with colleagues so that he could look after his young children in the mornings while his wife was out at work. On learning about the shift swaps, his employer told him that he was not permitted to change his hours of work in this way. H responded by writing to the employer pointing out the flexible working provisions and asking for a change to his shifts for childcare purposes. Shortly afterwards, he was informed that he was to be dismissed for refusing to work to the company's shift system. He subsequently brought an unfair dismissal claim under S.104.

The tribunal found that, although H had not made a request in writing in accordance with S.80F ERA, he had made it clear to his employer on a number of occasions that he was requesting flexible working for childcare purposes. Accordingly, the reason for his dismissal was his allegation that the employer was infringing his right to request flexible working. This amounted to an automatically unfair dismissal within the meaning of S.104.

Dismissals for asserting a statutory right are dealt with in detail in IDS Employment Law Handbook, 'Unfair Dismissal' (2010), Chapter 12, 'Dismissal for asserting a statutory right'.

Dismissal for refusing to accept new terms. There is considerable potential **4.60** for conflict where an employer is seeking to impose new terms and conditions on an employee who is unable to vary his or her working pattern because of, for example, caring responsibilities. One possible consequence would be that the employee resigns and claims constructive dismissal (see 'Constructive dismissal' below). However, it may be that the employee simply refuses to accept the new terms and the employer feels that it has no option but to dismiss. In such circumstances, an employer's obligations in respect of ordinary unfair dismissal under S.98 ERA and the flexible working procedure under S.80F should not be conflated – liability under one provision does not automatically lead to liability under the other. An example:

- **Harrison v Bowater Windows Ltd t/a The Prime Connection** ET Case No.1306479/03: BW Ltd began negotiations on a new package of terms and conditions which would have seen H's working hours change. H had three young children and the new hours would have made it impossible for him to collect them from school. His request under S.80F to continue working his existing hours was refused. The company's written response cited the cost of providing necessary health and safety and supervisory cover as being unjustifiable, but in evidence the manager who refused the request said that any such request would have been refused because management had made it clear that the new hours were to be imposed. When H refused to accept the new terms, he was dismissed. The employment tribunal found the dismissal fair for 'some other substantial reason' under S.98 ERA as BW Ltd had been entitled to seek to change working practices in order to exploit a new market. However, due to the total lack of consideration that was given to H's request for flexible working, the tribunal upheld the complaint under S.80H and awarded H eight weeks' pay.

Dismissals for 'some other substantial reason' under S.98 are discussed in IDS Employment Law Handbook, 'Unfair Dismissal' (2010), Chapter 8, 'Some other substantial reason'.

Unfair constructive dismissal. If an employer acts perversely in dealing with **4.61** a flexible working request or refuses a request on plainly unreasonable grounds, an employee may be able to establish a breach of contract giving him or her grounds to resign and claim unfair constructive dismissal. For a constructive dismissal claim to succeed, the employer's breach must constitute a fundamental breach of contract – see IDS Employment Law Handbook, 'Unfair Dismissal' (2010), Chapter 1, 'Dismissal', under 'Constructive dismissal – fundamental breach'.

In Clarke v Telewest Communications plc ET Case No.1301034/04 an employment tribunal found that TC plc had breached the implied duty of trust and confidence. Not only had it failed to comply with time limits set out in the Procedural Regulations, but in predetermining the outcome of both meetings with C, it had also failed to give C's request due consideration. In the tribunal's view, such conduct was likely to destroy or seriously damage trust and confidence. Moreover, C had made it clear in her resignation letter that she was resigning for reasons connected with the employer's failure to allow her to adopt a more flexible working pattern. As a result, the tribunal was satisfied that she had resigned in circumstances which amounted to an unfair constructive dismissal.

4.62 There is scope for overlap between unfair constructive dismissal and discrimination claims where an employee has resigned following the refusal of a flexible working request based (directly or indirectly) upon a protected characteristic. In Shaw v CCL Ltd 2008 IRLR 284, EAT, S resigned after her request to return to her sales post on a part-time basis following maternity leave and to only work within 100 miles of her home was rejected. The employment tribunal found that the refusal amounted to direct and indirect discrimination, but that the resignation was not in response to this discrimination but to the rejection of the flexible working request. Since the employer had been entitled, under the flexible working procedure, to refuse the request, the tribunal reasoned that the resignation was not in response to a breach of contract and it accordingly dismissed her unfair constructive dismissal claim. However, on appeal, the EAT ruled that the tribunal had been wrong to draw such a distinction. In its view, CCL Ltd's outright rejection of S's part-time working request for discriminatory reasons constituted a failure to maintain trust and confidence between the parties and thus amounted to a fundamental breach of contract. S had resigned in response to CCL Ltd's decision to reject her application, and she had done this promptly, four days after the rejection of her appeal. Accordingly, all the elements were in place to find a constructive dismissal and her appeal was allowed.

Two further examples:

- **Littlejohn v Transport for London** ET Case No.2200224/07: L, who held a managerial position at TfL, put in a flexible working request before her return to work from maternity leave, seeking a change from full-time work to working two days in the office and one day at home. TfL refused her request, taking the view that a job-share would not work. L resigned and succeeded before the tribunal with her claims of unfair constructive dismissal and indirect sex discrimination. The tribunal found that TfL had not provided justification for refusing L's request. In reaching this conclusion, it took into account the following matters: TfL did not believe that a job-share would work but had not actually considered whether it was workable in practice; it was concerned about its ability to recruit to a part-time position but the evidence showed that L's was a popular job and finding someone part time could have been explored; the tribunal did not accept that L's management function was incapable of being performed by two individuals; TfL had failed to look into alternatives that would have allowed L to remain in her job; and L was only asking for part-time work for one year and TfL could have allowed this for a trial period

- **Dilonell v Lloyds Pharmacy Ltd** ET Case No.3200789/12: D was employed as a pharmacist by LP Ltd from 2007. In 2011 she took long-term sick leave, having suffered a miscarriage. LP Ltd informed her that upon her return to work in May she was being transferred to another pharmacy where she would have to work Saturdays. In June D submitted a flexible working application, requesting that she work Monday to Thursday, 9 am to 6 pm, which was refused, and she appealed. The appeal was upheld to the extent that D was taken off the Saturday rota but LP Ltd did not implement the hours she had requested in her original request. Instead, she was told that she would have to work until 8 pm Mondays to Thursdays at a store in Braintree, which was some distance from her home, even though she had always made it clear that her childcare commitments required her to finish work no later than 6 pm. D did work at the store in question but complained about her working conditions and when she was subsequently called to a disciplinary hearing for, among other things, being late for work, she resigned. The tribunal found that D had suffered direct sex discrimination in relation to her application for flexible working, the decision to require her to work every Saturday and the way in which her final transfer was handled. It also upheld her constructive dismissal claim. There was evidence that other pharmacists were not required to work every Saturday and that the employer had used locums to cover Saturday working, which was no more expensive than using permanent employees. LP Ltd did not approach D's flexible working application as an opportunity to work with D to achieve the best possible solution for both. Rather it used it as an opportunity to push back against what it saw as a challenge to its authority. D did not have a right to flexible working. However, LP Ltd was required to properly consider her application. In the tribunal's opinion, it had not done so. It gave no reason why it was considered more appropriate to dispatch D to Braintree, when there were other vacancies she could have filled. The inescapable conclusion

223

was that LP Ltd was punishing D for making a flexible working application and for being off sick following her miscarriage.

4.63 None of the cases mentioned above should be regarded as authority for the proposition that discriminatory treatment inevitably breaches the implied term of mutual trust and confidence. Arguably, it appears self-evident that an act of discrimination will fatally undermine the relationship between employer and employee. However, the possibility remains that acts of inadvertent and non-culpable discrimination (such as unintentional indirect discrimination) might not automatically give rise to a claim of constructive dismissal. As always, tribunals will be expected to judge each case on its merits. For further discussion of this general point, see IDS Employment Law Handbook, 'Discrimination at Work' (2012), Chapter 26, 'Dismissal', under 'Relationship between discriminatory and unfair dismissals – reasonableness'.

4.64 Discrimination claims

When handling flexible working requests, employers must be careful to consider not only the flexible working provisions set out in Part VIIIA of the ERA but also any discrimination law implications. As mentioned previously, the right to request flexible working operates independently of existing employment law rights. Therefore, employees whose flexible working requests have been turned down, or who do not qualify for the right (because, for example, they have insufficient continuity of service or have already made a request within the previous 12 months), will not be prevented from bringing discrimination claims under the Equality Act 2010 (EqA), based upon one (or more) of the protected characteristics, i.e. age, disability, gender reassignment, marriage and civil partnership, pregnancy and maternity, race, religion or belief, sex and sexual orientation.

There are two types of discrimination claim that can flow from the refusal of a flexible working request. The first is a direct discrimination claim under S.13(1) EqA, where the claimant alleges that the request was dealt with in a manner different to how it would have been treated if the claimant did not have the protected characteristic at issue. The second, more common, form of claim (so far as flexible working applications are concerned) is for indirect sex discrimination under S.19 EqA. Indirect discrimination arises where an employer applies a provision, criterion or practice (for example, a requirement for staff to work full time or at certain hours) which puts persons sharing a particular characteristic at a particular disadvantage, puts the claimant at that disadvantage, and cannot be justified as a proportionate means of achieving a legitimate aim.

4.65 Note that, while 'pregnancy and maternity' is a protected characteristic under S.4, it is not a 'relevant' protected characteristic under S.19. Thus, while a refusal of a mother's flexible working request may give rise to an indirect sex discrimination claim, there is no prospect of an indirect pregnancy/maternity discrimination claim. An employee is not, however, prevented from bringing a direct discrimination claim based upon pregnancy/maternity.

What follows is a brief summary of discrimination law as it applies in the context of flexible working. For a full discussion of this complex area of law, see IDS Employment Law Handbook, 'Discrimination at Work' (2012).

Direct discrimination 4.66

Direct discrimination occurs where 'a person (A) discriminates against another (B) if, because of a protected characteristic, A treats B less favourably than A treats or would treat others' – S.13(1) EqA.

Cases of direct discrimination in relation to flexible working are fairly rare. Such a claim would be likely to arise where, for example, an employer takes the view that only flexible working requests from women will be considered. In these circumstances, a man whose request for flexible working in order to care for a child is turned down would be entitled to bring a direct discrimination claim based on the protected characteristic of sex. As noted under 'Indirect discrimination' below, men are highly unlikely to be able to claim indirect sex discrimination if such a request is turned down, given that women are more likely than men to have primary responsibility for childcare. However, they may have more success when claiming direct discrimination, as the following cases demonstrate:

- **Armstrong v DB Regio Tyne and Wear Ltd** ET Case No.2500602/11: the employer undertook a review of working practices that led to A being removed from a 'support roster' that had enabled him to meet his childcare commitments. When A's subsequent request for flexible working was turned down he brought a claim of sex discrimination. An employment tribunal, finding in favour of A, noted that two women with childcare commitments had been allowed to stay on the support roster, and determined that a hypothetical female comparator in A's position would have been treated more favourably than him, since the assertions of women as to their difficulties in meeting childcare needs were accepted more readily than those of their male counterparts. It followed that the employer had directly discriminated against A because of his sex

- **Pietzka v PricewaterhouseCoopers LLP** ET Case No.1603520/12: P was employed by PwC LLP to work a five-day week. He was promoted to manager in July 2010. Later that year he raised the issue of flexible working, asking if he could work a four-day week for childcare reasons. However, he was told that, given his role in the business and the level of work he carried out, it was not possible for him to be allowed to work flexibly.

225

He raised the issue again in August 2011, this time asking to reduce his working week by 50 per cent. His request was not agreed but he was told that a formal application to work 75 per cent of his contractual hours would be supported. An employment tribunal accepted P's evidence that his manager's attitude towards him changed after he began requesting flexible working. In particular, he spoke of flexible working harming P's career prospects. He found it difficult to accept that P would wish to put family issues above work. There was no evidence that such harm had been caused to the prospects of women who had taken up flexible working at PwC LLP. Indeed P's manager had been supportive of flexible working requests from female colleagues. P's path to flexible working was more difficult than it had been for female employees. Furthermore, once P's request was granted PwC LLP wished to exercise greater control over whether the flexibility arrangement would continue than in other cases. On the basis of those facts the tribunal upheld P's direct discrimination claim.

4.67 **Direct discrimination by association.** Carers of a child or an elderly or disabled person who are refused flexible working may have a claim for direct discrimination on the grounds of disability/age, as the definition of direct discrimination in S.13 EqA embraces 'discrimination by association'. This is discussed further under 'Parents and carers – discrimination by association' below.

Note that there is no possibility of a claim for *indirect* discrimination by association as S.19 EqA is clearly worded to require that the complainant have the protected characteristic at issue.

4.68 **Indirect discrimination**
As indicated above, indirect discrimination arises where an employer applies a provision, criterion or practice (PCP) (for example, a requirement for staff to work full time or at certain hours) which:

• puts, or would put, persons sharing a particular characteristic at a particular disadvantage

• puts, or would put, the claimant at that disadvantage, and

• cannot be shown to be justified as a proportionate means of achieving a legitimate aim – S.19 EqA.

Case law has established that in order to successfully justify a claim of indirect discrimination, the employer must show that it has carried out a balancing exercise, weighing the business's need to impose the PCP against the discriminatory effect of that PCP. This process requires the employer critically and objectively to evaluate its business decisions where discrimination is obvious or likely.

The question of justification should be considered in tandem with the permitted **4.69** grounds for refusing a flexible working request under S.80G(1)(b) ERA. Those grounds are: the burden of additional costs; the detrimental effect on ability to meet customer demand; the inability to reorganise work among existing staff; the inability to recruit additional staff; a detrimental impact on quality; a detrimental impact on performance; insufficiency of work during the periods the employee proposes to work; planned structural changes; and any other ground the Secretary of State may specify by regulations – for further details see 'Handling flexible working requests – grounds upon which employer can refuse request' above. This list is by no means definitive when it comes to justification under the EqA. However, it provides some guidance as to the matters that may constitute justification with respect to discrimination claims.

In contrast to claims under the flexible working provisions, employment tribunals must actively assess the legitimacy of the employer's business reasons for the refusal to see if they can be objectively justified. Having an apparently sound business reason for denying an employee's application to work part time, for example, is not sufficient in itself – the employer must also consider whether the reasons for insisting on full-time work are strong enough to overcome any indirectly discriminatory impact. In particular, an employer should consider whether there are any alternatives that would achieve the same aim without being as disadvantageous to an individual.

While the test for justification has always been set out by statute, it is largely a **4.70** matter of fact for tribunals to determine whether the employer has satisfied the statutory test. Unlike in unfair dismissal cases, there is no 'room for manoeuvre' for employers or, to put it another way, no range of reasonable responses. An employment tribunal should make its own judgment, upon a fair and detailed analysis of the working practices and business considerations involved, as to whether the PCP at issue is justified – Hardys and Hansons plc v Lax 2005 ICR 1565, CA. This has the effect of restricting the ability to challenge a tribunal's conclusion on appeal, and also means that it would be unwise to regard the outcome of cases that turn largely on their own facts as constituting precedents of any sort.

Two examples of flexible working cases in which the justification defence succeeded:

- **Burston v Superior Creative Services Ltd** ET Case No.72892/95: the employer's refusal to allow B to work three days a week was found by the employment tribunal to be justified. B had wanted to reduce her role from five to three days a week by carrying out sales work only while a part-time replacement was employed to carry out the general administration that had previously taken up two days of her working week. However, sales had been poor before B's maternity leave and the employer was entitled to demand that she spend more than three days per week on sales in future

227

- **Conway v Dairy Crest Ltd** ET Case No.2312942/10: DC Ltd was a national business with 131 depots. It employed seven auditors to ensure that the depots complied with its operations standards. Auditors could be sent anywhere in the UK and were required to stay away from home for significant periods of time. Following her return from maternity leave, one of the auditors, C, applied to work part time at sites within reasonable travelling distance of her home to fit in with nursery opening hours. She made it clear that she was no longer willing to stay away overnight except on rare occasions. DC Ltd refused her request and C claimed indirect sex discrimination. It was not disputed that the PCP of staying away overnight put women at a particular disadvantage, and the employment tribunal accepted that C had suffered a personal disadvantage. However, the legitimate aim of the PCP was to maximise the time that auditors spent on-site and to ensure that the small team of auditors could be sent anywhere in the country. If C only worked within reasonable daily travelling distance of her home, there would not be enough work for her. Furthermore, if she did not stay away overnight she would be unable to maximise her time on-site and it would take her longer to complete an audit. The tribunal concluded that the discriminatory effect of the PCP was justified by the needs of the business.

4.71 **Operational needs.** Operational needs and/or organisational efficiency are frequently relied upon to justify an employer's refusal to grant flexible working arrangements. An employer is, however, unlikely to succeed in establishing objective justification if it fails to give serious consideration to a request for flexible working (where this raises potential issues of indirect discrimination) or to conduct a proper assessment of its operational needs. This is illustrated by the following cases:

- **McGarr v Ministry of Defence** ET Case Nos.2300464/02 and another: Lieutenant Colonel M, a barrister serving with the Adjutant General's Corps within the Army Legal Service (ALS), sought permission from the Director of the ALS to apply for an appointment as a part-time Chair of the Appeals Service Tribunal. Her request was rejected on the basis of the Army's historical practice of permitting only those members of the ALS holding the rank of colonel or above to undertake the duties of part-time judicial office. The MoD argued that the policy was justified on the ground that it was necessary to preserve 'operational effectiveness'. Dismissing this argument, the employment tribunal held that the MoD's reaction to M's wish to undertake judicial duties 'has throughout borne all the hallmarks of an institutional knee-jerk reaction to what it saw as a threat to its established way of doing things'. The tribunal found that no proper assessment had been made by the MoD 'as to the extent to which its operational requirements, including overseas deployment, might be adversely affected by permitting officers below the rank of colonel to undertake part-time judicial duties.

No real attempt was made to gauge the numbers of officers likely to take advantage of such a policy and no sensible consideration given to the practical reality that, however high the degree of interest in part-time judicial office amongst officers below colonel rank, appointment to it is far from guaranteed and follows a lengthy selection process'

- **Littlejohn v Transport for London** ET Case No.2200224/07: L, who held a managerial position at TfL, put in a flexible working request before her return to work from maternity leave, seeking a change from full-time work to two days in the office and one day working from home. TfL refused her request, taking the view that a job-share would not work. L resigned and succeeded before the tribunal with her indirect sex discrimination claim (as well as an unfair constructive dismissal claim). The employment tribunal found that TfL had not provided justification for refusing L's request. In reaching this conclusion, it took into account the following matters: (i) TfL did not believe that a job-share would work but it had not actually considered whether it was workable in practice; (ii) it was concerned about its ability to recruit to a part-time position but the evidence showed that L's was a popular job and finding someone part time could have been explored; (iii) the tribunal did not accept that L's management function was incapable of being performed by two individuals; (iv) TfL had failed to look into alternatives that would have allowed L to remain in her job; and (v) L was only asking for part-time work for one year and TfL could have allowed this for a trial period

- **Stone v Cineworld Cinemas plc** ET Case No.1804043/11: S was employed as an operations manager at a cinema. She was required to work shifts starting at various times between 8.30 am and 4 pm. In June 2010 S asked to work a restricted shift pattern following her return from maternity leave. Her partner's working pattern involved three weeks away followed by three weeks at home. Since childcare was not available in the evenings, S wanted to restrict her availability to daytime shifts during the three weeks when her partner was working away. She would be available to work any shifts during the following three weeks, when he was at home to look after their child. She offered to work this pattern on either a full-time or a job-share basis but her request was refused. The employment tribunal accepted that, while the requirement to work the full range of shifts across each working week placed women at a particular disadvantage, the employer had a legitimate aim – namely, the smooth, efficient and economic running of the business. S's proposal to restrict her shift availability while continuing to work full time would require her colleagues to work more evening shifts and would limit her ability to provide cover at short notice. The employer was therefore justified in requiring S to work across all shift patterns if she remained a full-time operations manager. However, S's proposal to work the restricted shift pattern in a job-share had a more limited impact on the

229

company because the job-sharer would be available to discharge the role in the evenings during the three-week periods when S was restricted to daytime hours. Any detrimental effect on the business would be minimal, whereas the discriminatory impact of refusing the proposal was very severe, meaning in practice that S could no longer continue in her job. The company had never seriously considered the job-share suggestion, nor had it explored the practical possibility of finding a suitable job-share partner. In those circumstances, the means adopted by the company to fulfil its legitimate aim were not proportionate.

4.72 **Costs.** The question of whether, and to what extent, cost considerations can constitute a legitimate aim is a perennially thorny one. According to the established 'cost plus' principle, which has been endorsed on a number of occasions by the EAT, cost can be cited by an employer as one of a number of factors justifying indirect discrimination but cannot be relied on in isolation. However, recent case law has called that principle into question and there are likely to be further judicial developments in this area. This is discussed in IDS Employment Law Handbook, 'Discrimination at Work' (2012), Chapter 17, 'Indirect discrimination: objective justification', under 'Legitimate aim – costs'.

It is worth noting that the burden of additional costs is, on its own, enough to justify an employer's refusing a statutory request for flexible working – S.80G(1)(b)(i) ERA (see 'Handling flexible working requests – grounds upon which employer can refuse request' above). Accordingly, where a claimant has brought claims under both the EqA and the ERA in relation to a refusal of a flexible working request, the employer could find itself in the peculiar position of losing an indirect sex discrimination claim on the basis of the 'cost plus' rule while successfully defending a claim based on the flexible working provisions contained in the ERA.

4.73 **'Curing' discrimination upon appeal**
In Little v Richmond Pharmacology Ltd 2014 ICR 85, EAT, the EAT considered whether a successful internal appeal could 'cure' a prima facie case of indirect sex discrimination arising out of an employer's initial rejection of a flexible working application. During her maternity leave, L had requested part-time working on her return to work. RP Ltd turned this application down on the basis that it was not feasible for its sales executives to work part time. L brought an internal appeal against this decision but then resigned before a hearing could be arranged. R asked L to reconsider her decision to resign and arranged an appeal hearing which she attended. At this hearing, R agreed to L's part-time working arrangement, on a three-month trial basis, to begin following her return from maternity leave. However, L did not accept this offer and instead confirmed her resignation. An employment tribunal dismissed L's claim of indirect sex discrimination holding that, in light of RP Ltd's decision at the appeal hearing, she had not suffered a disadvantage.

230

In upholding the tribunal's decision, the EAT rejected L's contention that she implicitly withdrew her appeal when she resigned; as the tribunal had pointed out, L had attended the appeal hearing. The EAT held that 'an internal appeal process, consensually pursued, forms part and parcel of the employer's decision-making process', and further noted that RP Ltd's initial decision to reject L's request for part-time working was expressed to be subject to her right of appeal and, to that extent, the decision was conditional. L exercised her right of appeal and her flexible working request was allowed. This meant that L did not suffer any disadvantage or detriment as the PCP – namely full-time working – would not be applied to her until she had completed her maternity leave. The EAT was at pains to point out that this case was particularly fact- and claim-sensitive. L had not claimed constructive dismissal as a result of indirect sex discrimination. Her claim was that she had been subjected to a detriment when her application to work part time was initially rejected by RP Ltd. A key factor which led to the conclusion that L did not suffer any form of personal disadvantage or detriment was that she was still on maternity leave and had not returned to work when the decision was made at the appeal hearing to allow her to work part time. The EAT also emphasised that L had attended the appeal hearing. It remains to be seen, therefore, whether a claimant who opts to entirely disengage from the appeal process, but nevertheless has the rejection of his or her flexible working application overturned on appeal, will similarly be held to have not suffered a personal disadvantage.

'Competing' requests
4.74

Since the right to request flexible working is now available to all eligible employees, it is highly likely that an employer will at some point receive multiple, competing requests from two or more employees. As noted under 'Handling flexible working requests – prioritising competing requests' above, the flexible working provisions do not give priority to any particular group of employees. Where the employer is unable to accommodate all the requests, the question will arise whether the employer should give preference to requests from certain groups of employees, such as parents and carers (who prior to 30 June were the exclusive beneficiaries of the statutory right to request flexible working).

During consultation, the Government stated that formally prioritising certain groups of employees would be counterproductive, as this would reinforce the perception that flexible working is primarily for parents and carers and would not promote a culture where flexible working is a legitimate ambition for all employees. However, it also accepted that some employers may wish to take employees' personal circumstances into account if they have to prioritise between competing requests. The Government therefore decided that employers would not be required to prioritise competing requests according to a particular hierarchy of concerns (for example, childcare or care commitments) but would be allowed to take account of any other factors they considered relevant in the event that they had to choose between requests. Where the employer does prioritise, it still has to show that it could not accommodate all the requests for business reasons. However, this is unlikely to allay fears among employers that they could potentially leave themselves open to allegations of discrimination where they prioritise some requests over others.

4.75 Employers should be particularly mindful not to discriminate against employees on the ground of sex by prioritising, for example, mothers, without being able to objectively justify the discriminatory treatment. But sex discrimination claims are not the only type of claim that can arise out of a refusal to grant flexible working and complaints may be based on other prohibited grounds, such as race, disability, age, sexual orientation or religion or belief. During the consultation the Government acknowledged that employers were concerned about the risk of inadvertently discriminating against employees where they take into account the reasons for the changes sought and prioritise competing requests. However, in the response to the consultation it took the view that employers are already well accustomed to dealing with this risk because discrimination legislation requires them to consider whether refusing a flexible working request will disadvantage an employee given their personal characteristics.

The Acas Code has little to say on how to deal with competing requests, simply stating that an employer must not discriminate against an employee when considering a flexible working request. The Acas guide points out that when employers receive more than one request, they are not required to make value judgements about the most deserving. An employer should consider each case on its merits, looking at the business case and the possible impact of refusing a request – see 'Handling flexible working requests – prioritising competing requests' above.

4.76 An employer will not necessarily escape liability for discrimination simply by deciding to refuse all flexible working requests. In Hacking and Paterson and anor v Wilson EATS 0054/09 (an appeal from a tribunal decision to reject an application by the employer to strike out the claim) the EAT had to consider whether an employer's practice of refusing all flexible working requests from its property managers potentially had an indirectly discriminatory impact on women. The Appeal Tribunal decided that the appropriate pool for comparison was restricted to property managers who wanted to work flexibly. But it rejected the employer's argument that this automatically meant that there would be no indirect discrimination, since everyone in the pool would have received a negative response. The fact that all of them would have received a negative response did not mean that all would have suffered what could properly be characterised as a disadvantage or that the disadvantage to them would necessary have been the same. It was important to look at the nature of the consequences of the negative response and the tribunal should consider whether the refusal of the claimant's request gave rise to a particular disadvantage, something that would depend on the consequences – for the claimant – of a refusal. It went on to observe that people (both male and female) seek flexible working for different reasons, which include, for instance, enabling them to combine jobs, pursue other interests or follow educational courses. A negative response to the request for flexible working may accordingly give rise to differing effects. It followed that, when the case returned to the employment tribunal, the claimant would have to address the issue of whether or not the refusal of the request for flexible working put women at a 'particular disadvantage'. (Note that this case is discussed further in the section 'Parents and carers' below, under 'Mothers – disparate impact'.)

Parents and carers   4.77

Although the statutory right to request flexible working is now available to all eligible employees, it is likely that the majority of those requesting flexible working will be parents and carers attempting to juggle their caring responsibilities with work. In this section we consider the particular issues facing these employees.

Mothers. It is well established that an employer's rejection of a woman's request 4.78 for part-time or other flexible working arrangements can give rise to a claim of indirect sex discrimination. The rationale behind such a claim is that, since women are more likely than men to have primary responsibility for childcare, a refusal to allow flexible working – or, for that matter, the imposition of working arrangements that are incompatible with school or nursery hours – amounts to the application of a PCP that puts women at a particular disadvantage.

That said, not every refusal of a flexible working request will put a woman looking after children at a disadvantage. In Hillson v Everything Everywhere Ltd ET Case No.1701210/12, for example, H was employed by EE Ltd as a customer service representative in a call centre. She had two young children and in 2010 she made a flexible working request to work three days a week, which was granted. Towards the end of 2011 EE Ltd realised that, in order to meet customer call demand, it needed to change working patterns so that people worked shorter hours over more days. It embarked on a period of consultation and then published a new rota pattern, asking employees to state their preferences as to how many hours per week they worked. After H had made known her preferences, EE Ltd wrote to inform her that she had been allocated shifts from 8 am to 2 pm, on five days a week, and every other week one of the days would be a Sunday. H refused to work those hours, stating that the new working arrangement was an unreasonable change to her existing hours. She made a flexible working application to work from 8 am to 4 pm three days per week, stating that she could only work a three-day week because of childcare. EE Ltd could not accommodate this but offered her four-day

233

working on reduced hours. She rejected this offer and resigned, claiming that EE Ltd had discriminated against her as a working mother by failing to offer reasonable flexible working. An employment tribunal noted that the nub of the case was EE Ltd's failure to allow H to work a three-day shift pattern. In other words, the PCP at issue was the company's refusal to allow H to continue working three days per week. In this regard, the tribunal noted that there was no evidence to suggest that women are put at a particular disadvantage by being required to work four, rather than three, days a week. The premise of such an assumption is that women are more likely to have childcare responsibilities. In the instant case the tribunal observed that the four-day shift pattern which EE Ltd sought to implement would have allowed E to drop off and collect her children from school, whereas her previous three-day working pattern commencing at 8.15 am and finishing after 4 pm did not do so and required her to arrange childcare to drop off and collect her children. It was not clear why the four-day shift pattern disadvantaged E personally, other than that she preferred to complete her weekly working hours within three days, rather than four. If the PCP relied upon was EE Ltd's blanket application of the new shift system to all employees, again the tribunal had heard no evidence to suggest that this put women in particular at a disadvantage as compared with men. Indeed, given the wide variety of different shifts with different part-time hours within the shift system, the process seemed well able to cope with part-time childcare-related requests, and did not appear to have any adverse effect on women generally.

4.79 *Disparate impact.* In the past, it has tended to be assumed that women suffer a disparate impact when it comes to the rejection of flexible working requests. In London Underground Ltd v Edwards (No.2) 1999 ICR 494, CA, the Court of Appeal held that, in determining whether a shift system was indirectly discriminatory, it was legitimate for an employment tribunal to take into account the fact that women were far more likely than men to be lone parents with childcare responsibilities. And more recently, in Chief Constable of West Midlands Police v Blackburn and anor 2008 ICR 505, EAT (an equal pay case), Mr Justice Elias, then President of the EAT, suggested that an employment tribunal was entitled, in considering the disparate impact of a measure, to rely on the 'common knowledge' that women have greater childcare responsibilities than men. This suggests that a claimant will not necessarily be expected to provide statistical evidence to show that the PCP places women at a particular disadvantage.

However, not all divisions of the EAT have been willing to endorse the assumption that full-time working or certain shift patterns place women at a disadvantage without more. In Sinclair Roche and Temperley and ors v Heard and anor 2004 IRLR 763, EAT, for example, the Appeal Tribunal held that an employment tribunal had not been entitled to conclude that women have the greater responsibility for childcare in our society and that as a consequence a

234

considerably larger proportion of women than men are unable to commit themselves to full-time working. The EAT suggested that it was not appropriate to make such a generalisation in relation to men and women solicitors, or men and women working in high-powered and highly paid jobs in the City.

More recently, a decision of the EAT in Scotland has suggested that, where the **4.80** employer operates an absolute bar on flexible working arrangements, establishing that the bar puts women at a particular disadvantage may be difficult. In Hacking and Paterson and anor v Wilson EATS 0054/09 the Appeal Tribunal held that, in circumstances where the employer operated a policy whereby all requests by property managers for flexible working were to be refused, the correct pool for comparison in determining disparate impact was not all property managers, but only those who, at the relevant time, wanted flexible working to be available. The EAT went on to state that the fact that all those property managers would have received a negative response to a request for flexible working did not mean that all would have suffered what could properly be characterised as a disadvantage or that the disadvantage to them would necessarily have been the same. Rather, it is necessary for a tribunal to look at the negative consequences of the refusal. It is not, in the EAT's view, 'inevitable' that women will be disproportionately adversely affected by a refusal to grant flexible working. It noted that society has changed dramatically and that many women now return to full-time work after childbirth and more men take on childcare responsibilities. Moreover, while the childcare arrangements available to some women are such that they cannot work full time, other choose not to work full time. A negative response to the request for flexible working may, accordingly, give rise to differing effects. Where the effect is on an employee who is able to work full time but does not wish to do so, it is difficult to see that it would be correct to talk in terms of that employee being disadvantaged. Where the effect does amount to a disadvantage, the question of whether it amounts to a particular disadvantage that is liable to be experienced by women as opposed to men then arises.

In our view, the EAT has somewhat exaggerated the effect of changes to childcare arrangements in recent years. Although more men do now take on childcare responsibilities, the distribution of those responsibilities is still skewed heavily towards women. While a tribunal is not obliged to take into account 'common knowledge' and would be entitled to demand evidence from a claimant that she, and others of her sex, are put at a particular disadvantage by an employer's approach to flexible working, that evidence should not be particularly hard to come by in the majority of cases. The greater area of dispute is surely whether the PCP in relation to working hours can be objectively justified. Two examples:

- **Giles v Geach and anor t/a Cornelia Care Homes** ET Case No.3100720/06: in January 2005 G, who worked part time, was told that she must switch

235

to full-time work in the office from April. G's suggestions of job-sharing or working the additional hours from home were refused. The tribunal had no doubt that the defence of justification was not made out. Rejecting the employer's argument that the cost implications of G working at home would be enormous, the tribunal noted that the employer had taken no steps to assess those costs or the health and safety implications of such an adjustment. Furthermore, its argument that G was at risk of making errors through lack of concentration arising from childcare responsibilities if she worked at home was based on 'wholly outdated stereotypical attitudes'

- **Chandler v American Airlines Inc** ET Case No.2329478/10: C, who had worked for AA since 1998, was employed as a lead agent at the time she made an application for flexible working following the birth of her second child. Her application was refused, but AA agreed to a reduction in her working hours on her return in April 2009. AA carried out a review of its passenger services in July 2009 and as a result the post of lead agent was abolished and post-holders were invited to apply to become operational coordinators or team leaders. C applied for a post as team leader and was successful, but AA informed her that the post was full time, and although it would honour her hours and roster pattern for a trial period of four months, it would expect her to increase her hours to full time at the end of that period. She told AA that she was not in a position to work full time, and at the end of the trial period she was given a choice: she could work full time, consider a job-share as an operational coordinator, consider suitable alternative employment or accept a redundancy package. She accepted redundancy under duress and brought a claim of sex discrimination. On the basis of its recognition that significantly more women than men have primary responsibility for childcare, the employment tribunal held that a requirement to work full time was to the detriment of women and was not a proportionate means of achieving AA's legitimate aim of improving management. AA had accepted before the tribunal that the post could have been undertaken other than on a full-time basis, although not on the hours that C had been working. It followed that there was a less discriminatory alternative to the requirement to work full time, which could not therefore be justified.

4.81 Further support for our view can be found in Thompson v Helphire Ltd ET Case No.1401502/12, where T contended that judicial notice should be taken of the fact that more women than men have primary responsibility for childcare when assessing whether H Ltd's restriction on flexible working was indirectly discriminatory. Placing reliance upon the decision in Hacking and Paterson and anor v Wilson (above), H Ltd argued that, while that presumption might once have been justified, it was no longer necessarily so. However, the tribunal was prepared to have regard to established demographic trends, as reflected in the Equality and Human Rights Commission's Code of Practice on Employment and in the preponderance of decided cases, and held that women are more likely to be disadvantaged than men by the application of a requirement that roles are not amenable to part-time or job-share working arrangements.

If, contrary to our view, specific proof of disparate impact is required in this context, it is worth noting that the choice of relevant pool can have a significant impact on the outcome. For example, it is generally a good deal easier to establish that a requirement to work full time places women at a particular disadvantage if the pool consists of all potential applicants for a job rather than merely a cross section of a particular workforce. In the latter case, the proportion of women who are put at a disadvantage by the PCP may be so small in number as to make it impossible to say that the application of the requirement has any discriminatory effect in practice. Where the selected pool happens to include a relatively small number of women, it may be that none of these, apart from the claimant, has childcare responsibilities or faces other impediments to full-time working.

Nevertheless, there are numerous cases in which claimants have succeeded in **4.82** establishing, on the basis of statistics relating to a relatively small pool, that a PCP relating to working patterns places women at a particular disadvantage. In Bradley v West Midlands Fire and Rescue Authority ET Case No.1304700/06, for example, B was a single mother who worked as a firefighter. A new shift pattern was introduced making it harder, and, in her opinion, all but impossible on some occasions, to organise her childcare. Although B's family was able to provide some support, she submitted a request for flexible working, which was refused. Before the employment tribunal, the employer disputed the extent of the difficulties that B was experiencing with the new shift system. The tribunal referred to statistical evidence concerning applications for flexible working and exemption from the new shift pattern among the relevant section of the workforce. It also took judicial notice of the fact that a significant majority of single parents are women. On that basis, it held that the new shift pattern put women at a particular disadvantage compared to men, and that it had put B at that disadvantage. In reaching this conclusion, it reminded itself that the statutory test only requires the claimant to prove a 'disadvantage' and that it was not the case that she must show that compliance with the PCP was impossible. B's indirect discrimination claim was, however, ultimately dismissed on the ground that the application of the discriminatory PCP was a proportionate means of achieving a legitimate aim and was therefore justified.

National statistics are frequently relied upon by claimants in indirect sex discrimination cases concerning part-time and flexible working. For example, in Trainer v Penny Plain Ltd ET Case No.2510846/05 the tribunal, in accepting the argument that a PCP to work full time has a disparate impact on women, took into account statistics published by the Equal Opportunities Commission (EOC) (now merged into the Equality and Human Rights Commission) in

237

'Investigation into Flexible and Part-Time Working' (2005), which found that 'flexible and part-time working is female dominated'. Similarly, in Clarke v Telewest Communications plc ET Case No.1301034/04 a claimant was entitled to rely on statistics compiled by the EOC to successfully argue that a requirement that she work evenings and weekends indirectly discriminated against her. The first set of statistics in question was published in 'Facts about Women and Men in Great Britain 2004', and supported the widely accepted conclusion that a greater proportion of women in the workforce worked part time owing to their childcare responsibilities. The second report, 'Evening and Weekend Working – 2000 and 2004', highlighted that in 2004 11 per cent of female employees with dependent children worked evenings and weekends in their main job, compared with 18 per cent of male employees with dependent children.

4.83 *Women returning from maternity leave.* It is common for women returning from maternity leave to request to work part time (or different hours). They may succeed in a complaint of indirect sex discrimination if the employer cannot show any objective justification for a refusal to allow a return on different terms. Two examples:

- **Sidpra v Smile Publishing Ltd** ET Case No.3202027/03: during her maternity leave S raised the possibility of returning part time, working for one day a week. Her employer replied in writing saying that it was not able to accommodate her wish to return for one day a week, and the letter concluded with thanks for her work for them and wishing her well for the future. The letter was followed two weeks later by a cheque for holiday pay and her P45. She had tried on many occasions to contact her employer by telephone, but nobody was available to speak to her until shortly before she received her P45. At no time did the employer discuss with S whether she would be able to work for more than one day a week. A tribunal upheld her discrimination and unfair dismissal claims. Having made up its mind that one day a week would not work, the employer made a conscious decision that it was not going to discuss the matter further with S to see if a mutually acceptable compromise could be reached. That amounted to direct discrimination. There was also indirect discrimination in that the employer might have had grounds for not accepting S's request to work for just one day a week, but that was not the same as showing that the requirement to work full time was justified. The employer was not prepared to consider whether S could have been employed for something between one and five days a week

- **Warren v Maple House Independent Montessori School Ltd** ET Case No.2300997/04: W worked as a full-time teacher until she went on maternity leave in summer 2003. She hoped to return to teaching at the school on a part-time basis but the employer decided that part-time work could only be offered to W for three months, after which time she would have to revert to full-time working. W refused to accept that condition and the employer withdrew the offer of three months' part-time work. A tribunal upheld W's discrimination claim. Her employer had failed to investigate the possibility of making part-time working feasible, and by insisting that W could only come back on a part-time basis if she agreed to revert to full-time working after three months, it removed the possibility of carrying out an empirical trial. The employer thus failed to establish justification.

However, in the absence of a contractual term the employee has no 'right' to return on different terms. Whether or not a discrimination claim can be made out will depend entirely on the circumstances, as the following cases demonstrate: **4.84**

- **Riggs v Parker Bath Ltd** ET Case No.3103163/02: R was employed full time until 2001, when she went on maternity leave. She asked if she could return part time, working mornings, and her employer had no objection in principle provided appropriate arrangements could be made. It sought to employ another person to work on a job-share basis but was unable to recruit anyone by the time R was due to return from maternity leave. R was therefore told that part-time work was not available and that if she did not return to work she would be in repudiatory breach of contract. R refused to return to full-time employment and her employer regarded her as having resigned. R's sex discrimination claim failed because her employer had a genuine need that outweighed the discriminatory effect of the refusal to accede to her request. Her claims of unfair dismissal and breach of contract also failed. Since her contract required her to work full time, her refusal to do so amounted to a repudiation of the contract. Her employer was entitled to accept the breach as discharging it from further performance of the contract

- **Browning v HSBC Bank Ltd** ET Case No.1101477/07: B was employed as a commercial manager. She indicated that on her return to work following maternity leave she wanted to work three days a week but the employer said that that would not be possible because of the need to meet customer demand. B declined an offer to work reduced hours over five days and she was subsequently offered a senior clerical role on a temporary basis, pending a suitable managerial role becoming available, and was told she would retain her managerial status, pay and benefits. She rejected the offer. Her manager was determined not to lose her and persuaded the employer to create a new role for her, which she accepted. However, she resigned soon afterwards and claimed discrimination and constructive unfair dismissal in relation to her employer's handling of her return to work. The tribunal dismissed her claims. The employer had applied a criterion that commercial manager posts had to be carried out over five days a week, but this was legitimate given the need to provide customer satisfaction: the tribunal accepted that business customers expected instant access to their commercial manager,

239

especially when they had urgent matters to discuss. The employer attempted to employ B in a suitable alternative role, and the tribunal concluded that the employer had acted reasonably in this regard

- **Andrews v Rapid Electronics Ltd** ET Case No.1500748/03: A asked to work for 24 hours a week on her return from maternity leave. Her employer replied that it would need to discuss and agree the precise job content with her. On her return, and as a result of the change in hours, her role had changed somewhat and she subsequently resigned and claimed unfair constructive dismissal, sex discrimination and breach of Reg 18. She said she would have considered returning on a full-time basis had she been told that that was the only way she could maintain her position. The tribunal decided that on the facts A had never sought to exercise her right to return to her original job and it was justifiable for the employer to feel that it was unreasonable for her to 'cherry pick the best parts' of her previous job. However, she had been unfairly constructively dismissed as a result of the way she was treated during meetings to discuss the issue on her return.

4.85 **Fathers.** Men are unlikely to be able to claim indirect sex discrimination if their request for flexible working in order to care for a child is turned down, since, as noted above, women are more likely than men to have primary responsibility for childcare. Nevertheless, as discussed under 'Direct discrimination' above, men are more likely to be successful in claiming direct discrimination by showing that an actual or hypothetical female comparator is (or would be) treated differently.

4.86 **Carers of disabled or elderly people.** The availability of an indirect sex discrimination claim where a request is made in order to care for an adult is less clear cut. A claimant would need to show that a refusal of flexible working in these circumstances puts people of his or her sex at a particular disadvantage compared with people of the opposite sex. Tribunals are less likely simply to assume that the caring burden falls more heavily on one gender than the other, so some evidence of particular disadvantage is likely to be required.

Statistics suggest, however, that more women than men have caring responsibilities. A press release from the Office for National Statistics (ONS), 'Inequality in the provision of unpaid care in England and Wales' (2013), revealed that women were more likely to be carers of sick, disabled and elderly people than men. According to the 2011 Census, 5.41 million people provided unpaid care in England. Of these, around 3.12 million were female (58 per cent) and around 2.29 million were male (42 per cent), representing 11.8 per cent of the total female population and 8.9 per cent of the total male population in England. In Wales a similar gender inequality existed, with 0.21 million females (57 per cent) and 0.16 million males (43 per cent) providing unpaid care. Of the total population in Wales, 13.8 per cent of females and 10.6 per cent of males provided some level of unpaid care. The ONS also reported that the amount of unpaid care provided increases with age. Those aged 50 to 64 provide the most care and this is also the age group with the greatest gender inequality, with 24 per cent of women aged 50 to 64 providing unpaid care, compared with 17 per cent of men in the same age group. Managers should therefore treat requests for flexible working from carers of the elderly/disabled in the same way as those from carers of children, in order to avoid claims of indirect sex discrimination.

Discrimination by association. As noted under 'Direct discrimination' **4.87** above, carers of a child or an elderly or disabled person may have a claim for direct discrimination because of disability/age, as the definition of direct discrimination in S.13 EqA embraces 'discrimination by association'. This is because direct discrimination is defined as less favourable treatment 'because of a protected characteristic', and so does not require that the complainant actually have the protected characteristic at issue. So if, for example, an employer refuses a flexible working request from an employee seeking to care for a disabled relative, that may amount to direct disability discrimination if it can be shown that the reason for the refusal was in some way motivated by the fact of disability.

However, this analysis does not support a right not to be discriminated against because a person has caring responsibilities per se. To establish discrimination by association with a disabled person, a comparison needs to be made between the treatment of a worker requesting flexible working to care for someone with a disability and the treatment of a worker seeking flexible working to care for someone who does not have a disability, e.g. a non-disabled child. Only if the employer was more sympathetic to those with childcare responsibilities than those who had to care for someone with a disability would direct discrimination arise.

For a fuller discussion of this topic, see IDS Employment Law Handbook, 'Discrimination at Work' (2012), Chapter 15, 'Direct discrimination', under 'Discrimination by association'.

Disabled employees
4.88

Employers must give serious consideration to requests from disabled employees to alter or reduce working hours where it would help to alleviate a substantial disadvantage. Otherwise, they could well fall foul of their duty to make reasonable adjustments under S.20 EqA (see IDS Employment Law Handbook, 'Discrimination at Work' (2012), Chapter 21, 'Failure to make reasonable adjustments'). Three examples:

- **Caen v RBS Insurance Services Ltd** ET Case No.1801133/09: C was employed as a claims handler. In 2002, she suffered a nervous breakdown and it later transpired that she was also suffering from agoraphobia. As a result of this condition, C found it increasingly difficult to work a standard

241

working day because – owing to her anxieties – she did not want to travel to work when there were a lot of other cars on the road. Consequently, the employer permitted C to work from 6.30 am to 2 pm. This arrangement worked well until the Ministry of Justice proposed changes to the way in which claims would be administered by insurance companies such as the employer. This led to changes in the way C's office was run and she was told that she would have to work more normal hours, starting no earlier than 7.30 am. This caused C to become paranoid and she suffered anxiety attacks each morning before going to work. Eventually, C was dismissed and she pursued a number of claims, including that the employer had failed in its duty to make reasonable adjustments. Upholding the claim, the tribunal considered that once the concept of flexibility was agreed, there was no logical basis for saying that 6.30 am was inappropriate, but 7.30 am was appropriate. The employer had not demonstrated why starting at 6.30 am would not work and had thus failed in its duty to make reasonable adjustments

- **Mansoor v Secretary of State for Education and Employment** ET Case No.1803409/97: M worked as a clerical officer in a job centre. Until 1994 he worked on flexitime. Thereafter, because of his poor timekeeping record, he was required to work fixed hours. M had colitis and informed the employer that it was impossible for him to get to work at the scheduled start time because of his condition. He gave the employer permission to contact his GP and his consultant for confirmation. Notwithstanding that, the employer decided disciplinary action was warranted. At no time was M required to see the employer's medical adviser. Eventually, M was dismissed on account of his poor timekeeping and attendance. A tribunal found that the employer had failed to comply with the duty to make reasonable adjustments to accommodate M's disability. Adjustments could easily have been made by shortening M's hours or by removing the requirement to work fixed hours. Indeed, there was evidence to support the view that M would have been willing to work shorter hours and take a pay cut. However none of these possibilities was acted upon by the employer

- **Ewing v TSYS Managed Services EMEA and anor** ET Case No.1317604/12: E began a probationary period of employment with TMSE as a call centre operative. During his induction he revealed that he suffered from rheumatoid arthritis, a disability under the EqA. Although he took prescribed drugs to help control his condition, variations in weather and temperature could have an immediate and debilitating impact upon his mobility, thus causing timekeeping and attendance problems. TMSE had a strict attendance policy – comprising a 3 per cent allowance for absence or lateness – breach of which might result in disciplinary action. Due to his disability, E's attendance exceeded the 3 per cent allowance. Having identified that E had certain difficulties as a result of his disability, TMSE had discussions with E as to how it might support him. As a result, E was provided with an ergonomic mouse, ergonomic keyboard and a backrest for his chair. E suggested that he should be allowed to work flexible hours of his own choosing of between 35 and 40 per week. However, TMSE rejected this proposal, believing that it would put the business at risk and place a burden on E's colleagues. In October TMSE decided that E had failed his probationary period because of his poor attendance record and he was dismissed. The employment tribunal accepted that a call centre will inevitably rely on staff being in attendance when required. It noted that some adjustments were discussed and some implemented and that TMSE had given the appearance of a concerned employer. However, it found that the consequences of E being given greater flexibility were never properly explored. There was no discussion with other shift members to see how E might be accommodated or any suggestion that an increased tolerance would be granted E with regard to attendance and lateness which could then have been monitored over an extended probationary period. Such steps might have resulted in E remaining in TMSE's employment or, at worst, demonstrating that his continued employment was impractical. By failing to properly consider the flexible working option, TMSE was in breach of its duty under S.20 EqA. In addition, his dismissal was directly discriminatory because TMS had formed the view that E's disability precluded any likely improvement in his attendance record.

4.89 While shorter working hours may amount to a reasonable adjustment in some cases, employers should avoid making stereotypical assumptions about the abilities and capabilities of disabled people and should not simply reduce working hours without consulting the employee. For example, in Coombes v The Bradford Exchange ET Case No.2303160/06 the employee had a chronic condition involving bone deformity, which meant that he walked with a stick and led to high levels of disability-related absence. The employer suggested reducing the employee's working hours, but he rejected the suggestion. A reduction was then imposed on him. An employment tribunal found that the change was not a reasonable adjustment, and it was made because of the employee's disability, with the result that it amounted to disability discrimination.

It is not only the times at which an employee begins and finishes work and the total number of hours worked that should be looked at when considering what reasonable adjustments can be made – an employer may also need to amend shift patterns and rotas if their effect is to cause a substantial disadvantage to a disabled employee. In Stevenson v Severn River Crossing plc ET Case No.1402306/10 S was employed as a toll collector, a job that required a lot of stretching and bending down, particularly for low vehicles. She began to suffer from osteoarthritis in 2007 and in December 2009 she was diagnosed with fibromyalgia. An occupational health report in June 2008 recommended that S be allocated to work at those toll booths that largely dealt with heavy goods vehicles (HGVs), because the height of those vehicles reduced the amount of bending required. Subsequent reports recommended that S be allowed to start working no earlier than 8 am to enable the effect of her medication to wear off, and that heating should be provided in the toll booth. S maintained that the heating provided was inefficient and that her shift patterns meant a large amount of bending was still necessary. An employment tribunal determined that the employer had failed to make the reasonable adjustments of having a systematic approach to the rotas in order to ensure that S was placed in the lanes having a high degree of HGV traffic and of providing adequate heating.

4.90   As the provisions of the Working Time Regulations 1998 SI 1998/1833 demonstrate, working hours do not simply constitute the time at which an employee starts and finishes work: they also include the rest breaks to which an employee is entitled. The Regulations provide for a break of 20 minutes in any shift of over six hours, but an employer may need to consider providing additional or longer breaks to a disabled employee if his or her disability causes a greater degree of fatigue than generally experienced by people who do not have that disability. The Equality and Human Rights Commission's Employment Code provides the following example: 'A worker has recently been diagnosed with diabetes. As a consequence of her medication and her new dietary requirements, she finds that she gets extremely tired at certain times during the working day. It is likely to be a reasonable adjustment to allow her to take additional rest breaks to control the effects of her impairment' – para 17.15.

The question of whether allowing a disabled employee to work from home would be a reasonable adjustment is dependent upon the individual circumstances of the case and tribunals will need to examine the nature of the work being undertaken. For example, in Secretary of State for Work and Pensions (Job Centre Plus) and ors v Wilson EAT 0289/09 the EAT held that allowing W (who suffered from agoraphobia and panic attacks) to work from home was not a reasonable adjustment. It was highly relevant that the work she undertook involved face-to-face contact with customers and required access to confidential information that was centrally held. (Note that this could also be a reasonable basis for turning down a request to work from home made by an employee.)

4.91   **Elderly employees**
The Modern Workplaces consultation noted that many workers approaching retirement would like to continue with some form of part-time or flexible working and that flexible working can enable employees to phase their retirement in a way they find helpful. While this sounds like good practice, it is not without legal difficulties.

Employers could well encounter difficulties when deciding how to prioritise competing requests from younger and older workers (quite apart from workers with childcare and other responsibilities). An employer who offers flexible working only to older workers is likely to open itself up to complaints of age discrimination by younger employees. However, it is possible that an employer would be able to objectively justify its decision (by showing that it is a proportionate means of achieving a legitimate aim) and therefore avoid liability. For example, it could be argued that offering older employees flexible working gives retiring employees the opportunity to share their knowledge and skills and helps both employers and employees to manage the transition to retirement. Conversely, employers may find it difficult to objectively justify a failure to offer flexible working to its older workers.

Note that employers can justify direct age discrimination under the EqA. This **4.92** is a unique aspect of the protection against age discrimination in that it does not apply to any of the other protected characteristics. Age discrimination is fully discussed in IDS Employment Law Handbook, 'Discrimination at Work' (2012), Chapter 5, 'Age'.

Religious employees   4.93

An employee whose working hours prevent him or her from meeting a religious commitment – such as attending a session of worship or observing a day of rest – may argue that the working hours are indirectly discriminatory. If the employer refuses the employee's request for flexible working to accommodate this, it will have to show that the arrangements as to working hours are objectively justified.

The following cases show that insisting on a particular pattern of work may be justified where the employer can point to compelling business or organisational reasons in support of its policy:

• **Mayuuf v Governing Body of Bishop Challoner Catholic Collegiate School and anor** ET Case No.3202398/04: M was a mathematics teacher and a follower of the Maliki School of Islam. It was an essential requirement of his religion that he attend Friday prayers at a mosque. Following his appointment in April 2002, M was free during period five on a Friday afternoon, permitting him to attend mosque. However, in 2003 mathematics was identified as a priority area for improvement and it was decided that all year 11 students would be taught at the same time so that they could move up or down a set according to their ability. A new timetable was issued to reflect this strategy and thereafter M was required to teach on Friday afternoons. He brought a claim of indirect religious discrimination. The employment tribunal took into account the fact that there had been a decline in GCSE mathematics results; that there was a real and genuine need to teach year 11 classes at the same time to facilitate transfer between sets; that rewriting the timetable to accommodate M would have been practically impossible; and that engaging a supply teacher would have damaged continuity and entailed significant costs to the school (although, in the tribunal's view, cost

245

was a secondary consideration). The tribunal balanced those factors against the discriminatory effect on M, for whom missing Friday prayers was a 'most serious matter', and concluded that the PCP of teaching period five on Fridays was justified as a proportionate means of achieving a legitimate aim

- **James v MSC Cruises Ltd** ET Case No.2203173/05: J was a practising member of the Seventh-day Adventist Church. As such, she abstained from secular work on the Sabbath in order to worship, teach, learn and celebrate. In September 2005 she successfully applied for a position with MSC Ltd, which sold and marketed cruise holidays. However, on receiving the offer letter, she explained that she could not work on Saturday as this was the Sabbath. MSC Ltd responded that if J could not work on Saturdays then she would be unable to take up the offer of employment. J brought an indirect religious discrimination claim. An employment tribunal found the relevant disadvantage caused by the PCP of Saturday working but decided that it was justified. It accepted the employer's evidence that trading on Saturdays was an essential feature of the tourism industry, since this was when couples were most likely to be available jointly to explore holiday opportunities and make immediate decisions. It also had regard to the fact that Saturday working was not popular among existing staff; that a rota had been put in place to share the burden equally; and that the employer reasonably believed that any exceptions would create tension among colleagues

- **Patrick v IH Sterile Services Ltd** ET Case No.3300983/11: P was employed as a technician by IHSS Ltd, which provided a round-the-clock instrument sterilisation service to hospitals. He was a committed Jehovah's Witness and at the beginning of his employment came to an arrangement with his managers that he would not be required to work on Sundays. Following a business decision to minimise reliance on agency staff, taken with a view to reducing costs and maintaining quality, the company required its employees to work weekend shifts. As a result, P was expected to work at least one in every two Sundays and this affected his ability to worship and perform other duties at the Kingdom Hall. He brought a claim of indirect religious discrimination. The employment tribunal accepted that P was placed at a particular disadvantage compared with non-religious people by the requirement to work on Sundays. However, the company had the legitimate aim of fulfilling its contractual obligation to its customers to provide sterile laboratory services on a Sunday. Assuming the obligation to work on Sundays was distributed equitably among the small pool of staff, it was a proportionate means of achieving that aim.

4.94 However, the following cases illustrate that it is not enough for employers simply to cite business or operational needs. They should also be prepared to demonstrate that, before insisting on the relevant PCP, they explored ways of accommodating the employee's request:

- **Edge v Visual Security Services Ltd** ET Case No.1301365/06: the employment tribunal ruled that a committed Christian who made it clear to his employer prior to being employed that he did not wish to work on Sundays for religious reasons was indirectly discriminated against on the ground of religion when he was required to do so from time to time. The requirement to undertake occasional Sunday working was a PCP and could not be objectively justified in this case. In the tribunal's view, although the employer could show a legitimate aim – i.e. 'the need of the business to carry out security work on Sundays' – it could not show that the requirement was a proportionate means of achieving that aim. The principal reason why the employer was not willing to rearrange its affairs to enable E to avoid working on Sundays 'was that it was simply too much trouble'

- **Estorninho v Jokic t/a Zorans Delicatessen** ET Case No.2301487/06: E, a practising Catholic, was employed as a chef. He followed the Catechism of the Catholic Church, which obliged him to abstain from work on Sundays, and he had been recruited on the basis that his religious beliefs ruled out Sunday working. The business became increasingly busy and, several months after his employment began, E was told that he would in future be required to work on Sundays. When he refused to do so, he was dismissed. The employment tribunal held that the PCP of Sunday working put Catholics at a particular disadvantage and could not be shown to be a proportionate means of achieving a legitimate aim. The increase in business potentially gave rise to a legitimate business need and it was proportionate to ask E to work extra shifts. However, the employer had produced no evidence that requiring E to work on Sundays was the only way in which the upturn in business could be dealt with. It was neither proportionate nor legitimate to issue such an instruction without first discussing the matter with the other chef or looking at other ways of providing cover

- **Fugler v Macmillan-London Hairstudios Ltd** ET Case No.2205090/04: F, who was Jewish, argued that his employer applied a PCP of discouraging employees from taking holidays on Saturdays. The employment tribunal accepted that, since the Jewish Sabbath is on a Saturday, and in 2004 Yom Kippur, an important Jewish festival, was also on a Saturday, this PCP put Jewish employees at a disadvantage. With regard to justification, the tribunal noted that the employer had a legitimate aim to serve clients on a Saturday, which was its busiest day. It was necessary, however, to perform a balancing exercise between the importance of the employer's aim and the discriminatory effect. Given that Yom Kippur is such an important day in the Jewish calendar, the tribunal concluded that the employer should have considered how it could rearrange F's duties and customers for that particular Saturday. It therefore upheld F's claim.

4.95 Where the employer has given serious consideration to the employee's request and explored alternative ways of accommodating his or her religious beliefs, the justification defence is more likely to succeed. For example, in Cherfi v G4S Security Services Ltd EAT 0379/10 C, a Muslim, worked for G4S as a security guard in Highgate, where the client required all security officers to remain on-site throughout their shifts. Consequently, he was refused permission to travel to Friday prayers at a mosque in Finsbury Park. However, there was a prayer room on-site and C had the option of working on Saturday or Sunday rather than Friday. C claimed that the PCP of requiring him to remain at work during Friday lunchtimes constituted indirect religious discrimination. An employment tribunal held that, although the PCP placed C at a disadvantage as a practising Muslim by preventing him from attending prayers in congregation, G4S would be in danger of financial penalties or even losing its contract with its client if a full complement of security staff was not on-site throughout the day. It was not practicable to obtain cover for C's lunch break because this would have entailed paying the replacement for a whole shift. Furthermore, C had refused a variety of arrangements offered to accommodate his requirements. Thus, the tribunal found that the PCP was a proportionate means of achieving a legitimate aim – namely, meeting the operational needs of the business.

On appeal, the EAT upheld this decision. In its view, the tribunal had carried out the necessary balancing act, having considered both the reason why G4S refused to allow C to leave the site on Friday lunchtimes and the impact on C. The discriminatory effect of the PCP was limited to preventing C from attending congregational prayers during working hours. C was not prevented from praying at the Highgate site, and nor was he prevented from working on a Friday or pressured to accept work on a Saturday or Sunday. In view of this, and also having regard to the alternatives that had been open to C, the conclusion as to justification was one that the tribunal was entitled to reach.

4.96 For further discussion of these issues, see IDS Employment Law Handbook, 'Discrimination at Work' (2012), Chapter 11, 'Religion or belief', in the section 'Manifestation of religion or belief', under 'Is a right to manifest protected by S.10 EqA? – time off for religious observance'.

5 Zero-hours and other 'atypical' contracts

Zero-hours contracts

Casual and seasonal workers

Annualised hours contracts

On-call contracts

Among the more significant changes in the UK labour market over the last 30 **5.1** years has been the rise of more flexible forms of working. One driver for this has been the desire of many workers to have greater flexibility in order to fit work around their personal, social and family lives – the statutory right to request such changes is considered in Chapter 4, 'Flexible working'. Another has come from employers seeking to build a workforce that can better respond to fluctuations in demand, emergencies and other unexpected events.

In this chapter, we consider a number of working arrangements that are used by employers seeking to create a more flexible workforce:

- zero-hours contracts – contracts under which the employer offers no guaranteed hours

- casual and seasonal workers – where an individual supplies labour or services to another under an irregular or informal working arrangement

- annualised hours contracts – where, rather than stipulating that a worker or employee is expected to work a set number of hours in a week, the contract sets down the number of hours that must be worked over the course of a year

- on-call contracts – contracts that make provision for the worker or employee to be called into work on short notice.

Zero-hours contracts
5.2

Few employment law issues in recent memory have attracted as many column inches as zero-hours contracts. The recent Government consultation on exclusivity clauses in such contracts received over 30,000 responses. Legislation is in the pipeline, and as a general election year approaches, the major political parties are setting out further policy proposals on the matter. This can all seem a bit baffling to employment lawyers, because the actual impact of the zero-hours contract on this practice area has, thus far, been minimal. There are no

---

249

legislative provisions specifically covering zero-hours contracts (unlike part-time, fixed-term and agency contracts) and not much in the way of case law.

Essentially, a zero-hours contract is a contract under which the employer does not guarantee a minimum number of hours to the worker. There are many circumstances where this type of working arrangement suits both employer and employee. For example, people reaching retirement age may well be happy to work a few hours here and there, mothers with young children may wish to work on an ad hoc basis, and students may only want to work in the evenings and during their holidays. However, for many workers, zero-hours contracts are imposed on them and can lead to insecurity and worry over whether there will be enough work to provide sufficient funds to pay household bills, etc.

Below, we explore what is meant by 'zero-hours contracts'. We then consider the employment status and associated rights of those working under such contracts, before exploring the proposals for a ban on exclusivity clauses.

5.3 What are zero-hours contracts?

Unlike terms such as 'part-time worker' and 'fixed-term employee', the term 'zero-hours contract' does not appear in any legislation (other than in draft form – see 'Proposals for reform' below) and there is no settled definition under the common law. Read literally, 'zero-hours' refers to any contract for work where the employer does not guarantee a minimum number of hours. In other words, 'zero-hours' is just a novel way of describing one type of contract that engages a 'casual worker' (see 'Casual and seasonal workers' below). Such contracts can range from a simple oral agreement to call when work is available, to a lengthy written contract with clauses covering matters such as the terms of payment, confidentiality, discipline and grievances, and data protection.

A House of Commons Library briefing note, 'The rise and fall of zero-hours contracts', published in May 2014, uses a slightly more specific definition, describing a zero-hours contract as 'a type of contract used by employers whereby workers have no guaranteed hours and *agree to be potentially available for work, although are not obliged to accept it*' (our stress). This definition suggests that a zero-hours contract is one under which there is no obligation on either party in relation to the assignment and acceptance of working hours. As mutuality of obligation is now regarded as fundamental to a contract of employment, on the face of it a zero-hours contract and a contract of employment must be mutually exclusive. However, the reality is that some zero-hours contracts will be contracts of employment – see 'Employment rights under zero-hours contracts – are zero-hours staff employees?' below.

5.4 Although case law has made few, if any, inroads into defining what a zero-hours contract is, the EAT in Borrer v Cardinal Security Ltd EAT 0416/12 gave some indication as to what it is not. B worked for CS Ltd as a security guard. His contract stated that he could be required to work at any of the company's assignments and would be paid the rate applicable to the assignment to which he was allocated. In relation to hours of work it stated: 'Your working hours will be specified by your line manager.' B usually received a weekly text message from his manager confirming where he would be working the following week. B worked 48 hours per week for over two years, guarding the premises of CS Ltd's various clients. A client raised concerns about him and he was encouraged to take annual leave while an alternative placement was found. He was then offered a few short-term placements for a few days per week. B resigned because of CS Ltd's failure to offer him 48 hours of work per week. The tribunal concluded that CS Ltd was not obliged to offer him a set number of hours per week and he was effectively engaged on a zero-hours contract. He had therefore not been constructively dismissed or suffered an unlawful deduction, and was not entitled to notice pay. Overturning that decision on appeal, the EAT stressed that neither the contractual wording in respect of hours of work, nor the fact that B would be texted his shift pattern on a weekly basis, supported the conclusion that he had no guaranteed hours. The true agreement between the parties, considering the evidence as a whole and by reference to the specific findings made by the tribunal, was that B had a contractual entitlement to work 48 hours per week. His remuneration for those hours of work would depend on the rate applicable to the assignment to which he was allocated. In light of that conclusion, the case was remitted for the tribunal to consider the constructive dismissal claim.

Prevalence of zero-hours contracts. The lack of a common definition of 'zero- **5.5** hours contract' has led to uncertainty over the prevalence of these arrangements. The Labour Force Survey (LFS) put the number of employees on zero-hours contracts at 583,000 in the final quarter of 2013. However, in April 2014 the Office for National Statistics (ONS) published its 'Analysis of employee contracts that do not guarantee a minimum number of hours', based on a sample of 5,000 businesses surveyed in a two-week period in January 2014, which indicated that there were around 1.4 million employee contracts that do not guarantee a minimum number of hours. Moreover, the ONS analysis estimated that there were a further 1.3 million zero-hours contracts that did not provide any hours of work over the two-week window.

The reason for the substantial difference between the LFS and ONS figures is partly a result of differences in the object of measurement, with the ONS survey measuring the number of *contracts* at UK firms providing no guaranteed hours, while the LFS looks at the number of *people* working on these types of contract. As some individuals will have more than one job, the number of zero-hours contracts is likely to be higher than the number of 'zero-hours' workers. However, the ONS figures chime broadly with the CIPD's 'Labour Market Outlook: Spring 2014', which estimated that around one million people were employed on zero-hours contracts. It seems, therefore, that the LFS may be underestimating the number of individuals working with no guaranteed hours.

251

5.6 Employment rights under zero-hours contracts

In its 'Consultation: zero hours employment contracts' (December 2013), the Government expressed concerns about a lack of transparency over the rights enjoyed by zero-hours staff. However, given the wide range of contracts to which the label 'zero-hours' can be applied, there is no one-size-fits-all approach to the question of employment rights. Instead, it is necessary to ascertain the employment status of the person working under the contract: employee, worker or self-employed, which will then determine the employment rights available.

'Employees' enjoy significantly more employment rights than 'workers', who in turn enjoy far more rights than the self-employed. Thus, there are some attractions for employers in seeking to keep the workforce as casual as possible. However, employers would be mistaken to assume that zero-hours contracts are an effective means of bypassing all employment law.

5.7 A full discussion of the topic of employment status falls outside the scope of this Handbook and can instead be found in IDS Employment Law Handbook, 'Contracts of Employment' (2009), Chapter 1, 'Basic requirements', under 'Who is an employee?' and 'Specific categories of worker'. Below, we briefly consider the meaning of 'worker' and 'employee' in the context of zero-hours contracts and set out the main rights afforded to each.

5.8 **Workers.** Section 230(3) of the Employment Rights Act 1996 (ERA) defines a 'worker' as 'an individual who has entered into or works under (or, where the employment has ceased, worked under) – (a) a contract of employment, or (b) any other contract, whether express or implied and (if it is express) whether oral or in writing, whereby the individual undertakes to do or perform personally any work or services for another party to the contract whose status is not by virtue of the contract that of a client or customer of any profession or business undertaking carried on by the individual'.

The first part of this definition establishes that anyone who is an employee is also a worker. The second part is broad in scope, and will cover the vast majority of individuals on zero-hours contracts. The only circumstances likely to prevent 'worker' status arising are:

- where the contract does not require personal service – i.e. the person reaching the agreement with the employer has an unfettered right to send a substitute to perform the work (note, however, that courts will be alive to the possibility that a 'substitution clause' is a sham – see 'Sham clauses' below)

- where the person performing the work contracts with the employer as a professional or business dealing with a client or customer – examples of this would include a barrister who contracts with a client to provide personal services, or a plumber in business on his or her own account who does the work personally.

Those working under zero-hours contracts are often identified as independent **5.9** contractors or subcontractors, but provided that their factual circumstances meet the S.230(3) definition, they will be workers.

Rights under the ERA. A number of key provisions in the ERA are only **5.10** available to employees. However, the following rights also apply to workers:

- the right not to suffer unauthorised deductions from wages in accordance with Part II of the ERA – see IDS Employment Law Handbook, 'Wages' (2010), Chapter 3, 'Protection of wages – 1', and Chapter 4, 'Protection of wages – 2'

- the right not to be subjected to a detriment on one of a number of prohibited grounds set out in Part V of the ERA. These include making a protected disclosure – see IDS Employment Law Handbook, 'Whistleblowing at Work' (2013), Chapter 5, 'Detriment'; and raising working time complaints – see IDS Employment Law Handbook, 'Working Time' (2013), Chapter 7, 'Enforcement and remedies', under 'Complaints to tribunals – unlawful detriment'. (Note that all statutory provisions affording the right not to be subjected to a detriment – including those which appear in legislation other than the ERA – apply to workers.)

Right to be accompanied. Under S.10 of the Employment Relations Act 1999 **5.11** (ERelA), where a worker 'reasonably requests' to be accompanied at a 'disciplinary hearing', the employer must permit the worker to be accompanied by a 'companion'. The companion – chosen by the worker – may be a trade union representative or a fellow worker – S.10(2A). In addition to the right to be accompanied, a worker also enjoys protection from being subjected to a detriment for seeking to exercise the right, or to accompany a colleague who is exercising the right – S.12 ERelA. See IDS Employment Law Handbook, 'Unfair Dismissal' (2010), Chapter 6, 'Conduct', under 'Disciplinary proceedings – right to be accompanied'.

Working time and holidays. The S.230(3) ERA definition of 'worker' is **5.12** replicated in Reg 2(1) of the Working Time Regulations 1998 SI 1998/1833. Under these Regulations a worker employed on a zero-hours contract has the right to:

- a 48-hour limit on the average working week – Reg 4. However, a zero-hours worker, like any other worker, can sign a contractual waiver agreeing to work more than the weekly limit

- 5.6 weeks' annual leave, paid at the rate of one week's pay for each week of leave – Regs 13 and 13A. If a worker has no 'normal working hours', the rate of holiday pay is calculated by reference to the worker's average weekly remuneration (including overtime) over the 12 weeks prior to the calculation date (the first day of leave). The practice of rolling-up holiday

253

pay, which used to be prevalent in respect of zero-hours contracts, has been held to be contrary to EU law, so a zero-hours worker should receive holiday pay at the time the leave is taken

- daily and weekly rest breaks – Regs 10–12.

As mentioned above, workers also have the right not to be subjected to a detriment for seeking to enforce their rights under the Regulations.

For detailed discussion of the rights conferred by the Working Time Regulations, see IDS Employment Law Handbook, 'Working Time' (2013).

5.13 *National minimum wage.* The S.230(3) ERA definition of 'worker' also appears in S.54(3) of the National Minimum Wage Act 1998. A worker operating under a zero-hours contract will be performing 'time work' within the meaning of Reg 3 of the National Minimum Wage Regulations 1999 SI 1999/584 and as a result will be entitled to be paid the applicable rate of the minimum wage for any time spent working.

There is evidence – in the form of enforcement action taken by HM Revenue and Customs – that some employers have been denying zero-hours workers their full rights to the minimum wage. There appear to be particular problems around travelling time, with some zero-hours contracts in the social care sector specifying that workers will only be paid for the time visiting service-users, and not for time spent travelling between assignments. This is unlawful, as any time a worker spends travelling for the purpose of duties carried out by him or her in the course of his or her work must be treated as time spent working. For full details, see IDS Employment Law Handbook, 'Wages' (2010), Chapter 5, 'The national minimum wage', under 'Hours of work for NMW purposes – travelling time'.

5.14 Working under a zero-hours contract is sometimes equated with being 'on call'. However, this synonym is problematic where employment law is concerned, because 'on call' has a more specific meaning in relation to the national minimum wage. Zero-hours staff will enjoy the right to be paid for time spent waiting to be called into work if it fits into the meaning of on-call time under the national minimum wage legislation. This is considered later in this chapter under 'On-call contracts'.

5.15 *Protection for part-time workers.* The Part-time Workers (Prevention of Less Favourable Treatment) Regulations 2000 SI 2000/1551 use a definition of 'worker' identical to that in S.230(3) ERA – see Reg 1(2). However, the Regulations may not, in practice, be particularly valuable to zero-hours workers. Reg 5 sets out the right for a part-time worker not to be treated less favourably than a comparable full-time worker:

- as regards the terms of his or her contract, or

254

- by being subjected to any other detriment by any act, or deliberate failure to act, of the employer.

Crucially, however, a 'comparable full-time worker' must be employed 'on the same type of contract' – Reg 2(4)(a)(i). For these purposes, an employee and a worker are regarded as being employed on different types of contract – Reg 2(3). So, a worker on a zero-hours contract could not rely on Reg 5 to claim that he or she had been treated less favourably than a full-time *employee*, because the two roles are not comparable.

The rights of part-time workers under the 2000 Regulations are discussed in detail in Chapter 3, 'Part-time workers'.

Discrimination. Section 39 of the Equality Act 2010 (EqA) sets out the duty on **5.16** employers not to discriminate against job applicants and 'employees'. However, this obligation is actually very wide, because 'employment' for the purposes of the Act includes not only a 'contract of employment or apprenticeship', but also 'a contract personally to do work' – S.83(2) (see IDS Employment Law Handbook, 'Discrimination at Work' (2012), Chapter 28, 'Liability of employers, employees and agents', under 'Who is protected?'). This definition is wider than that of 'worker' in S.230(3) ERA, because it would include a genuinely self-employed individual who contracts personally to do work.

The protection from discrimination guaranteed by the EqA may prove particularly important for pregnant women working on zero-hours contracts. S.18 EqA provides that a person discriminates against a woman if, during the 'protected period', he or she treats her unfavourably because of the pregnancy or because of an illness suffered as a result of it. So, for example, it would be unlawful for an employer to reduce the number of hours it offers to a zero-hours worker once she announces her pregnancy. Note that the 'protected period' for these purposes covers the duration of the pregnancy, the two weeks' compulsory maternity leave, and any time spent on ordinary or additional maternity leave. However, since the right to ordinary and additional maternity leave is only enjoyed by employees, this effectively means that those working 'under a contract personally to do work' are only protected during pregnancy and the compulsory maternity leave period.

Employees. An 'employee' is defined in S.230(1) ERA as 'an individual who **5.17** has entered into or works under (or, where the employment has ceased, worked under) a contract of employment'. However, there is no statutory definition of a contract of employment – it is a matter that has been left entirely to the common law (for a full consideration of the relevant case law, see IDS Employment Law Handbook, 'Contracts of Employment' (2009), Chapter 1, 'Basic requirements', under 'Who is an employee?'). In determining whether such a contract exists, the courts will look at all aspects of the relationship – this is known as 'the multiple test'. That said, in Carmichael and anor v

255

National Power plc 1999 ICR 1226, HL, the House of Lords endorsed the concept of an irreducible minimum of three elements without which no contract of employment can exist: control, mutuality of obligation and personal performance.

If a contract does not oblige an employer to offer work, and the other party to the contract is not obliged to accept any work that is offered, then it is strongly arguable that it lacks the mutuality of obligation necessary to form a contract of employment. On the face of it, therefore, a zero-hours contract will be a contract for services, not an employment contract, thereby affording only worker status to the person working under it. However, that doesn't fully square with the view, held by both the Government and Acas, that some zero-hours staff are employees – see the Department for Business, Innovation and Skills consultation document, 'Consultation: zero hours employment contracts' (December 2013); the Acas Policy Discussion Paper, 'Give and take? Unravelling the true nature of zero-hours contracts' (May 2014); and the House of Commons Library briefing note, 'The rise and fall of zero-hours contracts' (April 2014). Nor does it correspond to the results of the CIPD research, 'Zero-hours contracts: myth and reality' (November 2013), which reported that 63 per cent of employers regarded zero-hours staff as employees, while only 19 per cent classified them as workers.

5.18 Clearly, some employers have taken the view that it is better to treat all staff as employees rather than have a two-tier workforce of employees and zero-hours workers. Additionally, there are a number of circumstances in which an agreement that guarantees no work – even one that expressly states that it is not a contract of employment – might nevertheless be held to amount to a contract of employment:

- where the clause indicating that there is no obligation to provide or accept work does not reflect the true intentions of the parties – see 'Sham clauses' below

- where a regular pattern of work develops, and a court implies an umbrella or global contract of employment, which persists between assignments – see 'Casual and seasonal workers – are casual staff employees?' below

- where each individual assignment under the zero-hours arrangement amounts to a contract of employment – see 'Casual and seasonal workers – are casual staff employees?' below.

5.19 *Additional rights enjoyed by employees.* If a zero-hours contract is a contract of employment, then the employee working under it will enjoy a greater degree of employment protection than if he or she had simply been a worker. These rights include:

- the right not to be unfairly dismissed – see IDS Employment Law Handbook, 'Unfair Dismissal' (2010). (Note that, other than in cases of automatically unfair dismissal, this right is subject to a two-year qualifying period)

- the right to a statutory redundancy payment – see IDS Employment Law Handbook, 'Redundancy' (2008). (Note that this right is subject to a two-year qualifying period)

- rights under the Transfer of Undertakings (Protection of Employment) Regulations 2006 SI 2006/246 – see IDS Employment Law Handbook, 'Transfer of Undertakings' (2011) for details

- the right to request flexible working (see Chapter 4, 'Flexible working'). Despite its name, the statutory right is simply a right to request a contractual variation: the variation does not have to involve more flexible working arrangements than currently enjoyed. Thus, an employee working under a zero-hours contract could, somewhat paradoxically, use this statutory right to request fixed hours. (Note that this right is subject to a qualifying period of 26 weeks' continuous employment)

- the right to time off for ante-natal care under Part VI of the ERA – see IDS Employment Law Handbook, 'Maternity and Parental Rights' (2011), Chapter 1, 'Time off for ante-natal care', under 'Right to time off for ante-natal care'

- rights to statutory maternity leave and pay, paternity leave and pay, adoption leave and pay and parental leave – see IDS Employment Law Handbook, 'Maternity and Parental Rights' (2012). (Note that the rights to statutory maternity pay, statutory paternity leave and pay and statutory adoption leave and pay are all subject to a qualifying period of 26 weeks' continuous employment, and the right to parental leave is subject to a one-year qualifying period)

- the right to a written statement of particulars of employment under S.1 – see IDS Employment Law Handbook, 'Contracts of Employment' (2009), Chapter 3, 'Written particulars'

- the right to statutory notice under S.86 ERA – see IDS Employment Law Supplement, 'Notice Rights' (2006), Chapter 1, 'Rights to notice'.

5.20 As made clear, a number of the rights mentioned above are only available to employees who have completed a specified period of continuous employment. If a zero-hours contract is actually a global, or umbrella, contract of employment, then continuity will persist even when the employee is not working. However, if each period of work is covered by a separate contract of employment, with no overarching contract linking them and covering the periods when the individual is not working, then he or she may have difficulty establishing continuity of employment. A gap between contracts of at least a week will

257

operate to break continuity unless it can be seen as a temporary cessation of work or an arrangement whereby the individual in question is to be regarded as continuing in employment – S.212(3) ERA. The rules governing continuity of employment are examined in depth in IDS Employment Law Handbook, 'Continuity of Employment' (2013), Chapter 1, 'The basic framework', and Chapter 2, 'Breaks in employment where there is no contract'.

5.21 **Sham clauses.** The definition of worker in S.230(3) ERA only applies where the individual performing the work undertakes to do so 'personally'. The requirement of personal service is also fundamental to a contract of employment – see IDS Employment Law Handbook, 'Contracts of Employment' (2009), Chapter 1, 'Basic requirements', in the section 'Who is an employee?', under 'Multiple test – personal performance'. Some contracts include a 'substitution clause', purporting to allow a party to the contract to provide a substitute to perform work in his or her place. The attraction of such a clause is that, if there is no requirement of personal service, any person performing work under the contract will not have the status of worker or employee, and will therefore enjoy none of the rights attendant upon such status.

Similarly, many zero-hours contracts include an 'obligations' clause, disavowing any obligation on the employer to make work available, and any corresponding obligation on the worker to accept offers of work. These clauses have developed in part as a response to case law which established that mutuality of obligation is a key aspect of any contract of employment – see IDS Employment Law Handbook, 'Contracts of Employment' (2009), Chapter 1, 'Basic requirements', in the section 'Who is an employee?', under 'Multiple test – mutuality of obligation'.

5.22 There is no statutory bar on substitution clauses or obligations clauses. However, the courts have been alive to the possibility of such clauses being a 'sham'. In Autoclenz Ltd v Belcher and ors 2011 ICR 1157, SC, the Supreme Court endorsed a line of case law to the effect that the standard for proving a 'sham' clause in the employment context is not as stringent as it is in ordinary contract law. In the context of commercial contracts, a clause will only be disregarded as a sham if it is the product of the contracting parties' common intention to deceive others. However, in Autoclenz, the Supreme Court held that cases such as Firthglow Ltd (t/a Protectacoat) v Szilagyi 2009 ICR 835, CA, indicated that no such intention to deceive is required in an employment context. Here, a clause may be disregarded if it simply fails to represent the true intentions of the parties. An employment tribunal should discern the true intentions or expectations of the parties (and therefore their implied agreement and contractual obligations), not only at the inception of the contract but at any later stage where the evidence shows that the parties have expressly or impliedly varied their agreement.

258

In the Autoclenz case, one of the clauses which was held to be a 'sham' stated that there was no obligation on A Ltd to offer work or on the claimants to accept it – a common clause in zero-hours contracts. However, the evidence before the tribunal showed that the four essential contract terms agreed between the parties were: (i) that the claimants would perform the services defined in the contract for the employer within a reasonable time and in a good and workmanlike manner; (ii) that they would be paid for that work; (iii) that the claimants were obliged to carry out the work offered and the employer undertook to offer work; and (iv) that the claimants must personally do the work and could not provide a substitute. The Supreme Court held that the tribunal clearly found that these were the true terms of the contract and it was entitled to disregard the terms of the written documents in so far as they were inconsistent. The contract, as performed, was a contract of employment.

The true intention of the parties came under scrutiny in Pulse Healthcare Ltd v **5.23** Carewatch Care Services Ltd and ors EAT 0123/12 where the claimants had each signed documents entitled 'zero-hours contract agreement'. These used the term 'employee' and included clauses on payment, deduction from 'salary', uniforms, annual leave, sickness, termination on notice and pension, all of which were couched in terms appropriate to a contract of employment. However, the documents also contained a number of provisions consistent with a more casual working relationship: work was to be done at such times and hours as agreed, there was no obligation to offer work, and the employer retained the right to reduce working hours whenever necessary. In response to claims of unfair dismissal, CCS Ltd argued that the claimants lacked sufficient continuity of employment, pointing to the lack of mutuality of obligation in the written terms of the zero-hours contracts. However, the EAT upheld the employment tribunal's finding that the 'zero-hours' clauses in the contracts did not reflect the true agreement between the parties. The purported 'zero-hours workers' were in fact employees working under global, or umbrella, contracts of employment. What made the claimants' case particularly compelling was the nature of the work they carried out. They were engaged as carers to provide critical care to a single patient on a shift system around the clock. The EAT considered it 'fanciful' that such care would have been provided through reliance on ad hoc arrangements and that it would have been 'unrealistic' to reach any conclusion other than that the claimants worked under contracts of employment.

Proposals for law reform **5.24**

During the course of 2012 and 2013 the issue of zero-hours contracts became the subject of increasing concern in the media, as campaign groups and trade unions sought to draw attention to the downsides of such working arrangements. In response, the Department for Business, Innovation and Skills launched a 'Consultation: zero hours employment contracts' in December 2013. However, it was clear from the outset that the Government had no intention of banning

259

these contracts. Instead, it sought to minimise 'abuse' and identify 'core standards that protect individuals', while seeking to increase 'transparency'. The consultation response, issued in June 2014, set out the Government's intention to legislate to ban exclusivity clauses in zero-hours contracts, a move which it expects to benefit up to 125,000 workers tied to such clauses.

5.25 **Ban on exclusivity clauses.** The Small Business, Enterprise and Employment Bill was introduced to the House of Commons on 25 June 2014. It proposes to insert new S.27A into the ERA, which will render unenforceable any provision of a zero-hours contract that prohibits the worker from working or performing services under another contract or any other arrangement, or from doing so without the employer's consent – S.27A(3). For these purposes, 'zero-hours contract' means 'a contract of employment or other worker's contract under which – (a) the undertaking to do or perform work or services is an undertaking to do so conditionally on the employer making work or services available to the worker, and (b) there is no certainty that any such work or services will be made available to the worker' – S.27A(1). An employer makes work or services available to a worker if the employer requests or requires the worker to do the work or perform the services – S.27A(2).

The definition in S.27A(1) bears little relation to any of those that have been adopted for statistical purposes (see 'What are zero-hours contracts?' above). Furthermore, there must be doubts about whether it is sufficiently robust to achieve the purpose of preventing abuse of exclusivity clauses in zero-hours contracts. On the face of it, an employer could take a contractual arrangement outside the definition simply by guaranteeing an extremely limited number of hours – for example, a guarantee of one hour of work a year would, on a literal construction of the definition, mean that there was a 'certainty' that work will be offered. Moreover, in so far as we are aware, the term 'certainty' is not one that has previously been used in employment legislation, and its introduction is likely to lead to some disagreement as to how high a hurdle it represents.

5.26 But even if a contract is caught by S.27A(1), the actual ban on exclusivity clauses only provides limited protection. S.27A(3) states that: 'Any provision of a zero hours contract which (a) prohibits the worker from doing work or performing services under another contract or under any other arrangement, or (b) prohibits the worker from doing so without the employer's consent, is unenforceable against the worker'. This would protect a worker from the *contractual* consequences of ignoring an exclusivity clause: the employer would not be able to seek an injunction or damages for breach of contract. However, there is no corresponding provision affording workers the right not to be subjected to a detriment for working elsewhere. Realistically, an employer unhappy that one of its zero-hours workers is performing work for another employer is not going to resort to costly legal action. Far simpler is the option afforded by the zero-hours nature of the arrangement – the employer can decline to offer the worker further work.

Assuming the ban on exclusivity clauses passes into law in its current form (as outlined above), it may present issues for certain employers with regard to confidential information and trade secrets. For example, if a zero-hours worker who is privy to sensitive commercial information also works for a competitor organisation, there is a risk that the information may fall into the wrong hands. However, an employer can protect itself in this regard by including appropriately drafted restrictive covenants in the zero-hours contract. For full details, see IDS Employment Law Handbook, 'Contracts of Employment' (2009), Chapter 5, 'Employee competition and confidentiality'.

Power to make further regulations. The second zero-hours provision included **5.27** in the Small Business, Enterprise and Employment Bill, S.27B ERA, is an enabling power allowing for future regulations 'for the purpose of securing that zero hours workers, or any description of zero hours workers, are not restricted by any provision or purported provision of their contracts or arrangements with their employers from doing any work otherwise than under those contracts or arrangements' – S.27B(1). This is still very much limited to preventing abuse of exclusivity clauses and could not be used to give greater protections to workers on zero-hours contracts. Regulations under S.27B could, for example, impose financial penalties on employers, introduce a right to compensation for workers, and modify zero-hours contracts, non-contractual zero-hours arrangements, and other workers' contracts – Reg 27B(5).

The enabling power in S.27B(1) applies to 'zero hours workers', a term which covers a wider range of individuals than just those engaged on 'zero hours contracts' as defined in S.27A (see above). 'Zero hours workers' are defined in S.27B(2) as '(a) employees or other workers on zero hours contracts; (b) individuals who work under non-contractual zero hours arrangements; (c) individuals who work under workers' contracts of a kind specified by the regulations'. The contracts that can be specified are 'those in relation to which the Secretary of State considers it appropriate for provision made by the regulations to apply, having regard, in particular, to provision made by the worker's contracts as to income, rate of pay or working hours'. This suggests that the Government is well aware of the possibility that employers might seek to evade the ban on exclusivity clauses by offering a guarantee of only a minimal number of hours, but is not yet convinced of the need for anti-avoidance measures.

Casual and seasonal workers   5.28

The terms 'casual worker' and 'casual labour' encompass a wide range of circumstances. In this Handbook, we use these terms to describe the situation where an individual supplies labour or services to another under an irregular or

261

informal working arrangement. This might be under a 'zero-hours contract' (see 'Zero-hours contracts' above), as part of a 'bank' of temporary staff, or it may simply be a one-off job. It may also include work which is offered on a seasonal basis: such as a shop worker recruited to cover the busy Christmas period, or an ice cream vendor engaged for the summer months. Examples of this type of work abound in the tourist industry, in agriculture, in the restaurant business and in the construction industry. Indeed, any industry where the employer's needs are intermittent, precarious or dependent upon unforeseeable factors will make use of casual labour.

Casual staff will generally qualify as 'workers' within the meaning of S.230(3) ERA so long as they provide personal services under a contract and the other party to the contract is not a client or customer of a profession or business carried out by the individual in question. A worker enjoys a number of important employment rights, including the right to paid annual leave and to the national minimum wage. For a discussion on the scope of S.230(3) and a list of the rights enjoyed by workers, see the section 'Zero-hours contracts' above, under 'Employment rights under zero-hours contracts – workers'. In addition, casual staff – at least those who work under a contract that requires personal performance – will be able to take advantage of the protection from discrimination afforded by the EqA. See IDS Employment Law Handbook, 'Discrimination at Work' (2012), for full details.

5.29 Are casual staff employees?

Casual workers are generally classified as independent contractors rather than employees. It is a characteristic of these relationships that there is no obligation to provide work and no obligation to accept it. Workers are free to work when they wish and employers are free to hire when they wish. Claims by casual staff to employee status therefore generally fail through lack of mutuality of obligation, an essential prerequisite for the existence of a contract of employment – IDS Employment Law Handbook, 'Contracts of Employment' (2009), Chapter 1, 'Basic requirements', under 'Who is an employee?'.

However, informal working relationships encompass a wide variety of different arrangements. On the one hand, an individual may supply the odd day's work to a number of different employers; on the other, an individual who began working on a casual basis may end up working, for example, every summer for the same employer over a period of many years. Where a working arrangement settles into an informal but regular pattern over a period of time, it may be possible for the worker to argue that a contract of employment exists.

5.30 A casual worker may be classified as an employee if either:

- he or she can point to the existence of a 'global' or 'umbrella' contract of employment, which continues to exist during periods when he or she is not working. If a global contract exists, the employee will be able to establish continuity of employment under S.212(1) ERA and therefore accrue the qualifying service necessary for various employment rights (see further the section 'Zero-hours contracts' above, under 'Employment rights under zero-hours contracts – employees')

- each separate assignment amounts to a contract of employment – in other words, the worker is employed under a series of individual contracts of employment. The difficulty with this approach, in contrast to the 'global' approach, is that it may not be possible to establish sufficient continuity of employment for the purposes of many rights under the ERA, including unfair dismissal. A gap between contracts of over a week will operate to break continuity unless it can be seen as a temporary cessation of work or an arrangement whereby the individual in question is to be regarded as continuing in employment – S.212(3) ERA. The rules governing the computation of continuous employment can be found in IDS Employment Law Handbook, 'Continuity of Employment' (2012).

Global or 'umbrella' contracts. In the case of a global contract, the question 5.31 will be whether there is an obligation to provide and perform any work which becomes available and whether that obligation continues during non-working periods; in other words, whether mutual promises as to future performance have been made.

An important case in this area is Hellyer Brothers Ltd v McLeod and ors; Boston Deep Sea Fisheries Ltd v Wilson and anor 1987 ICR 526, CA, which concerned a number of trawlermen, many of whom had worked for the same employer for the whole of their working lives. They would be taken on for each voyage, the duration of which would vary from several weeks to several months. The period of time in between voyages also varied, but was often not more than a few days. At the end of each voyage they were discharged by mutual consent. In January 1984 the employer decommissioned all its trawlers and the trawlermen subsequently claimed redundancy payments. The issue for the Court of Appeal was whether they were employees under a contract of employment. The Court held that there were no facts from which it could properly be inferred that the men had ever placed themselves under a legally binding obligation to make themselves available for work in between crew agreements or to refrain from seeking or accepting employment from another trawler owner during such periods. In addition, there was no continuing obligation on the employer to offer employment to any particular individual. There was no 'continuing overriding arrangement which governed the whole of [the parties'] relationship and itself amounted to a contract of employment'.

Mutuality of obligation was also absent in O'Kelly and ors v Trusthouse Forte 5.32 plc 1983 ICR 728, CA, where the workers were wine butlers in a large hotel and were known as 'regular casuals'. They were given preference in the work rotas over other 'casual' staff and had no other work. Nonetheless, the Court

263

of Appeal agreed with the tribunal that they were not employed under contracts of employment, either in the sense of there being a global contract in place or in the sense that each stint of work was carried out under a contract of employment. Although the relationship had many characteristics of an employment contract, one essential ingredient was missing: mutuality of obligation. The workers had the right to decide whether or not to accept work and were free to obtain work elsewhere: the fact that it would not have been in their interests to do so was another matter. Neither was the employer under any contractual obligation to provide any work, although in fact it regularly did so. The Court concluded that the workers were hired under successive contracts for services.

In Clark v Oxfordshire Health Authority 1998 IRLR 125, CA, the Court of Appeal held that a nurse who was retained by a health authority to fill temporary vacancies in hospitals did not have a global employment contract spanning her various individual engagements because there was no mutuality of obligation during the periods when she was not working. The fact that C was bound by an ongoing duty of confidentiality even during non-working periods was insufficient, since any such obligation would have stemmed from previous single engagements, and no continuing obligation whatever would have fallen on the health authority. However, the Court did accept that the mutual obligations required to found a global contract of employment need not necessarily consist of obligations to provide and perform work: for example, an obligation on the one party to accept and perform work and an obligation on the other party to pay a retainer during periods when work was not offered would be likely to suffice.

5.33　Similarly, in Carmichael and anor v National Power plc 1999 ICR 1226, HL, the House of Lords held that casually employed tour guides, when not actually working, had no contractual relationship at all with the tour guide operator because there were no mutual obligations to offer and perform work. The documents that existed simply provided a framework for a series of successive ad hoc contracts of service or for services, which the parties might subsequently make. Their Lordships said that 'the parties incurred no obligations to provide or accept work, but at best assumed moral obligations of loyalty in a context where both recognised that the best interests of each lay in being accommodating to the other'.

The decisions in the above cases mean that it will be difficult for many casual workers to establish the existence of a global contract of employment. However, as the House of Lords stated in Carmichael, the determination of employment status may depend on an evaluation of factual circumstances as well as on the construction of written documents. This raises the possibility that, if the course of dealings between the parties gives rise to mutual expectations that work will continue to be provided, this may amount to sufficient mutuality of obligation to found the basis of a global contract. Indeed, this was the case in Nethermere (St Neots) Ltd v Gardiner and anor 1984 ICR 612, CA, in which the Court of Appeal, albeit reluctantly, upheld a tribunal's decision to the effect that the long-standing relationship between homeworkers and the company for which they worked had developed into a global contract obliging the company to provide and pay for work and the workers to accept the work provided.

It is clear, however, that terms conferring mutual obligations cannot normally **5.34** be implied into a contract contrary to obvious express terms. Thus, in Stevedoring and Haulage Services Ltd v Fuller and ors 2001 IRLR 627, CA, the Court of Appeal held that a casually employed docker, who worked for an employer expressly on the basis that no mutual obligation as to the provision and acceptance of work existed, could not be an 'employee'. Courts and tribunals should, however, be alive to the possibility of 'sham' terms that misrepresent or conceal the parties' true intentions – see the section 'Zero-hours contracts' above, under 'Employment rights under zero-hours contracts – "sham" clauses'.

The Court of Appeal recently reviewed the requirements for a global contract in Stringfellow Restaurants Ltd v Quashie 2013 IRLR 99, CA. Lord Justice Elias referred to Nethermere (St Neots) Ltd v Gardiner and anor (above) and Carmichael and anor v National Power plc (above) as authority for the principle that, for a global contract to exist, it is necessary to show that there is at least 'an irreducible minimum of obligation', either express or implied, which continues during the breaks in work engagements. He pointed out that the significance of the irreducible minimum is that it determines whether a contract exists at all during the periods of non-work. Assuming that there is a contractual basis for the parties' relationship, then the extent of the obligation, and the presence of factors such as control, will determine whether the contract is one of employment.

Specific contracts. A casual worker who does not benefit from the mutuality **5.35** of obligation necessary to establish a 'global' contract of employment based on a long-standing relationship may nonetheless be able to establish sufficient mutuality of obligation in relation to each specific engagement entered into as part of that relationship. If so, the worker may be regarded as an employee in respect of each engagement, even though the employment relationship ends when each engagement is completed – see McMeechan v Secretary of State for Employment 1997 ICR 549, CA.

In Cornwall County Council v Prater 2006 ICR 731, CA, the Council operated a home tuition scheme, under which tuition was provided to school children for as long as necessary. Although there was no obligation on the Council to provide work or on a tutor to accept it, once a pupil enrolled there was a mutual expectation that the tutor would complete the assignment and the Council would pay the teacher for that work. P began working as a tutor in 1988 and was awarded a post as an employee in 1998. She was paid in all but 14 months over that period. The Court of Appeal upheld a tribunal's decision that P's employment with the Council stretched back to 1988. If P had sought to show that there was a long-term or global contract of employment, the fact that the Council was not obliged to offer her any work and that, if it did, she was not obliged to accept that offer would, no doubt, have defeated her claim. But P instead successfully argued that the individual engagements, once entered into, constituted contracts of employment and so there was no need for her to establish an overarching mutuality of obligation throughout the ten-year period. Any gaps between assignments were temporary cessations of work within the meaning of S.212(3)(b) ERA, which preserved her continuity of employment.

5.36   The Prater case was followed in North Wales Probation Area v Edwards EAT 0468/07, where the EAT held that a sessional relief worker was an employee. However, a different conclusion was reached in Little v BMI Chiltern Hospital EAT 0021/09. There, the working relationship between a bank theatre porter and the hospital for which he had worked for 16 years was regulated by a series of written agreements in which he was described as an independent contractor. The tribunal found that there was an absence of mutuality of obligation between the parties and that the written agreements accurately reflected their intentions. On appeal, the claimant submitted that he was employed under a succession of contracts of service rather than a global contract and that the mutual obligations that came into being during each period of work gave rise to a contract of employment. The EAT disagreed, holding that the hospital's policy of sending home bank theatre workers halfway through a shift when not required negated a specific contract of employment. Furthermore, the documentary evidence clearly envisaged that there would be no mutuality of obligation. This case could be distinguished from Cornwall County Council v Prater (above) and the Edwards case because the work could be withdrawn during the claimant's shift and he was not entitled to payment for the remainder of the shift. Accordingly, there was no obligation on the hospital to provide him with work even under the specific, individual contracts. While there was a contract in place when the claimant worked, it was – in fact and law – a contract for freelance services and not one of employment.

The Little case should be treated with some caution, however. In Drake v Ipsos Mori UK Ltd 2012 IRLR 973, EAT, His Honour Judge David Richardson noted that if Little were treated as authority for the proposition that a right to terminate work at will is inconsistent with a contract of employment, it would be contrary to the result and reasoning in McMeechan v Secretary of State for Employment (above), which was not cited in Little. As for the case before him, HHJ David Richardson overturned an employment judge's decision that D, who worked on an 'assignment by assignment' basis, was not an 'employee' during the periods of work. The handbook issued by IM UK Ltd stated that the acceptance of any individual assignment would give rise to a 'verbal contract' that the job would be completed to a deadline, but the employment judge found as a fact that no penalties or disciplinary sanctions were ever imposed when a worker did not complete an assignment. The judge had treated the fact that an individual contract arising under these arrangements was 'terminable at will' as a determining factor in his conclusion that the contract was not one of employment. This was an error of law. The case was remitted for a fresh hearing on whether the obligations that did exist within each contract were such as to give rise to 'employee' status.

Interestingly, the Court of Appeal in Pola v R (Health and Safety Executive) 2009 EWCA Crim 655, CA, had to consider the question of whether a casual worker, who was not obliged to turn up to work on any particular day, was nonetheless properly characterised as an employee during the periods he did in fact work for the purposes of health and safety law. Under the Health and Safety at Work etc Act 1974 it is necessary to determine whether or not a worker is an employee in order to ascertain what health and safety responsibilities are owed to him or her by the employer. The Court found that the relevant workers were expected to work for the whole of any day on which they turned up, and would be paid for the day in full. Consequently, they were employees during each day on which they worked. **5.37**

Annualised hours contracts **5.38**

Under a 'typical' full-time working arrangement an employee will be contracted to work between 35 and 40 hours a week. Over the course of the year, that equates to between 1,820 and 2,080 hours of work. Some employers may find that, while they have ample work over the course of the year to fill those hours, there are significant peaks and troughs. To an extent, periods where it is known in advance that there will be little work available can be catered for by requiring staff to take paid annual leave at a time of the employer's choosing; summer and Christmas shut-downs remain common across a range of industries. But there remains the problem of responding to an upturn in demand – the employer might have to pay overtime, or resort to recruiting temporary staff. For some employers, the solution has been to introduce annualised hours contracts – i.e. contracts that specify the number of hours to be worked in a year, rather than in a week.

What are annualised hours contracts? **5.39**
As the name suggests, annualised hours contracts mandate the number of hours that must be worked over the course of a year in return for an annual salary, with a degree of flexibility as to when those hours are worked. They appeal to certain employers – particularly those operating a shift system – because, compared with contracts which divide up hours on a weekly basis, they offer a

267

way of avoiding, at least to some extent, the twin perils of paying staff for idle time and for overtime.

Annualised hours are a form of flexible working and, as such, an employee may request a change from a standard working week to an annualised hours agreement where it suits him or her to do so – see Chapter 4, 'Flexible working', for full details of the right to request flexible working. However, moves towards this particular method of flexible working are more often made by employers seeking to match their staffing levels to the predicted demand for products or services. Many annualised hours working arrangements come about by way of a collective agreement with recognised trade unions. In such circumstances, the clauses relating to hours and pay are incorporated into the individual employees' contracts of employment.

5.40 While the zero-hours and casual contracts considered earlier in this chapter will most likely give rise to 'worker' status, those working under annualised hours contracts will more than likely be employees. The inclusion within the contract of the number of hours of work that must be performed over the year suggests that there is mutuality of obligation persisting throughout. Furthermore, the employer is likely to retain a significant degree of control over when the hours are worked and how the work is done, and the worker will generally be required to provide personal performance.

5.41 Working time considerations

The flexibility afforded by an annualised hours working arrangement is tempered by the employer's obligations under the Working Time Regulations 1998 SI 1998/1833. The following considerations apply:

- workers enjoy the right to a 48-hour limit on the average working week. Although workers can opt out of this right in writing, they must do so individually – an opt-out cannot be incorporated by way of a collective or workforce agreement. For further details, see IDS Employment Law Handbook, 'Working Time' (2013), Chapter 2, 'The 48-hour week'

- the scheduling of hours under an annualised hours contract must take account of the mandated rest periods under the Regulations: even if a worker has opted out of the 48-hour week, he or she is entitled to a daily rest period of not less than 11 consecutive hours in each 24-hour period during which he or she works for his or her employer; and an uninterrupted weekly rest period of not less than 24 hours in each seven-day period during which he or she works for his or her employer. This is in addition to the right to a 20-minute rest break in each shift of over six hours. For further details, see IDS Employment Law Handbook, 'Working Time' (2013), Chapter 3, 'Rest periods and rest breaks'

268

- the calculation of holiday pay may be more challenging where annualised hours contracts are concerned, as the right to paid annual leave under the Regulations is expressed in terms of weeks – all workers are entitled to 5.6 weeks' paid leave each year, remunerated at the rate of one week's pay for each week of leave. For further details, see IDS Employment Law Handbook, 'Working Time' (2013), Chapter 4, 'Annual leave', under 'Calculating holiday pay'.

In Cook and ors v C2C Rail Ltd EAT 0604/05 the employer and various trade **5.42** unions reached a collective agreement to introduce a new rostering system. Each employee moved to an 'annual hours contract' under which he or she would be rostered to work 1,930 hours – equivalent to 52 times a 37-hour working week – and paid an annual salary in 13 equal instalments. In respect of holidays, employees would not be rostered to work on 126 days during the year, which equated to two 'free' days per week, plus 22 days' 'fixed free time'. No provision was made for additional holiday payments on top of the salary. C and four other employees brought claims of unlawful deductions from wages, arguing that the contract entitled them to be paid a fixed sum for an hour's work, and so they should have been paid an additional sum to reflect the 22 days' holiday. However, the EAT agreed with an employment tribunal that the construction advanced by the claimants was 'not the way an annual hours contract would be expressed'. The contract did not set an hourly rate of pay, other than in specifying how pay would be calculated for overtime in excess of the 1,930 hours. Instead, it set an annual salary and allowed the employees to book off 'fixed free days'.

Overtime under annualised hours **5.43**

Employers seeking to introduce annualised hours contracts may well do so out of a desire to avoid paying overtime to meet periods of high demand. The greater flexibility provided by rostering hours on an annualised basis means that peaks and troughs can be better managed, and annualised hours agreements usually only make provision for the payment of overtime once the annual figure of hours has been exceeded. Under an annualised hours arrangement, an employee working extra shifts is simply getting through his or her hours that bit faster, and he or she is only likely to have the opportunity to work paid overtime towards the end of the year once the contractual hours have been completed.

In Ali and ors v Christian Salvesen Food Services Ltd 1997 ICR 25, CA, A and his fellow claimants had been hourly-paid workers who were paid at a higher rate for any overtime that they worked. After reaching a collective agreement with the recognised unions, the employer introduced an annualised hours system, under which the employees were paid a standard weekly wage throughout the year based on a 40-hour week. Overtime at the higher rate would only be paid at the end of the pay year if the employee in question had

269

worked more than 1,824 hours. The claimants were made redundant some six months into the working year. None had reached the overtime threshold but all had worked in excess of an average 40 hours a week. The employer, however, refused to remunerate them for those extra hours and the claimants brought unlawful deduction from wages claims. The tribunal dismissed the claims, finding that there had not been any deduction from wages because there was no express term in the contracts to cover overtime payments in circumstances where employees were dismissed before the end of the year. The tribunal was not prepared to imply a term into the contracts of employment to this effect, as it was not necessary to do so in order to make the contract work. The EAT disagreed. It considered that the lack of any express term covering early termination was an oversight, and that had this been drawn to the attention of the parties when they reached the agreement, they would have agreed that a term should be inserted into the agreement to ensure that overtime was payable to employees who worked during only part of the year.

5.44　On further appeal, the Court of Appeal restored the decision of the employment tribunal. A collective agreement negotiated across a broad range of issues for a substantial workforce had to be clear and concise in order to be readily understood by all who were concerned with its operation. It was to be expected that the parties to such an agreement would not wish to legislate for every contingency. Therefore, should any topic be left uncovered by the agreement, the natural inference was not that there had been an omission which required judicial correction, but rather that the topic had been intentionally left out of the agreement on the basis that it was considered to be too controversial or too complicated to justify any variation of the main terms of the agreement in order to take account of it. While the omission of any reference to what happened if contracts were terminated before the end of the pay year might, at first sight, appear to be surprising, it became less so when consideration was given to the immensity of the task that would be involved in covering every potential situation on termination. To devise terms that covered all contingencies would require an unacceptable degree of elaboration. It was therefore difficult, if not impossible, to devise a term which the negotiating parties would have agreed on had they decided to make provision for a particular set of circumstances.

While the Court of Appeal's decision was good news for employers, in that it was not thought necessary to imply a term to pay the employees for the additional hours they had worked, it also underlines the importance to all parties of the need to include express provisions wherever possible, given that the courts will be reluctant to assume that any omission is an oversight. The need for clarity works both ways. If, for example, the employees in the Ali case had been dismissed at a time when they had worked 50 per cent of their annual hours, but had received 60 per cent of their annual salary, they would not have been required to reimburse the employer for the overpayment.

270

On-call contracts

5.45

The demands of certain jobs mean that it is necessary for the employer to put in place contractual arrangements that ensure that workers who are not working are nevertheless 'on call' and can be summoned into work to deal with an emergency or a sudden upturn in demand. For example, an accident and emergency ward in a hospital needs the ability to call in extra doctors and nurses to deal with a crisis.

There is no uniform version of an 'on-call contract'. Rather, there are a wide range of contractual arrangements that include provision for a worker to be 'on call'. One of the crucial questions in respect of such arrangements is whether the worker is entitled to be paid for time spent on call. There are two broad circumstances in which an entitlement to be paid might arise:

• if the written terms of the contract stipulate payment – for example, many contracts agreed under the NHS 'Agenda for Change' include provision for on-call payments

• if the on-call time counts as time spent working for the purposes of the national minimum wage – see 'National minimum wage' below.

In addition to the question of whether the worker is entitled to be paid for **5.46** any time spent on call, there is also the matter of whether that time counts as 'working time' for the purposes of the Working Time Regulations 1998 SI 1998/1833. In this regard, two decisions of the European Court of Justice (ECJ) concerning on-call doctors have proved hugely influential – Sindicato de Médicos de Asistencia Pública (SIMAP) v Consellería de Sanidad and anor 2001 ICR 1116, ECJ, and Landeshauptstadt Kiel v Jaeger 2004 ICR 1528, ECJ. In those cases, the ECJ established that time when a worker is required to be present at a place determined by the employer and to be available to provide services to the employer immediately in times of need will count as working time for the purposes of the EU Working Time Directive (No.2003/88), which the Regulations implement. A full consideration of case law on this point can be found in IDS Employment Law Handbook, 'Working Time' (2013), Chapter 1, 'Scope and key concepts', under 'Working time – call-out and stand-by'.

National minimum wage

5.47

The National Minimum Wage Regulations 1999 SI 1999/584 set out four categories of work, each with different rules for the calculation of relevant hours: time work, salaried hours work, output work and unmeasured work. Salaried hours workers and time work workers will be regarded as working when they are on call, i.e. when they are available at or near a place of work for the purpose of doing work and are required to be available for such work.

271

However, they will not be regarded as working if their home is at or near their place of work and they are entitled to spend the time on call at home – Regs 15(1) and 16(1).

Where a worker is entitled to sleep at or near his place of work when on call, and is provided with suitable facilities for sleeping, only time when the worker is awake for the purpose of working is treated as time work or salaried hours work – Regs 15(1A) and 16(1A).

5.48 A worker will only need to rely upon Regs 15(1) and 16(1) to apply the NMW if he or she is on call but *not* working. If he or she is actually working, then the entitlement to be paid the minimum wage arises under Reg 3 (in the case of time work workers) and Reg 4 (in the case of salaried hours workers). This was made clear by the Court of Appeal in British Nursing Association v Inland Revenue 2003 ICR 19, CA. In that case, the BNA provided a telephone service at night from home and required the workers concerned to be available between 8 pm and 9 am in order to take telephone calls and respond to them by locating and assigning a nurse from a pool of available staff to provide emergency cover as required. Between calls, the night workers were free to spend the time as they wished and were paid for each shift they worked. The Court of Appeal held that the nurses were to be regarded as working throughout their shifts for the purposes of the Regulations even though they were free to do as they pleased between telephone calls. Such work was to be regarded as 'time work' within the meaning of Reg 3.

A fuller consideration of the case law in this area can be found in IDS Employment Law Handbook, 'Wages', Chapter 5, 'The national minimum wage', under 'Hours of work for NMW purposes – on-call working'.

6 Apprentices

Apprenticeships have long been thought to be in decline in the UK. Many **6.1** people think of them as being mainly relevant to manufacturing, construction and skilled crafts, and so a decline in these industries has led to an assumption that the number of apprenticeships available has also dropped. However, apprenticeships are now available in a much wider range of sectors than previously, including software development, banking and finance, business administration and healthcare, and this diversification has meant that significant numbers of young people still work under apprenticeship arrangements.

There are (broadly) two forms of apprenticeship. On the one hand, there is the 'traditional' contract of apprenticeship, the form and legal status of which is governed by case law going back hundreds of years. On the other, there is the apprenticeship agreement (formerly known as the 'Modern Apprenticeship'), the form and legal status of which is governed – in England and Wales – by the Apprenticeships, Skills, Children and Learning Act 2009 (ASCLA). As Government funding for apprenticeships is channelled through schemes that comply with the statutory arrangements, there is less incentive these days for employers to go down the common law route. Nonetheless, there may still be traditional schemes in existence and we consider both kinds of apprenticeship in this chapter. Furthermore, the common law principles may apply to 'modern' apprenticeships in Scotland and Northern Ireland, which are not covered by the ASCLA rules.

We begin by looking at the common law concept of a contract of apprenticeship **6.2** – in particular, the similarities and differences between a contract of apprenticeship and a contract of service. We then consider the ASCLA scheme and the legal status of apprenticeship agreements governed by it, before turning to the employment rights and protections that are available to apprentices under both schemes – these are now identical, given that both common law apprentices and those working under ASCLA-compliant schemes are treated for employment law purposes as 'employees'. Finally, we briefly review the funding arrangements for off-the-job training of apprentices under Government-backed schemes.

—————————————————————————————————— **273**

Note that, to avoid confusion, we use the term 'contract of service' throughout this chapter to denote what is more commonly known as a contract of employment. This is because the Employment Rights Act 1996 (ERA) defines a contract of employment as a contract of service *or* apprenticeship. A 'contract of service' should be distinguished from a 'contract for services', a term generally used to describe a contract between an employer and an independent, self-employed contractor.

6.3 Contracts of apprenticeship

Although a contract of apprenticeship is treated in the same way as a contract of service for many statutory purposes, the two types of contract are significantly different. In Wallace v CA Roofing Services Ltd 1996 IRLR 435, QBD, Mr Justice Sedley (as he then was) noted the demise of the traditional contract of apprenticeship but disagreed with commentary that suggested that the distinction between a contract of service and one of apprenticeship had become one of little practical significance. While there may be no significant difference between the two in terms of access to statutory rights, given their assimilation in the ERA and other employment protection legislation, the common law position as regards termination differs between the two. This difference is discussed under 'Termination' below but first we highlight the salient features of a contract of apprenticeship.

6.4 Characteristics of the contract

Unlike a contract of service, which has as its object the performance of work, the primary purpose of a contract of apprenticeship is training. Therefore, there is no need for the mutual obligations of work and pay that characterise a contract of service. In Dunk v George Waller and Son Ltd 1970 2 QB 163, CA, Lord Justice Widgery observed: 'A contract of apprenticeship secures three things for the apprentice: it secures him, first, a money payment during the period of apprenticeship, secondly, that he shall be instructed and trained and thus acquire skills which would be of value to him for the rest of his life, and, thirdly, it gives him status, because the evidence in this case made it quite clear that once a young man, as here, completes his apprenticeship and can show by certificate that he has completed his time with a well-known employer, this gets him off to a good start in the labour market and gives him a status the loss of which may be of considerable damage to him.' Although not intended to be an exhaustive list of the essential elements of a contract of apprenticeship, this indicates the manner in which such a contract differs from a contract of service.

As for the form of the contract, it is well established in relation to contracts of service that the label which the parties put on the working arrangements is not determinative, so the fact that the contractual documents do not themselves use the word 'employment' will not prevent a court or tribunal finding that there is a contract of service. The same is true of contracts of apprenticeship, in that the parties' failure to use the word 'apprentice' in agreeing the work and training arrangements will not of itself mean that the contract is not one of apprenticeship – see, for example, Chassis and Cab Specialists Ltd v Lee EAT 0268/10.

There is no formal need for 'consideration' under a contract of apprenticeship. **6.5** The doctrine of consideration requires that something of value pass from each party to the other when a contract is performed. Thus, if A promises B that he or she will perform a service, that promise will only be enforceable as part of a contract if A is to receive something of value in return. In the context of a contract of service the consideration is usually the work provided by the employee and the salary paid by the employer. Under a contract of apprenticeship, the training given by the employer to the apprentice is provided without any apparent consideration, since the apprentice is not required to do any work for the employer other than that which furthers his or her training. Before the Apprentices Act 1814 came into force it was common for an apprenticeship to be formalised as a deed, which is the legal form used to create a binding obligation in the absence of consideration. Since the Act removed this requirement contracts of apprenticeship are generally concluded in much the same form as contracts of service. It could therefore be argued that such contracts are invalid for want of consideration. However, the common law recognises certain kinds of contract that do not require consideration in both directions and it is generally accepted that a contract of apprenticeship is one such.

In any event, it is arguable that a contract of apprenticeship does provide something of value to the employer. In Edmonds v Lawson and ors 2000 ICR 567, CA, the Court of Appeal held that a pupillage agreement – under which a would-be barrister is provided with training in chambers – could be a valid contract compliant with the doctrine of consideration. The Court observed that nothing that a pupil does under the agreement could be viewed as providing consideration in return for the training, since a pupil is not obliged to do anything that does not contribute to his or her professional development. Nonetheless, viewing the matter more broadly than simply as an individual relationship between pupil and pupil-master, the Court accepted that pupillage arrangements were of benefit to the chambers as a whole. It took the view that the agreement of the claimant and other pupils to undertake pupillage at chambers provided a pool of selected candidates who could be expected to compete with each other for recruitment as tenants. Thus, pupils provide consideration for the offer made by the chambers by agreeing to enter into the close, important and potentially very productive relationship which pupillage involves.

An analogous argument might well be made with regard to apprenticeships in **6.6** general (although the Court of Appeal in Edmonds went on to reject the pupil barrister's argument that a pupillage agreement actually amounted to a contract of apprenticeship or an equivalent contract). An employer taking on an

275

apprentice is certainly in a very similar position to a pupil-master taking on a pupil, in that it has an interest in having available a pool of well-trained workers. This is the employer's 'recoupment' on its outlay on training and this benefit is industry-wide. Indeed, in Wallace v CA Roofing Services Ltd (above), Sedley J recorded his 'appreciation of the value of apprenticeships to the industry as a whole and of the contribution made by employers such as the defendants to the maintenance of an industry's accumulated experience and skills'.

6.7 Need to be in writing

There is some uncertainty over whether a contract of apprenticeship needs to be in writing. This was a requirement under S.2 of the Apprentices Act 1814, to which much of the case law refers – see, for example, MacDonald v John Twiname Ltd 1953 2 QB 304, CA. However, that Act was repealed in 2004 and there has since been no case law (to our knowledge) that considers whether there is still any necessity for a common law contract of apprenticeship to be in writing.

Cases decided before the repeal appeared to accept that even if a contract of apprenticeship is required to be in writing, an oral agreement will still be enforced if it is acted upon. In Wallace v CA Roofing Services Ltd (above) the High Court accepted that a common law contract of apprenticeship had come into existence on the basis of oral agreement. Sedley J summarised the law to the effect that while enforceability depends on the contract being in writing, an employer who has acted on an oral contract of apprenticeship will be held to it as if it were in writing. The Court of Appeal put it in a slightly different way in Edmonds v Lawson and ors (above) when it took Wallace and MacDonald as authority for the proposition that 'an oral contract of apprenticeship, although legally valid, is unenforceable unless and until acted upon'. However the principle is formulated, it is clear that a written contract is not essential, and if a court or tribunal can find clear agreement on oral terms, which are subsequently put into effect, then it can find an enforceable contract of apprenticeship.

6.8 It is interesting to note in this regard that S.230(2) ERA, which defines 'contract of employment' for the purposes of many statutory employment rights, envisages the possibility of a contract of apprenticeship being oral. It provides that a contract of employment means 'a contract of service or apprenticeship, whether express or implied, and (if it is express) whether oral or in writing'.

6.9 Status of 'modern' apprenticeships

Successive Governments have made it a matter of policy to increase the take-up of apprenticeships and have established various statutory schemes to this end. The question then arises whether these 'modern' apprenticeship arrangements qualify as traditional, common law contracts of apprenticeship. The answer has generally been 'yes', at least in relation to the Government-funded schemes in place before the ASCLA came into force.

276

In Whitely v Marton Electrical Ltd 2003 ICR 495, EAT, for example, the EAT held that a 'modern apprenticeship agreement', under which an employer agreed to employ an apprentice for the duration of his training, was a common law contract of apprenticeship. And in Flett v Matheson 2006 ICR 673, CA, the Court of Appeal held that a Government-funded Modern Apprenticeship was also subject to the common law rules on apprenticeship. There, an apprentice who entered into a tripartite 'individual learning plan' under the electrical industry's Modern Apprenticeship training scheme was held to have been engaged under a traditional contract of apprenticeship. The tripartite nature of the agreement – between the apprentice, the employer and a Government-sponsored training provider – did not deprive the relationship between employer and apprentice of a long-term character which persisted until the end of the training period contemplated. Although the employer did not provide the academic part of the training, it was required to give the claimant time off to obtain it and to fund the cost of attendance at classes. In the course of its judgment, the Court of Appeal warned that since such tripartite agreements are capable of amounting to contracts of apprenticeship, and thus of potentially attracting substantial damages if ended prematurely, there is a need for transparency in arrangements of this sort so that employers clearly understand their obligations.

The Flett decision was followed in Lloyd v Federal Mogul Sintered Products **6.10** Ltd (in administration) ET Case No.1308388/03, where the tribunal awarded an apprentice who had signed a 'modern apprenticeship pledge' £20,000 for breach of contract after he was dismissed before the end of his apprenticeship contract due to poor attendance. The tribunal noted that L's career was prematurely destroyed by the employer, which, despite the membership and advice available from an engineering federation, did not appreciate the special protection given to L as an apprentice. But for the employer's inherently unfair absence policy, L would probably have completed his apprenticeship and become a skilled engineer.

It is therefore beyond doubt that modern apprenticeship schemes can, in principle, give rise to common law contracts of apprenticeship. However, this is not the case in respect of apprenticeship agreements concluded in England and Wales under the ASCLA as S.35 of that Act expressly states that such agreements are to be treated for all purposes as contracts of service, not contracts of apprenticeship. Thus, the case law cited above is now of only limited application, since any apprenticeship that complies with the ASCLA conditions – which it must do if it is to be eligible for state funding – will not give rise to a contract of apprenticeship. However, the case law will still be relevant to the few apprenticeship arrangements that are set up outside the ambit of the statutory scheme and in Scotland and Northern Ireland, where Modern Apprenticeship arrangements are still in operation. The case law may also be relevant to those cases where there has been non-compliance with one or more of the ASCLA conditions, in which case the resulting agreement may give rise to a common law contract of apprenticeship. This issue, and the ASCLA scheme generally, is considered in more detail under 'Apprenticeship agreements' below.

6.11 Termination

Perhaps the most significant difference between a contract of service and a contract of apprenticeship is the restricted provision for lawful termination in respect of the latter. In the normal course of events, a contract of apprenticeship, being fixed-term in nature, will terminate on the date, or at the end of the period, specified in the contract. It is a feature of contracts of apprenticeship that they cannot usually be terminated earlier except in cases of serious misconduct by the apprentice. In Wallace v CA Roofing Services Ltd (above), Sedley J had to decide whether an orally agreed contract of apprenticeship included a provision allowing the employer to terminate the apprenticeship in case of a downturn in work – i.e. in a redundancy situation. He held that there was no such agreement on the facts and went on to give the obiter view that such flexibility could not be accommodated in a common law contract of apprenticeship in any event. In his view, the inclusion of a clause allowing for early termination in case of redundancy would mean that the contract is not a true contract of apprenticeship. Although it may be possible to create a contract that is subject to early termination for redundancy but is otherwise one of apprenticeship, it would require clear words to produce that result once the contract has been described as one of 'apprenticeship', as understood in the industrial context. Lord Justice Pill expressly concurred in this view in the Court of Appeal in Flett v Matheson (above), noting that 'once a contract has been categorised as one of apprenticeship, with a specific period of training contemplated, the right to dismiss on the ground of redundancy should not readily be implied'.

In Whitely v Marton Electrical Ltd (above) the EAT held that a 'modern apprenticeship agreement', under which the employer agreed to employ the apprentice for the duration of his training, was a common law contract of apprenticeship and could not be terminated before the end of the training period. Although there was a provision in the agreement requiring the apprentice to comply with the employer's ordinary terms and conditions of employment, that did not mean that the employer could rely on those terms as to notice of termination. Even assuming that the terms applied, wherever they were inconsistent with those of the apprenticeship agreement, the terms of that agreement had to prevail.

6.12 **Frustration.** Although contracts of apprenticeship can rarely be terminated prematurely, they may come to an early end by reason of frustration. Briefly, a contract will become frustrated when an unforeseen event makes performance of the contract impossible or radically different from what the parties originally intended – Davis Contractors v Fareham UDC 1956 AC 696, HL.

In FC Shepherd and Co Ltd v Jerrom 1986 ICR 802, CA, the Court of Appeal held that the contract of an apprentice who received an indeterminate sentence of imprisonment in a young offenders' institution was frustrated. At the time the sentence was imposed the contract of apprenticeship had over two years left to run. Lord Justice Mustil specifically rejected the argument that the fact that the joint industry board's rules laid down a specific procedure for termination meant that the contract could not become frustrated. In his view, the existence of specific rules could not mean that the employer's obligations were incapable of being discharged by frustration, but he did acknowledge that the existence of a termination provision should inhibit the court from being too ready to find in favour of frustration.

Frustration is considered in more detail in IDS Employment Law Handbook, 'Contracts of Employment' (2009), Chapter 10, 'Termination by operation of law', under 'Frustration'.

Remedy for wrongful termination. The limited scope for early termination 6.13 makes its effect felt when it comes to assessing damages for wrongful termination of a contract of apprenticeship. Whereas damages for wrongful dismissal under a contract of service are generally limited to the amount the employee has lost by way of notice pay, damages for wrongful termination of a contract of apprenticeship may give rise to substantial damages for lost earnings during the remainder of the apprenticeship and for the potential diminution of the apprentice's future prospects. As Lord Justice Widgery put it in Dunk v George Waller and Son Ltd 1970 2 QB 163, CA, damages can be sought for 'the loss of teaching, the loss of instruction and the loss of status'.

In Flett v Matheson (above), the Court of Appeal had to consider whether the employer's responsibility on termination of an 'individual learning plan' (ILP) – which the Court held to be a contract of apprenticeship – was limited to making reasonable efforts to find another employer willing and able to continue the apprentice's training. The Court concluded that the employer's liability was not so limited and that it was obliged to employ the apprentice for the contemplated period of the apprenticeship, subject to the express provisions for termination set out in the ILP. Although some training under the apprenticeship was to be provided by a third party this did not deprive the relationship of a long-term character that persisted until the end of the training period. Furthermore, although the ILP allowed the employer to seek an alternative employer if it could not continue with the arrangements itself, it also provided that until such a transfer had been arranged and registered, the employer would remain responsible for ensuring that all of its obligations to the apprentice were satisfied. Thus, if the employer's attempts to find an alternative employer failed, the obligation on the original employer would remain and it would not be entitled to dismiss the apprentice other than as expressly provided for in the ILP.

279

6.14 Apprenticeship agreements

A drive to improve the quality and take-up of apprenticeships has been on the political agenda for the past 20 years, albeit with the emphasis shifting between quality and inclusivity at different times. This drive has largely manifested itself in the establishment of state-funded apprenticeship schemes. The last Conservative Government sought to revive apprenticeships and, to that end, introduced Modern Apprenticeships in 1994 (later rebranded simply as 'Apprenticeships' in 2004). These were generally three years in duration and provided for an NVQ Level 3 qualification. The Labour Government that took office in 1997 was also keen to promote apprenticeships but was concerned that the Level 3 standard (equivalent to two A-levels) excluded too many young people. It therefore introduced apprenticeships at NVQ Level 2 (equivalent to five GCSEs), which were essentially a rebranding of the Youth Training Schemes that had previously served 16- and 17-year-olds who had left full-time education. By 2009, the majority of those aged between 16 and 18 who were in Government-funded apprenticeships were in Level 2 apprenticeships, the number in Level 3 apprenticeships having declined gradually. The number of firms employing apprentices did not increase over this period.

It was in this context that the Apprenticeships, Skills, Children and Learning Act 2009 (ASCLA) was introduced. This Act sets out the framework for Government-funded apprenticeships in England and Wales and specifies the conditions they must satisfy to be recognised under the Act. These provisions came into force on 6 April 2011.

6.15 Statutory conditions

The main statutory conditions that apply to an apprenticeship agreement in England and Wales are set out in S.32(2). These require that:

- under the agreement, the apprentice undertakes to work for another

- the agreement is in the prescribed form (see 'Prescribed form' below)

- the agreement states that it is governed by the law of England and Wales

- the agreement states that it is entered into in connection with a qualifying apprenticeship framework (see 'Apprenticeship frameworks and standards' below).

It is notable that these conditions do not include a minimum duration. Although the relevant framework agreement will indicate the length of the training period, and the employer will be obliged to specify the fixed term in the apprenticeship agreement itself (see 'Prescribed form' below), there is no particular provision as to duration in the 2009 Act. The National Apprenticeship

Service states that an apprenticeship under the statutory scheme typically lasts between one and four years.

Prescribed form. The requirement that the agreement be in the prescribed **6.16** form is supplemented by the Apprenticeships (Form of Apprenticeship Agreement) Regulations 2012 SI 2012/844 (the 'Form of Apprenticeship Agreement Regulations'). Under Reg 2(1), for an apprenticeship agreement to comply with the ASCLA it must be in the form of either:

- a written statement of particulars of employment given to an employee for the purposes of S.1 of the Employment Rights Act 1996 (ERA), or

- a document in writing in the form of a contract of employment or letter of engagement where the employer's duty under S.1 ERA is treated as met for the purposes of S.7A ERA.

The agreement must therefore include all the information that must be included in the employee's written particulars of employment under S.1 ERA, such as the date employment began, rate of remuneration, hours of work, holiday and sick pay entitlement, and notice requirements. In the case of employment that is not permanent the particulars must also include the period for which it is to continue or, if for a fixed term, the date on which it is to end. This requirement is particularly significant for apprenticeship agreements since they are designed to last for a fixed term. (For full details of the written particulars required under S.1 ERA see IDS Employment Law Handbook, 'Contracts of Employment' (2009), Chapter 3, 'Written particulars', under 'Required particulars'.)

In addition to the S.1 particulars, the apprenticeship agreement must include a **6.17** statement of the skill, trade or occupation for which the apprentice is being trained under the apprenticeship framework – Reg 2(2).

Certain minor modifications of Reg 2 apply in respect of apprenticeships relating to Crown employment, service in the armed forces and as House of Lords and House of Commons staff – see Regs 3 and 4.

Apprenticeship frameworks and standards. The requirement in S.32 ASCLA **6.18** that the agreement is entered into in connection with a 'qualifying apprenticeship framework' is amplified by S.32(6), which provides that a qualifying framework is either a recognised English framework or a recognised Welsh framework. These are defined in Ss.12–22 and are, in essence, the 'curriculum' for apprenticeship training. According to the National Apprenticeship Service, the framework will typically include a knowledge-based element, a competence-based element, transferable or functional skills, a module on employee rights and responsibilities and a module on personal learning and thinking skills.

The ASCLA allows the Secretary of State to designate a person responsible for issuing an apprenticeship framework relating to a particular sector. That person can then issue frameworks so long as they meet the standards established by

281

Ss.23–31 of the Act and by further regulations made under those sections. These standards set out the minimum requirements for an apprenticeship framework and include, among other things, a requirement for both on-the-job and off-the-job training and for the attainment of specific qualifications and technical competencies. These requirements vary according to the level of apprenticeship undertaken – intermediate, advanced or higher. The full detail of these standards (in relation to English apprenticeships) is set out in the document, 'Specification of Apprenticeship Standards for England', issued by the Department for Business, Innovation and Skills.

Note that framework requirements are to be removed in relation to English apprenticeships from 2015 – see 'Proposals for reform' below.

6.19 Conditions for variation. Under S.34, there is a restriction on the parties' ability to agree any variation to the apprenticeship agreement that would result in the agreement ceasing to be an apprenticeship agreement – i.e. any variation that would mean that S.32(2) ASCLA or the Form of Apprenticeship Agreement Regulations are not satisfied. Such a variation will have effect only if, before it takes effect, the employer gives the apprentice written notice stating that the agreement will cease to be an apprenticeship agreement if the variation takes effect. (As to whether the agreement will then become a contract of apprenticeship, see 'Legal effect of failure to comply with ASCLA conditions' below.)

6.20 Proposals for reform. The process by which an apprenticeship is recognised under Chapter 1 of the ASCLA is to be reformed in relation to English apprenticeships. Provisions in the Deregulation Bill, which is due to receive Royal Assent in 2015, will insert a new Chapter A1 into the 2009 Act. This will introduce a new 'approved English apprenticeship'. The statutory conditions for such an apprenticeship will be much the same in substance as the current Chapter 1 provisions governing apprenticeship agreements. However, some of the complexity of the conditions will be removed. Among other things, the requirement for an apprenticeship to comply with a specific 'apprenticeship framework' will no longer apply. Instead, the apprenticeship will have to meet one of the general apprenticeship standards approved by the Secretary of State, which will be developed by employers in the relevant industries. These changes will not entail any change to the legal status of apprentices. Section A5 of the new Chapter A1 will replicate the effect of S.35 ASCLA, making it clear that an approved English apprenticeship, like an apprenticeship agreement, has the status of a contract of service. The Government's intention is that all new apprenticeships will be approved English apprenticeships from 2017/18.

Note that these changes will not apply to Welsh apprenticeships, which will remain governed by the existing provisions in Chapter 1 ASCLA.

Legal status of apprenticeship agreement 6.21

Whereas 'Modern Apprenticeships' were capable of being traditional common law contracts of apprenticeship (see 'Contracts of apprenticeship – status of "modern" apprenticeships' above), apprenticeship agreements under the ASCLA are not. S.35(1) states that 'to the extent that it would otherwise be treated as being a contract of apprenticeship, an apprenticeship agreement is to be treated as not being a contract of apprenticeship'. In other words, even though an apprenticeship agreement might, if analysed under common law principles, meet the definition of a traditional contract of apprenticeship, it will not have that status at common law or for any other purpose. Subsection (2) goes on to provide that, 'to the extent that it would not otherwise be treated as being a contract of service, an apprenticeship agreement is to be treated as being a contract of service'. In other words, even though, on a common law analysis, the apprenticeship agreement might be lacking one or more of the crucial features of a contract of service – for example, the minimum mutual obligations – the agreement shall nonetheless be treated as a contract of service. The distinction is reinforced by S.32(2) ASCLA, which states that it is a condition of an apprenticeship agreement that the apprentice 'works' for the employer. This would not be the common law understanding of the apprentice's obligation under a traditional contract of apprenticeship, which has as its primary purpose the training of the apprentice rather than the doing of work for the employer.

The most significant effect of Reg 35(1) is that it reduces employers' potential liability for breach of an apprenticeship agreement. S.35(3) states that the provision applies 'for the purpose of any enactment or rule of law', which means that both statutory and common law rules are affected. As discussed in the section 'Contracts of apprenticeship' above, under 'Termination – remedy for wrongful termination', early wrongful termination of a common law contract of apprenticeship can lead to a substantial award of damages. S.35 ensures that this is not the case for apprenticeship agreements and so a wrongfully dismissed apprentice who seeks a contractual remedy will be limited to the damages available for wrongful termination of a contract of service, which are likely to be substantially less. For a fixed-term contract of service, the available damages are, in principle, the wages that would have been payable for the rest of the term. However, if there is a break clause in the contract, giving the employer power to terminate on notice – as is the case with ordinary contracts of service – then damages will be limited to the notice period. As with ordinary contracts of service, the apprentice's most valuable remedy for wrongful termination of an apprenticeship agreement would be a claim for unfair dismissal – assuming that the apprentice has accrued the minimum two years' service required to bring such a claim. This is discussed under 'Statutory employment rights and protections – unfair dismissal' below.

283

6.22 Note that the ASCLA conditions apply only to English and Welsh apprenticeships. The Act does not apply to the Modern Apprenticeship arrangements in Scotland and Northern Ireland and therefore does not affect the legal status of apprenticeships concluded in those jurisdictions. Accordingly, apprenticeships in Scotland and Northern Ireland may yet be subject to the common law principles discussed under 'Contracts of apprenticeship' above.

6.23 Legal effect of failure to comply with ASCLA conditions

Section 35(2) ASCLA – which provides that an apprenticeship agreement is to be treated as a contract of service – only applies to an 'apprenticeship agreement' as defined in S.32. This means that a contract or agreement that purports to be an apprenticeship agreement but which – for whatever reason – does not comply with the formalities listed in S.32 and with the Form of Apprenticeship Agreement Regulations will not automatically be deemed to be a contract of service, although it would nevertheless be open to a court or tribunal to find that the agreement has that status.

The more significant issue for employers is the possibility that a purported apprenticeship agreement that does not comply with the ASCLA will be treated as a contract of apprenticeship instead. If so, then the requirements under S.32 take on some importance. For example, the requirements that the agreement state that it is governed by the law of England and Wales and that it is entered into in connection with a qualifying apprenticeship framework may seem like minor technical details but, if either statement is absent, the resulting agreement would potentially be a contract of apprenticeship, along with all the associated liabilities.

6.24 As far as we are aware, there are no reported cases on the specific question of whether a purported apprenticeship agreement that does not comply with the formal requirements of the ASCLA is or may be a contract of apprenticeship. That question must be analysed in light of the case law discussed under 'Contracts of apprenticeship – status of "modern" apprenticeships' above, particularly those decisions that relate to Modern Apprenticeships. Several cases have held that Modern Apprenticeship arrangements gave rise to traditional contracts of apprenticeship, including the leading Court of Appeal decision in Flett v Matheson 2006 ICR 673, CA. Given that the ASCLA scheme is the current version of the Modern Apprenticeship programme in England and Wales, it would be tempting to conclude that an apprenticeship agreement that complies with the ASCLA scheme in all but formality must be a contract of apprenticeship. However, some of the case law suggests that it may not be as straightforward as that. For example, in Chassis and Cab Specialists Ltd v Lee EAT 0268/10 the EAT hesitated before deciding that a Modern Apprenticeship gave rise to a traditional contract of apprenticeship because the agreement at issue was for a two-year period only. The EAT noted that traditional apprenticeships are typically of longer duration. It also suggested that the 'comparatively low level' of qualification being worked towards (NVQ Level 2) pointed away from a common law contract of apprenticeship. On the facts of the case, the EAT was nonetheless satisfied that a contract of apprenticeship was made out. However, in a future case involving an apprenticeship agreement providing for similarly low-level qualifications over two years or less, the result would not necessarily be the same.

Other factors make it unlikely that a 'defective' apprenticeship agreement could be construed as a traditional contract of apprenticeship. For one thing, it is common for employers to include provision for termination in an apprenticeship agreement that would be more akin to a contract of service than a contract of apprenticeship. Such agreements routinely include provision for termination on notice, or by reason of redundancy, poor performance or misconduct. Such wide powers of termination are inconsistent with the much more onerous obligations assumed by an employer under a common law contract of apprenticeship. Furthermore, a prudent employer would usually include a provision in the agreement expressly stating that it is a contract of service and is not intended to give rise to a contract of apprenticeship. Although labels are never conclusive in contractual interpretation, such a description would undoubtedly help the employer in arguing that no contract of apprenticeship can be inferred on an objective analysis.

6.25 From the apprentice's point of view there is a danger that by working under a non-compliant apprenticeship agreement he or she would end up with no formal recognition that he or she had completed the apprenticeship. Under Ss.1 and 2 ASCLA, a person is deemed to complete an apprenticeship if he or she has completed a course of training and work under the applicable apprenticeship framework, having entered into an 'apprenticeship agreement'. If the conditions laid down by S.32 ASCLA and the Form of Apprenticeship Agreement Regulations are not satisfied in relation to the agreement then it will not be considered to be an 'apprenticeship agreement' for the purposes of Ss.1 and 2 and so the completion conditions will not be satisfied. This means that the apprentice would not be entitled to an apprenticeship certificate, which attests to the completion of a statutorily recognised apprenticeship, despite having fulfilled the prescribed learning and training requirements.

There is a power under Ss.1(5) and 2(5) for the Secretary of State to issue regulations laying down alternative completion conditions where the person works otherwise than under an apprenticeship agreement. It would, therefore, be possible for secondary legislation to provide for the situation where an apprentice satisfies the relevant learning and training requirements but, for whatever reason, the apprenticeship agreement is not in the required form. However, the regulations so far issued under this power do not address this specific situation. The situations so far covered are those provided for in the

Apprenticeships (Alternative English Completion Conditions) Regulations 2012 SI 2012/1199 and include:

- certain apprenticeships in specified sectors completed while the apprentice was working as a self-employed person or working 'otherwise than for reward' – Reg 3. The Government consultation, 'The Future of Apprenticeships in England: Funding Reform Technical Consultation', notes that this provision covers certain apprenticeships 'traditionally based on non-employed arrangements', such as share fishermen and women, film crews and those involved in certain sports

- apprentices who have been dismissed for redundancy – Reg 4. This provision enables redundant apprentices to complete their apprenticeships and have them formally recognised. The key requirements are that the apprentice had already begun a course of training while working under the apprenticeship agreement, had completed the training within six months of the redundancy, and worked 'otherwise than for reward' in relation to the apprenticeship framework while completing the training

- apprentices who have completed a course of training with a view to competing in the Summer or Winter Olympic Games or Paralympic Games or the Commonwealth Games – Reg 5.

Similar provision is made in relation to Welsh apprenticeships by the Apprenticeships (Alternative Welsh Completion Conditions) Regulations 2013 SI 2013/1468.

6.26 Statutory employment rights and protections

Although the common law status of a 'traditional' apprentice is different to that of a 'modern' apprentice under the statutory scheme that applies in England and Wales, there is no significant difference between the statutory employment rights and protections available to each. The stipulation in S.35 ASCLA that an apprenticeship agreement is to be treated as a contract of service for the purpose of any enactment or rule of law means that ASCLA apprentices are entitled to the same employment rights and protections as an employee. And because a contract of employment is generally defined to include a (common law) contract of apprenticeship (as well as a contract of service), traditional apprentices are covered to the same extent. The most important statutory provisions in this regard are:

- S.230(1) and (2) ERA, which provides, among other things, that a person who has entered into or works under a contract of service or a contract of apprenticeship is an 'employee' for the purpose of the Act. The status of 'employee' entitles an individual to the benefit of all the protections offered by the ERA, including the right to a written statement of employment particulars, the right not to be unfairly dismissed and the right to a redundancy payment

- S.295(1) of the Trade Union and Labour Relations (Consolidation) Act 1992, which is in materially the same form as S.230(1) and (2) ERA. 'Employees' under this Act benefit from, among other things, protection from detriment and dismissal for reasons related to trade union activities and the right to information and consultation in relation to collective redundancies (although apprentices may be excluded by virtue of their fixed-term status – see 'Fixed-term employee protections' below)

- S.83(2) of the Equality Act 2010, which ensures that the protection from discrimination and harassment in relation to 'employment' extends to those working under a contract of employment or apprenticeship. All apprentices are therefore entitled to protection from discrimination on the ground of age, disability, gender reassignment, marital status, race, religion or belief, pregnancy or maternity, sex and sexual orientation.

Furthermore, apprentices are covered in the same way as employees in respect **6.27** of working time protections and the right to paid annual leave under the Working Time Regulations 1998 SI 1998/1833; in relation to employers' duties under the Health and Safety at Work etc Act 1974 and the Management of Health and Safety at Work Regulations 1999 SI 1999/3242; and with regard to rights to maternity, paternity and adoption pay and leave and sick pay.

In short, an apprentice who works under a contract of apprenticeship or under an apprenticeship agreement that complies with the ASCLA is in no better or worse position in terms of statutory rights than an employee. This is subject to one notable exception – the rights contained in the Fixed-term Employees (Prevention of Less Favourable Treatment) Regulations 2002 SI 2002/2034 – see 'Fixed-term employee protections' below. There are also a few areas where the statutory rights may apply to apprentices in a slightly different way because of the inherent nature of apprenticeship agreements.

National minimum wage
6.28

An apprenticeship rate of national minimum wage (NMW) was introduced in October 2010 and currently stands at £2.68 per hour (rising to £2.73 in October 2014). The rate applies under Reg 13 of the National Minimum Wage Regulations 1999 SI 1999/584 to an apprentice who works under a contract of apprenticeship, which includes an apprenticeship agreement, and who is either within the first 12 months of that employment or has not reached the age of 19. Accordingly, an apprentice can be paid the apprentice rate only until the age of 19, unless he or she has not by that time worked for more than a year under the apprenticeship agreement. An apprentice who is 19 or over

287

and who is not in the first year of the apprenticeship is entitled to the appropriate adult rate of NMW, which is £5.03 up to the age of 21 and £6.31 for workers aged 21 and over (£5.13 and £6.50 respectively from October 2014).

6.29 Fixed-term employee protections

The Fixed-term Employees (Prevention of Less Favourable Treatment) Regulations 2002 SI 2002/2034 ('the FTE Regulations') set out a number of rights and protections available to employees working under a 'fixed-term contract'. The most significant of these are the right not to be treated less favourably than a comparable permanent employee (Reg 3); the right not to be dismissed or subjected to detriment for taking action or asserting rights under the Regulations (Reg 6); and the right to have a series of fixed-term contracts 'converted' into a permanent one, subject to various conditions (Reg 8). (For further details see Chapter 2, 'Fixed term employees'.)

The FTE Regulations cover contracts of employment which contain provision for termination, in the normal course, on the expiry of a specific term, on the completion of a particular task, or on the occurrence or non-occurrence of any other specific event – Reg 1(2). As both contracts of apprenticeship and apprenticeship agreements are usually fixed-term employment contracts, they would ordinarily be covered. However, apprentices are expressly excluded from the scope of the FTE Regulations by virtue of Reg 20, which provides that the Regulations 'shall not have effect in relation to employment under a fixed-term contract where the contract is a contract of apprenticeship or an apprenticeship agreement (within the meaning of S.32 ASCLA)'. Originally, this provision simply referred to a 'contract of apprenticeship', which meant that ASCLA apprentices, who are deemed to work under contracts of service, were still covered. However, Reg 20 was amended with effect from 9 January 2013 and both kinds of apprenticeship are now specifically excluded. Thus, the prohibition on less favourable treatment, the protection from dismissal and detriment and the right to have a series of fixed-term contracts converted to a permanent contract do not apply to any apprentices.

6.30 The effect of the exclusion from the right to conversion to a permanent contract under Reg 8 is to exclude all periods during which the individual was working in excluded employment from the calculation of the four-year minimum period – Hudson v Department for Work and Pensions 2013 ICR 329, CA. In that case, which concerned individuals on Government training schemes who are also excluded from the scope of the Regulations, the Court of Appeal held that a claimant who was employed on a series of fixed-term training contracts could not aggregate those contracts with a later contract of employment to establish the four years' employment required to trigger Reg 8. Applying the same reasoning to apprenticeships, an apprentice who completed a three-year apprenticeship and was then given a one-year contract of employment could not assert the right to a permanent contract on the basis of the four years' total employment.

There is some doubt, however, about the scope of the general exclusion in other respects. Reg 20 implies that the FTE Regulations *as a whole* do not apply to apprentices. This would mean that not only do the specific protections for fixed-term employees not apply but also the consequential amendments to legislation provided for in Schedule 2 would not take effect – the Regulations may be treated as never having been enacted at all. This gives rise to a little uncertainty, particularly as regards amendments to the ERA. Para 3 of Schedule 2 to the Regulations inserted a new definition of 'limited-term contract' into S.235(2A) and (2B) and amended the definition of 'dismissal' in S.95(1)(b) so that the termination of a limited-term contract by virtue of the limiting event (such as the expiry of the relevant period) would count as a 'dismissal' for the purpose of unfair dismissal protection. These amendments made explicit the fact that fixed-term employees have the right to claim unfair dismissal even when their contracts terminate in the normal course of events. If the FTE Regulations are treated as not applying in the case of an apprentice, it becomes questionable whether an apprentice can avail him or herself of the benefit of these amendments.

Whatever the answer, this uncertainty should not have any significant effect in **6.31** practice. Even if it is assumed that Reg 20 deprives the FTE Regulations of any effect whatsoever in relation to apprentices, an apprentice may still rely on the unamended (pre-2002) version of S.95(1)(b) ERA. This provided that a person was dismissed if he or she was 'employed under a contract for a fixed term and that term expires without being renewed under the same contract'. This unamended version still comfortably covers individuals on fixed-term contracts, including apprentices. The amendments in Schedule 2 to the Regulations really only had the effect of making it clear that *other* types of limited-term contract were also covered by S.95(1)(b). There should therefore be no doubt that the termination of a contract of apprenticeship or an apprenticeship agreement by virtue of its fixed-term clause amounts to a dismissal for the purposes of the ERA, regardless of whether or not the ERA is read in light of the amendments made by the Regulations.

There is also some uncertainty over whether an apprentice selected for redundancy for asserting rights as a fixed-term employee or doing anything in relation to the FTE Regulations can claim unfair dismissal. Although Reg 6 states that it is unfair to dismiss an employee for asserting rights under the FTE Regulations, the Reg 20 exclusion makes it clear that this protection does not apply to apprentices. However, there is another route by which dismissal may be rendered automatically unfair. Under S.105 ERA an employee's dismissal for redundancy will be deemed to be automatically unfair if the employee was selected for redundancy for one of the reasons listed in that section. Para 10 of

Schedule 2 to the Regulations adds to this list the reasons specified in Reg 6(3), which include the fact that the employee alleged that the employer had infringed the Regulations. Such an allegation need not be well founded, so long as it is not made in bad faith. The reasons specified in Reg 6(3) also include the fact that the employee assisted another employee in a complaint under the Regulations. Thus, an apprentice who asserts mistakenly but in good faith that he or she has rights as a fixed-term employee, or who gives evidence in proceedings under the Regulations, and who is then selected for redundancy for that reason, could claim to have been automatically unfairly dismissed by virtue of S.105 ERA. However, this will only be the case if the Schedule 2 amendments to existing legislation take effect despite Reg 20. As with the amendments to S.95 ERA discussed above, if Reg 20 is read as preventing the Regulations taking effect *at all* in relation to an apprentice, then the amendment to S.105 must be treated as never having happened and there would be no right to claim unfair redundancy selection in these circumstances.

6.32 ## Unfair dismissal

Although the protections of the FTE Regulations do not apply to apprentices, the expiry and non-renewal of an apprentice's fixed-term contract still counts as a dismissal under S.95(1)(b) ERA – see North East Coast Shiprepairers Ltd v Secretary of State for Employment 1978 ICR 755, EAT. This means that an apprentice who completes his or her apprenticeship and is not taken on as an employee may seek to claim unfair dismissal and/or a redundancy payment (on which see 'Redundancy' below). Dismissal on expiry of a fixed-term contract is treated in the same way as express dismissal for unfair dismissal purposes and so the employer will need to go through the usual dismissal procedure in relation to the termination of an apprenticeship. This involves identifying a reason for dismissal – usually 'some other substantial reason' – and applying the usual standard of the reasonable employer, which may entail warning the apprentice of the imminent dismissal and, in appropriate cases, looking for alternative employment – see S.98 ERA. However, it should be borne in mind that the right to claim unfair dismissal is limited to those with two years' continuous service, which may exclude many apprentices – see S.108 ERA.

Even where an apprentice is taken on in employment directly after the apprenticeship, there is still, arguably, a dismissal. S.95(1)(b) ERA provides that there is a dismissal for ERA purposes when a 'limited-term contract... terminates by virtue of the limiting event without being renewed *under the same contract*' (our stress). If an apprentice moves from apprenticeship to full employment then, although his or her 'employment' may be said to have been continued, it will not be under the same contract. This analysis is supported by the employment tribunal's decision in Tantum v Travers Smith Braithwaite Services ET Case No.2203585/12 that a trainee solicitor was dismissed when her training contract expired and she was given a new fixed-term contract as a qualified solicitor. Although a solicitor training contract is not an apprenticeship, it is broadly analogous, and so the same reasoning might well apply to an apprentice whose apprenticeship terminates and who is taken on as a permanent (or fixed-term) employee. However, there would be very little for the former apprentice to gain by bringing an unfair dismissal complaint in these circumstances since the dismissal would invariably be fair for 'some other substantial reason'. Even if the dismissal were procedurally unfair there would be no compensatory award, given the offer of further employment.

There is also the question of dismissal during the course of what would **6.33** otherwise be the fixed term of the apprenticeship. Although 'early' dismissals are not compatible with traditional contracts of apprenticeship, it is quite common for apprenticeship agreements to make provision for early termination in much the same way as an ordinary contract of service, providing for dismissal with (or exceptionally without) notice in cases of misconduct, incapability, failure to meet training requirements, etc. Contractual provision for such dismissals does not necessarily mean that the dismissal will be fair, however. Fairness depends on the question of reasonableness under S.98(4), which requires consideration of all the circumstances, including the size and administrative resources of the employer's undertaking, 'equity' and 'the substantial merits of the case'. Although there are, to our knowledge, no reported cases on the fairness of dismissal during the lifespan of an apprenticeship agreement, these general considerations would allow a tribunal to take into account the fact that an apprentice is in a different position to an ordinary employee. For example, a tribunal may consider that the implications of dismissal from an apprenticeship are more serious than from employment, as the apprentice's ability to complete his or her training is potentially jeopardised, and so employers may be expected to be more tolerant of mistakes and poor performance.

In the absence of case law on this topic it is impossible to predict how tribunals would deal with unfair dismissal cases brought by ASCLA apprentices. In 1981, an industrial tribunal considering an unfair dismissal claim brought by a common law apprentice recognised the 'special position' of an apprentice and applied an accordingly higher standard to the employer – Neve v Brookway Engineering Ltd ET Case No.1196/56. It found the dismissal for poor performance unfair, having taken into account, among other things, the fact that the employer did not try to contact the apprentice's parents before dismissing. Although this is an old case and, being a tribunal decision, sets no precedent, it does indicate that tribunals may be receptive to the suggestion that different standards apply to an employer's treatment of an apprentice than to its treatment of an ordinary employee.

The law on unfair dismissal is discussed in depth in IDS Employment Law Handbook, 'Unfair Dismissal' (2010).

291

6.34 Redundancy

The dismissal of an apprentice for redundancy – whether on the expiry of the fixed term or during the course of the contract – may give rise to a right to a redundancy payment under S.135 ERA if the apprentice has accrued two years' employment. However, if the apprentice's employment is terminated and not renewed at the end of the fixed term then the employer will usually be able to assert 'some other substantial reason' for dismissal under S.98(1)(b), instead of redundancy. In North East Coast Shiprepairers Ltd v Secretary of State for Employment 1978 ICR 755, EAT, a common law apprentice's contract terminated at the end of the apprenticeship and he was not offered further employment. The EAT did not doubt that there was a dismissal for the purpose of the statutory right to a redundancy payment but concluded that the dismissal was not for redundancy. It endorsed the reasoning of the tribunal below to the effect that the apprentice's complaint was that he had not been taken on as a permanent employee. However, there is no right to a redundancy payment on the refusal of employment and the EAT thought it reasonable to assume that Parliament did not intend there to be such a right.

The right to consultation over collective redundancies under S.188 of the Trade Union and Labour Relations (Consolidation) Act 1992 (TULR(C)A) can, in theory, cover apprentices in their capacity as employees. However, they will usually be excluded in their capacity as fixed-term employees. Employers are required to inform and consult the workforce when they propose to dismiss as redundant 20 or more employees at one establishment within a period of 90 days or less but, under S.282 TULR(C)A, the expiry of fixed-term contracts on their agreed expiry date do not count towards this 20-employee threshold. Therefore, the termination of apprenticeship agreements in accordance with their fixed terms will not contribute to triggering the employer's duties under S.188 TULR(C)A.

The law on redundancy is discussed in depth in IDS Employment Law Handbook, 'Redundancy' (2011).

6.35 Funding for training

The current scheme for the state funding of the external training element of an apprenticeship involves funds being routed directly to the training provider. The Skills Funding Agency allocates a budget to designated training providers, who then provide training to apprentices as part of their apprenticeship agreements. The Government does not, however, fund all of the training costs. Funding policy varies between England, Wales, Scotland and Northern Ireland. In England, the Government commitment is to fund 100 per cent of the training costs for apprentices aged 16–17 and 50 per cent of the cost for those aged 18–24. Training for those aged 25 or over is funded at a lower rate.

Unfortunately, the funding arrangements are notoriously complex and it is not at all clear how they work in practice. The uncertainty was highlighted by the Richard Review, a report commissioned jointly by the Secretary of State for Education and the Secretary of State for Business, Innovation and Skills in 2012. In its response to the Review, the vocational award organisation City and Guilds noted that employers of all sizes struggle to understand the rules. It observed that although the current funding rules require an employer contribution, this is 'largely ignored' by training providers. The Richard Review echoed this view, noting that very few providers collect fees from employers and commenting that this could be because the provider can cover the full costs of the training with its Government budget. However, other employers have reported that they make a substantial contribution to external training costs. The EEF's experience is that many employers contribute towards the cost of external training and some meet the entire cost. Whatever the reason for this difference of view, it is clear that the current funding system is by no means transparent. This lack of clarity led City and Guilds to call for more funding to be routed directly to employers.

In addition to the cost of external training there is the cost to the employer of **6.36** internal, on-the-job training, plus the usual costs of employment. These may be offset, to some extent, by the lower national minimum wage rate that applies to younger apprentices. In addition, the National Apprenticeship Service (NAS) offers a grant (subject to eligibility and availability) of £1,500 for small and medium-sized employers who recruit individuals aged between 16 and 24 through the statutory apprenticeship programme. An individual employer can receive up to ten grants in total. However, the NAS states that this initiative is due to expire in December 2014.

Plans for funding reform   6.37

Following the Richard Review, the Government decided to change the way that the external training aspect of apprenticeships is funded. The Review concluded that the current system is too 'provider-driven' and insufficiently responsive to employers' needs. Its solution was to make employers the customers of the training providers by routing state funding for external training through the employer. The onus will therefore be on employers to ensure that training is of sufficiently high quality for their purposes and trainers will (in theory at least) be incentivised to respond to business needs.

In July 2013, the Government launched an initial consultation on making such a change in England. (The planned funding reforms do not currently extend to Wales.) Then, in a follow-up 'technical' consultation issued in March 2014, the Government indicated that it had decided to implement a model that would rely on HMRC systems. It put forward two options. One would be to make payments to the employer through the PAYE system, with special provision for smaller employers who do not have sufficient PAYE liability from which to

293

deduct the Government contribution to training costs. The other would be to create an Apprenticeship Credit, which would give employers an online account from which to fund their training needs. Whichever mechanism is chosen, it is likely that the administrative burden on employers will increase under the new scheme. Although it is unclear how many employers currently obtain all of their external training from state-funded sources, at least some do, and these employers will notice the biggest change when they are obliged to manage their own training procurement individually.

6.38 The consultation also indicates other policies that are likely to have a cost impact on employers. For a start, the new scheme implements a policy of co-investment, under which the Government only partially meets the cost of the training and the employer is expected to make up the difference. Although this will not necessarily affect employers who already pay for some or all of their external training themselves, it will affect those who currently use only fully state-funded sources. The consultation document notes that funding will be linked to apprentices' performance and/or achievements and that there will be no funding available for internal training – i.e. where the employer itself provides the personnel to fulfil the off-site training element of the apprenticeship. There will also be a maximum Government contribution to training costs, which will vary between apprenticeship standards.

Although the technical consultation does not give any specific figures, it does acknowledge that there will be a financial impact on employers. For example, it points out that younger apprentices currently attract full funding for their apprenticeship and that this will no longer be the case when enforced co-investment is introduced. The consultation proposes to address this specific shortfall – and to recognise the greater level of supervision, guidance, education and induction required for younger workers – by making an additional, one-off payment in respect of 16- and 17-year-old apprentices. The payment will be made once the apprentice has completed the first three months of the apprenticeship.

The legislative underpinning for the changes will be included in the Deregulation Bill, which is due to receive Royal Assent by February 2015. The consultation indicates that the new funding scheme is intended to be brought into operation in 2016.

7 Employee shareholders

Employee shareholder status

Rights of employee shareholders

Enforcement and remedies

Tax implications

TUPE transfers

Termination of shareholder status

In October 2012 the Chancellor of the Exchequer, George Osborne, announced **7.1** plans for the introduction of a new kind of 'owner-employee' employment contract under which an individual waives certain employment rights in return for tax-free shares. The theory was that having a financial stake in the company for which they work would encourage employees' participation in the business and drive up productivity. While described as a 'voluntary' scheme open to new employees, the reality is that individuals are likely to be offered such terms on a 'take it or leave it' basis. The Government issued consultation on the scheme but despite a negative or mixed response from 92 per cent of respondents, it decided to proceed with its initiative and included the newly named 'employee shareholder' status as part of the Growth and Infrastructure Bill that had its first reading in the House of Commons on 18 October 2012. The progress of the Bill was not smooth. The House of Lords rejected it twice and finally gave consent on 25 April 2013 only after a number of amendments to the employee shareholder provisions were agreed, including a requirement that an individual receive independent legal advice before agreeing to work on such terms.

The provisions were finally brought into force on 1 September 2013 by S.31 of the Growth and Infrastructure Act 2013, which added a new S.205A to the Employment Rights Act 1996 (ERA). In summary, the scheme allows employees to give up certain employment rights, including the right to claim ordinary unfair dismissal, in return for at least £2,000 worth of free shares in the employer's company, which are subject to a number of favourable tax concessions. Existing employees cannot be forced to take up employee shareholder status (although they are free to do so), but employers are entitled to offer only employee shareholder contracts to new recruits.

It is difficult to gauge how many employee shareholder contracts are in existence **7.2** as there appear to be few government statistics available showing the rate of take-up. However, indications are that, apart from high-earning senior executives using the scheme to maximise tax savings, take-up has been minimal.

295

In January 2014 the *Financial Times* reported that the Department for Business, Innovation and Skills (BIS) had received only 19 enquiries about the scheme in the six months to the end of December 2013. Indeed, the Deputy Prime Minister Nick Clegg, speaking at a Westminster Press Conference on 6 January 2014, appeared to call for the scheme to be abolished in favour of income tax cuts for the low paid.

In this chapter we set out the definition of an 'employee shareholder' and describe the procedure that the parties must follow in order to reach a legally enforceable agreement. We then outline the employment rights that are affected before considering what remedies employees have if they are dismissed or subjected to a detriment for refusing to accept employee shareholder status. Finally, we take a brief look at the tax and other shareholding issues that can arise as a result of employee shareholder status. It should be borne in mind, however, that consideration of any company or tax law implications fall outside the scope of this Handbook.

7.3 **Government guidance**. BIS has issued guidance on employee shareholder employment status ('the BIS Guidance'), which can be found on its website. Complementary guidance on the tax treatment and value of the shares is available from HM Revenue and Customs.

7.4 ## Employee shareholder status

Unlike the nebulous definition of 'employee' on which many of the statutory rights contained in the ERA rest, 'employee shareholder' has a precise statutory meaning. S.205A(1) ERA states that an individual will be an employee shareholder where the following conditions are satisfied:

- he or she is or becomes an employee of a company limited by shares – S.205A(1). (The company can be a UK-registered company, a European company (Societas Europaea), or an overseas company – S.205A(13))

- the company and the individual agree that the individual is to be an employee shareholder – S.205A(1)(a). The agreement does not have to be in writing, although it would seem prudent to draw up a written contract to avoid future disputes

- in consideration of that agreement, the company issues or allots to the individual fully paid up shares in the company, or its parent company, which have a value on the day of issue or allotment, of no less than £2,000 – S.205A(1)(b). (Note that there is no limit on the number or value of shares the employee shareholder can receive but the tax exemptions are restricted to £50,000 worth of shares (see 'Tax implications' below))

- the company gives the individual a written statement of the particulars of the status of employee shareholder and of the rights which attach to the shares – S.205A(1)(c), and

- the individual gives no consideration other than by entering into the agreement – S.205A(1)(d). In other words, as the BIS Guidance points out, the individual must not pay anything or contribute in any way towards the shares.

Any job applicant or existing employee can become an employee shareholder. **7.5** However, existing employees cannot be forced to take up employee shareholder status and are protected from dismissal and unlawful detriment if they refuse – see 'Enforcement and remedies' below, under 'Unfair dismissal' and 'Unlawful detriment' respectively. Employers are entitled to offer only employee shareholder contracts to job applicants, although the BIS Guidance states that a job applicant does 'not have to apply for or accept an employee shareholder job'. How much choice he or she has in reality is another matter, since an individual seeking work may be compelled to accept whatever terms of engagement are on offer. Job applicants have no statutory protection if they refuse to accept employee shareholder status and are not offered the job as a result, unless they have been discriminated against in the process – see 'Enforcement and remedies – discrimination' below.

Once an individual becomes an employee shareholder, that status will not change even if he or she subsequently sells or otherwise disposes of his or her shares. It can only change with the agreement of both parties. If an individual ceases to be an employee shareholder while still employed, he or she will remain an employee and will presumably by able to rely on the statutory rights he or she gave up when accepting shareholder status. If he or she retains the shares in these circumstances they will cease to be exempt from income tax and capital gains tax – see further 'Termination of shareholder status' below.

Share valuation. The value of the shares refers to the actual market value **7.6** within the meaning of Ss.272 and 273 of the Taxation of Chargeable Gains Act 1992 at the time the employee shareholder acquires them. Since an individual is not an employee shareholder unless he or she receives at least £2,000 worth of shares, an accurate valuation of the shares is essential to establishing whether or not that status has been achieved.

Agreement procedure
7.7
An agreement to enter into an employee shareholder contract will have no legal effect unless the written statement provided in accordance with S.205A(1)(c) contains certain specified information. In addition, the individual must receive independent legal advice and a seven-day cooling off period must elapse before the agreement is 'live'. This procedure applies to both new employee shareholders and existing employees who agree to change status.

297

Parties entering into an employee shareholder agreement should follow a strict sequence of actions if the agreement is to be valid:

- the individual must be given a written statement of the particulars in accordance with S.205A(1)(c). Details of the terms of the proposed contractual agreement should also be provided, since the individual is entitled to advice 'as to the terms and effect' of the agreement' (see bullet below)

- the individual must receive advice from a relevant independent adviser as to the terms and effect of the agreement (at the company's expense – S.205A(7)), and

- seven days must elapse between the day on which the individual receives the advice and the day the agreement takes effect (the 'cooling off period') – S.205A(6).

7.8 A failure to follow these steps, or to complete them in the correct order, would render any employee shareholder agreement ineffective and the individual would simply be a normal employee, not an employee shareholder. As the agreement is ineffective, he or she would almost certainly have to return any shares received under it. However, if the employee is permitted to keep the shares, they would be subject to income tax and capital gains tax in the normal way.

7.9 **Written statement.** The written statement must include the following information:

- a statement that the employee shareholder would not have the employment rights specified in S.205A(2) (see 'Rights of employee shareholders' below) – S.205A(5)(a)

- the increased notice periods that apply under S.205A(3) and (4) if the employee shareholder wishes to return to work during a period of maternity, adoption or additional paternity leave – S.205A(5)(b)

- whether any voting rights attach to the employee shares – S.205A(5)(c)

- whether the shares carry any right to dividends – S.205A(5)(d)

- whether the shares would, if the company were wound up, confer any rights to participate in the distribution of any surplus assets – S.205A(5)(e)

- if the company has more than one class of shares, an explanation of how rights attaching to the employee shares differ from those that attach to the shares in the largest class (or next largest if the employee shares fall within the largest class) – S.205A(5)(f). (Note that the legislation gives no indication of whether the 'largest' class of shares is determined according to the number of shares or their value, or by some other criterion)

- whether the employee shares are redeemable and, if they are, at whose option – S.205A(5)(g)

- whether there are restrictions on the transferability of the shares and, if so, what those restrictions are – S.205A(5)(h)

- whether any of the requirements of Ss.561 and 562 of the Companies Act 2006 are excluded in the case of the employee shares (i.e. the existing shareholders' right of pre-emption which gives existing shareholders first refusal on any new shares that are issued) – S.205A(5)(i), and

- whether the employee shares are subject to 'drag-along' or 'tag-along' rights and, if so, what they mean – S.205A(5)(j). 'Drag-along rights' are the right of the majority shareholders, where they are selling their shares, to require the minority holders to also sell theirs, while 'tag-along rights' refer to the right of minority shareholders to sell their shares on the same terms as the majority – S.205A(13).

The company is, of course, entitled to include additional information in the written statement if it so wishes. For example, a company may wish to specify what happens when the employee shareholder leaves employment.

Independent advice. The requirement for an individual to obtain legal advice **7.10** is aimed at preventing companies taking advantage of employees or prospective employees who may otherwise unwittingly give up their employment rights. S.205A(6)(a) provides that an employee shareholder agreement will have no legal effect unless the individual has received independent legal advice on its terms and effect. The company must pay 'any reasonable costs incurred by the individual in obtaining the advice', whether or not the individual goes on to become an employee shareholder – S.205A(7). There is no indication as to what would amount to 'reasonable' costs' in this context and the BIS Guidance suggests that the employer and the individual should clarify this at the outset.

'Relevant independent adviser'. The advice must be from a 'relevant independent **7.11** adviser' as defined in S.203(3A) ERA for the purpose of S.203(3)(c) (which governs settlement agreements). This definition includes:

- qualified lawyers

- trade union officials who are certified in writing by the trade union as competent to give advice and as authorised to do so on behalf of the trade union, and

- advice centre workers who have been certified in writing by the centre as competent to give advice and as authorised to do so on behalf of the centre,

provided the adviser is not also advising the employer and, in the case of an advice centre worker, that he or she does not charge the individual for his or

299

her services. However, it does not cover financial advisers or accountants, who might arguably have a greater understanding of the tax implications of employee shareholder status.

The scope of S.203(3A) is discussed in detail in IDS Employment Law Handbook, 'Employment Tribunal Practice and Procedure' (2014), Chapter 3, 'Conciliation, settlements and ADR', in the section 'Settlement agreements', under 'Statutory requirements – relevant independent adviser'.

7.12 *Scope of advice.* Section 205A(6)(a) simply states that the individual must receive advice 'as to the terms and effect of the proposed agreement'. This raises the question: should the advice cover the tax implications involved or is it limited to the employment law ramifications? Separate tax provisions relating to employee shareholder agreements specify that payment for the advice required by S.205A(6) is exempt from income tax. 'Relevant advice' for this purpose means:

- advice, other than tax advice, which is provided for the purposes of S.205A(6)(a) (advice as to terms and effect of employee shareholder agreement), and

- tax advice which is so provided and consists only of an explanation of the tax effects of employee shareholder agreements generally – S.326B Income Tax (Earnings and Pensions) Act 2003.

This suggests that information on the tax implications of the agreement is optional and, if given, should be limited and generalised. However, the fact that the income tax exemption is limited to tax advice that consists of an explanation of the tax effects generally implies that the advice under S.205A(6) may be more wide-ranging – albeit that any payment by the employer for the advice would not be exempt from income tax. Certainly, the need to be advised as to the *effect* of an agreement would seem to encompass at least some targeted tax advice.

7.13 **Cooling off period.** Another concession made by the Government in order to gain the House of Lords' agreement to employee shareholder status was the addition of a seven-day cooling off period to allow the individual to consider the proposal. Accordingly, S.207A(6)(b) ERA specifies that an employee shareholder agreement has no effect until seven days have passed since the day on which the individual received the independent advice. Presumably either side can pull out of the agreement during this time, although the provision is squarely aimed at giving job seekers/employees time to consider whether they wish to accept or reject the proposed agreement in light of the advice received. The seven days begin on the day after the day on which the advice is received.

Rights of employee shareholders 7.14

An individual who enters into an employee shareholder agreement agrees to give up certain employment rights in return for shares in the employer's company. The rights given up are:

- the right to request study or training leave under S.63D ERA (which is unpaid and applies only if the employer has 250 or more employees)

- the right to request flexible working under S.80F ERA (unless the request is made within 14 days of the individual's return to work following a period of parental leave under S.76 ERA – S.205A(8)) (see Chapter 4, 'Flexible working')

- the right not to be unfairly dismissed under S.94 ERA (except, inter alia, where the dismissal is for one of the 'automatically' unfair reasons, or is discriminatory – see 'Unfair dismissal' below)

- the right to a redundancy payment under S.135 ERA (see IDS Employment Law Handbook, 'Redundancy' (2012)) – S.205A(2).

The exception that applies in respect of the right to request flexible working under S.76 ERA was inserted to reflect the fact that this right derives from European law and cannot be contracted out of.

In addition to the loss of the above statutory rights, certain notice requirements **7.15** are modified for employee shareholders. He or she must give:

- 16 weeks' notice (instead of eight) of his or her intention to return to work during a maternity leave period (under Reg 11 of the Maternity and Parental Leave etc Regulations 1999 SI 1999/3312) or adoption leave period (under Reg 25 of the Paternity and Adoption Leave Regulations 2002 SI 2002/2788) – S.205A(3)

- 16 weeks' notice (instead of six) of his or her intention to return from additional paternity leave (under Reg 30 of the Additional Paternity Leave Regulations 2010 SI 2010/1055) – S.205A(4).

In all other respects, employee shareholders should be treated as normal employees. Furthermore, an employer can choose to offer employee shareholders contractual rights that are similar to (or more generous than) those provided for by statute. So, for example, the agreement may include a contractual entitlement to a redundancy payment.

Unfair dismissal 7.16

As noted above, one of the statutory employment rights employee shareholders sign away is the right to claim unfair dismissal – S.205A(2)(c). However, this is subject to three exceptions:

301

- automatically unfair dismissals – S.205A(9)(a)

- discriminatory dismissals – S.205A(9)(b)

- dismissals where S.108(2) applies (suspension on health and safety grounds) – S.205A(10).

7.17 **Automatically unfair dismissals.** Under S.205A(9)(a) an employee shareholder retains the right to claim unfair dismissal if the dismissal is regarded by Part X ERA – whether under the provisions of that or any other Act – as 'automatically' unfair. A dismissal is regarded as automatically unfair when the reason itself is enough to establish unfairness and there is no need for a tribunal to consider whether dismissal falls into one of the potentially fair reasons in S.98(1) and (2) ERA, or whether it was reasonable under S.98(4). For example, dismissals for making a protected disclosure or for engaging in trade union activities are automatically unfair.

There is a long and ever-expanding list of automatically unfair reasons for dismissal, since each new statutory employment right that is introduced is generally accompanied by protection against dismissal for enforcing that right (and the creation of employee shareholder status is no exception – see 'Enforcement and remedies – unfair dismissal' below). A full list of automatically unfair reasons for dismissal can be found in IDS Employment Law Handbook, 'Unfair Dismissal' (2010), Chapter 10, 'Automatically unfair dismissals'. In the vast majority of cases, the usual qualifying period of employment for claiming unfair dismissal (currently two years) is waived. Thus, an employee shareholder is protected against certain types of dismissal from day one.

7.18 **Discriminatory dismissals.** Under S.205A(9)(b) an employee shareholder retains the right to claim unfair dismissal where the dismissal amounts to a contravention of the Equality Act 2010. Under that Act it is unlawful to discriminate against an employee because of a 'protected characteristic'. The protected characteristics covered by the Act are: age, disability, gender reassignment, marriage and civil partnership, pregnancy and maternity, race, religion or belief, sex and sexual orientation. For a detailed discussion on discrimination law, see IDS Employment Law Handbook, 'Discrimination at Work' (2012).

7.19 **Health and safety dismissals.** Employee shareholders retain the right to claim unfair dismissal after one month's service if the reason for dismissal is a requirement or recommendation that he or she be suspended from work because of a health and safety risk from certain hazardous substances as specified in S.64(3) ERA – S.205A(10).

302

Enforcement and remedies 7.20

The creation of a new employment status as opposed to a new employment right means that there are few corresponding enforcement provisions. If disputes do arise they are likely to do so in the context of another claim that the individual wishes to pursue. For example, an individual wishing to claim a statutory redundancy payment may assert that an employee shareholder agreement was invalid. In these circumstances, he or she would have to issue a claim for redundancy in an employment tribunal and the question of whether or not he or she was an employee shareholder would arise as a preliminary issue.

The Growth and Infrastructure Act 2013 did, however, introduce two new rights for existing employees to accompany the introduction of employee shareholder status – the right not to be unfairly dismissed and the right not to be subjected to a detriment for refusing to enter into an employee shareholder agreement. Job applicants and employees are also protected under existing legislation from being discriminated against in respect of employee shareholder status.

Unfair dismissal 7.21

Under S.104G ERA a dismissal will be automatically unfair if the reason, or principal reason, for it was that the employee refused to accept an offer by his or her employer to become an employee shareholder. In common with other forms of automatically unfair dismissal, there is no qualifying service necessary for bringing a claim under S.104G – S.108(3)(gm). However, the claim must be submitted within three months of the effective date of termination or, where that was not reasonably practicable, within such time as the tribunal considers reasonable – S.111(2). The time limit may be extended to allow for early conciliation – S.207B.

If the claim is successful, the employment tribunal may make an order for reinstatement or re-engagement under S.113. If no such order is made, then the tribunal will make an award for compensation calculated in accordance with Ss.118–126 – S.112(4). For full details of the remedies available, see IDS Employment Law Handbook, 'Unfair Dismissal' (2010), Chapter 14, 'Remedies'.

Unlawful detriment 7.22

Under S.47G(1) ERA an employee has the right not to be subjected to a detriment by any act, or any deliberate failure to act, by his or her employer on the ground that the employee refused to accept the employer's offer to become an employee shareholder. This section does not apply if the detriment is a dismissal, in which case the claim should be brought under S.104G (see 'Unfair dismissal' above) – S.47G(2). The burden of proof is on the employer to establish the ground on which any act, or deliberate failure to act, was done – S.48(2).

303

The claim must be submitted within three months of the date of the act or failure to act to which the complaint relates or, where it is part of a series of similar acts or failures, within three months of the last of them – S.48(3)(a). However, the tribunal can extend the time limit where it was not reasonably practicable for the complaint to be presented within the three months and it was presented within such further period as the tribunal considers reasonable – S.48(3)(b). The time limit may also be extended to allow for early conciliation – S.48(4A).

7.23 For the purposes of S.48(3), where an act extends over a period the 'date of the act' means the last day of that period – S.48(4)(a). A deliberate failure to act will be treated as done when the act was decided on – S.48(4)(b). An employer will be taken to have decided on a failure to act when it does an act inconsistent with doing the failed act or, if it has not done an inconsistent act, when the period within which it might reasonably have been expected to do the failed act expires.

If an employment tribunal finds a complaint under S.47G to be made out, it must make a declaration to that effect and may make a compensatory award – S.49(1). The amount of compensation is that which the tribunal considers just and equitable having regard to the infringement and any loss which is attributable to the act, or failure to act – S.49(2). It includes any expenses reasonably incurred by the claimant and the loss of any benefit that he or she would have had if he or she had not been subjected to the detriment in question – S.49(3).

7.24 The claimant has a duty to mitigate his or her losses and the tribunal will take this into account when assessing the amount of compensation, if any, to be awarded – S.49(4). If he or she had caused or contributed to the act complained of, the tribunal shall reduce the amount of compensation by such proportion as it considers just and equitable – S.49(5).

It should be noted that S.47G does not protect an employee shareholder who is treated less favourably than non-shareholder colleagues because of his or her employment status – for example, by being denied certain benefits or given less desirable work. Nor does it protect an employee who is not an employee shareholder from less favourable treatment compared with employee shareholder colleagues. However, if the individual is given or denied employee shareholder status because he or she has a protected characteristic and suffers less favourable treatment as a result, he or she may be able to bring a discrimination claim under the Equality Act 2010 (EqA) (see 'Discrimination' below).

7.25 Discrimination

Employee shareholders are not prevented from bringing claims under the EqA. Thus, if they suffer discrimination because of a protected characteristic, they can claim in the normal way – see IDS Employment Law Handbook,

'Discrimination at Work' (2012). Similarly, they can claim protection from less favourable treatment under the Fixed-term Employees (Prevention of Less Favourable Treatment) Regulations 2002 SI 2002/2034 and the Part-time Workers (Prevention of Less Favourable Treatment) Regulations 2000 SI 2000/1551. These two sets of Regulations may be of particular relevance where an employer only offers employee shareholder status to full-time permanent staff. The Fixed-term Employees Regulations are discussed in Chapter 2, 'Fixed-term employees', while the Part-time Workers Regulations are discussed in Chapter 3, 'Part-time workers'.

Tax implications

7.26

Individuals who agree to employee shareholder status receive in return shares worth at least £2,000 which are exempt from income tax and capital gains tax. The tax provisions relating to employee shareholder shares are contained in the Income Tax (Earnings and Pensions) Act 2003, as amended by Schedule 23 to the Finance Act 2013. They specify that an employee shareholder who receives the minimum £2,000 of shares will not be liable to pay income tax or national insurance contributions on those shares, provided that he or she does not have a 'material interest' of more than 25 per cent in the company. This is because the individual is deemed to have made a payment of £2,000 for the shares. Nor will the employee shareholder pay income tax on the proceeds if he or she sells the shares back to the company. He or she will also be exempt from capital gains tax on disposal of the shares provided they were worth no more than £50,000 when acquired.

The normal rules for income tax and national insurance contributions apply to any shares received in excess of £2,000. The deemed payment only applies on the first occasion on which an individual acquires 'qualifying shares' under an employee shareholder agreement with his or her employer.

HMRC has produced guidance on the tax treatment and value of shares, which is available on its website.

TUPE transfers

7.27

One issue that remains uncertain is what happens when an employee shareholder's employment transfers under the Transfer of Undertakings (Protection of Employment) Regulations 2006 SI 2006/246 (TUPE). Reg 4(1) provides that a TUPE transfer does not terminate the contract of employment of 'any person employed by the transferor and assigned to the organised grouping of resources or employees that is subject to the relevant transfer'. The Regulations define a contract of employment as 'any agreement between an employee and his employer determining the terms and conditions of his employment'; and 'employee' has a wider definition than elsewhere, being an

305

individual who works 'under a contract of service or apprenticeship or otherwise' – Reg 2(1). There is therefore little doubt that an employee shareholder will transfer under TUPE in the normal way and will retain his or her status as such, since that continues even if the shares have been disposed of. The real issue here is what happens to the shares. Does the employee shareholder retain his or her shares in the transferor company (if it still exists) or will the transfer force him or her to dispose of the shares, given that he or she is no longer employed by the transferor (see 'Termination of shareholding agreement' below)? Furthermore, since the effect of TUPE is to treat the employee as if he or she had always been employed by the transferee, is the employee shareholder entitled to equivalent shares in the transferee company? If so, potential buyers might think twice about acquiring a failing company that employed a significant number of employee shareholders.

The TUPE Regulations are discussed in detail in IDS Employment Law Handbook, 'Transfer of Undertakings' (2011).

7.28 Termination of shareholder status

Section 205(A)(12) ERA gives the Secretary of State power to make regulations dealing with the buying back of employee shares where an individual 'ceases to be an employee shareholder or ceases to be an employee'. However, no such regulations have been made to date and the matter is therefore left to the parties.

There is no requirement for an employee shareholder agreement to include provisions relating to the buyback of shares, but equally nothing to prevent their inclusion. The BIS Guidance states that: 'Your written statement should make it clear what will happen to the shares when you leave the company', but there is actually no statutory requirement for it to do so. Equally, it is not mandatory for the company's articles of association to deal with the matter. In the absence of any written agreement, an employee shareholder may be entitled to retain his or her shares on leaving the company or on termination of the employee shareholder agreement. It would therefore seem advisable for the parties to agree at the outset how the shares should be dealt with in these circumstances.

7.29 Similarly, there is nothing in the statutory provisions that requires the parties to specify how shares are to be valued in the event that the company buys them back. This too is left to the parties to agree. In a written answer to Parliament, Jo Swinson (Under Secretary of State for Employment relations, consumer and postal affairs) stated that 'it will be up to the employer and employee owner to determine the conditions for buy-back including how to establish a fair price' (House of Commons Debates 18 December 2012, Hansard col.729W).

8 Posted workers

The EU Posted Workers Directive (No.96/71) ('the PWD') is concerned with **8.1**
the protection of workers' rights within the framework of the free movement
of workers and services within the European Economic Area (EEA). It provides
that workers who are posted by their employers to perform temporary work in
other EEA states should enjoy protection based on the same 'floor of employment
rights' as is available to other workers employed in the 'host' country – i.e. the
country of temporary destination. Paras 13 and 14 of the Preamble to the PWD
refer to these rights as 'a nucleus of mandatory rules for minimum protection
to be observed in the host country' and 'a "hard core" of clearly defined
protective rules'. In so providing, the Directive attempts to remove legal
uncertainties surrounding the terms and conditions of employment of posted
workers during their posting while, at the same time, balancing the freedom of
undertakings to provide cross-border services. It seeks to strike this balance by
requiring EEA states to ensure that the minimum standards of employment
conditions which prevail in the host country are applied to posted workers in
respect of the stipulated core protections, including most minimum rates of
pay, annual leave and working time.

The PWD was published in January 1997 and its provisions were required to
be implemented by the relevant Member States on or by 16 December 1999.

Application of PWD to Iceland, Liechtenstein, Norway and Switzerland. **8.2**
The Agreement on the European Economic Area, which came into force on
1 January 1994, brings together the EU Member States and the three non-EU
members of the European Free Trade Association (EFTA) – Iceland, Liechtenstein
and Norway – into a single market, commonly referred to as the 'Internal
Market'. The EEA Agreement provides for the inclusion of EU legislation
covering four fundamental freedoms – the free movement of goods, services,
persons and capital – and guarantees equal rights and obligations within the
Internal Market for citizens and economic operators in the EEA. Since the

— **307**

coming into force of the Agreement, all EU labour law measures, including the PWD, are extended to the non-EU EFTA states. Accordingly, Iceland, Liechtenstein and Norway are obliged to ensure that the Directive's provisions are applied whenever an undertaking from another EEA state posts workers to work temporarily within their territories.

Although Switzerland is not part of the EEA, Swiss nationals also have the same free movement rights as EEA nationals by virtue of a 2002 bilateral agreement between the European Community and the Swiss Confederation. Under that agreement broadly similar rights and obligations as those that apply under the PWD are conferred on Swiss nationals who are posted to work in an EEA Member State and on Swiss companies that post such nationals.

8.3 Note that for the purposes of this chapter, references to a 'Member State' or an 'EEA state' are references to current members of the EEA (i.e. the 28 Member States of the EU and the three non-EU members of the EFTA.) These are: Austria, Belgium, Bulgaria, Croatia, Republic of Cyprus, Czech Republic, Denmark, Estonia, Finland, France, Germany, Greece, Hungary, Iceland, Ireland, Italy, Latvia, Liechtenstein, Lithuania, Luxembourg, Malta, the Netherlands, Norway, Poland, Portugal, Romania, Slovakia, Slovenia, Spain, Sweden and the UK.

8.4 **Outline of rights guaranteed by the PWD.** Under Article 3 PWD, posted workers are entitled to the terms and conditions of employment laid down by the host Member State's laws, regulations or administrative provisions in relation to the following matters:

- working time (maximum work periods and minimum rest periods)

- minimum paid annual holidays

- minimum rates of pay (including overtime rates)

- standards applicable to agency workers

- health, safety and hygiene at work

- pregnancy and maternity protection and the employment of children and young persons

- equality of treatment between men and women and other anti-discrimination provisions – Article 3(1)(a)–(g).

These matters are examined in greater detail under 'Rights under PWD' below. There is nothing to prevent an employing organisation established in the sending country applying working conditions that are *more* favourable to posted workers. Indeed, Article 3(7) PWD expressly states that its provisions 'shall not prevent the application of conditions of employment which are more favourable to workers'. Having said that, a jurisprudence has evolved from decisions of the European Court of Justice (ECJ), the effect of which is to preclude the imposition of terms and conditions that go beyond the listed matters in Article 3(1) if this would interfere disproportionately with the economic freedoms underpinning the European single market. For more details, see 'Rights under PWD' and 'Conflict between PWD and single market freedoms' below.

In addition to the matters specifically covered by the PWD, clauses of collective **8.5** agreements and arbitration awards that 'have been declared universally applicable' across a geographical area apply to posted workers employed in the industries or professions to which those agreements relate in so far as the relevant collective terms concern the core protections set out in Article 3(1) – Article 3(8) and (10). A similar but less restrictive right applies to collective agreements and arbitration awards relating to the building and construction industry provided that these too have been declared to be universally applicable – Article 3(1) and (8) (read in conjunction with the Annex to the Directive). This reflects the importance of posted working to the construction industry where there is a widespread practice of posting workers from one country to another in connection with the construction of infrastructure projects and the like. Both these sets of provisions are discussed in more detail under 'Rights under PWD – collective terms and arbitration awards' below.

Scope of chapter. Workers can be posted to any country in the world. However, **8.6** in this chapter we are solely concerned with the posting of workers within the EEA, to whom the PWD applies.

Background to Posted Workers Directive   8.7

Articles 45, 49, 56 and 57 of the Treaty on the Functioning of the European Union (TFEU) respectively provide for the free movement of workers within the EU, a right to freedom of establishment (e.g. to set up and manage undertakings) and a prohibition on restrictions on freedom to provide services. These economic freedoms underpin the concept of the single market and, because of them, the provision of cross-border services has grown and flourished across the EU. However, as membership of the European Community expanded in the 1980s, it was recognised by the European institutions that the exploitation of these rights and freedoms gave rise to a number of potential problems. These included a lack of clarity as to which country's laws applied to a worker posted from one country to another; the potential for exploitation of foreign workers by employing them on worse terms and conditions than indigenous workers; and the undermining of local terms and conditions via the use of 'cheaper' foreign workers. It was therefore considered desirable to introduce a directive requiring coordination between Member States on key rules that would apply when workers were posted from one undertaking within the EEA to another.

309

Prior to the adoption of the PWD in 1996, European law did not provide for any restriction on employers located in a Member State from seeking to utilise the freedom to provide services guaranteed under what are now Articles 56 and 57 TFEU by posting workers to another Member State. Only in the sphere of social security was there any regulation. However, concerns about the lack of employment regulation came into sharp relief at the time of the accession of Spain and Portugal to membership of the then European Community (now European Union) in 1986. Issues emerged that forced the ECJ to consider whether it was permissible for a Member State to lay down legal stipulations regarding the terms and conditions on which posted workers could be employed when temporarily working within its territory.

8.8 One of the strongest influences on the decision to provide EU-wide regulation in this matter was the ECJ's decision in Rush Portuguesa Limitada v Office National d'Immigration 1991 2 CMLR 818, ECJ. RPL was a building and public works undertaking with a registered office in Portugal. It entered into a sub-contract with a French company for work in France. In order to facilitate and complete that contract it found it needed to bring its own Portuguese workforce into France. However, RPL failed to obtain the work permits that were mandatory under the French Labour Code and as a result became liable to pay financial penalties. RPL sought to challenge these on the basis that they breached the fundamental freedom to provide services guaranteed under the EU Treaty. In particular, it argued that, as the production capacity of any undertaking was subject to the availability of its workforce, any conditions restricting that workforce inevitably limited its freedom to provide services. Following the referral of the case to the European Court, the ECJ ruled that restrictions on the right of entry of workers to another Member State were prohibited in so far as they went beyond what is reasonable and proportionate, but that 'Community law does not preclude Member States from extending their legislation, or collective labour agreements entered into by both sides of industry, to any person who is employed, even temporarily, within their territory, no matter in which country the employer is established; nor does Community law prohibit Member States from enforcing those rules by appropriate means'.

8.9 Social dumping

The principal mischief sought to be addressed by the PWD is the practice of 'social dumping', whereby service providers in the sending country apply their labour standards to undercut service providers in the host country. Without an enforceable obligation to ensure that the same basic standards operated by the host country are applied to both indigenous and posted workers, a company located in the sending country could arrange to deploy workers in the host country with the sole purpose of driving down labour costs there and thus securing tenders at the expense of the host country's own employers and workers. The purpose of the Directive is therefore to implement a more level playing field.

However, there is substantial evidence to show that this objective aimed at preventing social dumping has not been fully achieved and that, with regard in particular to workers from the recent EU accession countries of Eastern Europe, the problem of social dumping remains a serious one. For example, Romanian agricultural workers have been deployed in Southern Italy on terms and conditions that are as impoverished as the physical conditions in which they are housed. Similar instances have given rise to a legitimate concern that fraud is being practised through the medium of 'shell' or so-called 'letter box' companies that maintain a formal legal presence in a particular country but which operate minimal economic activity within that country. Since there is no limitation under EU law on the type of company that can undertake the temporary posting of workers, organisations are free to deploy legal structures that serve to mask the reality as to the terms and conditions on which posted workers are engaged and the length of time for which they remain posted. Letter box companies also have the potential to facilitate sub-contracting chains and false 'postings' in order to circumvent national rules on social security and labour conditions.

It is concerns such as these that have led to the recent approval by the Council **8.10** of Ministers of a draft new Directive – the EU Posted Workers Enforcement Directive – aimed at beefing up the enforcement of the PWD. For more details, see 'Enforcement' below.

Incidence of posting workers within the EU   8.11
Between 2004 and 2007, the number of EU Member States increased from 15 to 25 with the admission of the Czech Republic, Estonia, Hungary, Latvia, Lithuania, Poland, Slovakia, Slovenia, Malta and Cyprus. This period coincided with a substantial increase in the number of posted workers across the EU – the European Commission estimating there to be around one million such workers in 2009. This figure is now believed to be in excess of 1.5 million – see 'Posting of workers in the European Union and EFTA countries: Report on A1 portable documents issued in 2010 and 2011'. (The reference to 'A1 portable documents' in the report's title is to the PD A1 certificate of posting that all companies are supposed to lodge along with a declaration from each individual posted worker that he or she will only utilise the social security provision of his or her resident country. These PD A1 certificates are supposed to be filed with the relevant social security or tax authorities of each Member State and are used for the purpose, inter alia, of monitoring posted working trends across the EU.)

According to the analysis of the PD A1 certificates, the main sending countries of posted workers in 2011 were Poland, Germany and France, followed by Romania, Hungary, Belgium and Portugal; and the main receiving countries were Germany and France, followed by the Netherlands, Belgium, Spain, Italy

311

and Austria. Compared with previous figures issued in 2009, the number of posted workers sent abroad in 2011 from Slovenia, Romania, Latvia, Estonia, Lithuania and Bulgaria increased in relative terms by 70 per cent. In absolute terms, the number of posted workers sent abroad from Germany, Poland, Hungary and Slovakia also increased. Similarly the number of posted workers received from abroad increased sharply between 2009 and 2011 in Austria, Norway and Germany (in excess of a 40 per cent increase) and – in absolute terms – also in Belgium, the Netherlands, Italy and Switzerland. Conversely, the number of workers posted to Spain and Greece decreased across the same two-year period, almost certainly due to the sharp decline in labour demand caused by the economic crises in those countries.

8.12 In the same period the UK had fairly low figures compared to the other more densely populated EU countries, in terms of both the number of workers posted from it and the number of workers posted to it. Posted workers from the UK mainly tended to go to France, but also to Germany, Italy and the Netherlands.

However, it is widely accepted that these official figures mask the real extent of posted working within the EEA. This is partly because there is considerable uncertainty about the extent to which the PD A1 certificates recorded by countries reflect the actual number of postings taking place. In 2010, the French Employment Minister estimated that there were between 220,000 and 330,000 posted workers employed in France who had not been declared. Such figures – if representative of other Member States – suggest that the scale of posted working is far greater than the official figures portray and it is reasonable to assume that many posted workers are unlikely to be enjoying the basic protections that the PWD is intended to secure.

8.13 **Construction and building sector.** According to the figures compiled for the Report on A1 portable documents issued in 2010 and 2011, it is estimated that around 55 per cent of posted workers within the EU are employed in the construction and building sector. The importance of the PWD in this context is underlined by the mention in the Annex to the Directive of activities specifically associated with that sector. These include excavation, earthmoving, building work, renovation, repairs, dismantling and demolition, maintenance, upkeep, painting and cleaning work. By virtue of Article 3(1) and (8), the terms of collective agreements or arbitration awards that have been declared universally applicable in respect of the profession or industry to which they relate, must, in so far as they concern the activities mentioned in the Annex, be extended to posted workers. For more details, see 'Rights under PWD – collective agreements and arbitration awards' below.

8.14 **Other sectors.** Posted workers are also heavily employed in the transport, telecommunications, entertainment, repairs, maintenance and servicing industries throughout the EEA.

Transposition of PWD into national law   8.15

Even before the official publication of the PWD in January 1997, several Member States – including Germany, Austria and France – had already introduced their own national legislation on the posting of workers so as to address distortions to competition and the adverse effects on the protection of workers resulting from the transnational provision of services. Once the PWD was finally adopted, the national laws of those countries were tweaked with a view to meeting the specific requirements of the Directive.

Other countries such as Spain, Denmark, Italy, the Netherlands and Sweden transposed the PWD into their national law by passing legislation specifically to implement the Directive prior to its coming into force in January 1999.

UK implementation   8.16

The UK, by contrast, did not deem it necessary to enact any specific implementing legislation. This is because the Government of the day took the view that it was sufficient that the domestic law already in place for dealing with the subject areas covered by the PWD applied to workers regardless of whether they were permanent or temporary and whether they were indigenous or posted from other countries to the UK. It was also the case that, in terms of enforcement, posted workers would be entitled to enforce their statutory rights by recourse to UK employment tribunals and the domestic courts in the same way as other types of worker.

This stance was unique to the UK and Ireland and is one that continued (and continues) to be adopted by subsequent UK governments, including the current coalition government. Even so, it was recognised prior to the Directive's implementation deadline of 16 December 1999 that many of the UK's existing enactments were subject to territorial restrictions that could operate to preclude posted workers from enforcing their rights. Therefore, a series of amendments were made to address this. The process began with the repeal of S.196 of the Employment Rights Act 1996 (ERA), which, up to then, had limited the application of the rights enshrined in that Act to employees who *ordinarily* worked in Great Britain. This territorial proviso was removed so that, in the words of Ian McCartney, Minister of State for Trade and Industry, UK law would 'extend employment rights to employees temporarily working in Great Britain and thus facilitate the implementation of the Posting of Workers Directive' (House of Commons debates, 26 July 1999). Amendment was also made to the Trade Union and Labour Relations (Consolidation) Act 1992 so as to remove the territorial restriction in that Act on rights to be consulted about collective redundancies. With regard to equal treatment of men and women and the prohibition of discrimination, the Equal Opportunities (Employment Legislation) (Territorial Limits) Regulations 1991 SI 1999/3163

313

introduced amendments to ensure that territorial barriers to the effective enforcement by posted workers of anti-discrimination rights and protections were also dismantled.

8.17 As a result of these amendments, workers posted to the UK can avail themselves of all the domestic statutory provisions that govern the core protections set out in Article 1(3) PWD. The protections concerning maximum working hours, rest periods and paid annual leave are enforceable under the Working Time Regulations 1981 SI 1981/1833, which contain no specific exclusions in respect of temporary or posted workers. The Health and Safety at Work Act etc 1974 applies to all persons employed in the UK, temporary or otherwise. The protection accorded to pregnant women and women who have recently given birth – as governed by various enactments including the ERA and the Social Security Contributions and Benefits Act 1992 – similarly makes no distinction between a posted worker and any other kind of worker. The protection of children and young people – as provided for by the Children and Young Persons Acts of 1933 and 1963 – apply regardless of whether or not the child/young person is a posted worker. The same also pertains to the right to equal treatment and protection against discrimination set out in the Equality Act 2010. And S.1(2) of the National Minimum Wage Act 1998, which states that 'a person qualifies for the national minimum wage if he is an individual who… is working, or ordinarily works, in the United Kingdom under his contract', adequately ensures that the right to minimum wage rates is not restricted to those who 'usually' work in the UK. Posted workers are thereby covered.

8.18 **Threat of infraction proceedings.** Notwithstanding the UK Government's confidence that the PWD has been fully and effectively transposed into UK law, it seemed for some time that infraction proceedings might be instituted against it. In 2003 a Communication issued by the European Commission complained that the situations covered by the PWD and the rights derived from it were not clearly enough defined in UK law. It also asserted that the jurisdiction clause in Article 6 of the Directive stipulating that PWD rights must be capable of effective enforcement in the territory where a worker is posted had not been properly implemented. However, the Labour Government of the day stood firm. In his reply to the Commission, the Minister for Small Business and Enterprise, Nigel Griffiths, cited European case law as authority for the proposition that the transposition of a directive does not require a separate legal instrument at national level so long as (i) national law guarantees that national authorities will effectively apply the directive in full; (ii) the legal position is sufficiently clear and precise; and (iii) individuals are made fully aware of their rights and, where appropriate, may rely upon those rights before the national courts. Mr Griffiths maintained that there was no clear case for reassessment of the UK transposition of the PWD as all three of these conditions had been met.

By November 2004, it was evident that no further follow-up action was to be taken by the Commission, leading to an expression of confidence by a Government Minister that this was because UK law was in full compliance with the PWD. In 2006 the 30th Report of the House of Commons Select Committee on European Scrutiny recorded that the Government took the firm view that the PWD had been 'fully implemented' in the UK because 'all employment law applies to workers posted here' (para 13.8).

Ongoing concerns about non-compliance. Even though the threat of **8.19** infraction proceedings has receded, murmurings continue about the alleged deficiency in the transposition of the PWD into UK law. Trade unions in particular have been (and continue to be) critical in this regard. For example, they are frustrated by the failure of successive UK Governments to make any provision pursuant to Article 3(1) and (8) PWD for extending the provisions of collective agreements to workers posted to work in the UK construction sector. Furthermore, the TUC has noted that 'the absence of a Government agency gathering information relating to the number of workers posted to the UK at any one time also undermines the enforcement of the Directive'.

The unions have also expressed discontent about rulings of the ECJ concerning the extent to which industrial action can be lawfully directed at ensuring that the terms of collective agreements are applied to posted workers as well as indigenous workers by companies operating transnationally. In these cases – discussed under 'Conflict between PWD and single market freedoms' below – the Court accepted that the right to strike was a fundamental freedom, but asserted that that right is not absolute in circumstances where strike action impedes an organisation's equally fundamental freedom to provide services as guaranteed by Articles 56 and 57 TFEU.

Who is a posted worker? 8.20

The definition of 'posted worker' is set out in Article 2(1) PWD. This states that: 'For the purposes of this Directive, "posted worker" means a worker who, for a limited period, carries out his work in the territory of a Member State other than the State in which he normally works.' The definition of 'worker' is that which applies under the national law of the host Member State – Article 2(2). Article 2 does not encompass anyone who seeks employment in another EU/EEA state of his or her own accord. Instead, it is restricted to those sent by undertakings to work temporarily in another Member State in connection with the provision of services. Such a posting can be effected in one of two ways: via a service contract between the posting company and the company receiving the relevant services, or through a temporary work agency operating transnationally.

Posting must be temporary. In view of the reference to working 'for a limited **8.21** period' in Article 2(1), it is apparent that the posting of a worker is expected to

315

be temporary. However, the PWD contains no explanation of what is meant by 'a limited period'. Presumably, a worker who ends up being posted for a very substantial period, or even indefinitely, would at some point cease, in the terminology of the Directive, to be regarded as 'normally working' in the state of origin and would cease to be a 'posted worker' (assuming that he or she was one in the first place).

8.22 Under European rules on the coordination of social security across Member States, a posted worker can, subject to limited exceptions, only remain affiliated to the regime of his or her country of origin for a maximum of 24 months – see EC Regulation No.883/2004, as amended by EC Regulation No.988/2009. If a posting is expected to exceed 24 months then normally the worker cannot elect to continue to be covered by his or her home country's social security regime. It has been suggested that this gives an indication of what was in the mind of the European legislators when drafting the PWD and that, on this basis, a posting of anything beyond two years would no longer be 'for a limited period'. However, it seems unlikely that such a hard-and-fast rule can be applied.

Under the EU social security rules, once a worker has ended a period of posting, no fresh period of posting can normally be authorised until at least two months have elapsed from the date when the previous posting period expired. However, there is no equivalent to this in the PWD. This opens up the possibility that a worker could be employed on a series of continuous postings – whether to the same or to different Member States – with little or no gap between them without this having any automatic consequence regarding his or her status as a 'posted worker'.

8.23 **Domestic law definition of 'worker' applies.** Article 2(2) PWD provides that 'the definition of a worker is that which applies in the law of the Member State to whose territory the worker is posted'. In the absence of an EU-wide standard definition of 'worker', an individual might therefore be regarded as a worker within the jurisdiction of one Member State but not in another. It is true that, generally speaking, the basic employment rights governed by Article 3(1) PWD – as to which see 'Rights under PWD' below – are extended in all Member States to all individuals engaged in any kind of employment relationship, so the scope for variation between different countries is fairly narrow. But that does not mean there will be absolute symmetry. Nor does the PWD expect or demand that that is the case. So it may be, for example, that an individual who would be regarded under UK law as having self-employed status (and thus not a 'worker') might be regarded differently under the law of another Member State. The question of whether the individual falls within the Article 2 definition of 'posted worker' would therefore depend on the law of the country to which he or she is posted.

It should be borne in mind that the purpose of the PWD is not to guarantee free-standing rights to posted workers that indigenous or permanent workers in the host country do not themselves have. Rather, it ensures that they are entitled to the same rights – but only in respect of the matters specifically listed in Article 3(1)(a)–(g). This means that if a Member State adopts different definitions of 'worker' in respect of different legal rights, a posted worker's entitlement to a particular right will depend on whether he or she qualifies as a 'worker' for that particular purpose. So if, for example, a 'worker' is defined in one way under a country's national minimum wage law and a different way under its law on working time, the posted worker will have to satisfy both respective definitions in order to qualify for both these rights. If, however, his or her employment status meets one definition but not the other, the worker's legal entitlements under the PWD will be confined to the rights for which he or she qualifies.

Non-EEA based workers. It is frequently assumed – wrongly – that to be **8.24** regarded as a 'posted worker' within the meaning of Article 2 a worker must be an EEA national based in the country from which he or she is posted. The assumption derives from the phrasing of Article 2(1), which speaks of a 'worker who, for a limited period, carries out his work in the territory of a Member State *other than the State in which he normally works*' (our stress). However, a worker can be a third-country national (i.e. have non-EEA nationality) and still be a posted worker within the terms of Article 2. As the cases discussed below establish, if a Member State applies a rule as part of its immigration law that unduly restricts the right of a non-EEA national from working within its territory in circumstances where the individual has lawful residency in the sending state, then such a restriction is likely to constitute a breach of the right to provide services within the meaning of Articles 56 and 57 TFEU.

In Vander Elst v Office des Migrations Internationales 1995 1 CMLR 513, ECJ, a Belgian demolition business based in Brussels habitually employed Moroccan nationals. These held Belgian work permits and were thus legally resident in Belgium. In 1989, having secured a one-month contract to carry out demolition work in Reims, the business posted a team of employees to France to carry out this work, including four Moroccans for whom the employer had obtained short-stay visas. However, French employment inspectors subsequently found that the Moroccan workers did not have the necessary French work permits to enable them to take up paid employment in France in accordance with the French Labour Code, as a result of which the owner of the Belgian company was ordered to pay a fine. The matter was referred to the ECJ, which ruled that the relevant stipulations of the Labour Code impeded the business's freedom to provide services under what are now Articles 56 and 57 TFEU.

In so holding, the Court stated that it was significant that the Moroccan workers **8.25** had been lawfully resident in Belgium, being the state in which their employer was established and where they had been issued with work permits. Although it was permissible for any Member State to regulate access to its labour market by non-EU nationals, the regulatory regime had to be no more than a proportionate restriction on the fundamental freedom accorded to individuals and undertakings to provide services. In this case, the requirement of the French Labour Code for a company to secure and pay for additional work permits in addition to the short-stay visas already obtained was held to be disproportionate. The ECJ concluded that: '[Articles 56 and 57 are] to be interpreted as precluding a Member State from requiring undertakings which are established in another Member State and enter the first Member State in order to provide services, and which lawfully and habitually employ nationals of non-Member countries, to obtain work permits for those workers from a national immigration authority and to pay the attendant costs, with the imposition of an administrative fine as the penalty for infringement.'

In R (Low and ors) v Secretary of State for the Home Department 2010 ICR 755, CA, the Court of Appeal considered a case where an Irish company had sought to post to the UK non-EEA nationals who, it transpired, had no lawful immigration presence in Ireland, the UK or anywhere else in the EEA. Although the Court was clear that it was a breach of Article 56 for so-called third-country nationals who are lawfully resident in one Member State to be unduly restricted by the operation of national immigration rules from being posted to work on a temporary basis in another Member State, the Court held that this principle did not apply in the case of non-EEA nationals who are not lawfully resident or entitled to work in the state of origin. In the words of Lord Justice Rix (giving the judgment of the Court): 'Undertakings from a country of establishment are... free to set up a branch in another Member State of the European Union and there recruit and employ workers who are lawfully present in and entitled to work in that country. Such workers may be nationals of any country in the world, as long as they are entitled to be present in and to work in the host country... What, however, the ECJ jurisprudence gives no support whatsoever to is the proposition that Article [56] gives to an undertaking in an EU country of establishment a novel and unique right, not enjoyed by such an undertaking in its own country and lacked by any and all undertakings in a host country, to employ workers who have no lawful presence or right to work either in the country of establishment itself, or in the host country, or indeed anywhere in the European Union. That would not be to allow the foreign undertaking to compete with national undertakings on a level playing field, but to give it a wholly new and unprecedented advantage.'

8.26 The Court of Appeal also considered the circumstances in which the employment of migrant workers and the posting of them to another Member State can amount to an abuse of EU law. In this case the alleged posting of the three non-EEA nationals was intended to facilitate a service contract between the Irish company and a Chinese restaurant in the UK. However, it emerged that the employees in question had never, in fact, resided in the Republic of Ireland and that the company had no previous history of employing any workers who were lawfully present in Ireland or the UK for the purpose of conducting commercial operations in either country. This gave rise to the clear suspicion that the company had been incorporated in Ireland with the sole aim of employing illegal nationals and arranging for them to be posted to the UK to enable them to secure the protection of Community law. The Court of Appeal upheld the High Court judge's decision that this was an abuse of European law. Rix LJ concluded that the Irish company had 'sought to put between the UK restaurant and its staff the fiction of an undertaking established in another Member State purportedly using its Article [56] freedom to bring or "post" its lawful employees to the UK for the purpose of its operations [there]. This is solely in order to attempt to translate those unlawfully present and illegally working in the UK into workers protected under Community law. The truth, however, is that the Irish company [had] no employees lawfully present as such in Ireland and [had] posted none to the UK. The whole thing [was] a charade, and the applications to the Secretary of State, as [the High Court judge] observed, were rightly referred to as spurious.'

The Low case serves to demonstrate that, although there is no absolute prohibition on a labour supply company being established in one Member State for the principal purpose of posting employees to another Member State (whether the employees in question are EEA nationals or otherwise), the courts are likely to scrutinise the activities of such companies very closely. Non-EEA nationals with no lawful right to reside and/or work in the EEA will not be regarded as posted workers for the purposes of the PWD. Nor can any company that employs them expect to get around this by arguing that the refusal to allow such employees to be posted constitutes a breach of the company's fundamental freedom to provide services within the meaning of Articles 56 and 57 TFEU.

Exclusion of merchant navy personnel. By virtue of Article 1(2), the PWD **8.27** does not apply to seagoing personnel employed in the merchant navy.

When does PWD apply? 8.28

Article 1(1) stipulates that the PWD will apply when, in the context of the transnational provision of services, an undertaking established in a Member State posts workers to the territory of another Member State in accordance with Article 1(3). Article 1(3) sets out three different scenarios (or 'transnational measures') that will trigger the application of the PWD. These are:

- where an undertaking established in one Member State has a contract to provide services to an undertaking in another Member State and, pursuant to that contract, posts workers to that other Member State

- where an intra-company transfer takes place – i.e. an undertaking located in one Member State posts a worker to an undertaking within the same group

319

of companies located in another Member State (typically, this would cover an intra-group international secondment)

- where an employment business or employment agency located in one Member State posts workers under a hiring or agency agreement to an undertaking or user established or operating in another Member State. (Note that Article 3(9) provides that Member States may provide that workers employed by such employment businesses/agencies must guarantee to posted workers the same terms and conditions that apply to similar agency workers in the Member State where the work is to be carried out.)

As is made clear in Article 1(3), in the case of each of the above scenarios the PWD will apply only if, during the period of the posting, there is an employment relationship between the posting undertaking (or, as the case may be, employment business/agency) and the worker. If the worker ceases to be employed by the undertaking or agency responsible for the posting, the PWD will no longer apply and the worker will lose the rights that it guarantees.

8.29 Rights under PWD

Article 3(1) PWD requires Member States to ensure that workers temporarily posted to their territory are entitled to the minimum terms laid down by law, regulation or administrative provision in relation to certain specified matters. These matters are outlined below.

8.30 Core rights and protections

The basic rights set out in Article 3(1)(a)–(g) PWD – referred to in para 14 of the Preamble to the Directive as 'a "hard core" of clearly defined protective rules' – comprise the following:

- *maximum work periods, minimum rest periods and minimum paid annual holidays* (Article 3(1)(a) and (b) PWD). In Jackson v Ghost Ltd and anor 2003 IRLR 824, EAT, the EAT accepted that, in the UK, these particular rights were secured by the Working Time Regulations 1998 SI 1998/1833, and that a worker posted to work in an undertaking established in the UK would be entitled to rely upon them

- *minimum rates of pay, including overtime rates* (Article 3(1)(c) PWD). This protection is secured by the National Minimum Wage Act 1998 and related regulations. It is clear from S.1(2)(b) of the 1998 Act that a person qualifies for the national minimum wage if he or she 'is working, or ordinarily works, in the United Kingdom under his [or her] contract'. In view of the words 'is working', it is clear that there is no requirement for the individual to be working other than on a temporary basis in the UK and that a posted worker would therefore be entitled to the UK national minimum wage while posted to the UK. (It is respectfully suggested that, in so far as the obiter

320

comments of His Honour Judge Peter Clark in Jackson v Ghost Ltd (above) suggest the contrary, they are incorrect)

- *conditions of hiring out workers, in particular the supply of workers by temporary employment undertakings* (Article 3(1)(d) PWD). In the UK, the Agency Workers Regulations 2010 SI 2010/93 apply to all agency workers assigned to do temporary work for hirers through temporary work agencies. Under these Regulations, such workers are entitled to access a hirer's collective facilities and amenities and to access information about its job vacancies from the first day of their assignment. In addition, after 12 weeks of working in the same role with the same hirer, they are entitled to the same basic working and employment conditions that they would have been entitled to had they been recruited directly by the hirer – for full details, see Chapter 1, 'Agency Workers'. These protections extend to workers posted to undertakings in the UK just as they do to indigenous agency workers

- *health, safety and hygiene at work* (Article 3(1)(e) PWD). The Heath and Safety at Work etc Act 1974 and the Health and Safety at Work etc Act 1974 (Application Outside Great Britain) Order 2001 (SI 2001/2127)) combine to ensure that posted workers are accorded the same health and safety protection in the UK as other workers

- *protective measures with regard to the terms of employment of pregnant women or women who have recently given birth, of children and of young people* (Article 3(1)(f) PWD). This includes protection afforded by the EU Pregnant Workers Directive (No.92/85). It also includes provisions dealing with risk assessments, alteration of duties and possible suspension from work on maternity grounds under Regs 16 and 17 of the Management of Health and Safety at Work Regulations 1999 SI 1999/3242 and Ss.66–70 of the Employment Rights Act 1996 and the provisions on automatic unfair dismissal contained in S.99 of the 1996 Act (i.e. dismissal for a reason relating to pregnancy, childbirth or maternity) – see Jackson v Ghost Ltd (above)

- *equality of treatment between men and women and other provisions on non-discrimination* (Article 3(1)(g) PWD). In the UK, posted workers are entitled to protection under the Equality Act 2010 (i.e. they enjoy the right not to be discriminated against, harassed or victimised because of their age, disability, gender reassignment, marriage or civil partnership status, pregnancy and maternity, race, religion or belief, sex (i.e. gender), and sexual orientation). It is arguable that posted workers would also be entitled to analogous anti-discrimination protection available to part-time workers under the Part-time Workers (Prevention of Less Favourable Treatment) Regulations 2000 SI 2000/1551

- *collective agreement terms that 'have been declared universally applicable' in respect of the profession or industry to which they relate* (Article 3(1),

321

(8) and (10)). In Rüffert v Land Niedersachsen 2008 IRLR 467, ECJ, the European Court decided that this did not cover a German law allowing the state government to give mandatory effect to a building sector collective agreement because it did not embrace all undertakings in the region and industry).

8.31 As previously stated, the PWD only requires that posted workers receive the same rights and protections as indigenous workers in respect of the matters set out above. This means that if there is no legal regulation on a particular matter, a posted worker would have no protection – he or she would not derive a free-standing right simply by reason of the fact that it is listed in Article 3. In practice, however, most of the rights listed in Article 3(1)(a)–(g) concern matters that are subject to mandatory EU directives in their own right. This means that all EU countries will (or should) have transposed into their national law substantive provisions pertaining to the 'hard core' protections set out in Article 3(1)(a)–(g). The main exception to this concerns the right to minimum rates of pay (discussed under 'Minimum pay rates and paid holiday' below) as there is no EU directive requiring Member States to enact such minima.

In Commission of the European Communities v Luxembourg 2009 IRLR 388, ECJ, the ECJ held that Article 3(1) PWD must be interpreted as setting out an exhaustive list of the matters in respect of which Member States must ensure that posted workers receive the same treatment as indigenous workers. Furthermore, the level of protection that must be guaranteed to posted workers is limited, in principle, to that provided for in Article 3(1)(a)–(g). This principle applies unless, pursuant to the law or to collective agreements in the state of origin, those workers enjoy more favourable terms and conditions of employment as regards those matters. However, the Court acknowledged that under Article 3(10), Member States have the right to apply to undertakings which post workers to their territory terms and conditions on other matters where public policy provisions are at stake. This provision is discussed further under 'Options and derogations' below.

8.32 **Minimum pay rates and paid holiday**
Minimum holiday pay and minimum rates of pay (including overtime rates) are included among the list of matters to which posted workers are entitled to the same treatment as indigenous workers under the laws of the country to which they are posted – see Article 3(1)(a) and (c) PWD.

There is no specific EU directive requiring Member States to introduce a minimum wage into its national law. Although many countries – including the UK – have made such provision on their own initiative, by no means all have done so. If, therefore, a worker is posted to a country where there is no national minimum wage, he or she will not secure entitlement to such a wage during the posting simply because it is a matter covered by the PWD.

322

Where a national minimum wage *does* apply, Article 3(1) makes it clear that the concept of minimum rates of pay is to be defined by the national law and/ or practice of the Member State to whose territory the worker is posted.

Allowances and bonuses. In Commission of the European Communities v **8.33** Germany 2005 3 CMLR 4, ECJ, the question arose of whether German law breached the PWD by excluding from the calculation of the minimum rates of pay payable to workers posted to Germany remunerative elements such as allowances and supplements that were paid by employers in other Member States in the construction industry. The possibility of breach arose because binding collective agreements providing for minimum rates to be paid to workers within that industry had been declared to be universally applicable to employers both in and outside of Germany. In ruling that the German law was in breach of the Directive, the ECJ accepted the European Commission's argument that obliging businesses when operating in other countries to include the disputed components in the calculation of minimum pay rates, but to exclude these in the case of businesses established in Germany, resulted in higher wages costs for foreign undertakings compared with those incurred by German companies.

On a more general point of interest, all parties in that case conceded that it was not necessary to take into account contributions to occupational pension schemes, reimbursements of expenses incurred by reason of the posting, and flat-rate sums calculated on a basis other than that of an hourly rate when determining whether the same minimum rates of pay and overtime have been applied to posted workers. Furthermore, the ECJ held that allowances for dirty, heavy or dangerous work did not have to be taken into account: it was entirely normal that if a worker was required to carry out additional work or to work under arduous conditions, compensation should be provided without this being taken into account for the purpose of calculating the minimum wage.

Legal guarantees of cost of living adjustments. In Commission of the **8.34** European Communities v Luxembourg (above) the European Court held that a requirement under Luxembourg national law for undertakings to ensure that the remuneration rates of posted workers be periodically adjusted to reflect increases in the cost of living impeded the freedom to provide services enshrined in Articles 56 and 57 TFEU. In its view, this was an additional requirement that went beyond the obligation on Member States under Article 3(1)(c) PWD to guarantee that posted workers receive the same minimum rates of pay as other workers. The contention that this additional requirement was justified as a derogation by reason of 'public policy' within the meaning of Article 3(10) – see 'Options and derogations' below – was rejected by the ECJ because no evidence had been advanced to show whether and to what extent the application of the requirement was capable of contributing to the policy objective of

323

protecting posted workers from the effects of inflation and ensuring good labour relations.

8.35 **Deductions.** There is nothing to stop an employer subjecting posted workers to deductions that do not apply to indigenous workers (e.g. deductions for accommodation and transport costs) provided these specifically relate to the posting. Article 3(7) PWD states that: 'Allowances specific to the posting shall be considered to be part of the minimum wage, unless they are paid in reimbursement of expenditure actually incurred on account of the posting, such as expenditure on travel, board and lodging'. There is evidence that this 'loophole' has been exploited by some unscrupulous employers in order to pay posted workers less than equivalent indigenous workers and drive down their labour costs vis-à-vis service providers established in the host country. Posted workers from the East European countries are particularly vulnerable in this regard.

While the PWD provides that 'minimum rates of pay' paid to a posted worker should be as defined by the national law and/or practice of the Member State to which he or she is posted, the options for the host country to define the term 'minimum pay' are not unlimited. In EFTA Surveillance Authority v Iceland 2011 IRLR 773, EFTA, the European Free Trade Court held that an Icelandic law requiring foreign undertakings which posted workers temporarily to Iceland to pay regular wages for sick leave was in breach of the PWD. Article 3(1)(c) of the Directive did not authorise a host state to impose its own system for determining all aspects of wages on undertakings posting workers to its territory. That provision was solely directed to regulating matters relating to *minimum* rates of pay. Hence, an entitlement to sickness pay that was not itself set at a minimum rate did not fall within the notion of 'the minimum rates of pay'. In this particular case, the sickness pay provided for in the instrument implementing the PWD into Icelandic law was neither a flat rate of minimum compensation, nor calculated by reference to a minimum wage. On the contrary, the sick pay entitlement corresponded to the regular wage the worker received under his or her employment contract. It followed that the national provision was incompatible with the Directive unless it could be justified under the exception for public policy laid down in Article 3(10) of the Directive, for which see 'Options and derogations' below.

8.36 **Holiday pay.** In Finalarte Sociedade de Construção Civil LDA v Urlaubs- und Lohnausgleichskasse der Bauwirtschaft 2003 2 CMLR 11, ECJ, the European Commission sought to challenge differences in the way a holiday pay scheme operated in respect of workers employed in the construction industry. Under the scheme all employers, including those that were established in other Member States and which deployed posted workers to Germany, were required to pay into a central fund. Holiday payments were then extracted from that fund whenever a worker took annual leave. However, in the case of indigenous workers it was their employer who claimed from the fund, whereas in the case of posted workers it was the worker (not their employer) who had responsibility for doing this. The ECJ ruled that this discrepancy was explicable by objective differences between businesses established in Germany and those established in other Member States in relation to the effective implementation of the obligation to provide holiday pay. In particular, where a business established outside Germany ceased to provide services there, the German authorities were no longer in a position to ensure that it had, in fact, accorded full holiday pay entitlement to its posted workers. It followed that it was more efficient for the fund to provide holiday pay directly to the workers and this justified the difference in the way the scheme operated in respect of such workers.

In the Finalarte Sociedade case the ECJ was also called upon to consider whether information disclosure requirements in connection with administration of the holiday pay scheme were contrary to Articles 56 and 57 TFEU. Even though these requirements were imposed only on undertakings established outside Germany, the Court accepted that they may be an appropriate measure to ensure protection for posted workers regarding entitlement to paid holiday. But it also observed that the disclosure requirements gave rise to additional expense and administrative burdens. The resulting impact on the freedom to provide services could therefore only be justifiable if the requirements were shown to be necessary to safeguard by appropriate means the overriding public interest in promoting the social protection of posted workers. Whether this was the case was a matter for the German national court to determine having regard to the principle of proportionality. The ECJ made it clear, however, that the duty to disclose specific documents to the host state could never be justified if that state were in a position to perform the necessary checks on the basis of documentation already required by the rules of the Member State in which the sending business was established.

Collective agreements and arbitration awards   8.37

The PWD contains two specific sets of provisions allowing for the terms of collective agreements and arbitration awards to be extended to posted workers. The first deals with agreements/awards applicable to the building and construction industry. By virtue of Article 3(1) and (8), any terms of such agreements or awards declared to be 'universally applicable' in respect of the profession or industry to which they relate, must, in so far as they concern the activities mentioned in the Annex to the Directive, be extended to posted workers. The activities listed in the Annex include excavation, earthmoving, building work, renovation, repairs, dismantling and demolition, maintenance, upkeep, painting and cleaning work.

The second provision is set out in the second indent of Article 3(10). This stipulates that 'this Directive shall not preclude the application by Member States, in compliance with the Treaty [i.e. the TFEU], to the national undertakings and to the undertakings of other States, on a basis of equality of treatment... terms and conditions of employment laid down in the collective agreements or arbitration awards within the meaning of paragraph 8 and concerning activities other than those referred to in the Annex'. The meaning of this provision may not be apparent given its rather convoluted wording. The reference to paragraph 8 is to Article 3(8), which defines the meaning of 'universal applicability' in the context of collective agreements and arbitration awards that have been declared to be universally applicable. Essentially, Article 3(10), when read with Article 3(8), permits a derogation from the minimum protected rights guaranteed by the PWD where this takes the form of *extending* to posted workers rights established in 'universally applicable' collective agreements/arbitration awards if this ensures they receive equal treatment with other workers covered by the agreements/awards. This provision has the potential for wider scope than its 'sister' provision in Article 3(1) (discussed immediately above) because, unlike that provision, it is not confined to agreements or awards concerning the activities listed in the Annex to the Directive – i.e. construction and building activities.

8.38 **Meaning of 'declared to be universally applicable'.** Both sets of provisions discussed above apply only where the relevant collective agreement or arbitration award has been 'declared [to be] universally applicable'. By virtue of Article 3(8), this means 'collective agreements or arbitration awards which must be observed by all undertakings in the geographical area and in the profession or industry concerned'. In the absence of a system for declaring agreements or awards to be of universal application, Article 3(8) goes on to state that Member States may, if they so decide, base themselves on:

- agreements or awards which are generally applicable to all similar undertakings in the geographical area and in the profession or industry concerned, and/or

- collective agreements which have been concluded by the most representative employers' and labour organisations at national level and which are applied throughout national territory.

Even where such conditions pertain, Article 3(8) makes it clear that the application of any 'universally applied' collective agreement or arbitration award by an undertaking to posted workers has to be designed to achieve 'equality of treatment' as between those workers and other workers covered by the same agreement or award in respect of the specific matters set out in Article 3(1). In other words, the provisions authorise the extension of additional rights or protections under the terms of universal collective agreements or arbitration awards only if those rights/protections are *sui generis* with the basic matters discussed under 'Core rights and protections' above. Moreover, the extension of rights and protections in this way will only be permissible if the purpose is to secure equality of treatment between posted workers and indigenous workers within the same profession or industry. In this regard, Article 3(8) states that 'equality of treatment' is deemed to exist 'where national undertakings in a similar position are subject, in the place in question or in the sector concerned, to the same obligations as posting undertakings as regards the matters listed [in Article 3(1)] and are required to fulfil those obligations with the same effects'.

This concept of 'universal application' of collective agreements is one that has **8.39** been interpreted strictly by the ECJ. In Rüffert v Land Niedersachsen 2008 IRLR 467, ECJ, the Court held that a German law requiring public sector contractors and sub-contractors to pay workers the minimum wage laid down by the local collective agreement was in breach of the freedom to provide services under what are now Articles 56 and 57 TFEU, as the impediment it placed on the ability of foreign undertakings to provide services in Germany was not objectively justified. The collective agreement in question was not one that Germany was entitled to impose under the PWD as it had not been declared 'universally applicable' within the meaning of Article 3(8). Nor was it capable of being treated as such – the agreement covered only a part of the construction sector falling within the geographical area of the agreement in that it was stated to apply only to public contracts and not to private ones. Accordingly, the minimum rate of pay that the provision of German national law sought to apply was not one that the state was entitled to impose. It followed that the foreign service provider in this case could not be compelled to pay Polish posted workers the same minimum rates of pay paid to local German workers under the collective agreement.

This ruling was soon followed by the decision in Commission of the European Communities v Luxembourg 2009 IRLR 388, ECJ, where the ECJ also struck down a legal stipulation that sought to confer on posted workers the benefit of Luxembourg's national law regulating collective agreements. That stipulation was held be outside the remit of Article 3(10) because it was not limited to collective agreements that had been declared to be universally applicable. Nor could the disputed provision be justified by reference to the separate 'public policy' derogation provided for by the first indent of Article 3(10), details of which are outlined under 'Options and derogations' below. In the ECJ's view there was no reason why provisions concerning collective agreements should per se and without more fall under the definition of 'public policy'.

In STX Norway Offshore AS and ors v Norwegian State 2012 2 CMLR 12, **8.40** EFTA, the European Free Trade Association Court considered a national law provision that aimed to secure for workers posted to Norway certain beneficial terms contained in a nationwide collective agreement covering the maritime construction industry. The terms related to maximum normal working hours and the payment of additional remuneration whenever work assignments required overnight stays away from home. The clauses in the agreement conferring these benefits had been declared to have universal applicability to the maritime construction industry in accordance with Norwegian law. In the course of a legal challenge to the extension of the collective agreements to posted workers brought by a number of maritime employers, the EFTA Court rejected the contention that, in order to be declared 'universally applicable', a specific proportion of employees employed within the relevant industry sector had to be covered by the collective agreement or arbitration award.

8.41 **Relevance to posted workers in the UK.** There is no recognised legal mechanism in UK law for declaring collective agreements to be universally applicable. This means that, in order for the PWD provisions concerning collective agreements to apply, it is necessary to establish within the terms of Article 3(8) that the particular agreement either (i) covers all similar undertakings in the same geographical area in respect of the profession or industry concerned, or (ii) has been concluded at national level and has national application. 'Local agreements' are potentially covered by the first of these methods of establishing universal application, and national agreements are self-evidently covered by the second.

Compared with the much greater incidence of collective bargaining in many EU countries, only about 35 per cent of the total UK working population is covered by a collective agreement, and this falls to below 20 per cent for employees in the private sector. In the public sector, however, collective bargaining still remains the norm, and many public sector jobs are covered by national agreements. With specific regard to the building and construction industry – the sector in which posted workers are most prevalent – the Unite trade union has been successful in negotiating national agreements with employers' representative bodies. Indeed, the union has a stated 'core policy' aim of seeking to ensure that all construction workers are directly employed under the terms and conditions of collective agreements relevant to their particular trade. Hence, the provisions of Article 3(1) and (8) PWD have potential widespread significance to workers posted to work in the UK construction industry.

8.42 **Options and derogations**

Article 3(2) PWD states that the obligations to confer on posted workers equal rights with regard to minimum paid holidays and minimum rates of pay (including overtime) do not apply if: (a) the period of the posting does not exceed eight days; and (b) the posting is for the purpose of fulfilling a contract for the supply of goods requiring skilled and/or specialist workers.

In addition, Article 3(3) authorises Member States not to impose compliance with the rules of domestic law governing minimum rates of pay when the length of the posting does not exceed one month. This option has not been taken up in the UK and there is therefore no derogation for short periods of work in this country. The same is true in Belgium, Germany, France, Finland, Greece, Ireland, Italy, the Netherlands, and Sweden.

Article 3(7) provides that the PWD shall not prevent the application of terms **8.43** and conditions of employment that are *more* favourable to workers. The purpose of this is to enable workers to benefit from terms and conditions of employment more favourable than those in force in the country in which the temporary work is performed. Certain Member States have reproduced Article 3(7) verbatim in their legal instruments transposing the Directive into their national law. But, as explained under 'Public policy derogation' below, this provision has been interpreted restrictively by the ECJ to preclude national laws of a host country from applying protections and rights on posted workers in respect of matters that go beyond those listed in Article 3(1) if the effect of so doing is to interfere disproportionately with an undertaking's freedom to provide services under Articles 56 and 57 TFEU.

Public policy derogation. The first indent of Article 3(10) authorises the **8.44** application to posted workers of 'public policy' provisions under domestic law on the basis of equal treatment. So, for example:

- in Spain, national law adds to the matters covered by the PWD an obligation to respect the privacy and dignity of workers, trade union liberties, the right of assembly and the right to strike

- in France, certain provisions must be complied with in addition to those set out in Article 3(1). These include a stipulation that wages will be payable on a monthly basis; a procedure governing the payment of wages and remittance of pay slips; written declarations with regard to hours of work, collective accommodation, accidents at work, and lay-offs due to bad weather; a requirement to make certain declarations prior to the inspection of workplaces; and the display of documents at building sites to the effect that a building permit has been obtained

- in Finland, the law applicable to posted workers includes freedom of association and the right of workers to assemble at the workplace; provisions regarding night work, shift work and Sunday working; and an obligation to remunerate workers who have been prevented from working for reasons for which the employer is responsible

- in Greece, the legal instrument transposing the PWD provides for the application of national rules governing the protection of personal data

- in Luxembourg, posted workers are entitled to a written contract of terms and conditions; protection in respect of fixed-term contracts and part-time working; and rights concerning lay-off due to bad weather or technical reasons. Luxembourg has also extended to posted workers legal provisions concerning the prevention of clandestine and/or illegal work, and

- in Sweden, national law provides for the application to posted workers of rules governing the right of association and bargaining, and a 'peace

329

obligation' in the case of collective agreements concluded with any Swedish trade union.

Belgium, Germany, Denmark, Ireland, Italy, the Netherlands, Portugal and the UK are among the countries that have not availed themselves of the Article 3(10) derogation.

8.45 Although, on its face, Article 3(10) appears to confer a wide discretion on Member States to impose conditions more favourable than those set out in Article 3(1), this option has been narrowly interpreted by the courts in a way that calls into question the legitimacy of some of the additional legal protections and obligations mentioned above.

In Commission of the European Communities v Luxembourg (above) the ECJ stated that the public policy exception in Article 3(10) was in the nature of a derogation from the provisions of Article 3(1), which sets out an exhaustive list of the matters in respect of which Member States may give priority to the rules in force in the host Member State in connection with the posting of workers. Moreover, the first indent of Article 3(10) was a derogation from the principle of freedom to provide services under what are now Articles 56 and 57 TFEU. In consequence, the derogation had to be interpreted strictly. The freedom to provide services, being a fundamental principle of the TFEU, may be restricted only by rules justified by overriding requirements relating to the public interest and applicable to all individuals and businesses operating in the territory of the Member State where the service is provided, and even then only in so far as the public interest is not already safeguarded by the rules to which the service provider is subject in the Member State where he/it is established. The ECJ asserted that the reasons which may be invoked to justify any derogation from the principle of freedom to provide services have to be supported by appropriate evidence or an analysis of the expediency or proportionality of the restrictive measure adopted by the state.

8.46 Applying these principles, the ECJ concluded that a number of additional rights and obligations contained within the Luxembourg legal instrument implementing the PWD into national law went beyond the minima set out in Article 3(1) and could not be justified by reliance on the 'public policy' derogation in Article 3(10). These included:

- a requirement that posted workers be given a written contract or document informing them of their terms and conditions

- the automatic upward adjustment of rates of remuneration to take into account increases in the cost of living

- the application to posted workers of rules relating to the treatment of part-time and fixed-term working

- a requirement relating to the imperative provision of national law in respect of collective agreements.

The Court's reasoning in respect of the second and fourth of these issues has already been summarised above under 'Minimum pay rates and paid holiday' and 'Collective agreements' respectively. With regard to the requirement to provide written evidence of terms and conditions, the Court pointed out that, in view of the provisions of the EU Proof of Employment Relationship Directive (No.91/533), this was already an obligation imposed on undertakings in respect of the workers they employed. This rendered the existence of the additional obligation redundant, and imposing it was likely to have a chilling effect on undertakings when it came to the exercise of their freedom to provide services in a different Member State. As for the extension of the rules relating to part-time and fixed-term work, the ECJ held that these were also likely to hinder the exercise of the freedom to provide services by undertakings wishing to post workers and were in any event rendered redundant given that Member States were already obliged to guarantee the principle of equal treatment in respect of these types of working pattern by virtue of the EU Part-time Workers Directive (No.97/81) and the EU Fixed-term Workers Directive (No.99/70) dealing with those matters.

In EFTA Surveillance Authority v Iceland 2011 IRLR 773, EFTA, the European **8.47** Free Trade Association Court relied on similar reasoning in respect of a rule of Icelandic law imposing a duty on any undertaking posting workers to Iceland to take out accident insurance on behalf of their employees. The Court ruled that the 'public policy' derogation in Article 3(10) PWD could be relied upon to justify imposing additional requirements on undertakings posting workers only if there was a genuine and sufficiently serious threat to a fundamental interest of society. That had not been established in this case. The insurance stipulation concerned terms and conditions of employment and was consequently subject to the limitations of Article 3 PWD. It made no difference whether the stipulation was classified as a rule of tort or insurance law. An obligation to take out such insurance fell outside the matters listed in Article 3(1) and was therefore incompatible with the Directive unless it could be justified under the public policy exception. In this case, no such justification could be made out because the insurance obligation was not crucial to the social order in Iceland in view of the limited number of posted workers registered in that country.

Conflict between PWD and single market freedoms   8.48

Article 56 TFEU stipulates that 'restrictions on freedom to provide services within the Union shall be prohibited in respect of nationals of Member States who are established in a Member State other than that of the person for whom

331

the services are intended'. Article 57 expands on what is meant by 'services' in this context, stating that these will 'normally [be] provided for remuneration, in so far as they are not governed by the provisions relating to freedom of movement of goods, capital and persons', and in particular will include '(a) activities of an industrial character; (b) activities of a commercial character; (c) activities of craftsmen; (d) activities of the professions'.

In an additional provision with particular relevance to posted working, Article 57 goes on to state that 'without prejudice to... the right of establishment [within the meaning of Article 49], the person providing a service may, in order to do so, temporarily pursue his activity in the Member State where the service is provided, under the same conditions as are imposed by that State on its own nationals.'

8.49 Employment terms and conditions

Article 3(7) PWD stipulates that the provisions of Article 3(1)–(6) 'shall not prevent application of terms and conditions of employment which are more favourable to workers'. At first glance, this appears to confer on Member States an unfettered discretion to confer on posted workers terms and conditions that are more advantageous than the basic rights provided for in Article 3(1). However, as discussed below, the fundamental freedoms enshrined in the TFEU – particularly the freedom of establishment and the freedom to provide services – regularly intrude to limit the capacity of Member States to make more favourable provision.

As the ECJ made clear in Commission of the European Communities v Luxembourg (above), Article 3(1) must be interpreted as setting out an exhaustive list of the matters in respect of which Member States must ensure that their posted workers receive the same treatment as indigenous workers. The ECJ also stressed that the level of protection guaranteed to such workers is, in principle, limited to that provided for in Article 3(1)(a)–(g) unless, under the law or collective agreements in place in the state of origin, those workers enjoy more favourable terms and conditions of employment as regards those matters – see 'Rights under PWD – core rights and protections' above.

8.50 In the context of posted working, any augmentation of rights, whether in respect of subject-matter or level of protection conferred, is permissible only if one of the following conditions is met:

- the more favourable terms are shown to be justifiable on the ground of 'public policy' pursuant to the derogation set out in the first indent of Article 3(10) (see 'Rights under PWD – options and derogations' above for details), or

- the terms are provided pursuant to a collective agreement or arbitration award that has been declared to be 'universally applicable' within the meaning of Article 3(8) and the second indent of Article 3(10) and the extension of the terms of the agreement/award to posted workers seeks to ensure that they receive equal treatment with other workers covered by the same agreement/award (see 'Rights under PWD – collective agreements and arbitration awards' above).

The European Court has consistently held that if a Member State's more generous provision does not satisfy one or other of these conditions, the additional provision will be regarded as erecting an unjustified barrier to the exercise of the freedom to provide services under Articles 56 and 57. Even if one of the conditions is met, the ECJ has ruled that it will nevertheless be regarded as impeding the full exercise of the freedom to provide services if the additional right is, in fact, one to which posted workers are already entitled under the law of the Member State in which their employer is established – see Criminal proceedings against Arblade and ors 2001 ICR 434, ECJ; and Finalarte Sociedade de Construção Civil LDA v Urlaubs- und Lohnausgleichskasse der Bauwirtschaft 2003 2 CMLR 11, ECJ.

This reveals that there is a tension between the PWD and the TFEU economic **8.51** freedoms in the context of posted workers' terms and conditions of employment. But this 'clash of rights' is also evident in two other areas, namely:

- the capacity of Member States to impose detailed monitoring and licensing obligations on service providers in connection with the posting of workers, and

- the extent to which strike action can lawfully be taken as a means of persuading service providers to agree to the extension of advantageous collective terms to posted workers.

These issues are considered separately below.

Monitoring, licensing procedures and immigration checks   8.52

The UK may be regarded as being particularly generous in its treatment of posted workers in one particular respect. Unlike many EEA countries, the UK does not impose licensing and authorisation requirements regarding posted workers within its territory, with the sole exception of transitional work authorisation arrangements in respect of Croatian nationals following the admission of Croatia to EU membership in July 2013. These are governed by Part 3 of the Accession of Croatia (Immigration and Worker Authorisation) Regulations 2013 SI 2013/1460.

In 2006 the then Parliamentary Under-Secretary of State for Employment Relations, Jim Fitzpatrick, commented that: 'We will not have to change our control measures, as we do not place unjustifiable or disproportionate requirements on foreign companies temporarily posting their workers to the UK... Monitoring and sanctions for non-compliance with the employment

333

rights specified by the Posted Workers Directive is identical to that available to domestic workers' (30th Report of the House of Commons Select Committee on European Scrutiny, 4 April 2006, para 13.10).

8.53 This laissez-faire attitude to the licensing of posted workers obtains only with regard to migrant workers who are *lawfully* employed in the sending country from which they are being posted to the UK. This was confirmed by the Court of Appeal in R (Low and ors) v Secretary of State for the Home Department 2010 ICR 755, CA, when rejecting an appeal against the refusal to permit three employees of a company incorporated in the Republic of Ireland to enter the UK for the alleged purposes of fulfilling a service contract between the company and a Chinese restaurant. All three employees had a history of immigration offences as a result of which they had been prohibited from working in the UK. The Irish company attempted to regularise the employees' otherwise unlawful status by applying for temporary residence permits for the duration of the service contract, but the applications were refused because they were suspected of being 'spurious'. The company then sought judicial review of the refusal decisions, asserting that, as employees of a company incorporated in a Member State, the claimants were entitled – pursuant to what are now Articles 56 and 57 – to enter the UK and reside there as 'posted workers' for the duration of the service contract. A High Court judge rejected the judicial review application and, on appeal, the Court of Appeal upheld that decision. It ruled that, as it could not be established that the employees were lawfully entitled to reside in any Member State, the immigration authorities were entitled to refuse them entry, and that this did not breach the company's rights under Article 56 regarding freedom to provide services.

8.54 **Procedures must be proportionate.** In general, a restrictive approach has been adopted by the ECJ in cases where Member States have sought to impose overly detailed licensing and monitoring procedures in connection with posted workers. In Commission of the European Communities v Grand Duchy of Luxembourg 2005 1 CMLR 22, ECJ, the Court ruled that an obligation on service providers of other Member States when posting workers to first obtain work permits and to provide minimum bank guarantees breached Articles 56 and 57 TFEU in that they were an inappropriate means of pursuing the public policy objective of preventing disturbance in the local labour market and went beyond what was required to pursue the objective of social welfare protection. The imposition of a simple duty on service providers to report details of their activities to the Luxembourg authorities would, in the ECJ's estimation, have been as effective and less restrictive than the licensing regime imposed by Luxembourg in this case. Nor could that regime be regarded as constituting an appropriate means of protecting workers since it involved formalities and delays that were liable to discourage the free provision of services through the medium of posting workers from other countries.

334

A similar conclusion was reached in Commission of the European Communities v Germany 2006 2 CMLR 23, ECJ. In that case, the European Court held that requirements and restrictions imposed on non-EU nationals as a condition of being allowed to be posted to work in Germany were unlawful because they were more burdensome than those that applied to EU nationals and could not be justified. In particular, the requirement for certain checks to be carried out beyond a simple declaration that the non-EU posted workers were lawfully resident in the state where the sending employer was established went beyond what was necessary to prevent an abuse of the freedom to provide services. And a separate requirement that such workers demonstrate that they had at least a year's prior employment with the posting employer was disproportionate to the objectives of protecting posted workers and safeguarding the host state's prerogatives regarding the domestic employment market and the prevention of social dumping.

In Re Criminal Proceedings against Santos Palhota and ors 2011 1 CMLR 34, **8.55** ECJ, the Member State concerned – Belgium – met with more success in showing that its monitoring procedures constituted a proportionate interference with the freedom to provide services as guaranteed by Articles 56 and 57. The ECJ accepted that obligations imposed on employers of workers posted to Belgium to file a declaration of posting prior to posting workers and to retain copies of relevant supporting documentation for filing with the authorities at the end of the posting constituted restrictions on the freedom to provide services. But it said that such restrictions could be justified if (a) they met an overriding public interest objective which was not already safeguarded by the rules in the Member State in which the service provider was established, and (b) the restrictions were appropriate for attaining that objective and did not go beyond what was necessary. In respect of the case before it, the Court held that the Member State's declaration procedure made it possible to monitor compliance by employers with the provisions of Article 3(1) PWD and thus pursued the public interest objective of the social protection of workers. However, the Court was less sanguine about Belgium's application of a registration procedure on foreign service providers entailing the delivery of a registration number that needed to be cited by a posted worker before he or she would be permitted to commence work. Such an administrative procedure went beyond what was necessary to ensure that posted workers were sufficiently protected.

Lawfulness of industrial action   8.56
The question has arisen of whether the right to take industrial action to persuade a foreign service provider to agree to extend the provisions of a collective agreement to workers it is intending to post to another Member State can be squared with the economic freedoms guaranteed to service providers under the TFEU.

335

While not dealing specifically with the issue of posted workers, the ECJ's decision in International Transport Workers' Federation and anor v Viking Line ABP and anor 2008 ICR 741, ECJ, has potentially important implications for dealing with the clash of fundamental rights in this area. The case concerned industrial action initiated by trade unions against a Finnish shipping company, Viking Line, after it had sought to 'reflag' one of its vessels in order to man it with a cheaper Estonian crew. The aim of the industrial action was to induce Viking to enter into a collective agreement with an Estonian union under which the Estonian crew members' terms and conditions would have been enhanced. Viking successfully applied for an injunction in the UK High Court restraining the industrial action on the ground that it would deter the company from exercising its freedom of establishment guaranteed by what is now Article 49 TFEU. Following an appeal, the case was referred to the ECJ, which acknowledged that the right to take collective action (including the right to strike) was fundamental and formed an integral part of the general principles of Community law. However, that right could be subject to certain restrictions and the fundamental nature of it was not such as to render the right to freedom of establishment inapplicable to the collective action at issue in the case.

8.57 The ECJ went on to hold that the effect of the industrial action against Viking made the company's exercise of its right to freedom of establishment less attractive or even pointless inasmuch as the action prevented it from enjoying the same treatment in the host Member State as other economic operators established in that state. It followed that the collective action constituted a restriction on freedom of establishment. Such a restriction could be accepted only if it pursued a legitimate aim compatible with the TFEU and was justified by overriding reasons of public interest. But even if that were the case, it would still have to be suitable for attaining the objective pursued and must not go beyond what was necessary in order to do so. In this regard, the ECJ observed that it was for the national court to examine whether, under the national rules and collective agreement law applicable to industrial action, the union had other means at its disposal to bring to a successful conclusion the collective negotiations entered into with the company that were less restrictive of freedom of establishment and whether the trade union had exhausted those means before initiating the action. In the event, the legal action was settled before the Court of Appeal had the chance to consider these issues in the light of the ECJ's judgment.

However, similar issues arose in Laval un Partneri Ltd v Svenska Byggnadsarbetareförbundet and ors 2008 IRLR 160, ECJ – a case that did entail posted workers. There, Swedish trade unions took collective action in the form of a blockade aimed at obliging a Latvian company to abide by a Swedish collective agreement applicable to building workers in respect of Latvian workers posted to Sweden. The ECJ was asked to consider whether such action interfered with the Latvian company's freedom to provide services under

Articles 56 and 57 TFEU. As in the Viking case, the Court recognised that the right to take collective action is a fundamental right which forms an integral part of the principles of Community law, but that that right may nonetheless be subject to certain restrictions. Furthermore, the ECJ confirmed that the right conferred by Article 56, in common with the freedom of establishment guaranteed by Article 49, applies to the actions of trade unions and not just to those of bodies governed by public law. The ECJ proceeded to hold that the collective action in question did constitute a restriction on the Latvian company's Article 56 rights, but that it was in principle capable of being objectively justified on the ground of protecting workers provided the action did not go further than was necessary. However, in light of the minimum protection provided for by the PWD, and the fact that Swedish law made no provision for a minimum wage or the applicability of Swedish collective agreements to posted workers, the ECJ concluded that collective action aimed at obliging the Latvian company to observe the terms of a collective agreement providing for better working conditions could not be objectively justified.

8.58 In both of these cases the ECJ noted that the TFEU makes provision for both economic freedom and social protection, and that where these two interests conflict, a balance must be struck. The ECJ's rulings are something of a double-edged sword so far as trade unions are concerned. On the one hand, the Court recognised the fundamental nature of the right to strike. On the other, it suggested that collective action taken against employers operating transnational undertakings might have to be justified.

Enforcement
8.59

Article 6 PWD states that: 'In order to enforce the right to the terms and conditions of employment guaranteed in Article 3, judicial proceedings may be instituted in the Member State in whose territory the worker is or was posted, without prejudice, where applicable, to the right, under existing international conventions on jurisdiction, to institute proceedings in another State.' Pursuant to this, most Member States have made it possible for posted workers to institute judicial proceedings in their domestic courts and tribunals when the worker is or was posted there in order to enforce the right to the terms and conditions of employment guaranteed by the Directive.

However, as previously discussed, neither the UK nor the Republic of Ireland has thought it necessary to introduce specific implementing provisions to spell out that posted workers have the right to bring legal action in the domestic courts and tribunals to enforce their PWD rights – see 'Transposition of PWD into national law – UK implementation' above. Instead, the approach has been to ensure that the existing legislative measures dealing with the core rights set out in Article 3(1) of the PWD apply to posted workers in exactly the same way as to indigenous workers.

337

8.60 Territorial considerations

Generally speaking, where an employee works for the same employer in a number of different European countries, or where the employee is temporarily seconded to a different employer in another country, the question of which country's domestic law is the applicable law to resolve an employment dispute is governed by international conventions. The basic rule, set out in Article 3 of the Rome Convention on the Law Applicable to Contractual Obligations 1980, is that an employment contract is governed by the law chosen by the parties if, as is usually the case, a choice of law clause exists in the contract. However, Article 6(2) of that Convention provides that the parties' choice of law cannot deprive the employee of the protection afforded by the 'mandatory rules' of the country in which the employee 'habitually carries out his work', unless the contract is more closely connected with another country. Article 3(3) explains that mandatory rules are those laws of a country which 'cannot be derogated from by contract'. In the UK this would include most statutory employment rights.

The 1980 Convention, which was signed by all EU Member States and implemented into UK law by the Contracts (Applicable Law) Act 1990, applies to contracts concluded before 17 December 2009. From that date, EU Regulation No.593/2008, known as 'Rome I', has replaced the Convention, but has changed little of substance.

8.61 As to which country's courts and tribunals can hear a claim, Article 6 PWD makes it clear that a posted worker is entitled to enforce his or her right to the terms and conditions of employment guaranteed in Article 3 by instituting judicial proceedings in the Member State in whose territory the worker is or was posted rather than in the country in which his or her work is habitually carried out. That said, the entitlement is expressed to be 'without prejudice... to the right, under existing international conventions on jurisdiction, to institute proceedings in another State'. Accordingly, under the Brussels Regulation on jurisdiction and the recognition and enforcement of judgments in civil and commercial matters (Council Regulation No.44/2001) – commonly referred to as the Brussels I Regulation – a posted worker also has the option of enforcing the rights secured by Article 3 in the Member State in which he or she normally works, which would usually be the country in which his or her employer (or agency) is established.

The law governing international jurisdiction, applicable law and forum is discussed in depth in IDS Employment Law Handbook, 'Employment Tribunal Practice and Procedure' (2014), Chapter 2, 'Tribunals' jurisdiction', under 'Territorial limitations'.

8.62 New Posted Workers Enforcement Directive

Partly arising out of widespread concern that the PWD is not operating entirely successfully to eradicate the mischief of social dumping, the European

Commission has decided that the best way to achieve more effective monitoring and observance of the PWD is to enact a new Directive specifically focusing on enforcement. The provisions of the resulting Enforcement Directive aim to ensure that enforcement and monitoring rules are better applied in practice, especially in certain sectors such as construction and road haulage where so-called 'letter box' companies are prevalent. These pursue no real economic activity within the country in which they are established and use false posting to circumvent national rules on social security and labour conditions. The new Directive also aims to improve the protection of posted workers' rights by preventing fraud, especially in subcontracting chains where posted workers' rights are not always respected.

Key provisions. The Enforcement Directive makes provision for: 8.63

- increasing the awareness of posted workers and companies about their rights and obligations as regards terms and conditions of employment

- improving cooperation between national authorities in charge of posting by imposing an obligation to respond to requests for assistance from competent authorities of other Member States within a time limit of two working days for urgent requests and 25 working days for non-urgent requests

- clarifying the definition of posting so as to increase legal certainty both for posted workers and service providers, and at the same time tackling 'letter box' companies that use posting to circumvent the provisions of the PWD

- defining Member States' responsibilities to verify compliance with the rules laid down in the PWD by, for example, designating specific enforcement authorities responsible for verifying compliance

- requiring posting companies to designate a contact person for liaison with the enforcement authorities; declare their identity, the number of workers to be posted, the start and end dates of the posting, the address of the workplace and the nature of the services to be provided; and to keep available basic documents such as employment contracts, payslips and time sheets of posted workers

- improving the enforcement of rights, and the handling of complaints by requiring both host and home Member States to ensure that posted workers – with the support of trade unions or other interested third parties – can lodge complaints and take legal and/or administrative action against their employers if their rights are not respected

- ensuring that: (i) administrative penalties and fines imposed on service providers by one Member State for failure to respect the requirements of the PWD can be enforced and recovered in another Member State; and (ii) the sanctions for failure to comply with the PWD are effective, proportionate and dissuasive.

339

8.64 **Adoption and deadline for implementation.** The Council of Ministers formally adopted the agreed text of the new Directive on 13 May 2014. The next stage is for the text to be published in the Official Journal, after which Member States will have two years and 20 days to implement its provisions. At the date of writing, the Directive has not yet been published in the Official Journal.

Case list

(Note that employment tribunal cases are not included in this list.)

McMeechan v Secretary of State for Employment 1997 ICR 549, CA   1.177, 5.35, 5.36

McMenemy v Capita Business Services Ltd 2006 IRLR 761, EAT;
  2007 IRLR 400, Ct Sess (Inner House)   3.40, 3.59, 3.71, 3.74

Manson and Johnston v (1) University of Strathclyde (2) Automated
  Microscopy Systems Ltd EAT 356/87   2.65

Mascellani v Ministero della Giustizia (Case C-221/13), ECJ   3.106

Matthews and ors v Kent and Medway Towns Fire Authority and ors
  2006 ICR 365, HL   2.37, 3.7, 3.50, 3.54, 3.64

Ministry of Defence v Wallis 2011 ICR 617, CA   2.17

Ministry of Justice (formerly Department for Constitutional Affairs) v
  O'Brien 2012 ICR 955, ECJ; 2013 ICR 499, SC; 2014 ICR 773, EAT   3.11, 3.21, 3.90

Mitchell v David Evans Agricultural Ltd EAT 0083/06   3.99

Montgomery v Johnson Underwood Ltd 2001 ICR 819, CA   1.174, 1.178

Moran and ors v Ideal Cleaning Services Ltd and anor 2014 IRLR 172, EAT   1.70, 1.71

Muschctt v HM Prison Service 2010 IRLR 451, CA   1.187

N

Nethermere (St Neots) Ltd v Gardiner and anor 1984 ICR 612, CA   5.33, 5.34

North East Coast Shiprepairers Ltd v Secretary of State for
  Employment 1978 ICR 755, EAT   2.66, 6.32, 6.34

North Wales Probation Area v Edwards EAT 0468/07   5.36

North Yorkshire County Council and anor v Laws EAT 1376/95   2.109

Nottinghamshire County Council v Lee 1980 ICR 635, CA   2.64, 2.73

O

O'Brien v Ministry of Justice 2012 ICR 955, ECJ ; 2013 ICR 499, SC;
  2014 ICR 773, EAT   3.12, 3.22

O'Kelly and ors v Trusthouse Forte plc 1983 ICR 728, CA   5.32

Österreichischer Gewerkschaftsbund v Verband Österreichischer
  Banken und Bankiers (Case C-476/12), ECJ   3.27, 3.76

P

Pfaffinger v City of Liverpool Community College and another case
  1997 ICR 142, EAT   2.72, 2.90

Pola v R (Health and Safety Executive) 2009 EWCA Crim 655, CA   5.37

Prakash v Wolverhampton City Council EAT 0140/06   2.79

Primary Fluid Power Ltd v Brislen EAT 0611/04   2.66, 2.70

Pulse Healthcare Ltd v Carewatch Care Services Ltd and ors EAT 0123/12   5.23

R

R (Low and ors) v Secretary of State for the Home Department
  2010 ICR 755, CA   8.25, 8.53

R (Manson) v Ministry of Defence 2006 ICR 355, CA   3.20

R (on the application of Elias) v Secretary of State for Defence 2006 IRLR 934, CA   3.21

R v Secretary of State for Employment ex parte Equal Opportunities
  Commission and anor 1994 ICR 317, HL   3.2

Re Criminal Proceedings against Santos Palhota and ors 2011 1 CMLR 34, ECJ   8.55

Revenue and Customs Commissioners v Thorn Baker Ltd and ors 2008 ICR 46, CA   2.15

345

Index

A

Acas
Code of Practice on Flexible Working, 4.7
conciliation, 2.143, 3.93, 4.50

Additional paternity leave
employee shareholders, 7.15

Adoption leave
agency workers, 1.166–1.168
zero-hours contracts, 5.19

Agency workers
see also **Collective facilities and amenities**
adoption leave, 1.166–1.168
Agency Workers Regulations 2010
agency workers, 1.63–1.65
annual leave
equal treatment, 1.21–1.23
BIS Guidance, 1.58
collective facilities and amenities, 1.72–1.79
commencement, 1.57
compensation, 1.140
contract with temporary work agency, 1.69
contracting out, 1.132
detriment, 1.21–1.22, 1.137
employment status, 1.57
equal treatment, 1.86–1.136
general, 1.3
health and safety at work, 1.171–1.173
hirers, 1.60
information on vacancies, 1.80–1.85
liabilities, 1.133–1.136
managed service contracts, 1.68
pay
equal treatment, 1.103–1.120
purpose, 1.57
remedies, 1.140
review of impact, 1.58
scope, 1.59–1.71
self-employment, 1.66
statutory defence, 1.135–1.136

supervision and direction of the hirer, 1.67–1.68
Swedish derogation, 1.114–1.118
temporary work agency, 1.61, 1.62
temporary workers, 1.70–1.71
time limits, 1.139
unfair dismissal, 1.138
working time
equal treatment, 1.121–1.123
annual leave, 1.121–1.123
bonuses, 1.110–1.112
contract terms
contents, 1.16
employment agencies, 1.17–1.18
employment businesses, 1.16
hirers, 1.19, 1.20
requirement, 1.15
variation, 1.16
definition, 1.63–1.65
detriment, 1.21–1.22, 1.137
discrimination
employment service providers, 1.162–1.163
equal pay, 1.158–1.163
principal, discrimination by the, 1.159–1.161
employment agencies, 1.4, 1.6–1.7
employment businesses, 1.4, 1.8–1.9
employment status
common law test, 1.176
importance, 1.174
problems of identifying status, 1.175
relationship with the employment business, 1.177–1.182
relationship with the end-user, 1.183–1.188
statutory definition of worker/employer, 1.174
equal treatment
anti-avoidance provisions, 1.101–1.102
annual leave, 1.121–1.123
basic principle, 1.86
basic working and employment conditions, 1.86

C

Capability
unfair dismissal
fixed-term workers, 2.80–2.81
Casual workers
bank of temporary staff, 5.28
employees, 5.29–5.30
examples, 5.28
global contracts, 5.31–5.34
meaning, 5.1, 5.28
specific contracts, 5.35–5.37
umbrella contracts, 5.31–5.34
workers, 5.28
zero-hours contracts, 5.28
Charges
see **Fees**
Child-minder agencies
exclusion from legislation, 1.12
Collective agreements
annualised hours contracts, 5.39
fixed-term workers, 2.127
posted workers, 8.37–8.41
Collective facilities and amenities
access, 1.72–1.79
benefits in kind, 1.74
BIS Guidance, 1.73
breach of regulations, 1.79
collective, 1.73
company cars, 1.74
comparators, 1.77, 1.83
examples, 1.73
facilities, 1.73
justification, 1.78
liabilities, 1.79
loans, 1.74
meaning, 1.73
provided by the hirer, 1.75
training, 1.76
Collective redundancies
apprenticeships, 6.34
fixed-term workers, 2.100–2.101
Companies
fees, circumstances of charge, 1.28
Company cars
collective facilities and amenities, 1.74
Comparators
collective facilities and amenities, 1.77, 1.83

equal treatment
agency workers, 1.77, 1.83, 1.128–1.129
fixed-term workers, 2.40–2.41
Compensation
Agency Workers Regulations 2010, 1.140
flexible working, 4.46–4.49
Compliance
see **Enforcement**
Conciliation
Acas
fixed-term workers, 2.143, 3.93, 4.50
Confidential information
employment agencies, 1.46
employment businesses, 1.46
hirers, 1.46
work-seekers, 1.46
Construction industry
posted workers, 8.13
Constructive dismissal
flexible working, 4.61–4.63
Continuity of employment
agency workers, 1.97–1.100
fixed-term workers
equal treatment, 2.30–2.31, 2.60
less favourable treatment, 2.30–2.31
successive fixed-term contracts, 2.106–2.119
successive fixed-term contracts
arrangement or custom, 2.115–2.116
collective agreements, 2.127
continuity of employment, 2.106–2.119
Fixed-term Employees (Prevention of Less Favourable Treatment) Regulations 2002, 2.106–119
gaining permanent status, 2.103–2.105
temporary cessation of work, 2.108–2.109
TUC concerns, 2.117–2.119
unpredictable gaps in employment, 2.113–2.114
Contract terms
agency workers
contents, 1.163
employment agencies, 1.17–1.183
employment businesses, 1.163

353

355

365